Praise for *Face to Face*

In *Face to Face*, the dean of North American Reformation scholars makes a succinct but profound presentation of Luther's theology in terms of *coram* relationships. Taking constructive account of other modern interpreters, Dr. Kolb offers his own compelling reading of Luther in historical context for the benefit of contemporary proclamation.

—Dr. Christopher B. Brown, associate professor of church history,
Boston University School of Theology

Of all of Robert Kolb's recent books, this one looks like a theological and devotional classic. It seems that Luther's ontology of Word is the perfect toolbox to reimagine our relationship with God, with creation, and toward ourselves. This book is like a theological antidote, like devotional soothing balm against self-centered ideological politicization of Christian faith, written as a long, pious meditation against the narcissistic superficiality of our paranoid times.

—Rev. Dr. Boris Gunjević, tutor in philosophy of religion
and Christian doctrine, Westfield House, Cambridge,
Cambridge Theological Federation

The Latin word *coram* cannot be used for today's popular worldview "facing reality." For the author, it means first and foremost "facing God," then "facing creation." It is not just a belief or a down-to-earth teaching for Christians, but a warning to all rising powers.

—Rev. Dr. Pilgrim W. K. Lo, professor emeritus
of systematic theology and Luther studies,
Lutheran Theological Seminary, Hong Kong

Bob Kolb is one of the most authoritative and trusted guides to the theology of Martin Luther in the English-speaking world. In this volume, he explores the Wittenberg reformer's relational view of reality and its foundation in the conversing God, who summons all of creation into loving relationship at every moment. Kolb invites the reader to come face-to-face with this God, even as Martin Luther did. A fascinating and important book that draws on a lifetime of scholarship and Christian discipleship.

—Dr. Ronald K. Rittgers, professor of the history
of Christianity, Duke Divinity School

The face is one of the key things that separates humans from all other animals: in a mysterious sense, we are our faces, and face-to-face encounters with others are always personal and relational. In this creative and ingenious work, Robert Kolb explores the significance of the face, and of the language of face-to-face encounter, in the theology of Luther. In so doing, he brings to life and to relevance the greatness of the reformer's thought in a new way that is of real significance for our contemporary discussions of what it means to be human, and especially to be human before God.

—Dr. Carl R. Trueman, professor of biblical and religious studies, Grove City College

With this book, which is sharp-sighted and convincing throughout, Robert Kolb once again presents a magisterial work on Luther's theology. Kolb leads us right into the core of Luther's understanding of the Christian religion: the assumption of the immediacy of the God-human relationship. Immediately addressed by God's law and gospel, man shapes his relationship to the world and fellow human beings—and to himself. Kolb thankfully elaborates this highly momentous basic idea of Luther in all its richness of facets and its existential implications. A great read as well as an inspiring one!

—Dr. Christian V. Witt, professor of Reformation History and director of the Institute for Late Middle Ages and Reformation, University of Tübingen

LUTHERAN QUARTERLY BOOKS

Editor

Paul Rorem, Professor Emeritus, *Princeton Theological Seminary*

Associate Editors

Timothy J. Wengert, Professor Emeritus, *United Lutheran Seminary (Philadelphia)*

Mary Jane Haemig, Professor Emerita, *Luther Seminary, St. Paul*

Mark C. Mattes, *Grand View University, Des Moines, Iowa*

Lutheran Quarterly Books will advance the same aims as *Lutheran Quarterly* itself, aims repeated by Theodore G. Tappert when he was editor fifty years ago and renewed by Oliver K. Olson when he revived the publication in 1987. The original four aims continue to grace the front matter and to guide the contents of every issue, and can now also indicate the goals of *Lutheran Quarterly Books*: "to provide a forum (1) for the discussion of Christian faith and life on the basis of the Lutheran confession; (2) for the application of the principles of the Lutheran church to the changing problems of religion and society; (3) for the fostering of world Lutheranism; and (4) for the promotion of understanding between Lutherans and other Christians."

For further information, see www.lutheranquarterly.org.

The symbol and motto of *Lutheran Quarterly*, VDMA for *Verbum Domini Manet in Aeternum* (1 Peter 1:25), was adopted as a motto by Luther's sovereign, Frederick the Wise, and his successors. The original "Protestant" princes walking out of the imperial Diet of Speyer in 1529, unruly peasants following Thomas Müntzer, and from 1531 to 1547 the coins, medals, flags, and guns of the Smalcaldic League all bore the most famous Reformation slogan, the first Evangelical confession: The Word of the Lord remains forever.

For the complete list of *Lutheran Quarterly Books*, please see the final pages of this work.

Face to Face

Face to Face

Martin Luther's View of Reality

ROBERT KOLB

FORTRESS PRESS
MINNEAPOLIS

FACE TO FACE
Martin Luther's View of Reality

Copyright © 2024 Fortress Press, an imprint of 1517 Media. All rights reserved. Except for brief quotations in critical articles and reviews, no part of this book may be reproduced in any manner without prior written permission from the publisher. Email copyright@1517.media or write to Permissions, Fortress Press, PO Box 1209, Minneapolis, MN 55440-1209.

All Scripture quotations, unless otherwise indicated, are from the New Revised Standard Version Bible, copyright © 1989 National Council of the Churches of Christ in the United States of America. Used by permission. All rights reserved worldwide.

Library of Congress Cataloging-in-Publication Data

Names: Kolb, Robert, author.
Title: Face to face : Martin Luther's view of reality / Robert Kolb.
Description: Minneapolis : Fortress Press, [2024] | Includes bibliographical references and index.
Identifiers: LCCN 2023041353 (print) | LCCN 2023041354 (ebook) | ISBN 9781506498324 (print) | ISBN 9781506498331 (ebook)
Subjects: LCSH: Luther, Martin, 1483-1546. | Reality.
Classification: LCC BR334.3 .K597 2024 (print) | LCC BR334.3 (ebook) | DDC 230/.41092--dc23/eng/ 20240116
LC record available at https://lccn.loc.gov/2023041353
LC ebook record available at https://lccn.loc.gov/2023041354

Cover design and illustration: Kristin Miller

Print ISBN: 978-1-5064-9832-4
eBook ISBN: 978-1-5064-9833-1

Contents

Foreword: For the Reader, to Understand the Book

This volume arises out of six lectures given in 2016 and 2017, in the course of the observance of the five-hundredth anniversary of the posting of the *Ninety-five Theses* on indulgences, one at Församlingsfakulteten in Göteborg, Sweden, four at a pastoral retreat of the New Jersey district of the Lutheran Church-Missouri Synod, and one at Concordia Seminary in St. Louis. I am most grateful to Anthony Steinbronn, at that time president of the Lutheran Church-Missouri Synod's New Jersey district and a long-time friend, for conceiving of the program for a pastoral retreat centering on Luther's "*corams.*" Over the years Tony has given me many insights into Luther's way of thinking and its value for a twenty-first century assessment of life. Those insights have grown out of his own rich pastoral experience and leadership in the church that demonstrate how apt Martin Luther's thinking is for our own time. My colleague Erik Herrmann has also given me so many insights into Luther as well as the invitation to deliver the 2017 Reformation lecture at Concordia Seminary. In addition, the text contains significant portions of a lecture given at Församlingsfakulteten (the Lutheran School of Theology) in Göteborg, Sweden, in 2016, entitled "How Did Luther Enter Dialogue with Society and How Does His Underlying Theology Apply to Us Today in a Secular Society?" This essay appears on the Församlingsfakulteten website in full. Conversations with colleagues on the faculty in Göteborg have also enriched my understanding of Luther and his significance in the twenty-first century.

Scholars have made much of Luther's speaking of human beings face to face, with God (*coram Deo*), and with other human beings or "the world" (*coram hominibus* or *coram mundo*). He did so at times with the Latin preposition *coram* ("in the presence of" or "face to face with"). Each of the chapters of this volume begins with an attempt to provide a Latin equivalent following this pattern for the specific aspects of those relationships discussed in the chapter. The Wittenberg reformer's relationship with God embraced his understanding of God as Hidden and God as Revealed. His understanding of God Revealed embraced both his understanding of God's person and his understanding of how God becomes present in believers' daily life through forms of God's word. Even though he seldom labelled it as such, Luther also reflected a great deal on his own view of himself, and so we can speak of Luther *coram seipso* or *meipso*, ("facing himself," or "myself").[1] Furthermore, Luther confronted and was confronted by Satan because he experienced the constant attacks of the Evil One; the devil did sneak up from behind, but Luther turned to stare and speak him down. He confronted God's law and God's wrath as well as the sin that Satan fosters with the name of Christ on his lips. He recognized that the world surrounded and enveloped his daily life, as a gift from God in the structures of community that God had ordained. He also took up the biblical usage of the "world" as human culture hostile to God, exercising its perversion of his good creation as a tempter in its own right. Finally, his conception of human life as shaped by the God who loves to converse and commune with his people led him to dwell often in his preaching and teaching on his relationships with others, both as individuals and in smaller social units, whom God had called him to serve. Risto Saarinen observes that "while Luther employs a rich variety of relational phrases, for instance, 'before God' (*coram Deo*) and 'for me' (*pro me*), he does not employ the concept of relation frequently."[2] That observation of the reformer's use of the word "relationship" may be because Luther used the Aristotelian category of *relatio* relatively seldom. In his preaching, lecturing, and writing the Wittenberg reformer certainly was constantly discussing relationships with God, himself, Satan, other human creatures, and nature as well. He used a variety of rhetorical means, including first- and second-person monologues and dialogues, to concretize the relational foundation of life and creation.

The Latin preposition *coram*—"face to face"—summarizes the view of reality that energized and directed Martin Luther's theological thinking and his practice of the godly life. This preposition captures Luther's

1. The term fashioned by Gerhard Ebeling in his *Lutherstudien*, volume 2, *Disputatio de Homine*, issued in three separate parts (Tübingen: Mohr/Siebeck, 1977, 1982, 1989). Luther himself spoke of a person's relationship with self in a sermon preached in Kemberg in 1531, WA 34,2: 108,24–109,5.

2. Risto Saarinen, "Martin Luther and Relational Thinking," in *Oxford Research Encyclopedia of Religion*, 1, 4–6. https://doi.org/10.1093/acrefore/9780199340378.013.344

permeating presupposition that God is personally engaging his entire creation in relationship, from his initial "let there be" of creation, throughout Scripture, in nature, within his church. Luther presented the Creator as the God of conversation and community, that is, "face to face" with his entire creation. "Coram" serves as an accurate reflection of Luther's understanding of the origin and end of all in the speaking person of the God of Israel, who came to earth as Jesus of Nazareth.

Luther regarded God as prepositional. The word *preposition* comes from the Latin and can be translated as "placed in the presence of." The German word for *preposition* is *Verhältniswort*, literally "relationship word." The Latin preposition *coram* designates the presence or relationship that brings objects or people "face to face." Luther's emphasis on the personal, relational nature of reality made use of this preposition—perhaps not so often as some modern interpreters of Luther would like to think, but in such significant ways that we can use it as a guide to his entire way of perceiving God and humanity. The preposition embodies his conviction that God is present and exercising his relationship with his creation continuously, without ceasing.

The volume brings together aspects of my research that have appeared in various venues over the years, with some more recent thoughts gleaned from my reading of Luther and with a special focus on the questions summarized in the title of the book. My own overview of Luther's thinking in much more traditionally organized form may help illuminate corners of this discourse for some readers.[3] Largely unmentioned in this study are a number of scholars whose overviews and insights into Luther's thought have formed my own and enabled me to read the Wittenberg reformer with more sensitivity to the rhythms of this thought. Among the most important of their works are those of Paul Althaus,[4] Bernhard Lohse,[5] Steven Paulson,[6] Oswald Bayer,[7] Hans-Martin Barth,[8] Paul Hinlicky,[9] and Reinhard Schwarz.[10] Biographical studies provide contextual framework; my favorite is that of Scott H. Hendrix.[11]

3. *Martin Luther, Confessor of the Faith* (Christian Theology in Context series; Oxford: Oxford University Press, 2009).
4. *The Theology of Martin Luther*, trans. Robert C. Schultz (Philadelphia: Fortress Press, 1966).
5. *Martin Luther's Theology*, trans. Roy Harrisville (Minneapolis: Fortress Press, 1999).
6. *Luther for Armchair Theologians* (Louisville, KY: Westminster John Knox, 2004).
7. *Martin Luther's Theology: A Contemporary Interpretation*, trans. Thomas H. Trapp (Grand Rapids, MI: Eerdmans, 2008).
8. *The Theology of Martin Luther: A Critical Assessment* (Minneapolis: Fortress Press, 2012).
9. *Luther for Evangelicals: a Reintroduction* (Grand Rapids, MI: Baker Academic, 2018).
10. *Martin Luther, Lehrer der christlichen Religion*, 2nd ed. (Tübingen: Mohr Siebeck, 2016).
11. *Martin Luther, Visionary Reformer* (New Haven: Yale University Press, 2015).

This study focuses only on Luther, and readers could gain the false impression that Luther thought alone. The theological faculty of the University of Wittenberg formed a team, to be sure under Luther's leadership, with Philip Melanchthon as co-captain, but with the participation of other immediate colleagues and a network spread across German-speaking lands and beyond. Without his team—or teams—Luther could not have produced the reform that issued from Wittenberg. In fact, the entire university, especially colleagues in the arts faculty, formed a laboratory in which intellectual experimentation and fermentation took place in various fields of learning that made an impact on German and European society. A study of precisely how this interaction functioned is needed to build on insights of scholars such as Timothy Wengert and Irene Dingel, who have shown how this team was formed and functioned.[12]

This study presumes that Luther had formulated the core of his theology by 1521 or 1522,[13] and that his subsequent writings, as well as some from before 1521, reflect this common core. Chronological sensitivity is necessary, nonetheless, because in certain instances the reformer's expression of that core takes on specific meaning from a very specific temporal situation. He never ceased experimenting with the best way to articulate God's message in Scripture for specific contexts as questions and issues shifted with changing historical circumstances. In general, however, the last twenty-five years of Luther's life maintain a fundamentally consistent presentation of the heart of the biblical message that shaped specific applications and experiments fitting for specific situations and times.

The form of the original oral lecture has not completely disappeared. This permits each chapter to be read as a somewhat independent essay though chapters are arranged to build on each other. But each can be read on its own. This arrangement has led, however, to some repetition. The study employs relatively extensive quotations from Luther's writings. Luther expressed his thought better than any commentator can. The flavor of his own delivery of his message is important for acquiring a sense of his genius and of the method of his thinking and teaching.

This modest volume is intended as a primer to Luther's thought. It has been written to invite readers in the English-speaking world into conversations regarding the foundation and framework of Luther's way

12. For example, Timothy J. Wengert, "Melanchthon and Luther / Luther and Melanchthon," *Lutherjahrbuch* 66 (1999), 55–88; Timothy J. Wengert, "The Wittenberg Circle," in OHMLT, 491–501; Dingel, "Freunde—Gegner—Feinde. Melanchthon in den Konfliktfeldern seiner Zeit," *Theologische Literaturzeitung* 135 (2010): 775–804.

13. See the introduction, pp. 19–37.

of thinking based on some of the scholarly discussions of the past half century. Readers will find here extensive citations from Luther to help give them a feel for the reformer's way of communicating to his own age, with his contemporaries. They will find summaries of how Luther strove through his engagement with the concerns of his day to transmit the Bible's conversation of God with its readers. If the book invites, stimulates, provokes fruitful engagement with this sixteenth-century conversation partner, it will have reached its goal.

—Mainz, the Festival of Saint Martin of Tours 2022,
Martin Luther's 439th baptismal birthday

Acknowledgments

The author is grateful for permission to republish significant elements of the following published essays:

Robert Kolb, "'What Benefit Does the Soul Receive from a Handful of Water?' Luther's Preaching on Baptism, 1528–1539," *Concordia Journal* 25 (1999), 346–363.

Robert Kolb, "'This is My Customary Procedure,' Says God: Martin Luther's Use of Dialogue and Monologue in his Lectures and Sermons," *Teach These Things. Essays in Honor of Wallace Schulz*, ed. Erik Rottmann (Versailles, MO: Wild Boar Books, 2008), 25–40.

Robert Kolb, "'The Armor of God and the Might of His Strength.' Luther's Sermon on Ephesians 6 (1531/1533)," *Concordia Journal* 43 (2017): 59–73.

This gratitude also extends to the New Jersey District of the Lutheran Church-Missouri Synod; Concordia Seminary, St. Louis; and Församlingsfakulteten in Göteborg Sweden for permission to transform lectures held for these groups into this book.

Abbreviations

BC	*The Book of Concord*, ed. Robert Kolb and Timothy J. Wengert (Minneapolis: Fortress Press, 2000).
BSELK	*Die Bekenntnisschriften der Evangelisch-Lutherischen Kirche*, ed. Irene Dingel (Göttingen: Vandenhoeck & Ruprecht, 2014).
EA	*Dr. Martin Luther's sa[e]mmtliche Werke* (Erlangen: Heyder, 1826–1857).
Joest, *Ontologie*	Wilfried Joest, *Ontologie der Person bei Luther* (Göttingen: Vandenhoeck & Ruprecht, 1967).
Lenker, *Sermons*	*The Complete Sermons of Martin Luther*, ed. John Nicholas Lenker (1905–1909; Grand Rapids, MI: Baker, 2000).
LW	*Luther's Works* (St. Louis/Philadelphia: Concordia/Fortress Press, 1958–1986).
OHMLT	*The Oxford Handbook of Martin Luther's Theology*, ed. Robert Kolb, Irene Dingel and L'ubomír Batka (Oxford: Oxford University Press, 2014).
Paulson, *Outlaw God*	Steven D. Paulson, *Luther's Outlaw God. Volume 1: Hiddenness, Evil, and Predestination* (Minneapolis: Fortress Press, 2018), *Volume 2.*

	Hidden in the Cross (Minneapolis: Fortress Press, 2019); *Volume 3. Sacraments and God's Attack on the Promise* (Minneapolis: Fortress Press, 2021).
WA	*D. Martin Luthers Werke* (Weimar: Böhlau, 1883–1993).

Introduction: Reality and the Apprehension of Reality

In 1998 Gerhard Ebeling summarized an important insight in his earlier analysis of Luther's way of thinking, calling attention to the reformer's recasting of the framework for viewing reality into a paradigm based on the personal relationship of the person of God to every one of his creatures, from human beings to stones and tree leaves. "Reality" is a term so all-encompassing that it cannot be viewed from outside; it can only be experienced. Therefore, Luther's "relational ontology" presumes his experience with God, especially as encountered in Scripture and in his own conscience and consciousness as well as his living among the vast variety of creatures of God, animate and inanimate. This view posits that God is the Creator of all that is real, and that he creates and re-creates through his speaking. God's word provides a key to the relationships that determine human existence and the existence of everyone and everything around us. Thus, Ebeling demonstrated, the concept of person or personhood—both God's and the human being's— undergirds the reformer's perception of reality. So do the associated aspects of interpersonal relationships in communication of one kind or another. Luther thus lays the basis for comprehending everything that a person encounters and takes as the "real," and it undergirds all investigation of the created substances in every corner of creation.[1]

Otto Hermann Pesch spoke of Luther's "intellectual style of performance" as existential—not in the sense of the twentieth-century philosophical movement[2] but as an orientation to Scripture and to life

1. Gerhard Ebeling, "Luthers Wirklichkeitsverständnis," *Zeitschrift für Theologie und Kirche* 90 (1993): 409–424, translated by Scott Celsor in *Lutheran Quarterly* 27 (2013): 56–75.
2. Cf. Risto Saarinen's comment, "Luther's view of relationality helps to understand what he means by the Christian's first-person involvement in phrases like 'my faith' and 'for my sake.'

that worked with the "category of relationship." Thomas Aquinas, as a representative of scholastic theologians, worked in contrast, Pesch contended, with "ontological categories of nature." Pesch described Aquinas's "concentration on God as creator and on the world as his creation" as a "sapiential" approach to theology, a view from above. In contrast, Pesch argued, Luther's focus developed out of the midst of actual experience in daily life, a focus on the sinner and on God as the one who restores righteousness to sinners.[3] Readers of Luther must keep in mind that his concept of God as creator and sustainer of all that exists through the mystery of his creative word lies at the foundation of all his teaching. He viewed creation as designed by God in specific forms that continue to be subject to his loving guidance and care. His recognition that relationship to God and relationships created by God frame what is real did not in any way weaken his trust in the biblical dictates for human behavior. All proper human activity flows from fearing, loving, and trusting in God and therefore loving others as one loves oneself (Matt 22: 37–39). He did not retreat with his convictions into Kantian exile.[4]

The oft-repeated opinion that Luther had no systematic theology arises from the fact that he produced no *Loci communes* or *Institutio*, as did Melanchthon and Calvin, to prepare preachers for their task. But his lectures on biblical books and his preaching proceed from his concept of the "*doctrina*" of the Holy Spirit as he harvested it from the apostles and prophets. Philip Watson, the English Methodist Luther scholar, cited the Swedish Lutheran Einar Billing's observation, that Luther's "different thoughts are not strung together like pearls in a necklace, united only by the bond of a common authority or perhaps by a chain of logical argument, but that they all lie close as the petals of a rose about a common center."[5] Luther proceeded to

He does not have the post-Enlightenment sense of subjectivity in the manner of Pietism or other individualist variants of modern Christianity. On the other hand, the ideas of passive attachment and the attribution of gift-like properties to a believer enable a robust first-person involvement in Faith." Saarinen, "Martin Luther and Relational Thinking," 1.

3. Otto Hermann Pesch, "Existential and Sapiential Theology—the Theological Confrontation between Luther and Thomas Aquinas," in *Catholic Scholars Dialogue with Luther* (Chicago: Loyola University Press, 1970), 61–81, 182–193.
4. On attempts to make sense of Luther within frameworks set by nineteenth century Idealism, see Risto Saarinen, *Gottes Wirken auf uns : die Transzendentale Deutung des Gegenwart-Christi-Motivs in der Lutherforschung* (Stuttgart: Steiner, 1989). Reiner Schürmann, *Broken Hegemonies*, trans. Reginald Lilly (Bloomington, IN: Indiana University Press, 2003) ventured an exploration of the relationship of Luther and Immanuel Kant.
5. Philip S. Watson, *Let God be God. An Interpretation of the Theology of Martin Luther* (Philadelphia: Fortress Press, 1966), 26.

organize his reading of Scripture on a different basis than the scholastic view of reality, dependent as it was on Aristotle's dependence on human reason. Luther listened to the word of the Creator before he turned to human reasoning. He thus differed from Aristotle in that he had found another foundation for his understanding of reality. God's creative word and the relationships that they brought into being framed his thought.

THE RECENT DISCUSSION OF LUTHER'S "ONTOLOGY"

For a more detailed investigation of Luther's concept of reality, readers must turn to the work of Wilfried Joest (1914–1995), professor at the University of Erlangen, who published a masterful, definitive study of Luther's "ontology," or view of reality, in German in 1967.[6] Every student who wishes to pursue this subject in depth should read it. It is true that some claim that Luther had no ontology, but that can be said only if the analysis of what human beings can identify as real is limited to the ways that ancient Greek philosophers found access to reality limited, to those things that rational human intuition or observation and experience can digest and integrate into a system. Some sensed an inborn knowledge of divine or eternal designs for all things, and others had confidence in human reason to interpret authoritatively their encounters with the reality around them. For Luther, that fell short of complete engagement with reality.

Risto Saarinen points out that the Erlangen professor "does not reduce Luther's ontological language into existential experience but constructs a theological ontology that is thoroughly relational." Saarinen summarizes Joest with three guiding theses. First, "a person is responsive, has everything he receives in the correlative relation of word and faith." Second, individuals live within an eschatological framework. That includes not only the future fulfillment of all God's promises but also the current battle against Satan and his entire horde of evils. Third, "a person has the center of his personhood outside of himself. He is 'excentric' (*exzentrisch*)." Saarinen contrasts the medieval "concentric" view of individual human beings as substances to be analyzed according to Aristotelian definitions with Luther's view of human personhood as taking place before God,

6. Wilfried Joest, *Ontologie der Person bei Luther* (Göttingen: Vandenhoeck & Ruprecht, 1967). The study by Eilert Herms, *Luthers Ontologie des Werdens. Verwirklichung des Eschatons durchs Schöpferwort im Schöpfergeist. Trinitarischer Panentheismus* (Tübingen: Mohr/Siebeck, 2023) is scheduled to appear after the completion of this manuscript.

in relationship to God, and oriented toward the Creator and creatures outside the self.[7]

Luther found the Bible's way of considering all that exists deeper and broader than Aristotle's system for describing God, human creatures, and the origins of everything else. The Wittenberg professor rejected speculation about eternal ideas as forms of that which is experienced in this world. He favored Aristotle's focus on the created order in the form in which Ockham and his followers had understood "terms," all that human language labels from the common human experience in the creation designed and maintained by God.[8] In contrast to the ancient Greeks, he began with the definite, historical beginning, when the Creator personally spoke all that exists into existence. Luther continued to use much of Aristotle's assessment of reality; for instance, he sometimes used the familiar logical categories of substance, quantity, quality, relation, place, time, situation, condition, the active, and the passive. For him, these categories encompassed only a part of reality within his own larger framework for observing the real.[9] Thus, he subordinated Aristotle's description of what constitutes this reality to the biblical framework. If one can speak of the human experience of everyday living in terms of "spheres" or "circles" of reality, as suggested by Robert Kegan,[10] then Luther viewed the relationship of the Creator to every creature as the all-encompassing sphere of reality, centered on its Creator. Individual creatures encounter this reality in the concrete sphere of experience and observation. There they discover God as he relates to his creation as its preserver and as each creature relates in its created character or quality to other creatures of the Creator. The problem with the scholastic theology that Luther had learned lay not in its concepts of the "causes" of things or in its natural scientific judgments, as it does for some modern people. Rather, the problem lay in its attempt to use

7. Saarinen, "Martin Luther and Relational Thinking," 3.
8. Graham White, *Luther as Nominalist: A Study of the Logical Methods Used in Martin Luther's Disputations in the Light of Their Medieval Background* (Helsinki: Luther-Agricola Society, 1994); Mark Mattes, "Luther's Use of Philosophy" in *Lutherjahrbuch* 80 (2013): 115–123; Sammeli Juntunen, "Luther and Metaphysics. What is the Structure of Being according to Luther" in *Union with Christ: The New Finnish Interpretation of Luther*, ed. Carl E. Braaten and Robert W. Jenson (Grand Rapids, MI: Eerdmans, 1998), 129–160. By the 1520s, Luther was expressing discomfort with elements of Platonic speculation over eternal ideas to which he had earlier not objected, WA 10,1,1: 196,14–197,21.
9. This evaluation is supported in large part by the analysis of Rudolf Malter, "Luther und die Geschichte der Metaphysik," in *Thesaurus Lutheri. Auf der Suche nach neuen Paradigmen der Luther-Forschung*, ed. Tuomo Mannermaa, Anja Ghiselli, and Simo Peura (Helsinki: Luther-Agricola Gesellschaft, 1987), 37–62.
10. Robert Kegan, *In Over Our Heads: The Mental Demands of Modern Life* (Cambridge MA: Harvard University Press, 1994).

Aristotelian categories to perform tasks that cannot really be performed in biblical fashion with these categories. Scholastic theologians had extended a proper use of Aristotle into realms that the ancient philosopher, who had no active concept of a personal Creator God, had not been able to grasp.[11]

Since Joest's work was published, the subject of Luther's ontology has aroused attention largely because of a proposal of Tuomo Mannermaa, a Finnish ecumenical theologian at the University of Helsinki. Mannermaa argued that Luther held a "real-ontic" understanding of the salvation of sinners. This "real-ontic" view defined salvation as a "deification" of sinners through faith in Christ. Mannermaa's concern for a "real-ontic" definition of the people of God arose in part out of the failure of purely existential views of biblical salvation advanced in the earlier twentieth century to provide a solid basis for genuine trust in the person or the work of Jesus.[12] The actual formulation of this view took place in the context of the dialogue between Finnish Lutherans and Russian theologians of the Eastern Orthodox tradition who were grounded in the thought of the fourteenth century archbishop of Thessalonica, Gregory Palamas (1297–1359).[13]

A warm front of support for Mannermaa's interpretation of Luther's doctrine of justification and a cold front of critique of it met in one of the liveliest discussions among Luther scholars in the past half century. The discussion has not centered on Mannermaa's insistence on the reality or ontological actuality of what God made human beings to be and how he intervened in the history of sinful humanity as Jesus of Nazareth. Indeed, critique has focused on his assertion that Luther taught that salvation in Christ meant the "divinization" of the believer. Opponents rightly demonstrate that Luther understood the forgiveness of sins to be the center of God's saving, righteousness-restoring action as a "humanization" (although he never used this term). Although Luther relatively seldom said "let God be God," Philip Watson rightly chose this line for the title of his study of the reformer's theological development.[14] It expresses his conviction that God is Creator and that creatures differ from him essentially as

11. Theodor Dieter, *Der junge Luther und Aristoteles. Historisch-systematische Untersuchungen zum Verhältnis von Theologie und Philosophie* (Berlin/New York: de Gruyter, 2001); Brian Gerrish, *Grace and Reason, a Study in the Theology of Luther* (Oxford: Clarendon, 1962).

12. For example, cf. Tuomo Mannermaa, *Der im Glauben Gegenwärtige Christus: Rechtfertigung und Vergottung. Zum ökumenischen Dialog* (Hannover: Lutherisches Verlagshaus, 1989); ET: *Christ Present in Faith. Luther's View of Justification*, trans. Kirsi Stjerna (Minneapolis, Fortress Press, 2005).

13. Reinhard Flogaus, *Theosis bei Palamas und Luther* (Göttingen: Vandenhoeck & Ruprecht, 1997).

14. Philip S. Watson, *Let God be God. An Interpretation of the Theology of Martin Luther*; cf. WA 10,1,1: 24,6.

products of his creative word. In effect, this plea also declared, "let human creatures be human." The reformer believed that the "very good" relationship of God with his human creatures in Eden reappears in the faith in Christ that forms the center of the believer's life. This relationship of faith constitutes what it means to be "saved."[15]

Criticism began with the observation that Luther spoke in terms supporting a concept of "divinization" very seldom in comparison to his employment of the frequency of contrasting descriptions of salvation that focus on renewal of the nature of Adam. For the most part, these terms appear very early in Luther's career, and often in ambiguous expressions.[16]

15. Compare among others, Flogaus, *Theosis bei Palamas und Luther*; Klaus Schwarzwäller. "Verantwortung des Glaubens. Freiheit und Liebe nach der Dekalogauslegung Martin Luthers," in *Freiheit als Liebe bei/Freedom as Love in Martin Luther*, ed. Dennis Bielfeldt and Klaus Schwarzwäller (Frankfurt: Lang, 1995), 133–158; William W. Schumacher, *Who do I Say That You Are? Anthropology and the Theology of the Theosis in the Finnish School of Tuoma Mannermaa* (Eugene, OR: Wipf & Stock, 2010); Timo Laato, "Justification: the Stumbling Block of the Finnish Luther School," *Concordia Theological Quarterly* 72 (2008), 323–346; Javier Garcia, "A Critique of Mannermaa on Luther and Galatians," *Lutheran Quarterly* 27 (2013): 33–55. Criticism of the formulation of the theology of "divinization" concentrated on the imprecision of assessment in Mannermaa's use of terms such as "faith" and in the absence of the concept of the performative or creative nature of God's Word in Luther's thought. The "Finnish" school's seemingly minimal attention to Luther's strong emphasis on the doctrine of creation and the nature of Creator as almighty Lord of all, along with something less than a clear affirmation of the reality-changing nature of God's word as the pronouncement in his promise of forgiveness, life, and salvation, contributed to the negative appraisal of this interpretation of Luther's soteriology.

    It must be noted that Mannermaa himself strove to offset a false impression of the "godness" of believers. He argued that retaining an understanding of the distinct nature of the substantial identities of the Creator and the human creatures preserved the integrity of each as the human being became divinized through faith into a super-human status. He observed that "Luther emphasized that the incarnation of the Word, or the Verbalization of the flesh, in no way may be understood as *substantial*, as a change in the substance of God or the human creature. With the use of the term substance Luther intends to say that God and human being remain the entities that they are in themselves. . . . God does not transform himself into the human being, and the human being does not transform himself into God. Both preserve their own substances, that is, what each is in and of himself." "Hat Luther eine trinitarische Ontologie?," in *Luther und Ontologie*, ed. Anja Ghiselli, Kari Kopperi, and Rainer Vinke (Helsinki: Luther-Agricola-Gesellschaft, and Erlangen: Martin-Luther-Verlag, 1993), 18.
16. Albrecht Beutel, "Antwort und Wort," in *Luther und Ontologie*, 70–93. Particularly, in regard to Scripture passages that speak of "believers being in Christ" and "Christ being in believers," it should be noted that both the Hebrew preposition "ב" and the Greek preposition "ἐν"—usually translated "in" in a spatial sense—also can mean "together with" or "in the company of," implying an intimate relationship of two entities that retain their own identity and integrity. Thus, such passages do not mean that the identity of one person is transferred to the other; cf. Albrecht Oepke, Art. "ἐν" in *Theological Dictionary of the New Testament*, ed. Gerhard Kittel, trans. Geoffrey W. Bromiley 2 (Grand Rapids, MI: Eerdmans, 1964): 541–543. Beutel notes that the term "divinization" does not occur in Luther's works and that related terms occur a total of thirty-three times in the one hundred volumes of his writing in the Weimar edition of

Furthermore, he recognized the "ambition of divinity" in every human being. This led him to write to Georg Spalatin during the diet of Augsburg in 1530 with a plea to admonish Philip Melanchthon not to think that he could solve all problems that confronted the Wittenberg reform effort there. "Remind Philip in my name continually that we are not to become as if we were God." Melanchthon should fight against "the innate ambition for divinity that was implanted by the devil in paradise. . . . We are to be human and not God."[17] Preaching on John 19:7 the previous year, Luther commented that Adam's sin in paradise was his wanting to be God himself, just as we try to make ourselves into children of God by making ourselves ultimate arbiters of the good. Luther labeled this the worst and most serious of sins, which expresses itself also in our attempts to justify ourselves through works.[18]

Within the "Finnish school" the discussion of his view of reality has moved into its third generation. Ilmari Karimies's meticulously argued contribution to the discussion of Luther's view of reality anchors this view in an understanding of faith in which God's speaking in Scripture and the human response of trust play a smaller role than scholars have usually held. He traces Luther's means of perceiving and understanding the "real" in the period between his first lectures on the Psalms and the Diet of Worms with selected documents from the period. The tradition of Platonism conveyed by Pseudo-Dionysius, the Victorines, and Bonaventure, was available to Luther in the writings of Jean Gerson. Karimies posits that in this period "for Luther faith has both a function as cognition of God and a function as an interpretative capacity with regard to the universe (i.e., the created world)."[19] "Luther holds that the content of faith cannot be mediated merely by the grammatical signification of words, but that the ontological elements must accompany the words." Precisely what these ontological elements are that are apprehended through "illumination given by the internal Word" and how

his works, 73. When Luther spoke of "union with Christ," he was often speaking of analogies, for example, the union of husband and wife, in which the union brings each to the fullness of their own identity and does not change the masculine or feminine identity of the couple but enhances the integrity and nature of each.

17. WA BR 5:415,41–45, Nr. 1612.
18. WA 28:349,15–16, LW 69:230–231.
19. Ilmari Karimies, *Martin Luther's Understanding of Faith and Reality (1513–1521): The Influence of Augustinian Platonism and Illumination in Luther's Thought* (Tübingen: Mohr/Siebeck, 2022), 18. Karimies is somewhat critical of Mannermaa's failure to define "faith" fully, a problem his study seeks to remedy. Karimies has abandoned the term "divinization" for the concept of "participation," without giving details of the nature of the believer's "participation" with Christ.

this apprehension takes place by illumination are not clear,[20] but this definition of the grasping of reality strikes tones very similar to what Luther later labeled *Schwärmerei*, which he firmly rejected.[21] However much Luther may have actually appropriated in his early teaching from Augustinian Platonism and related traditions, it is clear that already in 1518 with the Heidelberg Theses and certainly by 1520, Luther has come to new insights informed by his ever greater reliance on his interpretation of the Hebrew prophets' conception of God and his creation. The Old Testament presentation of God and creation did not integrate well with the Platonic schema, even if Christian Platonists retained some of its elements. The concept of an illumination of the sinner that altered the reality of the sinful individual apart from the word and trust in its promise diminished in Luther's maturing thought.

Nonetheless, in this discussion, sight dare not be lost of Karimies's concern that something real—in his word "ontological"—is involved in what God has made and what believers experience in their dealing with "reality." Luther's firm conviction that God had precisely defined the nature of the objects of his creative word, including human nature, remained a constant in his thinking. God's word set reality in place, and that reality includes his design for the relationship of his creatures, including his human creatures, to live within the order and peace, the structure that God created as the defining pattern of every creature. Luther firmly believed that the Creator's design and plan for human living as revealed in Scripture reflects the reality with which human beings must live. That plan builds upon the foundational axiom that before any other details or definitions of humanity are posited, human beings are created to "fear, love, and trust in God above all things." As his explanations of the other nine commandments in his Small Catechism affirm, all human obedience that pleases God stems from this fear, love, and trust.[22]

Luther's fundamental definition of humanity with these three terms, fear, love, and trust, grounds his understanding of human reality in the relational realities of God's personal interaction with other persons and with all of creation. Albrecht Beutel's summary of the discussions of the meaning of these three foundational emotions explains the function of this formulation in the word of judgment and the word of new life in love and trust in Christ. Fear does embrace the sense of awe and wonder

20. Karimies, *Luther's Understanding of Faith and Reality*, 339.
21. Amy Nelson Burnett, "Luther and the *Schwärmer*," in OHML1, 511–524.
22. Small Catechism, explanation to the first commandment, BSELK 863/864,3–10, BC 351.

that the Creator evokes in his human creatures, but as sinners their reverence must combine with dread and trepidation before their Maker. The reformer never explained why "love and trust" becomes the one word "love" in the explanations of the other commandments. Some have suggested a grammatical reason; "fear" and "love" take the accusative, and "trust" takes the dative or combines with a preposition (e.g., "in") in German. But Beutel also accentuates the distinction of law and gospel implied in pairing "fear" with "love."[23] Toward the end of his treatment of the Ten Commandments in his Large Catechism, Luther wrote,

> Thus, [God] demands that all our actions proceed from a heart that fears God, looks to him alone, and because of this fear avoids all that is contrary to his will lest he be moved to wrath. Conversely, he demands that our actions proceed from a heart that trusts in him alone and for his sake does all that he asks of us because he reveals himself as a kind father and offers us every grace and blessing. . . . Thus the First Commandment is to illuminate and impart its splendor to all others. . . . In this way this fear, love, and trust should impel us not to despise his Word, but to learn it, to hear it gladly, keep it holy, and honor it.[24]

CONSCIENCE AS THE PERCEPTION OF REALITY

As the organ through which human beings apprehend divine and created reality, Luther spoke of the "conscience." Johannes Mathesius recorded an observation of Luther from the autumn of 1540: "conscience is twofold: in relationship to God, it is about faith; in relationship to human beings, it is about love."[25] Luther understood the conscience as the active agent by which God's human creatures perceive the structure of reality as expressed in God's law, which governs human perception of how God works[26] and thus how reality functions. Behind his use of the term *Gewissen* in German lay two terms in the Latin vocabulary of the medieval church, *conscientia* and *synderesis*. From his teachers he had learned that the

23. Albrecht Beutel, "'Gott fürchten und lieben.' Zur Enstehungsgeschichte der lutherischen Katechismusformel," in Beutel, *Protestantische Konkretionen. Studien zur Kirchengeschichte* (Tübingen: Mohr Siebeck, 1998), 46–55.
24. BSELK 1042/1043,26–1044/1045,21, BC 429–430.
25. WA TR 5:40, Nr. 5273.
26. Cf. the definition formulated by the student colleague of Luther's mentor, Johannes von Staupitz, Johannes Altenstaig, in his theological dictionary, *Vocabularius Theologie* . . . (Hagenau: Gran, 1517), LIa-b, consulted at the Herzog August Bibliothek Catalog on January 24, 2022, http://diglib.hab.de/drucke/b-49-2f-helmst-1/start.htm.

synderesis, as the spark of the conscience, directed the individual's moral sense toward proper behavior on the basis of this synderesis's apprehension of reality.[27] Following Augustine, Luther thought of "conscience" as God's addressing his entire being, not only his reason or moral will but also his emotions, with his elucidation of reality. This conscience provides the thinking that governs interaction with God in faith and with his creation in love.

To be sure, Luther also often used the term "conscience" for the moral perception of individuals, for the hearing of the voice of the law with which God prescribes human behavior. But when he stood before Emperor Charles V at the Diet of Worms in 1521 and confessed that he was "convinced by the Scriptures" and was "in his conscience captive to God's Word,"[28] his usage of "conscience" reflected the predominant definition of late fifteenth century usage. This definition embraced his entire view of reality and his whole understanding of what is true—by this time, for Luther, shaped by Holy Scripture. (That had become clear to him and both his supporters and his opponents in the Leipzig Disputation two years earlier as he made clear his distrust of popes and councils.) In Worms, by binding himself to Scripture and his conscience to the word of God,[29] Luther took his stand on his comprehensive understanding of the reality that God had fashioned as Creator.[30] Luther designated this conscience also as the "heart," as Birgit Stolt has shown.[31] In 1520 Luther wrote that Christ has given this heart or conscience righteousness in God's sight—identity as God's child—through his liberating work that swallowed up sin and death through the resurrection.[32] God addresses the heart by speaking and thus determines human existence, Luther explained to his hearers in 1534: God has not placed Jesus Christ into the hands of believers or sketched his message for the eye to behold, but God has painted this Word into the heart.[33] Jonathan Reinert traces the development of Luther's understanding of the relationship of the heart to Christ. His earlier focus on the heart as the location of true repentance in his first lectures on the psalms turned into a general designation for the source of the fervent prayers of

27. Cf. Heiko Augustinus Oberman, *The Harvest of Medieval Theology* (Cambridge, MA: Harvard University Press, 1963), 65–66.
28. WA 7:876,1–878,8; LW 32: 106–114; cf. WA 7:838,4–8.
29. WA 7: 838,3–8, LW 32: 112.
30. Cf. Jakob and Wilhelm Grimm, *Deutsches Wörterbuch* (Leipzig, 1854–1961) 6: 6219–6242, consulted on October 11, 2021, at https://woerterbuchnetz.de/?sigle=DWB#1.
31. Birgit Stolt, *Martin Luthers Rhetorik des Herzens* (Tübingen: Mohr/Siebeck, 2000), 49–57.
32. WA 7: 59,24–60,9, LW 31: 357–358.
33. WA 37: 456,37–457,16.

the faithful. By 1520, the activity of Luther's "heart" embraced the entire trust and faithfulness of believers.[34]

His treatment of 1 Timothy 4:2 in 1528 demonstrates this usage. The expression the "searing" of conscience in that passage had puzzled some patristic and medieval commentators. Luther explained that consciences are seared and made unable to detect reality when Satan transforms their way of evaluating their world and themselves. The conscience, like the person who creates a god by placing trust in someone or something, creates its own "doctrine." Luther and his colleagues understood "doctrine" as the activity of teaching the dynamic word of God.[35] They believed that what Scripture teaches functions as "the body of doctrine."[36] It embraces an entire conception of the divine, the human, and the natural world and how each goes about doing what there is for it to do. Philip Melanchthon formulated the Wittenberg understanding of his "topics" within the body of doctrine in the final revision of his *Loci communes*, reflecting the understanding of Luther and his colleagues. These articles of faith or topics (*loci*) flow out of the biblical recitation of the actions of God and the story of his people; the topics simply summarize and codify God's intent, activity, and message for his people as it has unfolded in the narratives, preaching, and letters of his prophets and apostles. The church organizes the reports of God's actions for his people into topics to ease the proclamation of the messages of law and gospel, the teaching or doctrine of Scripture. Whereas philosophy works with demonstrable propositions, theology presents the revelation of God from what he has said in Scripture. This provides a most certain foundation for knowledge of God and his creation.[37] The intense dependence on what God has specifically said in Scripture rests in part on Luther's concept, derived from the fourteenth century philosopher and theologian William of Ockham, that no necessity—and most certainly no necessity accessible to human reason—shaped God's plans formulated in eternity for the nature and form of his creatures and the course of their history. Every thing and every person is designed by God and produced

34. Jonathan Reinert, "Das menschliche Herz und Luthers Theologie. Ein weiterer Blick auf den den Weg des werdenden Reformators," *Lutherjahrbuch* 88 (2021): 44–68.
35. On Melanchthon's use of doctrine as a "verbal noun," cf. Peter Fraenkel, "Revelation and Tradition, Notes on Some Aspects of Doctrinal Continuity in the Theology of Philip Melanchthon," *Studia theologica* 13 (1959):116–118 (97–133). His analysis describes Luther's usage as well.
36. Irene Dingel, "Philip Melanchthon and the Establishment of Confessional Norms," in Irene Dingel et al., *Philip Melanchthon. Theologian in Classroom, Confession, and Controversy* (Göttingen: Vandenhoeck & Ruprecht, 2012), 161–177.
37. *Melanchthons Werke in Auswahl*, 2.1, ed. Hans Engelland (Gütersloh: Bertelsmann, 1952): 167–172.

by God; God established in creation the proper identity or righteousness of everything. God is Lord of all.

Doctrines of demons also shape consciences, or false consciences, so that a monk spins out of his imagination an image of God that demands works for salvation, Luther asserted. He operated with this understanding of the vital, essential role of the conscience driven by God's word for the good human life. It expresses itself with a righteousness that God's word creates, the righteousness of faith or trust in Christ that brands God's children with "enthusiasm, concern, diligence, and ardor."[38] It rests on the reality that God gives humankind in his communication with his human creatures, in part in nature, but definitively in Scripture.

The Wittenberg professor's concordance-like command of Scripture enabled him to draw from every part of the Bible when constructing his depictions of the several kinds of relationships that define the existence and personhood of every human being. This triad of fear, love, and trust does appear in earlier medieval theologians' works, but Luther gives no indication that he was borrowing a citation when he combined the three, also before he wrote his catechisms.[39] These relationships inform and direct as believers in Christ practice living within the bonds that link individuals to God, to Satan and his destructive forces, to themselves, to the institutions and systems of earthly societies and cultures, to other individuals, and to the creation in general. When these relationships take the shape that God planned for them, they create and support life and our own personhood in the context of Edenic peace, order, and harmony. When sin perverts these relationships, life turns sour, and death looms over daily life. Only through Jesus Christ, Luther proclaimed, can God's human creatures be delivered from bondage to sin and death. Only through Jesus can they grasp life and fulfillment in his promise of life with God forever. Christ's work restored the relationship between human creature and Creator by restoring the believer's trust in God above all else.

LUTHER'S EPISTEMOLOGY OF THE CROSS

Because God speaks and creates relationships through his speaking, Luther could not separate "ontology," his understanding of reality, from "epistemology," his understanding of communication and the source of human knowing and learning. Apart from God's revelation in the several forms of

38. WA 26: 69,7–70,1. LW 28: 310–312.
39. Beutel, "Gott fürchten und lieben," 55–58.

his word, human beings may have some sense of the Divine, for instance, from the majesty of nature or the struggles of conscience. But they get to know God personally by listening to what he says to them. God speaks to them in the person of Jesus Christ and in the message of the prophets and apostles in Holy Scripture. At times, human beings relate to one another with feelings that they cannot put into words, for example with gestures or non-rational utterances. However, their ongoing relationships depend on the communication of something of these feelings in understandable language.

Luther grounded his perception of human ways of learning of reality, and understanding it, in the apostle Paul's assertion of an epistemology of the cross in 1 Corinthians 1 and 2. The demand for signs—that is, experimental evidence—voiced by the Jews, according to Paul, brings many blessings as people explored God's world, but it can produce no true knowledge of God. For the human assessment of the evidence would then govern the knowledge that is being sought, placing the human experimenter as the final arbiter over the God being investigated. The rational logic of the Greeks serves society in many ways, Luther often stated, but it cannot ascertain the truth about God or the heart of humanity without subjecting God to humanly-determined standards of evaluation. Yet, as a unique approach to learning and knowing set apart from these empirical and logical epistemologies, Luther affirmed this epistemology of the cross. In 1533, Luther's student Veit Dietrich edited his mentor's statement in a comment on Psalm 126 that his theology "is a theology of the cross" into an assertion that his theology was a "profession" of the cross. In this case "profession" probably had the sense of a verbal confession of the cross but perhaps as an entire way of life under the cross. The confession of the faith flows out of the premise that life-embracing knowledge of God centers in God's revelation of his disposition toward his human creatures and his modus agendi in dealing with them that is cruciform in Christ. In either case, his trusted student viewed Luther's use of the cross as an epistemology of the word of the cross.[40]

THE MYSTERIES OF GOD

Luther occasionally expressed delight that God had revealed himself and his will in paradoxes, to confound the arrogance of human reasoning in

40. WA 40,3: 193,19–23; cf. Robert Kolb, "Luther's Theology of the Cross Fifteen Years after Heidelberg: Luther's Lectures on the Psalms of Ascent," *Journal of Ecclesiastical History* 61 (2010): 69–85.

matters divine, and to bring believers to humble awe and wonder before God's majesty. Sometimes this delight is attributed to the nature of Ockham's assertion that God could have designed any world God wished, a belief that delivers human beings into an arbitrary world that has no rhyme or reason. This is patently untrue when one reads Ockham, and it does not describe Luther's understanding of paradox or mystery. To be sure, his Ockhamist instructors had taught that God almighty is absolutely responsible for everything. They had also presented a created world in which God holds to the ordained order and power that he has expressed in his *pacta* governing nature and human existence. Each *pactum* expresses God's obligation to reliably hold to what God has ordained (Ockham's *potential ordinata*), with miracles outside the obligated agreement no more often in Ockham than in Thomas Aquinas and other medieval thinkers. The beings whom God had created in his own image as fully responsible or accountable for abiding by his law are neither subject to an arbitrary world, nor are they able to make up rules for life that is properly human and God-pleasing. Steven Paulson effectively presents the nature of the Creator's absolute, ultimate responsibility for the design of an orderly world:

> If Luther learned anything from his Nominalist teachers, it was that God's hidden will was not arbitrary (illegal), but merely unpredictable. Luther never adopted the teaching of God's hiddenness in absolute power as something irrational, unhinged, wild, nihilistic, and generally opposed to law. Luther did not cultivate a wild God (whose ways cannot be surely known) in contrast to a domestic God who can be grasped by human reason. When Luther said he was an Ockhamist, or followed Biel, he was referring precisely to their epistemological and theological weddedness to the theory of both eternal and natural laws—the first law governing incomprehensible, eternal objects, and the latter law ruling temporal objects, which makes it possible for thought to reflect reality accurately.[41]

From 1518 on, Luther taught that what human beings can confidently know about God comes through his revelation of himself and his will in Jesus Christ and in the Holy Scripture. The Hidden God lies beyond human grasp, but within human grasp there are mysteries, God revealing something of himself and the reality in which human beings find themselves in ways that can be described but not rationally analyzed by human reason.

Although Luther used the word *mysterium* and its German equivalent *Geheimnis* relatively seldom, he recognized that the Creator's essence and

41. Paulson, *Outlaw God*, 2: 190.

modus operandi often exceed the capabilities of the creature, to say nothing of sinful creatures, whose perceptions and analytical capabilities have been weakened and even corrupted. Mysteries are formidable challenges to human thinking, objects that will not disappear, that draw observers into their orbit. They arouse a fascination that invites inquiry but defies our best efforts at taming or solving them. In his postil sermon of 1525 on 1 Corinthians 4:1–5, Luther struggled to define the Greek *mysterion* and thought it better to leave it as a foreign expression, equating it roughly with "secret" or "hidden." God has revealed his "mysteries" to the simple, according to Matthew 11:25, as Paul reminded the Corinthians (1 Cor 2:7–8), but not so that they can explain what God is doing. They were only to trust and confess God's work.[42]

Luther's epistemology took seriously the mysteries that God Hidden has revealed in proclamation apart from explanations that satisfy the criteria of human reasoning in any culture. Most Christians recognize that this *mystery of the Trinity* and the intricate relationships that join Father, Son, and Holy Spirit together constitute territory that lies off limits for human speculation. In the German publication of a 1523 sermon on Genesis 1:28, Luther noted that both ancient and modern theologians had tried to pattern the constitution of the human being after the three persons of the Trinity and dismissed such conjecture as nothing more than guesswork.[43] Attempts to explain or depict the Trinity through the use of analogies from human life applied to the "immanent" Trinity, God's inner being, only refashion God in human images. Attempts to dictate life on earth according to inventions of the inner relationships within the Trinity only find justification for what we want to see as proper human behavior or organization in the efforts of our own minds. Luther's recognition of the limits of human imagination led him to treasure and be content with the formulations of the ancient church regarding God, for they preserve the biblical teaching regarding the Trinity from falling subject to the play of rational searching.

The greatest *mystery*, Luther affirmed, took place in *the incarnation, death, and resurrection of Christ*, a stumbling block for reason but the source of life, salvation, peace, righteousness, redemption, strength, and wisdom (1 Cor 1:30).[44] In his preface to the postil of his disciple Johann

42. WA 10,1,2: 126,18–127,2. LW 75: 118.
43. WA 24: 49,23–50,19.
44. WA 10,1,2: 127,3–128,7, LW 75:118; cf. Klaus Schwarzwäller, *Cross and Resurrection: God's Wonder and Mystery*, trans. Ken Sundet Jones and Mark Mattes (Minneapolis: Fortress Press, 2012), 74–102.

Spangenberg, Luther marveled at the wonder of what Paul calls the mystery of who Jesus Christ is (Col 1:26–27, 1 Tim 3:16). This awesome action of God in his own person had illuminated Luther's life but remained hidden, foolish, for the wise of the world.[45] The *atonement* through Christ's death and resurrection also defies all human attempts to decipher how God's mind worked in planning the deliverance and restoration of sinners to his rule and family. Likewise, the fact that salvation takes place on the basis of trust in Christ instead of on the basis of human performance eludes the minds of people in every culture since cultures preserve themselves through human accomplishment and obedience. Therefore, the stewards of these mysteries must tirelessly proclaim them as mysteries and apply them as such to their hearers.[46] Only the Holy Spirit opens human minds to grasp these mysteries that reveal the disposition of the God of grace, not through analytical understanding but through faith.[47]

Just as mysterious as the Creator's divinity and his way of restoring sinners to himself for Luther, was the mystery of *what it means to be a human being* created in God's image.

The Ockhamist vision of the world God ordered in his *potentia ordinata* presumed that human beings are created in the image of God, with functioning thinking, willing, and feeling. It also presumed that God is almighty, the Creator of all things. With those principles, Luther encountered the mystery or paradox of the biblical writers' ascription of all responsibility for what takes place in this world to the Creator while insisting that human creatures exercise responsibility for what takes place in their sphere of responsibility. How God can be completely responsible for everything if human beings are held responsible by him for being the creatures God made them to be defies the imagination. Ockhamists solved this tension through the lens of a *pactum* (covenant). This pledge of God postulated that if a person initiated the relationship and met the conditions of creaturehood and the obligation to obey—at least, as best as one could—then that person could have a good relationship with God. Thus, God's exercise of his responsibility as set forth in God's covenant to bestow grace depended on human sinners first exercising their ability to perform as best as they could. Luther found this solution totally inadequate. He came to affirm in paradoxical fashion two complete responsibilities. Luther resolved this duality of two complete responsibilities with his distinction of law and

45. WA 53: 216–18; LW 60: 283–284.
46. WA 17,2: 115,28–35, LW 76: 295.
47. WA 17,2: 160,4–28, LW 76: 337–338.

gospel. Nonetheless, for him, the complete nature of being the human creature fashioned in the Creator's image remained a profound mystery.

The *mystery of the continuation of sin and evil in the lives of the baptized* shaped Luther's preaching and teaching profoundly. The question of how evil can exist in the world of an almighty, loving God and the dilemma of why some are saved and not others express the conundrum that Gottfried Wilhelm Leibniz labeled "theodicy," the human attempt to justify God. Such efforts are as old as Job and his friends and as fresh as world news today. The more pressing question for Luther, "Why are some saved and not others?" troubled him deeply. This quandary drove him to despair, he confessed, and then drove him to the cross. The cross "justifies" God—that is, proves his "righteousness"—Paul wrote in Romans 3:25–26. Luther found himself forced to be content with that. He turned to a frequently used medieval distinction of levels of knowledge of divine matters. Based on the schema of three revelatory lights, he mused that according to the light of nature those who do good go to heaven and those who do evil go to hell. But his own experience as a sinner given the gift of faith in Christ contradicted this light. The light of grace affirms that those who trust in Christ are saved while those who do not trust in Christ are not, yet faith is a gift from God, not a human accomplishment. Therefore, the reformer resigned himself to waiting for the light of glory to answer, even if not to explain, this dilemma.[48]

Instead, Luther repeated Paul's assertion that Christ's death justifies God (Rom 3:25–26). The cross arouses the hatred of sinners, for it offers a God who defeats evil in a despicable way, dying an impossible death, with a gift that no amount of individual suffering, to say nothing of individual performance, could ever come close to matching. It transports the human mind out of the realm in which it has been given dominion and into the sheer dependence on the word that proclaims the Lord in his own suffering and dying.[49] God's justification of sinners in Christ's death and resurrection demonstrates his own righteousness.

Luther found ways to be soberly realistic about the depth of the embedded evil that haunts every person. All people experience life as a continuous coping with the mysteries of sin and evil. Luther recognized both the willing disobedience of God's commands and the addictive nature of sinful habits. He took seriously the traps that larger systems of societal organization lay for especially the pious, but he attributed their transgressions to the decisions of sinful leaders of these systems, who failed to exercise

48. WA 18: 784,1–785–38, LW 33: 289–292.
49. Paulson, *Outlaw God*, 2:329–382.

their earthly callings faithfully. All such deviations from God's design for his creatures contradict the existence of the image of a benevolent Divine in the individual sinners. Some experience the Divine, whether they conceive of their Ultimate and Absolute as "it" or "him" or "her," as arbitrary and mean-spirited rather than benevolent. Luther had initially harbored such feelings himself. At the same time, Luther experienced the combat against all evils that the Holy Spirit was waging in his life and the lives of those around him, and he felt the weight of these struggles on himself. He knew that the decisive battle in that conflict had taken place as Christ fell on the battlefield of Golgotha and reclaimed life for himself and all his people in his resurrection.

God demonstrates his cleverness in his approach to the world which the Creator handed over to humans. Instead of accepting our judgment that human life can continue apart from its Creator and abandoning us, he sticks with his rebellious creatures. He accepts our ruining his creation on our own terms. He deals with the evil that we introduced in his own manner that defies both our desire for signs or empirical proofs and our confidence in our own powers of logic. Through the nonsense and impotence of the cross, he destroys the decrepit systems of human making from the inside. He becomes present in the midst of and under the domination of evil, and then he smashes it, devouring it in his death and resurrection.

God lends his presence to those who suffer, Luther experienced. The second person of the Trinity has been there and done that, with the intention of destroying evil by submitting to it and conquering it. The mystery of the *continuation* of sin and evil after Jesus's resurrection victory remains unsolved. Its "solution" is given not in resolution of every dilemma or control of every crisis. Luther found its resolution in the recognition that God operates in this counter-intuitive way that looks foolish and powerless to the world but is actually the means by which he ultimately brings evil to its end. Through this foolish-appearing, impotent-seeming modus operandi, Luther's *theologia crucis* asserts that God engages the Evil One and all the disruption and deception that he creates in fierce combat on the battlefields of the lives of his people.[50]

50. On the development of Luther's view of the cross and suffering and its practical application, see Ronald K. Rittgers, *The Reformation of Suffering. Pastoral Theology and Lay Piety in Late Medieval and Early Modern Germany* (Oxford: Oxford University Press, 2012), esp. pp. 84–124. On Luther's transformation and later abandonment of the term "purgatory" from his medieval view of its being a place for purgation after death to a description of the trials caused by the *Anfechtungen* of Satan, world, and even God, see Min Hwan Kim, "Luther's View of Purgatory," Ph.D. dissertation, the Toronto School of Theology, University of Toronto, 2022.

One example suffices to display Luther's attitude toward each of God's mysteries. He did not gaze at the ineffable Trinity or peer into unsolvable puzzles, but he fixed his eyes and ears instead on Christ. He knew that some Wittenberg parishioners apparently were wondering if the bodies of those who had been eaten by wild animals or burned could possibly come back to life. He answered, "Yes!" In preaching on the raising of Lazarus, Luther's amanuensis Georg Rörer noted that the preacher said that Christ "will call me with a single word out of the dust and worms and cause my body to shine like the sun."[51] "Some drown in water and are eaten by fish. Some hang on the gallows and are consumed by the ravens. Some are burned in fire,"[52] but all will arise out of the earth like seeds that come to life as plants. If God had been able to assemble his human creatures in the beginning, he will be able to defy chemical dissolution in whatever form when putting them back together. The miracle of the new resurrected body needed no explanation, Luther believed. It was sufficient to live in the sure and certain hope of that body's resurrection in Christ. Unsettling though every confrontation with evil is, Luther rested in the promise of the presence of the person of his Creator, who had come in human flesh to liberate him from imprisonment in any and every evil.

The mysteries remain unexplained, but Luther addressed the existential situations in which they arise with his distinction of law and gospel. Ultimately, he pointed to the reality of the person of the present Christ, the Creator at hand, in the lives of his people.

THE ROOTS OF LUTHER'S WAY OF THINKING

Luther's initial perception of God, himself, and the world arose out of the piety of the medieval Western church. He experienced this practice of the Christian faith while growing up in the parish of Saint George in the booming mining town of Mansfeld at the end of the fifteenth century. His understanding of what it means to be Christian in his childhood and youth reflected the Germanic appropriation of the message brought by missionaries to northern Europe some eight hundred to a thousand years before Luther was born. The conversion of the first Christians in Luther's native Thuringia had occurred on the basis of political decisions made by Frankish conquerors or local rulers. These conversions took place without sufficient personnel to catechize and

51. WA 49:51,4–19.
52. WA 49: 426, 21–35.

preach in a way that would cause the people to abandon the old structures of religious thinking and practice. While some elements of the biblical faith seeped into the thinking of Luther's ancestors, their faith fell into certain structures of their ancestral religion. Throughout medieval Europe, popular Christian culture exercised a powerful influence in shaping elite Christian culture. While theology may shape popular piety to some extent, the converse is also true. In Luther's case, for example, popular piety also shaped the theology that he had absorbed in university and cloister.

The English historian Keith Thomas labels medieval Christianity a religion of "a ritual method of living, not a set of dogmas."[53] This way of conceiving the Divine and the Human focused the practice of religion by both individuals and the community not on God's gracious approach to human beings but on their own performance of, above all, sacred rituals and other religious activities. Three aspects in the amalgam of traditional religious structures and the Christianity imported into northern climes from Mediterranean churches shaped this ritualistic-hierarchical interpretation of being Christian. The first is that human performance plays a key role in winning the favor and support of divine power(s). The second is that the most important of these activities was the performance of sacred rites, religious practices and activities, generally conducted properly only by or under the supervision of the religious personnel—the hierarchy, embodied for most people in their local priest. Third, because none believed that human performance could adequately or completely close the gap between human frailty and divine omnipotence, substitutes for what Paul Hiebert called "the excluded middle" of traditional religions[54] quickly found their place in popular piety. Traditional gods took on the names of Christian saints, and Christian saints assumed functions of traditional gods.[55] The traditional divine domain of the person-like intermediaries—generally regarded as gods—under the rule of a distant and unreachable chief god evolved into the realm of the saints, real and invented persons, usually with super-human feats in their past and super-human powers in the present. It seemed difficult to believe that the King of Heaven could

53. Keith Thomas, *Religion and the Decline of Magic* (New York: Scribner's, 1971), 76.
54. Paul Hiebert, "The Flaw of the Excluded Middle," *Missiology* 10 (1982): 35–47. In his pleas for careful attention to the challenge of an excluded middle, Hiebert warns against making "Christianity a new magic in which we as gods can make God do our bidding" and do so through intermediaries, such as the saints, pp. 46–47. Hiebert's mature thought on this theme appears in *Transforming Worldviews: An Anthropological Understanding of How People Change* (Grand Rapids: Baker Academic, 2008).
55. Hiebert, "Flaw," 46–47.

really be interested in how many hairs each human head had and in the welfare of sparrows. God seemed distant; Christ, angry. But the saints, especially the Blessed Virgin, seemed to have the ability and disposition to help with daily life.

Bernd Hamm has called attention to the increasing attempts in the fifteenth century to bring God and his beneficial intervention into human lives ever closer to believers. The veneration of the Virgin Mary played the most prominent rule in these efforts to propagate a "theology of piety." Local and regional favorites and heroes of the faith, frequently early martyrs, joined her in assuming extensive influence over pious imaginations. This theology focused on Christ's suffering *with* us the woes of daily life rather than on the merciful Savior, who suffered "*for* us," died, and rose "*for* us."[56] In this way Christ offered a measure of comfort alongside the hope that the believer's participation in the ritual of the church was pleasing to God.

The power of the hierarchy, specifically the local priest, rested on his commissioning by the church as a special person, whose ordination was thought to have granted him the power to exercise the mediating role that bridged the gap between God and human creatures. The priest administered the connection of the past actions of God and the present dilemmas of his people, of God's saving actions in Jesus Christ and the contemporary sinners in village or neighborhood. Volker Leppin's analysis of the assigned task of the local priest highlights the priest's ritual re-presentation of the biblical story of salvation through the sacraments. When the priest performed the proper religious duties, he was reenacting God's reconciliation of his rebellious creatures on the basis of Christ's sacrifice in the sacrifice of the mass. In the sacrament of penance, the disobedience of Adam and Eve in Eden became real for the penitent, as did God's bestowal of a renewed relationship that demanded sweat of the brow and ushered in the pains and suffering of daily life.[57] The historical became the present, and the present was transported into the past; the congregation through its priest was able to participate in the events of the past. Only the priest could perform the sacramental actions in which all Christians were bound to participate in order to merit God's grace. Thus, he held power in the village or town even if he often earned resentment

56. Bernd Hamm, *Frömmigkeitstheologie am Anfang des 16. Jahrhunderts. Studien zu Johannes von Paltz und seinem Umkreis* (Tübingen:Mohr/Siebeck, 1982) depicts the piety as cultivated by Paltz.

57. Volker Leppin, *Repräsentation und Reenactment. Spätermittelalterliche Frömmigkeit verstehen* (Tübingen: Mohr Siebeck, 2021).

because of this and because of the people's contempt for the clergy's less than perfect conduct of life.

Thus, human performance, especially of sacred activities, defined the fate of the faithful, in daily life and in the life hereafter, even when it was taught that God's grace is also necessary for human efforts to become effective. Coming out of a Greco-Roman Christianity that depended on legal structures and human obedience to law to hold the world in order, the theologians of medieval German-speaking lands reinforced the popular beliefs that depended on human performance—especially of proper sacred activities—for salvation. Understanding the mass as the local priest's performance of a sacrifice for reconciling sinners to God and a means of channeling divine aid for daily life made sense to those schooled in the ritualistic-hierarchical religious perceptions of traditional religions. Luther's upbringing in the atmosphere of Mansfeld's practice of the faith ripened under the cultivation of his instructors in the cloister and the university when he lived in Erfurt as university student and Augustinian frater.

Luther certainly began his teaching career as a product of scholastic instructors at the university but also of the teaching and acculturation he received in the Augustinian cloister. His instructors in both cloister and university stood under influences from the University of Tübingen, where they had studied under, or in the wake of, one of the most influential German theologians of the late fifteenth century, Gabriel Biel. Biel's thinking grew out of the tradition of Ockham. As described above, the bedrock of Ockham's thinking lay in his belief in the omnipotence of God and his standing as the guarantor of order in human life, as he pledged in his *pactum* to those who merit his grace. Luther was taught to reject the view that governing reality stood an eternal law that maintained its own distinctive integrity standing eternally alongside the eternal God, even though it always accorded with God's will. Ockham posited that God had created all the laws that govern the universe and relationships among persons, the Divine and the human. Luther thought in Ockham's terms. Ockham had also absorbed from the Old Testament some sense of the goodness of creation that avoided slipping into a strongly spiritualizing assessment of the good—the spiritual—and not so good—the material—spheres. For Ockham, our expressions regarding the reality behind experience that human language describes lay not in the supernatural realm, which he acknowledged does shape what happens and exists on earth. Reality lay in what God, the Creator, had enacted in his act of creation and continued to accomplish there. Luther grasped such elements of Ockham's thought and never let go.[58]

While retaining some of these elements of his instructor's teaching, Luther departed sharply from the Ockhamist tradition because Ockham's teaching on the salvation of sinners diminished the role of grace. It left him in despairing uncertainty over his status in relationship with God. If he was certain of anything, he was certain of his own failure to meet God's initial demand for establishing peace between himself and sinners. With the ferocity of a child betrayed by parent or teacher, Luther abandoned Ockham's conception of the *pactum* governing salvation from sin. Ockham, and after him Biel and Biel's students who taught Luther in Erfurt, insisted that "by purely natural powers" sinners had to merit sufficient grace in order to enable them to perform truly good works. These works performed with the aid of grace were said to merit them the remission of eternal guilt and permit them to work off temporal punishment for their sins, either on earth or in purgatory. Luther was convinced that he had never done his best, or that which is in him naturally, to earn the grace he needed to convince God that he was righteous.

Luther's path out of this dilemma moved him through the 1510s. Ilmari Karimies argues that his concept of faith is key to his illumination that brought him close to God, a concept born of the Augustinian Platonic tradition found in later disciples of Augustine such as the Victorine monks and Bonaventure. Karimies does not explain, however, precisely how this solved the problem of his despair over his own unworthiness.[59] The research of Bernd Hamm and Volker Leppin has highlighted Luther's engagement with the school of Rhenish mystics around Johannes Tauler. In the mid to late 1510s, his reading of Tauler and his school bequeathed Luther a form of monastic devotion that highlighted God's grace given to the humble. These "Rhenish mystics" fostered in his thinking a dependence on his suffering Savior that led him out of Ockhamist efforts of performance of his own good works.[60]

58. Oberman's *Harvest of Medieval Theology* presents an authoritative exposition of Biel's thought. On Luther and Ockhamist principles, see Theo Dieter, "Luther as Late Medieval Theologian: His Positive and Negative Use of Nominalism and Realism," in OHMLT, 31–48; Theodor Dieter, *Der junge Luther und Aristoteles*, passim, esp. 175–193; and Bengt Hägglund, *Theologie und Philosophie bei Luther und in der occamistischen Tradition. Luthers Stellung zur Theorie von der doppelten Wahrheit* (Lund: Gleerup, 1955).
59. Karimies, *Luther's Understanding of Faith and Reality*, passim.
60. Cf. Leppin's overview, "Luther's Roots in Monastic-Mystical Piety," OHMLT, 49–61.

Luther took what the traditions of cloister and university offered him into the study of Scripture necessitated by his calling as professor of Bible at the University of Wittenberg. With the aid of biblical humanist scholars such as Desiderius Erasmus, Johannes Reuchlin, and Jacques Lefévre d'Ètaples he delved ever deeper into Scripture.[61] This struggle to find a safe haven with a gracious God led to his discarding some aspects of the traditions that had shaped him, whether popular piety, Augustinian Platonism, Rhenish mysticism, or Ockhamist theology. The struggle placed Luther in a new position as an interpreter and proclaimer of the biblical message. His reaction against every system that made human performance critical for salvation set the stage for his finding in Scripture that God speaks a re-creative word of promise to deliver sinners from their sin and restore them to being his children. That promise arises from, and rests on, the atoning work of Jesus Christ in his death and resurrection.

Some scholars have situated Luther's theology on a straight line somewhere between his medieval Catholic roots and the "completion" of his Reformation by John Calvin and his Reformed followers. One astute commentator on Luther's way of thinking, Philip Cary, concludes that "there are a number of points, most prominently in his sacramental theology, where Luther is closer to Catholicism than the Reformed tradition ever gets."[62] Several serious problems beset this view. This judgment ignores the profound differences with both Roman Catholic and Reformed approaches to sacraments, Scripture, the justification of sinners, and the life of the church that Luther's teaching on God's salvation of sinners, sacramental theology, and other key elements of his way of thinking reveal. Luther's understanding of the sacraments developed out of his rejection of the diminished role of trust in God's promise that he sensed in the theology that had convinced the common people that the sacraments bestowed the habitus of grace *ex opere operato*, that is, on the basis of ritual participation in the sacramental action. His rejection of the sacrifice of the mass, or of any human contribution to the impact of the sacraments on the believer, separates Luther from Catholicism both widely and deeply. Furthermore, Luther taught that the sacraments bestow salvation because God comes in them with his promise of forgiveness, life, and salvation in Christ, not through the material elements as such, or the human performance of the ritual of the mass. Therefore, on the sacraments and above all on the

61. Robert Rosin, "Humanism, Luther, and the Wittenberg Reformation," in OHMLT, 91–104.
62. Philip Cary, "Why Luther is Not Quite Protestant: The Logic of Faith in a Sacramental Promise," *Pro Ecclesia* 14 (2005): 447.

central, related, issue of justification of sinners through faith alone, Luther is not "on the medieval side of this divide."[63] Concerning Reformed views, Cary is correct in noting that Calvin diverges from Luther "in ways that can be described as narrow but deep." But those divergences also highlight vital aspects of Luther's understanding of God's way of salvation for sinners. Luther had absolute confidence that God had the power to arrange to have the body and blood of Christ given to recipients of the Lord's Supper in bread and wine. This confidence discloses his commitment to trusting Christ's Word in Scripture as well as his carefully formulated principles of distinguishing metaphorical from literal passages in it.[64] Just as important, Luther's belief that God actually exercises his power to forgive sins and create his own children out of sinners discloses his operational principle that the finite can indeed convey the infinite. This means that the ruling activity of God has at its disposal all of creation, from which he uses selected elements as his tools to accomplish his life-restoring will for sinners.[65] But on the issue of justification, which Luther regarded as "the article on which the church stands," he drew a sharp line excluding any role for human merit, and in this regard he is significantly closer to Calvin than to his medieval teachers.

The Wittenberg reformers worked hard to clarify the distinction between God's using human language and sacramental elements to convey his promise with its power and the faith that medieval Christians put in a power residing in material objects. These objects ranged from consecrated bread to a great number of holy places or things, including remnants of the saints, all of which were thought to exercise divine power in their lives. Luther strove to make clear that only those material elements that God had selected to aid in communicating his promise of forgiveness and life performed as instruments of the Holy Spirit. Words, water, and bread and wine have many uses, but God has chosen them to accompany the promise as a form of his power to save (Rom 1:17) as part of his multimedia communication. Therefore, the relationship among scholastic theologians, Wittenberg theologians, and Genevan theologians is better described as triangular rather than linear. This is true whether Luther is thought to be "the golden middle or mean," as some Lutherans propose,

63. Cary, "Why Luther is Not Quite Protestant," 464.

64. *That These Words of Christ, "This is my body"* . . ., WA 23: 139,4–147,27, LW 37: 61–66; *Confession concerning Christ's Supper*, WA 26: 318,1–32, LW 37: 207–208.

65. Amy Nelson Burnett, *Debating the Sacraments. Print and Authority in the Early Reformation* (New York: Oxford University Press, 2019), 303–310; Robert Kolb, *Martin Luther, Confessor of the Faith* (Christian Theology in Context series; Oxford: Oxford University Press, 2009), 141–151.

or a hero whose work needed completion by Calvin, or the continuer of medieval piety and thought in sanitized fashion.

THE MATURATION OF LUTHER'S THEOLOGY

To trace the roots and the path of development of the Wittenberg corner of this triangle, it is helpful to note a constellation of factors in Luther's own background. For most of the twentieth century, those scholars who focused on Luther's thought sought to identify a defining moment in which his theological development took a radical turn. These attempts reflected the particular ideas that their authors held to be critical for theology in their own time. At least in part, the search for a "conversion experience" that provides a key to Luther's thinking reflects the theological scene of the nineteenth century and its Romantic orientation. Leading figures of the "confessional revival," for instance, such as Wilhelm Löhe, Louis Harms, and Johann Hinrich Wichern, had told of critical conversion experiences. Rather than a sudden conversion experience, the process of Luther's maturing thinking came through a series of hard-fought battles between what he had been taught and what he was finding in his study of the biblical text. "I didn't learn my theology all at once. I had to ponder over it ever more deeply, and my spiritual trials [*Anfechtungen*] were of help to me in this, for one does not learn anything without practice. What kind of physician would that be who stayed in school all the time . . . Why shouldn't this be so in the case of the Holy Scriptures, too?"[66] In his preface to the Jena edition of Luther's works, Luther's confidant from early on, Nikolaus von Amsdorf, depicted the growth of his friend's convictions: "Luther searched the Scriptures; the more light and knowledge of God that he appropriated in faith, the stronger and firmer was his certainty and immovable conviction that his discovery was grounded in Scripture and that the raging and writing of his opponents was spiteful and ill-willed."[67]

Luther's theology matured within Erfurt's cloister and university life, the cradle of mystical-monastic piety and the Ockhamist world. His study of Scripture flowed together with his pastoral experience as an Augustinian brother bound to preach and hear confessions as an aid to local parish priests.[68] His own personality contributed to his sorting out the legacy

66. Table Talk, No. 352 (Fall 1532) in LW 54:50–51.
67. *Der Erste Teil aller Bu[e]cher vnd Schrifften des thewren/ seligen Mans Doct: Mart: Lutheri/vom XVII. jar an/bis auff das XXII.* (Jena: Christian Rödinger, 1555), preface.
68. On the order of Augustinian Eremites, their pastoral duties, their increasing interest in Augustine and Paul, as well as the use of humanistic methods and tools in the Erfurt cloister, see David

of his instructors. His appropriation of the skills of reading Scripture in the original Hebrew and Greek, as a part of the movement today labeled "biblical humanism," helped him form a new way of defining what it means to be a Christian. Immersion in the Psalms and Paul in the 1510s as a lecturer on Scripture gave rise to a fresh view of God, himself, and the realities of God's creation.

The roots of his developing theology had deeply penetrated the world of scholastic theology and its allegorical method of appropriating passages of Scripture for its formulation of doctrine. But his study in the Augustinian cloister in Erfurt also acquainted him with an approach to biblical exegesis that focused more on the literal sense of the text and the historical nature of God's revelation than was often the case in university lectures. The Erfurt Augustinians had included in their number an advocate of this more historical interpretive school, Hermann of Schildesche (1290–1357). Whether his manuscripts still lay in the Erfurt cloister's library at Luther's time is not clear, and other evidence of his continuing direct influence is not to be found in Luther's writings. But the strictly allegorical method of interpreting the Bible had alternative approaches in the Augustinian Eremite tradition, specifically in its Erfurt cloister.[69]

Amid his struggles, Luther's encounter with the writings of Johannes Tauler and others in the "Rhenish" school of monastic-mystical piety led him to find refuge in his own humility. From them he learned that he could in no way prepare himself to enter God's presence through his own efforts. Only in becoming totally humble before God could he please his Lord. Eventually, Luther found that the focus on his own humility did not supply the final answers to his dilemma. Nevertheless, the passive stance of these mystical thinkers made its mark on him even if he did move decisively beyond them. For instance, his infatuation with one of these writers, the author of the *Theologia Germanica* (so Luther entitled his edition of the booklet in 1516), finally dimmed because he came to recognize that its theology ultimately depended on the free movement in the human will to embrace God. For Luther, that solution did not work.[70]

Gutiérrez, *Geschichte des Augustinerordens* 2 (Rome: Historisches Institut des Augustinerordens, 1975): 116–154; Adalbero Kunzelmann, *Geschichte der Deutschen Augustiner-Eremiten 5, Die sächsisch-thüringische Provinz und die sächsische Reformkongregation bis zum Untergang der beiden* 5 (Würzburg: Augustinus, 1974): 4–104; and Eric L. Saak, *Highway to Heaven. The Augustinian Platform between Reform and Reformation* (Leiden: Brill, 2002).

69. Christopher Ocker, *Biblical Poetics before Humanism and Reformation* (Cambridge: Cambridge University Press, 2002), esp. 94–106, 224–238.

70. Volker Leppin, "Luther's Roots in Monastic-Mystical Piety," in OHMLT, 49–61; cf. Paulson, *Outlaw God*, 1: 58–61, 2: 245–256.

He never abandoned appealing to passages from the works of Bernhard of Clairvaux, but, in the words of Bernd Hamm, for Luther, "it was liberating to overcome the fixation on both outward pious actions and inward true love of God. He did this by listening to the absolving word of the gospel . . ."[71] Of Luther's engagement with Tauler and his school, Risto Saarinen argues, "Luther does not aim to practice mystical theology. He is primarily interested in deconstructing the natural and ordinary semantics of 'mine' or 'my own.' Before God the human person should be 'outside of himself' or 'external to himself' in the sense that he claims no natural powers, properties, or contributions."[72] As with his study of Ockham, Luther's reading of Tauler and other pious literature of the late medieval period altered his thinking as it was being reformed and refined on the forge of his biblical studies and his own experience.

When individuals slowly begin to realize that the foundations of life—their view of reality—set in place by parents and teachers are crumbling, they may indeed have moments in which sparks illuminate what had seemed very dark moments earlier. The old system that shaped Brother Martin's initial concept of his Christian identity broke down slowly for him. This student of Scripture and Augustinian pastor-frater encountered both the weight of the ideals of the medieval system of practicing the faith and the abuses of that system that had transformed ritual satisfaction of punishment through pilgrimages and other sacred activities, into cold cash transactions. Some semblance of faith had perhaps been able to play a role in performances of sacred activities, such as risking life to free the Holy Land, or gaining favor through visiting places, or venerating objects with the radiance of holy power. But when Luther heard from his penitents in Wittenberg and environs that plunking a coin into Johann Tetzel's box had rendered faith quite irrelevant, it changed the game. Whether the faithful were supposed to make the transactions through purchase of indulgences or masses or through the sweat of their spiritual brows in good works of all kinds, commercialized religion was the last straw for Luther. His personal conversations with God in reading Scripture and praying the psalms in the daily hours in the cloister had slowly led him to reject such dependence on his own performance of sacred activities. It led him to ever deeper insights into what God was telling him in the Bible. More and more in the 1510s, he dared to look at God face-to-face and listen to what he was saying without concentrating on whether he was making

71. Bernd Hamm, *The Early Luther: Stages in a Reformation Reorientation*, trans Martin J. Lohrmann (Grand Rapids, MI: Eerdmans, [Minneapolis: Fortress], 2020), 25.

72. Risto Saarinen, "Martin Luther and Relational Thinking," 7.

the proper response. Tetzel's indulgence preaching only greased the skids that were leading him to deconstruct the heart of the old religion and construct the message and way of life of the Reformation.

Luther had already begun to formulate a new vision of the content and method of theological education for the public in university disputations held in the twelve months between September 1516 and September 1517. The process received a special impetus from the dispute over pastoral issues raised by indulgences. In the early twenty-first century, the judgment expressed by Reinhold Schwarz has come to predominate Luther research: Luther's thought matured through key stages for over a decade, coming to a solid core around 1521.[73]

The Wittenberg professor never ceased to experiment with new formulations of elements of this core of teaching when new situations arose, as he noted in 1529 regarding his public pronouncements on the threat of the Osmanic Turk.[74] His pulpit in the churches and his lectern in the university served as laboratories for the apt application of God's word to his hearers. For example, his utterances on the relationship between the priesthood, or calling of all baptized believers, and the pastoral office shifted, but a high appreciation of each typifies his early thinking as well as his later views. His confession of the saving work of Jesus Christ and his critique of specific sins varied as the effective proclamation of law and gospel demanded, but his fundamental perceptions of both were set by 1522. Thus, instead of searching for an "evangelical breakthrough" or "tower experience," it is best to speak of Luther's "evangelical maturation."

Some scholars find the roots of his mature way of thinking in his earliest academic and homiletical ventures.[75] Stefani Leoni suggests that in his lectures on Augustine and Peter Lombard in 1509–1511 Luther was already accentuating the relational foundations of Luther's understanding of God.[76] According to Leoni, Luther shifted his view of reality from Aristotelian substantial analysis of the objects of human knowledge and inquiry to a biblical analysis grounded in relationships during the course of the first psalms lectures. Indeed, Luther never abandoned using Aristotle's principles of physics, basing descriptions of all objects of knowledge in terms

73. Reinhard Schwarz, *Martin Luther, Lehrer der christlichen Religion*, 2nd ed. (Tübingen: Mohr Siebeck, 2016), 22–23.

74. WA 30,2:107,5–108,15.

75. For example, Peter Iver Kaufman, "Luther's 'Scholastic Phase' Revisited: Grace, Works, and Merit in the Earliest Extant Sermons," *Church History* 51 (1982): 280–289.

76. Stefano Leoni, "Der Augustinkomplex. Luthers zwei reformatorische Bekehrungen," in *Reformatorische Theologie und Autorität. Studien zur Genese des Schriftprinzips beim jungen Luther*, ed. Volker Leppin (Tübingen: Mohr/Siebeck, 2015), 185–294, esp. 191–194.

of "substance" and "accident." In his 1522 postil, in his sermon on John 1 for Christmas day, he posited that the "light of grace" does not eliminate the "light of nature." Even the latter suggests that the human being and all human thoughts and powers have been created by the eternal word of God. This relationship with the Maker frames reality. Only sin obscures recognition of him in the sinner, who is by fallen nature inclined toward evil. Therefore, the natural light does not suffice to produce the good in sinners despite its continuing validity and use in other than spiritual matters.[77] Underlying this framework of investigation by "natural light" Luther found that the bedrock of life consists of the personal relationship of the Creator to all his created persons and things and their resulting relationships with each other. His daily human experience impressed upon him that if he was to have value himself and his neighbor was to be loved and served as one who has value, then ultimate reality must lie within personal structures and a relational framework.

A second stage in Luther's developing theology took form as he began to drive certain Ockhamist principles that he had learned from his instructors against others of their principles. Although membership in the Order of the Augustinian Eremites had never guaranteed a concentration on the study of the works of the Bishop of Hippo, the revival of interest in Augustine that was taking place when Luther entered the cloister made its mark on him.[78] During the course of his appropriation of Augustine's works, the nature of God as unconditionally gracious led him further in Augustine's direction since this God of love had no external rule book to hide behind. Augustine's concept of God's unconditional grace contradicted Ockham's program of human merit working its way into God's grace.

In addition, Augustine's teaching that God determined his relationship with believing sinners through the non-imputation of their sin impelled Luther toward another aspect of his thinking. God simply no longer regarded their sin as determinative of who they are and thus they were no longer defined by it. God's regard, his "imputation," not only created the reality of the person of faith by disregarding sin, as Augustine had taught. Luther came to recognize that God's imputation also regarded this person positively, as a child of God, forgiven of all sins. Thus, through his regard, delivered through his word in oral, written, or sacramental form, God performed an act of new creation.[79] The focus moved from the human

77. WA 10,1,1: 203,3–206,16.
78. As detailed in the works listed in note 57 above.
79. Erik Herrmann, "'Why then the Law?' Salvation History and the Law in Martin Luther's Interpretation of Galatians 1513–1522," Ph. D. Dissertation, Concordia Seminary, St. Louis, 2005.

being's obedience to the sinner's relationship with God. The sinner had become holy because God said so and viewed her as his child. Luther was turned from looking inward into himself to looking outward, toward the gracious God who revealed himself as Jesus Christ. The personal aspect of reality at its very root grew in Luther's thinking as he abandoned his medieval definition of being Christian through Augustine's drawing him into the conversation with the Scripture's God of conversation and community.

Not only Augustine's views were influencing Luther. A host of voices from the past fed into Luther's processing of his reading of the biblical text from the ancient fathers and commentators up to his own day. And yet David Steinmetz found that Luther demonstrated an "astonishing degree of independence from his teachers . . . from the very beginning. Luther is always more than the sum of the parts of his theological heritage. Luther learned from Staupitz, Trutfetter, Biel, and Paltz. . . . But [his] first work . . . carries an original and unforgettable stamp."[80]

The final stage arose within Luther's engagement within the thought of the apostle Paul as he lectured on Romans and Galatians, 1515–1517, and then moved on to lectures on the Epistle to the Hebrews and a second lecture course on the psalms, 1517–1521.[81] Augustine's influence was particularly important at the beginning of this stage, which was interrupted by his travel to Worms and stay at the Wartburg, 1521–1522. By the time Luther returned to lecturing at the university, several key hermeneutical principles had taken firm root to provide the framework for his exposition of Scripture and the address of its message to his contemporaries.

From his thinking on God's regard or view of reality as determinative of what is real, he recognized that, in Genesis, God's speaking had shaped the world. God not only created the world through his speaking, but his word also sustains every aspect of creation. For Ockham, God's word, found in both the Bible and the teaching of the church, determined ultimate truth. The truth regarding God himself and the humanity he had created in his own image lay beyond human reason's ability to master.[82] Luther abandoned the ultimate authority

80. Steinmetz. *Luther and Staupitz*, 141–142.

81. On the delicate interweaving of his various concerns regarding pastoral practice and the care of souls in this critical period of development, see Anna Marie Johnson, *Beyond Indulgences: Luther's Reform of Late Medieval Piety, 1518–1520* (Kirksville, MO: Trueman State University Press, 2017).

82. Volker Leppin, *Geglaubte Wahrheit. Das Theologieverständnis Wilhelms von Ockham* (Göttingen: Vandenhoeck & Ruprecht, 1995), 39–126; Volker Leppin, *Wilhelm von Ockham. Gelehrter, Streiter, Bettelmönch* (Darmstadt: Wissenschaftliche Buchgesellschaft, 2003), 47–86.

of the pronouncements of the church but accorded such authority to Scripture. The gospel of Jesus Christ, according to Paul, Romans 1:16, exercises power to save.

By 1519 Luther discovered in the concept of "promise" a construct that conveyed his conviction that God's pronouncement of forgiveness of sins through Christ's death and resurrection actually re-creates the determinative identity of those who trust his promise. God's word re-creates sinners on the basis of what Christ accomplished by dying and rising for God's chosen children.[83] Luther recognized that God is present in his word[84] and that his word concretely addresses human beings in oral, written, and sacramental forms. He believed that God is speaking to all readers in the words of Scripture as a person in conversation with readers and hearers. The oral culture in which he grew up experienced words on the hand-written or printed page as media of the spoken word.[85] Therefore, the reformer suffered or enjoyed personal engagement with his Lord as he read, taught, and preached from the pages of the Bible, as he heard his promise proclaimed by his colleagues, as he witnessed baptisms, recalling his own, and tasted the promise in the Lord's Supper.[86]

Luther probed the depths of the biblical concept of promise as pledge regarding the future. In God's mouth, this pledge or promise becomes a description of present reality. But Luther was only too aware of the continuation of sin and evil in the daily experience of the baptized. His perception that no explanation can comprehend why evil continues in the experience of God's people led to his conviction that the Christian

83. Oswald Bayer, Promissio *Geschichte der reformatorischen Wende in Luthers Theologie*, 2nd ed. (Darmstadt: Wissenschaftliche Buchgesellschaft, 1989), ET by Jeffrey Silcock, forthcoming; Robert Kolb, *Martin Luther and the Enduring Word of God. The Wittenberg School and its Scripture-Centered Proclamation* (Grand Rapids, MI: Baker Academic, 2016), 46–74.

84. In his current work on the Reformation concept of God's presence in his word, fundamentally in Scripture, Ronald K. Rittgers has sharpened my perception of this position in Luther and its significance. Rittgers views it as a form of "enchantment" and argues against the tradition of Max Weber and Ernst Troeltsch, as it has developed over the past century, with its interpretation of the Protestant Reformation as a de-enchantment or a demystification of the world. Cf. also the critical overview of Alexandra Walsham, "The Reformation and 'the Disenchantment of the World' Reassessed," *The Historical Journal* 51 (2008): 497–528. Rittgers argues that the presence of God and his activities as the gospel effects his power in proclamation from printed page or oral sources preserved and focused, even strengthened, the perception of human life in the hands of a source of power beyond human control.

85. William A. Graham, *Beyond the Written Word: Oral Aspects of Scripture in the History of Religion* (Cambridge: Cambridge University Press, 1987), 7, 29, 63, 150.

86. On God's being present in the conveying of the gospel of Christ, cf. Paulson, *Outlaw God*, 3:71–109.

life is a life of repentance.[87] Luther's own experience convinced him that he continued to fall into temptation daily, and his hearkening to God's word of absolution assured him that God regarded him as holy for Christ's sake. His formulation *simul justus et peccator* (at the same time a righteous person and a sinner) occurs relatively seldom in his writings, but the concept permeates his proclamation and instruction. This struggle with sin, as Paul had described it in Romans 7, necessitated this daily repentance.

Expressed in the first of the Ninety-five Theses, "the whole life of a Christian is a life of repentance,"[88] this fundamental thesis matured over the years into his affirmation of the continued impact of God's word in baptismal form on the Christian each day. Baptism initiates a life in which "the old Adam in us with all sins and evil desires is to be drowned and die through daily contrition and repentance, and on the other hand daily a new person is to come forth and rise up to live before God in righteousness and purity forever."[89] This life of repentance concretely practices his distinction of law and gospel, as the law reveals a person's sin and calls the sinner to abandon it and all false gods, as the gospel creates faith and thus takes possession of this reborn child of God. Luther viewed each sermon as a search expedition seeking the unrepentant and the repentant in order to apply the appropriate treatment to their specific dilemma.

Luther recognized that God has revealed both his own intention and action on behalf of sinners, which he labeled "gospel," and God's design for good human living, which he labeled "law." The reformer acknowledged that both terms have multiple meanings in Scripture, but using them in tandem became, for him, the key to reading Scripture. The law's presentation of God's will and plan for human living always accuses sinners and condemns them. The law is like a mathematical formula. It does not create reality but reports on what God has designed and made; it calculates what is there in the person it assesses. It is not inventive but only evaluative.[90]

Because of the mystery of the continuation of sin and evil in the lives of the faithful, the law's accusation calls us to daily repentance. Gospel speaks of what God has done for us, and law speaks of what we do as

87. On Luther's maturing shift to a new understanding of repentance, see Hamm, *Early Luther*, 85–109; cf. also Robert Kolb, "Old Adam, New Martin: The Fatal and Resurrecting Consequences of Baptism in Luther's Use of Romans 7," in *Simul: Inquiries into Luther's Expression of the Christian Life*, ed. Robert Kolb, Torbjörn Johansson, and Daniel Johansson (Göttingen: Vandenhoeck & Ruprecht, 2021), 63–78.
88. WA 1: 233,10–11, LW 31: 25.
89. Small Catechism, Baptism, question 4, BSELK 884/885,12–18, BC 360.
90. My pastor, Andrew Dinger, gave me this comparison as one more at home with mathematics than I.

his faithful, obedient children. The gospel comforts the repentant and re-creates them as children of God, who perceive themselves as children whose trust in Christ moves them to obedience to his commands. Luther encountered the person of his Lord as he heard, and as he proclaimed, both law and gospel.

The distinction of law and gospel as a key to what God has said to his human creatures in Scripture correlated with Luther's assessment of what it means to be human. He broke with the medieval teaching that ultimately God judges human beings on the basis of their obedience to his law even though medieval teachers all acknowledged that their keeping of the law arises at some point out of the aid of God's grace. Luther came to distinguish two kinds of human righteousness. This twofold righteousness or identity as child of God differentiates what constitutes the core identity of God's child and the relationship between Creator and human creature from the expression of that core identity in relationships of human creatures with each other and with the rest of God's creation. The core identity as child of God is not bestowed by obedience to the law of God but solely by God's gracious favor; it does create obedient children, who, recognizing God's goodness and their own belonging to his family, strive to act like children of God.

Luther formally presented this distinction in a work entitled *Treatise on Three Kinds of Righteousness* published in 1518 and developed it more precisely in his *Treatise on Two Kinds of Righteousness* of 1519. He initially distinguished the civil righteousness or identity of people from the twofold righteousness of Christians in relationship to God and in relationship to God's creatures. All his likely readers were Christians. This may be the reason why, despite his continuing belief that those outside faith in Christ can externally perform acts in accordance with God's law, Luther focused in the second treatise on the twofold nature of what constitutes human integrity. In 1519 he distinguished righteousness granted from outside ourselves (*justitia aliena*) from the righteousness we perform ourselves (*justitia propria*); later he labeled them passive and active righteousness (*justitia passiva / activa*). The former is the identity bestowed by the parents to whom we owe our origin; God alone creates and re-creates human beings and gives them the trust that stands at the heart of who they are. The latter is the identity that these children express as they meet parental expectations for them by following the rules this heavenly Father has laid down for his children.[91] These two aspects of his person composed

91. Robert Kolb, "Luther's Hermeneutics of Distinctions: Law and Gospel, Two Kinds of Righteousness, Two Realms, Freedom and Bondage," in OHMLT, 176–178.

the constitution of the person whom Luther perceived himself to be, in relationship to God and in every relationship to other people and to the rest of God's creation. The person who is righteous by trusting God's judgment that sin has been forgiven and new life inaugurated, by the very nature of this trust, wants and seeks to act as God's righteous child.[92]

Luther also perceived that human creatures live out and practice their passively received identities as God's children and their actively serving identities as these children in two dimensions of the life God that designed for them. Luther used the term *Reich*, usually translated as "kingdom," in several ways. He used it, on the one hand, as an expression of God's rule and Satan's rule, and on the other hand, he used it as a description of God's own rule in each of two spheres of life. The sphere of our relationship with God is what we might call the vertical dimension and Luther called "the heavenly kingdom" or "the kingdom of God's right hand." The sphere of our relationships with the rest of creation, including other people, is then the horizontal dimension of life, what Luther designated as "the earthly kingdom" or "the kingdom of God's left hand." In the former, Christians recognize their passively established righteousness and practice the active righteousness of giving witness to their Lord and praising him and praying to him. In the latter they recognize their passively given identity as children of God and actively act it out in service, love, and care for other people and for God's creation.

As this concept of God's word was developing, Luther outlined the foundation of his call for reform in theses designed to explain why he was advancing his new formulations of key biblical terminology; he composed these theses to explain his argument to his Augustinian brothers. He advertised "our theology" as a *theologia crucis* in the Heidelberg Theses of April 1518. The role of the cross of Christ set the distinction of God Hidden (*Deus absconditus*), who lies beyond the grasp of the creature—especially of the sinful creature—from the God Revealed (*Deus revelatus*). Human reason is baffled by many actions of the Hidden God and dares not venture into speculation and explanation of these actions. Only as God has revealed himself in Jesus Christ, and in the prophetic and apostolic writings through which God addresses humankind, can human beings recognize God as he really is. He does hide himself in a crib as baby and on the cross as a criminal as well as in the crypt as corpse. These are forms in which human reason does not expect God to appear. The theologians of the cross crucify their own dependence on reason and thus their own

92. Cf. Joest, *Ontologie*, 274–279, 298–320, and essays in *The Alien and the Proper: Luther's Twofold Righteousness in Controversy, Ministry, and Citizenship* (Irvine, CA: 1517 Legacy, 2022).

attempts to establish autonomy for themselves. Alone in the wisdom and power revealed in what seems foolish and impotent to human reason (1 Cor 1–2) can human creatures grasp how God is, and is present, in the fallen world. Therefore, instead of defining human beings as Aristotle's *animal rationalis*, Luther found true humanity centered in being a person who fears, loves, and trusts God above all things, an *animal fidens*.[93]

This view of God Hidden and Revealed and of human beings as people of trust rather than merely *animales rationales* appears most clearly in *On Bound Choice* of 1525, the Jonah commentary of 1526, and the Psalms lectures of the early 1530s, but it remained a guiding principle for other works throughout his career.[94] In addition to the axiom that God is to be found only in his revelation of himself and that human beings are defined, first of all by their trust in their Creator, and then by his design for their lives, Luther focused on the cross in his proclamation of Christ's atoning work. His account of the believer's experience of the cross of service in vocation and the cross of persecution and rejection by the world also reveal his use of the cross as a guide for interpreting Scripture and daily life.[95] In Luther's estimation, theologians of the cross recognize the boundaries of their engagement and let the Hidden God remain hidden. They recognize that the Holy Spirit governs the conversation with us, and so they listen all ears for what he tells them as his message flows out of Scripture into their world. In full trust and confidence, they throw themselves completely into the hands of God, revealed in Jesus Christ, and engage him in ongoing conversation in the face of both his blessings and the attacks of evil, especially the Evil One, (*Anfechtungen*) of all kinds.[96]

Christ's suffering on the cross provides not only the liberation of sinners from the domain of sin. It also sets an example for them and elucidates the nature of the believer's life in this world. In 1530, at the Castle Coburg, Luther preached on Christ's passion, noting that Christ by his suffering not only saved us from the devil, death, and sin but also that his suffering is an example that we are to follow in our suffering. The Holy Spirit supports us in this suffering by being present in daily life through his word in all its forms. Though our suffering and cross should never be so exalted that we think we can be saved by it or earn the least merit through it, nevertheless we should suffer as Christ suffered so that we may

93. Gerhard O. Forde, *On Being a Theologian of the Cross* (Grand Rapids, MI: Eerdmans, 1997).

94. Steven Paulson, *Luther's Outlaw God: Volume 1: Hiddenness, Evil, and Predestination* (Minneapolis: Fortress Press, 2018).

95. Cf. Forde, *On Being a Theologian of the Cross.*

96. On the critical role of Luther's Anfechtungen in his evangelical maturation, cf. Hamm, *Early Luther*, 37–58.

be conformed to him. God has ordained that we should not only believed in the crucified Christ but also be crucified with him (Matt 10:25, 38).[97]

ON LUTHER'S POLEMICAL "METHOD"

Much has been written, often in auxiliary comment on another subject, about Luther's practice of his call as teacher of the Bible, that is, a theologian of the church. His oath to serve the church as a teacher of Scripture, a part of his receiving the degree of *Doctor in Biblia*, determined his commitment to the Holy Scriptures. His approach to them arose not only out of his own personal crises of faith—all theology is autobiographical—but also out of his experience as an Augustinian friar, preaching and hearing confessions in the vicinity first of Erfurt and then of Wittenberg, and also engaging in what he deemed "mutual conversation and consolation of the Brothers"[98] in the cloister. He sought the clear meaning of the language of Scripture because he believed that the Holy Spirit had been effectively present in the origin of its texts and in their delivery. He experienced God's speaking to him from the words of the prophets and apostles and felt called to continue the conversation with hearers and readers as a "teacher of Bible." The availability of both the Hebrew Bible and Johannes Reuchlin's Hebrew grammar and dictionary opened up new and deeper vistas of what God was trying to tell him. The appearance of Erasmus's edition of the New Testament filled him with delight and drove him ever deeper into its texts. His knowledge of the Latin Vulgate and of the Hebrew and Greek texts of Scripture flowed into his gifts of artistic command of German and solid familiarity with the Latin of his university world, strengthened by his sense of effective rhetoric, to make him the proclaimer of Christ that he became.

A vital part of his theological method involved, as it has for the church throughout the ages,[99] rejecting the errors of the day upon which the truth of Scripture shed light. Polemic formed an essential element in his theology (as it does for every public thinker). Elements of his teaching were shaped by "binary opposites," to use the linguist's designation, usually in Luther's case not suppressed. Irene Dingel has shown how methods of the search for truth within the university communities of Europe, practiced in the public disputation of pro and contra handed down formally in the

97. WA 32:28,28–29,12, LW 51: 198.
98. BSELK 766/767,4–5, BC 319.
99. Hans-Werner Gensichen, *We Condemn, How Luther and 16th Century Lutheranism Condemned False Doctrine*, trans. Herbert J. A. Bouman (St. Louis: Concordia, 1967).

Sententiae of Peter Lombard, moved to the vernacular and to the populace as a result of the attacks on Luther and his defense against them elicited by the publication of his Ninety-five Theses on Indulgences.[100]

Truth was important to Luther's critics and to his own circle because they all believed that life in this earth has consequences for existence beyond death, and those consequences consisted of the difference between heaven in God's company and hell in devastating isolation from the Creator of life. A sense of betrayal haunted Western Christendom throughout the sixteenth century. The papal court felt that this Augustinian brother was betraying the pope and God himself with his radical reinterpretation of certain basic concepts of biblical teaching. Luther felt betrayed by the papacy, which he had regarded as the guarantor of God's truth. His growing disappointment with Pope Leo's court drove him finally to label the very institution of the papacy "Antichrist."[101] His colleague Andreas Bodenstein von Karlstadt perceived Luther's "go slow" policy in introducing practical reforms and his sacramental teaching as a betrayal of the original aims of the Wittenberg reform. Luther regarded Karlstadt as a brother turned betrayer because of his failure to realize what he himself had advocated at Luther's side in the years leading up to 1521. Ulrich Zwingli and Johannes Oecolampadius felt that Luther had betrayed reform as well by remaining stuck in medieval sacramental doctrine, and Luther felt betrayed by these two, who had praised his reform efforts, when they could not believe what he saw clearly on the biblical page. Polemic came naturally to those who felt that eternal life and eternal death were hanging in the balance and that the gospel was being undercut by their opponents.

The following chapters explore the nature of Luther's practice of thinking and preaching or teaching theologically, that is, biblically. These studies argue for the centrality, or fundamental nature of his understanding of reality, to be based on the relationships set in place by, and continuously experienced in the personal activity of, the omnipotent and omnipresent Lord, Creator, Deliverer, and Re-Creator, as he goes about confronting and engaging his human creatures in his world. Being *incurvatus in se* (turned in upon ourselves), results in the breakdown in the personal

100. On the significance of polemic as an instrument for determining the truth, see Irene Dingel, "Pruning the Vines, Plowing Up the Vineyard: The Sixteenth-Century Culture of Controversy between Disputation and Polemic," in *The Reformation as Christianization: Essays on Scott Hendrix's Christianization Thesis*, eds. Anna Marie Johnson and John A. Maxfield (Tübingen: Mohr/Siebeck, 2012), 397–408, and Irene Dingel, "Von der Disputation zum Gespräch," *Lutherjahrbuch* 85 (2018), 61–84.

101. Scott H. Hendrix, *Luther and the Papacy, Stages in a Reformation Conflict* (Philadelphia, Fortress, 1981).

relationship that God designed to stand at the core of human existence. The breakdown has ended for those who trust God's promise personified in God incarnate, Jesus of Nazareth, the Messiah. Only in face-to-face hearkening to God as he pronounces sinners liberated from their bondage to sin can the relaxed and truly human life burst out of this prison. Luther reminds us of this as he explores the corners and contours of human life as the persons God created human beings to be, in relationship with him and with the whole of his creation.

1.

The Reformer (Not Quite) Face to Face with God Hidden

Luther coram Deo abscondito

GOD OF MYSTERY, GOD OF MIGHT

Martin Luther's account of everything in nature and history placed all of reality in the hand of God because everything had begun with his speaking it into existence. The creation of reality in the beginning came through God's saying, "Let there be." Luther defined all that God has done and made, things in general, as words of God's language.[1] Neither the elements of nature nor human beings can claim existence independent of God. They exist only through his action, his activity. His word and hand embrace and guide all that God has created.[2] God then placed all things that he had spoken into existence and placed them in the dominion of his human creatures. They came late to the scene, at the end of the week. What the Creator had already prepared, he placed in their care. They had played no role in the origin of anything. They were simply given responsibility

1. WA 42: 35,39, LW 1: 47.
2. Thus, Risto Saarinen's comment that it may be misleading to call Luther's view of the relationship of the believer and the Creator an "ontology," while worthwhile caution, misses the larger framework of Luther's thinking in terms of God's creative as well as his re-creative activity; he did indeed "develop [a] full-fledged relational account of reality," through his concept of the creative word of God, also in its providential role. Cf. Saarinen's "Martin Luther and Relational Thinking," in *Oxford Research Encyclopedia of Religion*, https://doi.org/10.1093/acrefore/9780199340378.013.344, 113–114.

for taking care of God's world. Their dominion was to imitate his own lordship, a servant lordship that lifts up and sustains, not a dominion that tyrannizes and manipulates.

Luther never ceased to believe that God had brought forth every thing and every person, angelic and human, according to his plan. He was taught that God's covenant set a law in place as his reliable guide for practicing our humanity. He never abandoned his belief that God had designed the only life that would please him and be satisfying to his human creatures. He created the law to set before these creatures what this design is. He also believed that the rational human mind exercised care for God's gifts based on God's gift of reason. Aristotle held that reason operates based on an eternal, immutable law, accessible to human reasoning. Luther strove to live life on the basis of Scriptural revelation and his inborn sense of God's design for a sufficient life. The young Luther judged himself based on the law that God had decreed. He never ceased believing in the order that God placed into all creation, including human life, as a reflection of the peace of Eden to which God calls his human creatures to return.

Luther did not believe that the Creator is the Great Unknowable. Luther was convinced God has revealed himself clearly in the incarnation of his second person, Jesus of Nazareth, and as the Holy Spirit spoke through prophets and apostles. Far less clear and complete are the traces that God's creative activity has left in the created order. Human creatures, especially in their sinful state, cannot fully know God. God remains, in part, hidden, and God Hidden remains out of bounds for human reasoning. In his majesty the Hidden God defied the reformer's imagination, puzzled him in the way he dealt with human beings—especially believers—and terrified him as he considered his own sinfulness.

THE CONFRONTATION OF BROTHER MARTIN AND THE HIDDEN, MAJESTIC, AND ALMIGHTY GOD

The idea that God is more than meets the eye rose to prominence in Luther's thinking as he was struggling with the threat of God's judgment. It quickly embraced more than just that threat. The condemnation that God visited through his law was, in fact, for the young Augustinian brother quite clear. But other factors contributed to his forming the foundation of his concept of the *Deus Absconditus*, that God hides himself and remains God in spite of the fact that his actions contradict our expectations and presuppositions about him and his behavior.

Luther's ruminations on this fact appear explicitly in detail in his Heidelberg Theses prepared for his Augustinian brothers in April 1518, in order to meet the demand for an explanation of his heretical thoughts in his Ninety-Five Theses on indulgences published in the fall of 1517. At their meeting in Heidelberg in April 1518 he pointed to the contrast between what seems to be noble and proper human works, eligible for merit in God's sight, and God's way of acting, which seems "unattractive and appears evil." God's unconditional, gracious forgiveness gives the impression to sinners that he operates outside of, if not against, his law demanding proper performance. That Jesus's suffering and cross trump human works seems contradictory, improper, illegal.[3]

Some scholars suggest that the Heidelberg Theses are "pre-reformational" because they do not contain aspects of Luther's thought that became key in later years. For the most part, these scholars believe that "reformational" can be dated more or less precisely (depending on what element, or elements, of Luther's mature theology each scholar deems as the key to that mature way of thinking). Some scholars find that this contrast of God Hidden and God Revealed does not appear consistently throughout Luther's career. In fact, the contrast between the "more to God than meets the eye" and the God who appears broken and bloody on the cross grew sharper, and gained breadth and depth, in later works. The basic concept remained: there is much more to God than human reason can command. Some of that "more" instills, and some of it fosters, wonder at God's love. It may also produce awe and even terror by fostering a sense of vulnerability to this overwhelming power. This contrast between *Deus absconditus* and *Deus revelatus* remained an unshakable presupposition and pillar of Luther's thinking.

Luther's thinking expanded into the recognition that the person of the Creator, the Almighty, is the one who is what he is, as he told Moses (Exod 3:14). He is the one who identifies himself clearly in human language and historical actions as a loving, merciful person. This person can never, as Creator, be grasped and explained completely by creatures. They remain dependent on God's word, in fleshly and linguistic forms. Luther continued to acknowledge, as he emphasized in Heidelberg, that human reason, designed to help make our horizontal relationships work, fails to grasp the fact that his Creator as parent does the parental thing while expecting that his creatures will do the creaturely thing. Those expectations arise in the world and for the people whom God has created, and then, out of the nothingness of their sinfulness, re-created.

3. WA 1: 353,15–354,36, LW 31: 39–41. Cf. Paulson, *Outlaw God*, vol. 1.

In addition, Luther struggled increasingly with the contradictions between daily human—even Christian—experience and God's promise to give blessings, letting his goodness flow. From his Ockhamist instructors, Luther had learned that the *pactum*, established by God's *potentia ordinata*, his exercise of power as he had ordered it in his covenant, guaranteed certain standards and accountability on God's side of the relationship as well as on the human side. Luther could speak occasionally of God's immutability. God's person does not change. The important point, however, is that he is reliable. Stones can be relatively immutable; people are reliable. That is what Ockham meant with his placing the world under the covenants that God, in his complete divine freedom, had made as he decided what law and order he would write into the existence of his creation. Luther relied on God's reliability.

But in Scripture and in his own experience Luther found God exercising his responsibility for everything in contrary ways. He noted Joseph's experience and compared it with Jacob's: Both suffered in the process of being done to death so that they might get used to trusting his promises pure and simple, "with eyes shut," in the face of God's being nowhere in sight nor reach of sound. Believers experience that God hides himself, and they feel that they are perishing in the contradiction of the promise.[4] Among the worst of such experiences that believers face, the confrontation with their own sin strikes terror in the heart at the thought that "the Holy Spirit cannot abide with such a sinner as I am."

David also illustrated that experience for Luther. Preaching on Matthew 24,15–28, in 1537, the reformer did not pursue the question of why such a thing as David's sinning against Bathsheba and Uriah could happen. He only posited that despite David's greatness, God removed his support, and the king fell into sin. That demonstrated the power of Satan.[5] But lecturing on Psalm 51 in 1532, edited for publication in 1538, Luther asserted the necessity of God's promise coming to the contrite heart that believes that God is the father of mercy and all consolation (2 Cor 1:3). "The reliable means of purging, the most effective medicine that is necessary to cleanse the bones and conscience of the sinner, came to David, as it came to Paul and Peter." For the Holy Spirit caused them to repent, and they received the mercy of God.[6] David needed to be reduced to his own "purgatory," weighed down by the sorrow over his own sin and God's wrath, to be able to cling to God's faithfulness in showing mercy. As he wrote the

4. WA 44: 269,31–270,24, LW 6: 360–361.
5. WA 45:262,19–23.
6. WA 40,2: 415,24–417,17.

psalm, David knew from his own experience that he should bring other transgressors to repentance (verse 13).[7] David's story imposes the law most strictly, but Luther perceived the message of this narrative as comforting in its telling of God's merciful rescue as gospel. The reformer did not try to solve the contradictory nature of such a transgression occurring in one of his chosen children. Only Nathan's proclamation—not an explanation of how God works—could break through David's sin and David's despair. Only God's embrace in the prophet's declaration could pierce the darkness of the situation.[8]

Those contrary experiences—his own and those of the figures reported or reporting in Scripture—shifted Luther's focus from human experience and rationality to the person of his Lord. Such experiences turned him to the voice of his Creator that came in the apparent foolishness and impotence of the dying God-man on the cross (1 Cor 1 and 2). The feelings of wonder at God's almighty Godness, his perplexing and even offensive failure to honor his promises to keep the world in order, and his wrathful judgment blend in Luther's use of his distinction of God Hidden and God Revealed. The distinction framed and shaped his thinking to his dying day, an essential element in the *theologia crucis* that he had practiced all his days and claimed still in 1532 was "our theology."[9]

As Steven Paulson has shown, Luther briefly profited from his reading of Dionysius the Areopagite, who encouraged him to recognize the fact that God in his essence remains unknown and unsearchable. But Luther did not find satisfying the stance simply of awe that appreciates God's being God. For God also, in that which Luther could not grasp, terrified the poor Brother and offended his sense of justice and propriety. This turned Luther from gazing heavenward because he became convinced that his gaze could not pierce to the heart of Divinity. He looked instead to God on the cross and in the tomb, the very mention of which offends our imagination of the Divine and offends our sense of order, justice, and equilibrium.[10] But precisely there, coming to terms with all evil through

7. WA 40,2: 436,22–437,24.
8. Cf. Paulson, *Outlaw God*, 2: 271–328.
9. Cf. the introduction of this volume, pp. 35–37, and Robert Kolb, "Luther's Theology of the Cross Fifteen Years after Heidelberg: Luther's Lectures on the Psalms of Ascent," *Journal of Ecclesiastical History* 61 (2010): 69–85.
10. Steven D. Paulson, *Luther's Outlaw God*, 1: 31–33, 2: 189–205, 231–235, 243–245, and Steven D. Paulson, "Luther's Antidote to Apophatic Theology," *Lutheran Quarterly* 35 (2021), 249–272. Cf. Knut Alfsvåg, "Deification as Creatio ex nihilo. On Luther's Appreciation of Dionysian Spirituality," in *Hermeneutica Sacra. Studien zur Auslegung der Heiligen Schrift im 16.- und 17. Jahrhundert / Studies of the Interpretation of Holy Scripture in the Sixteenth and Seventeenth Centuries*, ed. Torbjörn Johansson, et al. (Berlin: de Gruyter, 2010), 59–84. On Pseudo-Dionysius, cf.

dying and reclaiming life by rising from his lying as cold, stiff corpse, God spoke to Brother Martin, by this time professor of Holy Scripture as well.

Therefore, Luther told his students that the greatest danger that they faced was the temptation to stray into heaven by speculating about God's power, wisdom, and majesty that lie far beyond human capacity to imagine. Such speculation, Luther knew from experience, would only lead to reliance on oneself instead of acknowledging one's createdness and dependence on the Creator. That would lead them to fall as Satan had, losing God and all that he has given. The despair that the professor knew only too well would envelop any such speculation. Luther referred his students to the person of Christ rather than to any attempt at rational elucidation, for such use of reason is bound to fail.[11]

Luther's experiences with this God who remained hidden in the fullness of his majesty and power provides a kind of case study of the encounters with the "Totally Other"—the "Holy" or the "Numinous"—as described in the theory advanced by the Marburg professor Rudolf Otto (1867–1937). Otto's theory reflected his research in lands of what we call the majority world. Otto identified the "irreducible moments" of religious conviction and experience to encounters with natural phenomena behind which lurk the *mysterium tremendum* [the mysterious that makes you shake in your boots] and the *mysterium fascinans* [the mysterious that draws you magnetically to itself].[12] Otto based his case on examples from traditional religions, but medieval Christianity exhibited many of the same characteristics that he encountered there.

According to Otto, this *mysterum tremendum*, which Luther would have associated with a natural knowledge of God, confronts human beings in God's demonstration of his overwhelming almighty power. It breeds the deep sense of what it means to be creature at the mercy of a divine person or force, who, or which, can wipe us from the face of the earth with a single thunderbolt or a breath of the wind. A sense of absolute awe envelopes human beings in the moments when this fear-provoking confrontation with the might of the Incomprehensible takes place. Parallel to this experience of the Absolute and Ultimate is the experience of the

Paul Rorem, *Pseudo-Dionysius: A Commentary on the Texts and an Introduction to their Influence* (New York: Oxford University Press, 1993).

11. WA 40,2: 77,11–20, LW 26: 28–29.

12. Rudolf Otto, *Das Heilige. Über das Irrationale in der Idee des Göttlichen und sein Verhältnis zum Rationalen* (Breslau: Trewendt & Granier, 1917), ET: *The Idea of the Holy: An Inquiry into the Non-Rational Factor in the Idea of the Divine and Its Relation to the Rational*, trans. John W. Harvey (1923, London: Oxford University Press, 1950). On Otto, see Paulson, *Luther's Outlaw God*, 1, 29–30.

mysterium fascinans, feelings of wonder that attract us at the same time to the Divine, which Otto called the "Numinous." No "God as buddy" here. People think that the Divine that commands wonder must have laid down a friendly law to secure their lives, a law that is well within the reach of human beings standing in the glow of an imagined Ultimate Good. Actual experience disabuses us sooner or later of this illusion.[13] In either terrifying or fascinating appearance, this is the Divine in a form that forces human creatures to take him, her, or it seriously! As a professor of comparative religions, Otto did not discourage rational inquiry into religious questions, but he recognized that the human reactions to the Divine feature elements that reason does not capture, elements that exceed its ability to grasp.

Whether our response to the Other fills us with awesome fear and dread or with enthralled wonder, it seems clear that this Being defies our mastery because it is our nature as creatures to be dependent on our Creator. This sense of createdness—of having come from somewhere and having some kind of goal that stems from outside of us—leads us to recognize our own ultimate lack of full control over life. It turns us to intermediaries for answers to daily problems. A frantic search for a suitable substitute for our Creator drives us to and fro, as we set our sails to every wind of an interpretation of reality that promises to fashion an idol that can stabilize and secure life (Eph 4:14). We discover that no amount of trying to play God or attain divinity, which is the essence of our sinfulness and our failure to enjoy the fullness of our humanity, can overcome this ultimate judgment of our own self. Luther combined this sense of his createdness and dependence with his discernment that he had not behaved well as this dependent creature. Indeed, he had fled from God's presence. He had developed an angry hatred toward the God whom he viewed as angrily hating him. God Hidden in the image forged by this conscience-plagued Brother scowled with wrath and revulsion at this sinner who, try as he might to keep God's law by his purely natural power, fell short in his own estimation and—he knew—God's.

Depictions of God in altar pieces that Luther had seen throughout his life confirmed the impression of a distant and angry God, functioning as part of a system to enforce moral order with the threat of punishment. He tried several devices supplied by the medieval church to cover his inner flawed self: attendance at mass, pious practices of various kinds, and the ultimate performance of monastic obedience. Just as God's true nature

13. Paulson, *Outlaw God*, 2: 185–190.

as his loving Creator was hidden from him, so he tried to avoid personal contact with the divine and hide the person he judged himself to be over against God's law and the church's regulations.

This search for the source of power sufficient to manage life for the best explains why traditional religions all either have stories of origin by an effecting, causal Something, or they posit the eternality of matter and search for an engaged organizing person or principle. Each of these systems places them in a dependent relationship to an ultimate power, some sort of eternally existing principle of keeping order. Human creatures usually are curious about their origins, immediate and ultimate, because origins tell us much about our present existence and identity and thus about the potential for our future.

Such concerns and questions may lose their pressing nature and may even diminish for many in an era in which they perceive no need for a Creator or a Preserver (person or semi-personal) since what many need seems always there. Modern Westerners wish to enforce just enough law and order to put and keep things in an organized, regular arrangement of the world that maximizes their own benefits. Even such people, however, may search for some story of origin in order to provide essential elements for establishing their identity and a means for expressing it. From questions relating to the effecting causes in ourselves and what we experience, we proceed to ask about what constitutes the realities around us.

Luther's late medieval environment expressed in its own unique form a general cultural phenomenon that Otto was trying to identify. So do cultures of the twenty-first century. Many of life's critical questions are answered by modern disciplines of physics and chemistry—although in line with the nature of the "scientific" or experimental method, always only tentatively. Other eras have had other theories and ways to produce such axioms. All strive to define the thatness or whatness of ourselves and what surrounds us. This matter needs form, design, plan. The design must come from somewhere or someone or a committee or Force. With these elements of explanation at hand, we search for the goal or meaning of it all. We crave not only a good explanation of our own existence and that surrounds us. We hope for respect from other people. All this constructs some sense of who each individual is. Luther recognized that, apart from God's revelation of himself, all this knowledge gives at best an inexact picture of what stands behind what we can touch and see, hear, taste, and smell.

Many modern accounts of reality have been formulated in desperation by individuals and fostered by groups seeking control in a world that no longer corresponds to the comforting environment of their youth. They seek solutions to the problems of change in special secret insights from gurus or in relationships to inanimate objects—magical gems or haunted places. Many of such later modern substitutes for God that seem to have powers to set troubled people at ease elude explanation in terms of natural science and traditional principles of reasoning. These semi-divine persons and objects are assigned powers and roles not subject to the standards of natural scientific inquiry, it is claimed. Their ability to help comes from their having a certain enchanting radiance that individuals sense or feel, on the basis of information received from others. The fascination of displays of power greater than one's own breeds and brews idolatries of many kinds. This essentially returns the people of the twenty-first century to the medieval world and its reliance on the proper human interaction with intermediate objects or persons in Hiebert's middle realm of the exercise of super-human or semi-divine powers. Too often Christians seem powerless to answer as they try to talk the language of their culture. Such conversations can be dangerous; Gerhard Forde observed that it is "precisely the attempt on the part of theologians and preachers to accommodate God to current modes of thought that led to unbelief, not the fear that God was truly God in majestic awesomeness. God was turned into a patsy not worthy of commanding belief."[14] Luther, his colleagues in Wittenberg, and his followers across Europe, along with other reformers of the sixteenth century, believed that the beings and objects that inhabited this "middle realm" fell easily into the role of idols for human beings. Luther's understanding of God's providential love and immanent presence obviated the need for this intermediate help unless it took the form of the aid of God's angelic messengers (who played a reduced role in Wittenberg piety).

A longing for a certain sense of security also accompanies this search for human origins and for whatever might provide the power to cope with life's problems for each day. That means that despite the desire for personal freedom to maneuver in our surroundings and manipulate our environment, we covet some feeling of a structure for daily life. That means that we yearn for boundaries, even if we insist that they be flexible enough to respond to our latest desires. We covet some sense that life has meaning and significance and that our life earns the respect of others. Medieval Europe had many fewer back-ups amid life's exigencies. No insurance systems, no elaborate medical facilities, no unemployment benefits offered

14. Gerhard O. Forde, *On Being a Theologian of the Cross: Reflections on Luther's Heidelberg Disputation, 1518* (Grand Rapids, MI: Eerdmans, 1997), 85 on Thesis 15.

safety nets to Luther's contemporaries, and so it is understandable why they sought security where they could imagine it might be found. But the medieval systems of identifying sources of such security and meaning, whether scholastic, monastic, or that of popular piety, left Luther groping and grasping for God, who remained largely hidden.

Caught between the presentation of the biblical message delivered by his teachers and his own sensitive perceptions of his own performance and person, Luther struggled with the despair that this conflict imposed upon him and with the terror that beset him when he contemplated his failure to fear, love, and trust in his Creator above all else that exists. Already in his early perception of a very personal and emotional God fostered by the psalms, Luther felt forced to "let God be God." The reformer only later came to realize that God's righteousness or true identity lies in his mercy and steadfast, loving kindness. Then he learned how foolish he had been to try to plumb the depths of the God who had plagued him with his demands and had no other word for him than the language of law's requirements.

Luther gradually moved away from simply regarding God as the One who was and had to be God, Creator, Almighty, angry father. That is why in 1531 he told his students to abandon speculation about his majesty since no one can bear to face God amid sin and death. The commentary on Galatians of 1535, taken from these lectures, calls attention to the infinite, incomprehensible nature of God that overwhelms human nature. Luther counseled his students, if they sought certainty regarding their salvation, to repudiate their "speculative sensibilities." Instead, they should grasp God as he has revealed himself in Christ. For God forbids his people to try to climb to heaven and to conjecture or hypothesize about his majestic nature.[15]

THE PERPLEXING AND OFFENSIVE GOD

Challenges to Luther's faith in the God whom he had come to know as a merciful and loving Lord did arise throughout his life. As the mature evangelical thinker that emerged from the struggles of the 1510s between his conscience and his Creator, Luther never abandoned his conviction that God's performance was not always consistent with the person he had come to know God to be through Jesus. Luther's bafflement reflected the unsolvable mystery of the continuation of sin and evil in the lives of the

15. WA 40,2: 77,3–6, 77,20–78,13, LW 26:29.

baptized. Our assessment of God's performance in a sinful world raises doubts about God's intentions, for our experience too often poses problems of "theodicy." Luther let God's justification of himself on the cross in the incarnate second person of the Trinity meet all questions raised by natural disasters or by humanly devised madness, meanness, malfeasance, or maleficence. In the absence of rational explanation for misfortunes and evils, Luther came to count on this divine person as an utterly reliable person, trusted despite his seeming failure to perform what Luther thought was right and just.

Luther struggled with such questions, both in his own pensive reflection and in his disputes with those who challenged him by citing episodes in the history of the church where many of his ideas were hardly to be found. He found a message for his contemporaries in the Holy Spirit's working with the brokenness of human life and the sinful twisting of God's word. The Holy Spirit's abiding presence in his church—where the holy dwells with the unholy, like the church's members who are sinful and holy at the same time—offered comfort in their own struggles. At the same time, the church's dreary history called them to repentance for their own conduct of the life of the church. Luther generally avoided "reasonable" solutions to these questions. In the final analysis, he had no explanation for why God manages his church in this manner.[16] In his theology of the cross he pointed out that God's way of working rests on what seems foolish and impotent to the world (1 Cor 1 and 2), on suffering and enduring persecution from Satan and his forces.

One set of challenges to the image that God projects when he shows his mercy arises from the natural and historical disasters that afflict believers and false believers alike without any seeming sense or purpose. God seems to have hidden himself and fled the human scene. Oswald Bayer observes,

> His [God's] hiddenness besieges us in the experience of blind and furious natural catastrophes, irredeemable injustices, innocent suffering, starvation and murder, in each and every war, and in the experience of incurable disease. "God" remains in these things, mostly anonymous and almost always veiled in the "divine passive" (*passive divinum*), no lover of life, but the accuser and denier—easily confused with the devil—in contrast to his revealed will and the gospel.[17]

16. Cf. Paulson, *Outlaw God*, 2: 118–147, for a fine analysis of Luther's meeting Erasmus on the battlefield of such questions about the use of church history
17. Bayer, "God's Hiddenness," *Lutheran Quarterly* 28 (2014): 274.

By 1518 Luther was warning his hearers and readers not to venture into the black hole that lies behind catastrophes, injustices, and suffering, the black hole in which the fullness of God's majesty and power had hid himself. God failed to give the reformer expected support in some instances. So, the reformer sometimes thought that God had forgotten him, acting like a modern neglectful parent who just does not come home to his children. But Luther also confronted those times when the God who is in total control of his creation took on a devil-like character as a dissatisfied and irate judge in the attacks Luther experienced.[18] Bayer comments, "Only when faith's journey is past and we live by sight will this monstrously biting and stinging discrepancy between God's terrible hiddenness and his love, as revealed through the Son in the Holy Spirit be expunged, overcome, and finally disappear." For the time being, "the *Deus absconditus* remains for the moment so dark and vague, that he can be mistaken for the Devil."[19] Then "divine hiddenness is not about absence but presence. The trouble for sinners with a hidden God is not distance, transcendence and emptiness, but God's overwhelming nearness, ubiquity, and immanence." Only preaching his loving presence into people's lives can make even his contrary nearness acceptable to his people and give them comfort.[20] But the dilemmas posed for human reason by this mystery of sin's persistence and the defiance of the ungodly to the Almighty God did not cease to torment Luther, as he explained in *On Bound Choice* (1525). To such questions he found no satisfactory explanation but only the more than satisfying person of his Lord Jesus Christ.[21]

The worst challenge to faith is indeed when God appears to be doing evil to those whom he had promised to rescue from their wandering ways and to restore them to his household. In *On Bound Choice*, Luther acknowledged that God Hidden offends. He had already wrestled with the offense of God's appearing as the enemy as he lectured on Jonah in the spring before he drafted his response to Erasmus in late 1525. The prophet's cry in 2:4 captured feelings Luther had had himself. Jonah, Luther paraphrased, told God of the despair he felt, terrified by his display of anger and his casting Jonah out of his presence. Luther labeled this the "deepest sighing and the greatest death," truly God's attack upon Jonah's faith. Yet Jonah could only hope in the Lord, and he uttered his cries of

18. WA 31,1: 249,25–31, LW 14:31.
19. Bayer, "God's Omnipotence," *Lutheran Quarterly* 23 (2009), 91. Cf. Bayer, "God's Hiddenness," 274.
20. Paulson, *Outlaw God*, 1, xxxiii.
21. WA 18: 784,1–785–38, LW 33:289–292. Cf. the introduction of this volume, pp. XX.

despair in prayer. He went face to face with the God who was seemingly condemning him and ended up expressing thanksgiving and faithfulness at the end of chapter one.[22] In the German translation of these lectures prepared for wider distribution in print, Luther equated the word "hell" with the terrors and trepidation of the dying, who measure their lives by the law. Hell is worse than these terrors, but the sense of being cast away from God overpowers the human imagination. Fear besets every corner of consciousness. The marvelous thing about Jonah is that despite these feelings he turned to God.[23]

Luther met God's *tentationes* with both protest and lament. Luther prescribed, according to Oswald Bayer, both Spirit-effected patience and equally Spirit-effected impatient lament and petition. In 1532 he told the Wittenberg congregation, referring to Romans 8:26,

> how I long for salvation. Deliverance from death. This call is beyond human formulation and human power, as it yearns only for deliverance from death. Thus, all Christians must experience the assured answer to this sighing and lament, and it resounds into heaven so that the Lord will come to give his aid.[24]

Luther exuded comfort in the face of all the distress and dilemmas that this mystery of sin and evil poses because he trusted in the person of God rather than in his own solutions to the evils of daily life. He trusted that God had achieved the decisive solution to the total problem of sin and evil through the death and resurrection of the incarnate second person of the Trinity. God had always been deeply involved in his creation, Luther perceived. In the face of evil, he lent his presence to his human creatures through the incarnation, in which God the Son became human. This divine Person suffering on the cross and leaving the tomb behind is ultimately who he claims to be: the God who faithfully preserves his people despite their unfaithfulness and who accompanies them in the midst of their vulnerability and even in their rebelliousness.

In his affirmation of God's omnipotence, which alone assured believers that their salvation lay only in God's choosing them and Christ's dying and rising for them, Luther recognized that God is responsible for everything, especially for the rescue and restoration of sinners, their re-creation as children of God. He had no first-hand experience of the council of the

22. Paulson, *Outlaw God*, 2: 63–108.

23. WA 19: 226,6–232,25., LW 19: 75–82.

24. WA 36: 560,9–12, cf. Oswald Bayer, "Toward a Theology of Lament," in *Caritas et Reformation. Essays on Church and Society in Honor of Carter Lindberg*, ed. David M. Whitford (St. Louis: Concordia, 2002), 217.

Trinity before the foundations of the world (Eph 1:4). Therefore, the Wittenberg professor depended on his own experience of the impossibility of his will's turning his actions into totally God-pleasing, proper actions to confirm that God alone bears the burden of this rescue and restoration. This seems to make it necessary to place responsibility for evil on God or at least to suggest that he permits it, a solution that does not make him any more just since he could prevent it. Yet Luther did not draw that conclusion. With his axiom that God is absolutely good, he placed responsibility for sin and evil squarely on human creatures. They do not merely lack something. Luther knew that his own evil disposition and deeds sprang from an active hostility to God. Therefore, he lived with the tension that the bound choices that his very active will made nonetheless bore the responsibility for his sin. He turned his gaze from beyond the bounds of human experience to the voice of God for his solution and came up with the proper distinction of law and gospel.

In *On Bound Choice* he confessed that this dilemma haunted him, but it also drove him to the foot of the cross, to await "the light of glory" since neither the "light of nature"—human reason—nor "the light of grace"—salvation by faith alone with faith dependent on God's gracious giving—provided satisfying answers.[25] Steven Paulson notes that Luther concludes here, "God is really hidden—and will never be found. But he is also not hidden, but most revealed, when preached. The trick is to hold the attempts to make these two—hidden, not hidden—as proof of the promise. The promise rather teaches how to separate them so that you struggle with God—and conquer."[26] Only in addressing the design of God as the demands of the law for responsible exercise of God's gift of humanity and only in addressing the gift of God as the re-creative gospel of Christ to those broken by the law's demands, could sense be made of life. This is a sense that did not correspond to rational analysis, but it is a sense that corresponds to human experience, Luther noted, when the Holy Spirit opens eyes and ears to the voice of the Lord.

GOD THE TERRIFYING JUDGE

Initially, however, the most terrifying thing about God, for Luther, lay less in such theodical problems. His terror stemmed from the evaluation of God's law, his standard which he fashioned as the plan for the good

25. WA 18: 785,26–38, LW 33: 292.
26. Paulson, *Outlaw God*, 3: 317.

human life and as the measure to evaluate the performance of his human creatures. In what seems to be an autobiographical echo of the apostle Paul's language in 2 Corinthians 12:2, Luther wrote in explaining his Ninety-five Theses on Indulgences in 1518 that he had "known a person" who asserted that he had frequently suffered the pangs of hell for brief periods of time. This experience of hell exceeded his ability to describe it in either spoken or written words, he stated. Thirty minutes, even six minutes, of such terror would kill a person, his very bones incinerated, in the face of the anger of God, reinforced by the rage of every other creature. He had found nowhere to flee, no support, neither from within nor from outside. He could hear only accusation. The sinner groaned with the naked desire for help, filled to the tiniest corner with the most bitter bitterness, horror, panic, and sadness.[27]

Luther's sensitive personality demanded from himself full compliance with the commands of his Creator. God had made him, and God continued to insist on conformity to his design for the person and performance of this creature of his. This led to an ongoing underlying dread that filled and possessed Brother Martin because he had some sense of who God is as the Creator of all. This sense nourished Luther's consciousness of the majesty and magnificence of God's person and a feeling of awe and wonder in his presence. But in his early years in the cloister, he sensed only dimly the outline of the God whom he got to know as he delved more deeply into Scripture. He avoided face-to-face confrontation with God as much as he could, but his attempts did not help.

By 1525 Luther had gotten to know God well enough to reflect honestly on his own attitude toward his Creator as he struggled with his own unworthiness and his resentful, rebellious thoughts when he brought himself into God's presence. Thus, he was not only describing the Israelites but also himself when he explained the second half of Exodus 19 to the Wittenberg congregation in September of that year. "Here you see what kind of a creature the human being is: when faith is absent, he has pure anger and hate against God." This text showed "how human beings stand over against God. They flee from him, are hostile to him, they blaspheme, for they run from him and are filled with fear of him as a strict judge, for they see no good in themselves."[28] The Israelites were shielded from the face of God (19;10–24), but Luther was not protected from his gaze. From his early years on, he was confronted face to face with this God who was

27. WA 1: 557,33–558,18, LW 31: 129–130.
28. WA 16: 417,29–418,12–13.

sorely displeased with Martin, even Brother Martin the Augustinian friar, because of his sinfulness.

Luther confronted the demands that he recognized had been placed on him by God's gift of life, demands that drove him into fear and loathing of God. Preaching on 2 Corinthians 3 in 1535, Luther compared Moses veiled with Moses unveiled, that is, the presentation of the law with devices built in for softening its demands, versus the raw, unveiled claim of God on the human being's life. The veil over Moses encouraged those who hear the law to take their sins less seriously, to show contempt for God by not fearing him. They become arrogant hypocrites. No one faces Moses unveiled without being driven to despair. That is the better Moses for sinners, Luther told his hearers, for he drives them to seek deliverance through the promise of Christ.[29]

As a maturing hearer of his gracious Lord, Luther did not cease experiencing God's taking the role of angry judge to call believers to repentance and to strengthen their faith in him. He continued to experience God's discontent and accusation with his straying from complete trust and the obedience it produced. Even after God had revealed his gracious disposition that became concrete in the incarnation, death, and resurrection of Jesus Christ, the second person of the Trinity, his Lord could keep this sinner's conscience on repentant tenterhooks with an angry visage. In his *Exposition of the Lord's Prayer* (1519), the reformer created a dialogue between the soul and God, in which God's discontent was repeated for every petition that the pious believer tries to pray correctly.

To the soul's plea to be delivered out of its miserable condition on earth, God replies in Malachi 1:6 that a child honors its father. "If I am your father, where is my honor? If I am your Lord, where is the awe and reverence due me? For my holy name is blasphemed and dishonored among you and by you, Isaiah 52 [:5]." The soul admits that this is true and asks for help in promoting God's name, only to hear "How can my name and honor be hallowed in you while your heart and mind are inclined to evil and captive to sin, Genesis 8[:21] and Isaiah 52 [:5] and since no one can sing my praise in a foreign land, Psalm 127[:4]?"

Undeterred, the soul concedes that it has not honored God's name but counts on placing all its powers under God's rule. God is not impressed. "Him whom I am to help, I destroy. Him whom I want to quicken, save, enrich, and make pious, I mortify, reject, impoverish, and reduce to nothing, Deuteronomy 32[:39]. However, you refuse to accept such a plan

29. WA 41: 434,18–435,35.

from me, my way of doing things, Psalm 78[:10–11]. How can I help you? What more can I do? Isaiah 5[:4]?" In a penitent spirit, the soul grants God's accusation and prays for aid in acting in accord with the divine will. God objects, "Your lips often voiced your love for me, while your heart was far from me [Isa 29:13]. When I intervened for you to make you better, you ran away. As I was working with you, you deserted me . . . Psalm 78[:9] . . . Those who were making a good start and moved me to deal with them turned their backs on me and fell back into sin and into my disfavor." The soul had to admit that this is true but prays for Jesus's sake that God destroy the sinful will and pour out grace for all Christians.

At this point in his life Luther viewed the fourth petition as a prayer for the proper teaching of the bread of life, God's word, and so God referred to Jeremiah 5 and other passages, as well as Matthew 7:6 and 15:26, responding indignantly to the sinner's plea, "You sin daily, and when I have my Word preached to you day and night, you do not hearken and listen, and my Word is despised." The soul pleads for forgiveness, and God says impatiently, "I forgive and redeem you so often; and you do not remain steadfast and faithful [Ps. 78:8]. You are of weak faith. You cannot watch and tarry with me a little while, but quickly fall back into temptation, Matthew 26[:40–41]."

The soul's prayer for aid against temptation earns the curt retort, with reference to Psalm 11:7, "I am just, and my judgment is correct. Therefore, sin dare not go unpunished. For that reason, you must endure affliction. That this brings you spiritual struggles is your own fault, for it compels me to punish and to guard against it." The soul persists to the end, throwing itself on God's mercy. Luther responds, "at the end, some may say, 'What am I to do if I cannot believe that I am being heard?' Answer: follow the example of the father of the person possessed in Mark 9 [:23–24]. When Christ said to him, 'Can you believe? All things are possible to him who believes,' the father cried with tears in his eyes, 'O Lord, I believe; help my faith when it is too weak." Luther concluded simply, "To God alone be honor and glory."[30]

In the face of God's justifiable and understandable anger and discontent with the bedraggled lives of even the faithful, Luther knew by 1519 that behind the wrath was the person of the God whose mercy took bodily form on the cross and in the resurrection. Luther recognized times when God remains Hidden and sinners with most repentant hearts still quake and quiver in his presence. But in those moments, they have faith to flee

30. WA 2:128,3–13019, LW 42:78–81.

to the cross and find God Revealed there. This treatment of the Lord's Prayer seems autobiographical. Luther had learned the answers God gives as he experienced *Anfechtungen*, the attacks of devilish doubt.

Luther could even speak of God's playing with his children as earthly parents tease their children to drill into them that sometimes parents' love is present despite contrary appearances. The heavenly Father may mask himself and give his children a scare to turn them from sin or to give them a delightful thrill. God's playful interventions in human lives challenge the faith of believers, "both in the presentation of conflicting claims from God but also in human struggle to lay hold of the promise [God gives faith]." The promise of grace in the face of the condemnation of his commands "is never a simple legal appeal but a struggle, wrestling with God . . ."[31] Luther drew both on God's "playing" with the patriarchs[32] and the telling of times when "Jesus often jests and plays in his words, yet in such a way as to demonstrate his seriousness in his goodwill toward them."[33] This play reflects Luther's theology of the cross in that it places believers in the dilemma of suffering the contradictory in their experience and turns them from such experiences to the person of the God they know they can trust. It turns them to him despite—or in the face of—events that seem incompatible with his love and his power. Trust in him and in the reliability of his person and promise—rather than the proof based on rational assessment of what is happening to them—governs their reactions and gives them confidence and even peace in the light of God's unpleasant playfulness.[34]

When God Hidden still intrudes into the life of one who has been turned to Jesus, Luther insisted, this God in hiding is not a different person or even a different, dissident, part of the personality of the one God. It was the same God acting out of his identity as a loving and merciful person, parent, in ways that defy the imagination of the sinful human creature. God is not two-faced. Our confusion about God's disposition toward us rises out of the fact that neither as creature nor as sinner can the human being comprehend in all respects what the Creator is up to.[35] Nonetheless, we may perceive what God is doing as the work of Satan in the Lord's testing of faith.

31. Christopher B. Brown, "*Deus Ludens*: God at Play in Luther's Theology," *Concordia Theological Quarterly* 81 (2017): 160 (153–170). Cf. Paulson, *Outlaw God*, 2: 109–113.
32. Vincent Kam, "Luther on God's Play with His Saints," *Lutheran Quarterly* 34 (2020): 138–151.
33. Brown, "*Deus Ludens*," 161–163.
34. Kam, "Luther on God's Play," 138–151.
35. WA 43: 459,24–32; LW 5:45.

AND THE HIDDENNESS OF THE GOSPEL

Luther did not plan to write a theology for the ages, and he would have been amazed and shocked to know that people five hundred years later would be reading his words and tossing about his phrases. He provided no chart to guide the hapless twenty-first century reader through his writings. It is therefore understandable that some are confused by his recognizing that his Revealed God reveals himself in hidden places and in ways that human reason only dimly perceives.[36] God came in the form of a baby although the last place to expect God is in a crib, a crying kid. God changed the course of history for the world and for individuals in the form of a criminal on a cross, hardly where we would expect to come upon God and recognize the Lord of history. God prepared for the biggest bang ever as he lies as a corpse in Joseph's crypt. God reveals himself in such a way as to block every pretense that our reasoning might have for pinning down our Maker. Already that crib in Bethlehem, to say nothing of the cross and the crypt in Jerusalem, provide a stone of stumbling, a rock of offense (Rom 9:33, 1 Pet 2:8).

This hiddenness of God in crib, cross, and crypt stared Luther in the face and set him at ease. As a young university student and Augustinian Brother, he had sensed God's presence from time to time, but he dared not look his Judge in the eye. Later in his struggles with the theodical questions of life or with existential situations in which God seemed nowhere to be found, he learned to call into the darkness. He used God's own promises to draw him near, peering through mysterious or experiential darkness into the face of the dying and rising Jesus, whom he trusted was present even if he seemed to have deserted the poor Martin. The reasons for terror in the face of his judge remained in Luther's acknowledgment of his own transgression and straying, but they vanished from his sight as God's mercy that showed itself in Jesus's presence "for him" triumphed in the end. His Creator's presence triumphed over his absence in determining what Luther experienced as the reality of human life.

36. On God's hiding himself during the career of Isaiah, including claiming the pagan ruler Cyrus as his messiah, see Paulson, *Outlaw God*, 1: 25–55.

2.

The Reformer Face to Face with Death, Sin, the Law and God's Wrath, and the Devil

Luther coram Morte, Peccato, Lege et Ira Dei, et Diabolo

LUTHER'S APPRAISAL OF HUMAN LIFE IN A SINFUL WORLD

Martin Luther could be surprisingly optimistic. He sometimes regarded only a tiny part of life as standing under the power of Satan.[1] In 1542, lecturing on Genesis 27:39–49, he informed his students of the earthly blessings which the patriarchs had enjoyed, including those which Isaac bestowed on Jacob (Gen 27:39–40), observing that God gives "sumptuously and luxuriously."[2] Commenting on his experience of daily life in his exposition of Genesis 32 on Jacob, he told his students that the entire flow of nature and life gives evidence of God's goodness in spite of the bad factors that they perceive.

Why should Luther not have been fairly content with daily life? By 1540 he presided over a satisfying family life. He was among the best paid people in Wittenberg. Thanks to his wife's shrewd stewardship, he seldom went hungry, even in the not infrequent times of scarcity in Wittenberg. He was enjoying relative safety even as an outlaw and heretic with death sentences from both pope and emperor hanging over

1. WA 44: 67,9–10, LW 6: 90.
2. WA 43: 523,16–524,31, LW 5: 138–140.

his head. Even if he had to contend with the threats of his emperor, Charles V, and neighboring prince Duke Georg of the other Saxony, or the curses and condemnations that King Henry VIII of England and Duke Heinrich of Braunschweig-Wolfenbüttel lodged against him, he walked Wittenberg's muddy streets and traveled electoral Saxony's rutted roads without much fear.

On the other hand, Luther could express a profound pessimism:

> God has cast us into the world under the devil's lordship, with the result that we have no paradise here, but expect every kind of misfortune for body, spouse, child, property, and reputation at every hour. When there is an hour in which we do not experience ten misfortunes, indeed if you can live out one such hours, you should say, "what a great blessing my God has shown me that every kind of misfortune did not befall me."[3]

Thus, Martin Luther was also soberly realistic about threats far greater from persons and forces more powerful than those of Emperor Charles V and Duke Georg, of King Henry and Duke Heinrich. He looked inside himself and saw his own sinfulness. He looked around and saw the temptations of Satan and the world. He looked up and saw the wrath of God and the condemnation of his law. He looked ahead and saw the fearsome promise of death. Luther took evil in all its forms more seriously than had most medieval theologians. He could do so in the end because he was no longer dependent on human power to confront any of those forms of misfortune and malevolence. He had an almighty God on his side, and this God had triumphed over evil and sealed its fate in all its forms. Luther did not try to explain the existence of Satan and sin despite his frustration with the unanswerable questions that the Evil One and all his agencies place before us.[4] Luther lived at peace because God in human flesh had won the war. This chapter treats in more detail his struggle with his own sin. That struggle took place within the context of his encounter with God's law and God's wrath, with death, and with the person whose impetus led to human sin, the devil.

Luther had a crystal-clear picture of his list of enemies. He faced ever more honestly and seriously the threat from his own sinfulness; from God's wrath as it expressed itself in the law's condemnation of sin; from the law's carrying out the just payment for sin in its wage, death; and from the foe behind all these threats, Satan.

3. WA 19: 644, 20–24.
4. WA 18: 784,1–785–38, LW 33: 289–292. On Luther's refusal to answer questions arising out of God's mysteries, see the introduction, pp. 13–19, and chapter 1, pp. 41–54.

LUTHER FACES DEATH

Death was without doubt for Luther the enemy, but its importance for his perception of life and his sense of the future sometimes has been exaggerated and misrepresented. For Luther, death had been defanged. It did not remain all so fierce any longer. In 1999 Harvard professor Richard Marius published his second biography of Luther, entitled *Martin Luther: The Christian between God and Death.*[5] This impressionistic study argues that Luther's fear of death was the primary driving force in his thinking and career. Marius's title clearly alludes to a volume by his former Harvard colleague, church historian Heiko A. Oberman, whose own Luther biography, *Luther: Man Between God and the Devil,*[6] had commanded great scholarly attention and respect. In principle, Marius did not like Luther's way of thinking; he labeled Luther's call for reform a "catastrophe in the history of Western civilization." "Our world would have been far better off had events taken a different course,"[7] he stated. Marius, in fact, made no pretension of writing a scholarly analysis. He chose to quote from the "early" Luther rather than from the reformer's mature thinking and admitted he did so because he found this early Luther more likable and interesting than the mature thinker.[8] It is also true that more of the reformer's works from his earlier years are accessible in English translations, which Marius often used without citing the standard scholarly edition of Luther's works, the Weimar edition.[9]

Marius contended that the fear of death dominated Luther's thinking. He alleged that the reformer's energies were channeled by "the need to conquer it so he could live day by day. His greatest terror, one that came on him periodically as a horror of darkness, was the fear of death—death in itself, not the terror of a burning and eternal hell awaiting the sinner in an afterlife."[10] For this claim and others in the book Marius failed to

5. Richard Marius, *Martin Luther: The Christian between God and Death* (Cambridge: Harvard University Press, 1999). What follows here reflects parts of my studies, Robert Kolb, "'Life is King and Lord over Death,' Martin Luther's View of Death and Dying," in *Tod und Jenseits in der Schriftkultur der Frühen Neuzeit*, ed. Marion Kobelt Groch and Cornelia Niekus-Moore (Wiesbaden: Harrassowitz, 2008), 23–45, and Robert Kolb, "'Ein kindt des todts' und 'Gottes Gast.' Das Sterben in Luthers Predigten," *Lutherische Theologie und Kirche* 31 (2007): 3–22.
6. *Luther: Man Between God and the Devil*, trans. Eileen Walliser-Schwarzbart (New Haven: Yale University Press, 1989), from the original German, Berlin 1982.
7. Marius, *Luther*, xii.
8. Marius, *Luther*, xii.
9. This is not the case in every citation of Luther, however. Marius did delve into the original texts at times.
10. Marius, *Luther*, xiii–xiv.

provide any citations from Luther's writings. His insistence that Luther's search for God arose only out of a simple fear of death[11] flies in the face of Luther's utterances that regarded all the evils that proceed from Satan's attacks on the human creature and human sin as part of the devil's master strategy. Marius himself recognized that "death, hell, the grave, and wrath are almost synonyms in Luther's rhetoric,"[12] that death "is always for him God's judgment on sin,"[13] and that in a comment in 1522 Luther combined his "great fears, of death, the devil, and hell."[14] Marius failed to sort out precisely what each of those foes meant for the reformer. In fact, the Wittenberg reformer's direct treatments of death very seldom mentioned the fear of death in comparison with his emphasis on the deliverance from death that the resurrection of Jesus Christ brings to God's chosen children.

Indeed, Luther recognized the nature of death as a tool of the devil, whom Jesus labeled a liar and a murderer (John 8:44). His lies deceived human creatures to death, the dying of the relationship with their Creator, the sustainer of life. Death places bodies in the grave. Death generates fear and sorrow. Luther knew this from personal loss of family, friends, and followers, having experienced grief himself at the deaths of his parents and two of his daughters.[15] His own terror at the threat of death in the face of a thunderstorm, he later claimed, had driven him into the cloister (although the decision rested on much more than one lightning bolt on his return to Erfurt in 1506).[16] He repeated the conventional medieval argument that excessive grief accomplishes nothing, but he did not discount sorrow over the loss of a loved one as had some medieval writers who relied on Seneca and other ancient Stoic thinkers.[17] Instead, he sensitively addressed the natural sorrow that accompanies the loss of a loved one with explicit articulation of the hope of life everlasting. The hurt Christians feel at this loss is natural: "it would not be good if the hurt were not present.

11. Marius, *Luther*, 106, 114. Marius cited Werner Elert's comment that the "melody of death" resounds through Luther's work, 60. On that page cited Elert explains death within the larger context of Luther's view of evil, see his *Morphologie des Lutherums. I. Theologie und Weltanschauung des Luthertums hauptsächlich im 16. und 17. Jahrhundert* (Munich: Beck, 1931), 16–17.
12. Marius, *Luther*, 203.
13. Marius, *Luther*, 313.
14. Marius, *Luther*, 334; see similar concessions to the opposing position, 64, 67, 191, 214.
15. Scott H. Hendrix, *Martin Luther: Visionary Reformer* (New Haven: Yale University Press, 2015), 272–273 and 216–217.
16. Hendrix, *Visionary Reformer*, 33.
17. Ute Mennicke-Haustein, *Luthers Trostbriefe* (Gütersloh, Gütersloher Verlagshaus, 1989), 104–106; Stephen Pietsch, *Of Good Comfort: Martin Luther's Letters to the Depressed and their Significance for Pastoral Care Today* (Adelaide: ATF, 2016), 27–100; Neil R. Leroux, *Martin Luther as Comforter: Writings on Death.* (Leiden: Brill, 2007), passim.

That would be a sign of a love grown cold."[18] "It is normal and right that a person should grieve, particularly when it concerns one's own flesh and blood, for God has not made us to be without feelings, to be like a stone or a piece of wood. Instead, it is his will that we weep and mourn. Otherwise, it would be a sign that we did not love our own."[19]

Individually, believers experience that death reveals God's wrath against sin.[20] That gives Christians a sense of fear that, because of Christ, they need not have.[21] Luther reminded his students in 1531 that they should lay aside their anxiety over their sin and their terror in the face of death by regarding them as empty. They should look upon death as nothing other than a hollow specter, deception invented by Satan. They should remember that Christ's conquering death and the devil had removed the seriousness of death's threat.[22] His early revision of the medieval "art of dying," his *Treatise on Preparing to Die* (1519), reminded readers that Christ had imprisoned death, indeed had consumed it. "Christ is the image of life and grace standing in opposition to the image of sin and death. [. . .] God be praised and thanked that he has overcome sin and death for us in Christ,"[23] the reformer wrote. In evening conversations at the Black Cloister, he often commented to colleagues, students, and visitors that he was prepared to place his body and soul into God's hands, trusting that God would free him from the frailties of earthly life.[24]

Contrary to Marius's picture of the fear-filled, aging Luther, the reformer himself told his hearers at table that he was anticipating being in the Lord's presence in heaven and lived in the hope of a blessed end. He did not believe that death could crush him.[25] Through God's almighty power, Christ's resurrection freed him from death's threats.[26]

18. WA Br 10: 664.
19. WA Br 8: 485.
20. WA TR 6: 300–301 Nr. 6970–6971.
21. WA TR 3: 186, Nr. 3140b.
22. WA 40,1: 444,30–445,36, LW 26: 285–286.
23. WA 2: 690;1–9; cf. 2. 691,12–21; 2: 697,14–30. Cf. Bernd Hamm, *The Early Luther. Stages in a Reformation Reorientation*, trans Martin J. Lohrmann (Grand Rapids, MI: Eerdmans, [Minneapolis: Fortress Press], 2020), 110–171. On the traditions of preaching the passion that developed out of this work and used it, see Jonathan Reinert, *Passionspredigt im 16. Jahrhundert. Das Leiden und Sterben Jesu Christi in den Postillen Martin Luthers, der Wittenberger Tradition und altgläubiger Prediger* (Tübingen: Mohr/Siebeck, 2022).
24. WA TR 3: 16, Nr. 3928. Cf. WA TR 1: 418, Nr.853; 1,422–423, Nr. 860; 4: 214, Nr. 4313; 6: 302, Nr. 6978.
25. WA TR 6: 301–302, Nr. 6974–6975, 6977–6978.
26. WA TR 1: 404–406, Nr. 832; 2: 210, Nr. 1764; 2: 358, Nr. 2197; 2: 599, Nr. 2675b; 4: 295, Nr. 4400; 4: 473, Nr. 4777; 4: 539, Nr. 4835–4836; 5: 447–448, Nr. 6031; 5: 280, Nr.5626; 5: 320–321, Nr. 5685; 5: Nr. 447–449, Nr. 6031; 5: 666, Nr. 6445; 6: 30–31, Nr. 6541.

For Luther, death had become a means of liberation from sin[27] and from all the weaknesses and pains of the body.[28] He emphasized that the faithful rely on the promises of their resurrection in Christ.[29] He urged his hearers to conduct their lives in that trust in Christ that prepares the way for death and in the confidence in his resurrection and their own that enables them to resist Satan's attempts to undermine their faith in Christ.[30] Luther held up the martyr Stephen as a model for Christians to follow in placing their lives in God's hands (Acts 7:59).[31] In the midst of their thoughts regarding death they were to fix their eyes on Christ, who clears away their sorrow over the thought of departing this world.[32] Dying in faith has lost its bitter taste since Christ has atoned for sin and become the life of believers.[33] Death had invaded the world fashioned by the Author and Lord of Life, but its invasion had been repulsed in Christ's resurrection. Fear of death arises also in the hearts of the faithful, there is nothing left to fear.

Luther knew that some in his day did not believe in the resurrection of the dead,[34] and therefore he proclaimed it with vigor. Preaching on Jesus's raising the son of the widow of Nain to life (Luke 7:11–17) in 1533, Luther constructed a conversation between God and death. God ignores death's grumbling and puts death in its place:

> Death, I am your death; hell, I am a plague upon you, [. . .] your bullet, the stone on which you will be ground to dust. Yes, I intend to be your hell. You have filled my people with fear, so they do not want to die. Watch out! I am on the other side. When you kill someone, I will kill you. You say, 'I have gobbled up that person, I have swallowed down Doctor Martin.' Boast as you will, death. In my eyes they are not dead whom you have killed, but they are asleep, and so softly that I can wake them with a finger.[35]

God took on death in a drama staged on a battlefield, presented in Luther's sermon on 1 Corinthians 15 in May 1545:

27. WA TR 6: 155, Nr. 6730.
28. WA TR 4: 200–201, Nr. 4203.
29. WA TR 5; 347, Nr. 3767; 6: 303, Nr. 6979.
30. WA TR 1: 246–247, Nr. 529.
31. WA TR 1: 45, Nr. 117. This material is excerpted from Robert Kolb, "'Life is King and Lord over Death,'" and Robert Kolb, "'Ein kindt des todts'".
32. WA TR 6: 303, Nr. 6979.
33. WA TR 3: 369, Nr. 3511, WA TR 6: 302, Nr. 6976.
34. WA 28: 429,22–430,32 436,24–30, LW 69: 286, 288.
35. WA 37: 150,14–20.

> Death has been knocked to the ground. It has lost its kingdom, power, and victory. It did have the upper hand and because of sin the entire world was subject to it, and all people had to die. Now it has lost its victory. Against death's kingdom and victory, our Lord God, the Lord of Sabaoth has won his own victory, the resurrection of the dead in Christ. For a long time, death sang, "Hurray! Triumph! I, death, am king and lord over all human beings. I have the victory and am on top." But our Lord God permits himself to sing a little song that goes, "Hurray! Triumph! Life is king and lord over death." Death has lost and is on the bottom. Previously death had sung, "Victory! Victory! Hurray! I have won. Here is nothing but death and no life." But God now sings, "Victory! Victory! Hurray! I have won. Here is nothing but life and no death. Death has been conquered in Christ and has died itself. Life has gained the victory and won."[36]

He then continued,

> That was the kind of song that we will sing in the resurrection of the dead when the mortal puts on immortality. At the present time death is choking the life out of us in miserable and manifold ways, one person by the sword, another by the plague, another by water, another by fire. Who can recite all the ways in which death eliminates us human creatures. Death lives, reigns, rules, takes the victory, and sings "I won, I won, I have the power and I hold the claim over all that lives on earth. I strike them all with death, young, old, rich, poor, highly placed and those on the lower rungs of society, nobles and those outside the nobility. I defy anyone who wants to take that from me. But death will soon sing itself hoarse, sing itself to death. Then, on Easter, there will be another song, "Christ is arisen, from agony. Then we will all be joyous, for Christ will be our comfort." Death, where is your sting? Where are you keeping the one who lay in the grave, the one you killed on the cross?"[37]

The practical application of this view of death was clear, as Luther noted in a sermon on Matthew 21: 1–9, in 1532. In it he affirmed that the dying Christian recognizes that dying in Christ, bearing his name through baptism, means going through death to be with him.[38] Death did not possess Luther. He lived in the confidence that he possessed the resurrection promise. His resurrected Lord intended to maintain his relationship to Martin into eternity.

36. WA 49: 768, 25–39, 769,19–32. Cf. Luther's description of the victory of Christ over Satan and death in his Large Catechism, second article of the Apostles Creed, BSELK 1054/1055,36–1058/1059,10, BC, 434–435.
37. WA 49: 768,25–39, 769,19–32.
38. WA 36: 376,4–10.

LUTHER FACES SIN

Death proceeds from sin, the devil's instrument for separating human beings from the person of their God. L'ubomír Batka has demonstrated the command of biblical definitions of sin that Luther exhibited in his writings. He translated the Hebrew *pescha* as "sin," "unrighteousness," or "transgression." *Aon* referred specifically to "unrighteousness in God's sight," but later he also defined the word as "misdeeds." The Hebrew *hattaa* he rendered as "original sin," the fundamental inclination against God. *Rascha* indicated for him "rude Godlessness, pride and a lack of fear of God, an active self-confidence of one's own righteousness and denial of sin"—evil.[39]

Luther's profound sense of human sinfulness arose from his sensing the personal offense that the Creator feels when rejected by the creatures he loves. The devil's deception aims at the separation of God's human creatures from their Creator. One of Luther's adaptations of medieval theological terminology to his understanding of Scripture transformed the term "original sin" or, in German, "inherited sin," from being only a historical report on the origin of the sinfulness of all humankind in the fall of Adam and Eve. For Luther it was that, too, but his definition of original sin deepened and intensified its significance over against medieval definitions. Original sin had become through that inheritance also the "root" sin from which blossomed all the actual sins of his daily life.[40]

It had indeed all begun in Eden. There, according to Luther, it was not human pride, as alleged by many medieval theologians and as John Milton would contend a century later in *Paradise Lost*. For Luther, what Satan induced in human hearts that produced sins is at its core doubt of God's word and defiance of his lordship. The reformer described what separated Adam and Eve from God in other ways, but doubt formed the underlying foundation for his definition of original sin. Doubt breaks the fundamental trust that constituted the human side of their relationship with their Creator. Luther's definition of what it means to be human in his explanation of the first commandment in the Small Catechism provides the counterpoint to his definition of the root sin: failing to fear, love, and

39. "Luther's Teaching on Sin and Evil," in OHMLT, 234–243; cf. 233–253, cf. chapter 5, pp. 173–177.

40. Robert Kolb, "Luther's Transformation of Scholastic Terms," in *Handing over the Goods: Determined to Proclaim Nothing but Christ Jesus and Him Crucified—Essays in Honor of James Arne Nestingen*, ed. Steven Paulson and Scott L. Keith (Irvine, CA: 1517 Publishing, 2018), 36–38 (21–38).

trust in God above all else. The origin of human sin—and the origin of the sins that interrupt the daily lives of believers on a continuing basis—lies in questioning what God has said and thus denying the lordship of the Creator. In 1530 he told hearers, "There is nothing to which the devil is so hostile as the beloved Word. The reason is that he can conceal himself beneath every created thing. Only the Word exposes him, so that he cannot hide himself and shows everybody how dark he is."[41]

God's command not to eat (Gen 3:1–7), Luther told his students in 1535, became the object of the serpent's attack, not only on God's order for his creatures but also on the link that bound them to God in a personal relationship. Every satanic attack that believers experience assaults God as well. The devil seeks to strike a lance through the hearts of the faithful to wound or kill God. The devil's question, "Has God really said?" served as the means by which he might bring Adam and Eve to put the very will of God itself up for grabs. Satan attacked the faith of Adam and Eve by destroying their trust in what God said and substituting Satan's own words for God's. The trust that oriented their lives turned from their Creator to their Murderer. Luther noted that once the devil had created doubt in the minds of Adam and Eve, he had no difficulties in taking over their thinking and their way of life.[42] This destroyed God's image in the human being by destroying their faithfulness to him.[43] The devil's deception turned them from the One who always tells the truth to the one whose person embodies duplicity and disruption.

Unbelief is the fountain out of which other sins flow; abandoning the word of God and doubting him produces all other sins, for it necessitates "the fashioning of idols, the denial of God's truth, the invention of new gods"[44] and thus the fashioning of new rules for life. Luther observed that Eve had not only rejected God's command but also distorted it by adding to it (Gen 3:3).[45] Thus, as Erik Herrmann observes, "Luther did not consider sin or evil in isolation, as a mere act of transgression of a set of rules or a conceptual standard of morality. Rather, in line with the psalmist, sin was defined *in relation* to another, indeed, *the* Other—the Maker of heaven and earth."[46] Sin arises out of the desperate attempt of those who turn their

41. WA 32: 36,33–37,1, LW 51: 206.
42. WA 42: 110,38–111,3, LW 1: 147.
43. WA 42: 110,7–17, LW 1: 146.
44. WA 42: 112, 20–22, LW 1: 149.
45. WA 42: 116,40–117,14, LW 1: 154–155.
46. Erik H. Herrmann, "Luther and the Importance of the Hebrew Heritage for His World of Thought," in *Simul: Inquiries into Luther's Expression of the Christian Life*, ed. Robert Kolb, Torbjörn Johansson and Daniel Johansson (Göttingen: Vandenhoeck & Ruprecht, 2021), 53.

backs on the One who designed their lives to explain and cope with reality apart from the foundation and core of all that exists, the Creator. Sin tries to live as a human being in an image that sinners create for themselves. But unlike living as God's images, the images we construct depend on stealing from other creatures the materials from which we try to create ourselves to please ourselves. It never works.

In this regard Luther emphasized that the ear has channeled into the human heart this doubt and spirit of rebellion. Doubt and rebellion blossom quickly into disobedience to God's commands and departure from the way of life he designed. Hermann points to the life-embracing nature of listening to the word of the Lord. "The great *Shema* of Hebrew calls upon God's people not only to hear but to do; for there is no word for 'obey' in Hebrew, only *šĕma*, only 'hear.' Thus, the 'hearing of faith' (Gal 3:2–5) and the 'obedience of faith' (Rom 1:5) are synonyms. It is precisely through hearing that the heart is changed—through the word of the Lord, faith is born in the heart."[47]

Human doubt of God's word and dismissal of his lordship turn to pride and arrogance, and pride and arrogance take form, Luther believed, in "wanting to be God himself." Adam had sinned in Eden by such aspirations to divinity and fell prey to Satan's provocation because he became dissatisfied with being the wondrous creature that God had fashioned in his own image. He sought divine status through the knowledge of good and evil. Luther recognized that all human beings since had followed Adam's example. With a gigantic hole at the center of life, where God fits perfectly, sinners must seek a substitute. They turn first to themselves. Finding the self inadequate, they fashion other substitutes. Finding any single one of the substitutes inadequate, they become polytheists, whether they lived in ancient Palestinian surroundings or are living in modern skyscrapers. Preaching on John 19:7 on March 6, 1529, Luther commented that Adam's initial sin was permitting Satan to move him in the wrong direction. Adam could not be satisfied with trusting his Creator and being the good creature that God had made in his own image. He desired to be God, with the accompanying knowledge of good and evil. That is the pattern of sin in every human being's life, Luther asserted. It centers on the fashioning of idols as substitutes for the Creator. In a mad search for someone or something worthy of our reliance, human confidence comes to an uneasy rest on wisdom, money, and property to attain the good. All sin arises out of the broken relationship, out of the refusal to be

47. Hermann, "Luther and the Hebrew Heritage," 56.

listening to the Creator.[48] Even when human beings find their own persons insufficient as substitutes for their Creator, the devil gladly cooperates in manufacturing idols for them without sinners even realizing it. He lends his aid to the process since altering or corrupting God's word introduces newly fashioned idols into the lives of God's people (Deut 32:17), Luther told his students in 1535.[49] Original sin is not so much accusation as simple diagnosis. At the heart of our existence a dead heart is beating feebly but pumping no lifeblood at all.

Luther recognized that even at his pious best, truly serious sin remained in him. He knew that to discount those transgressions that had less serious consequences for other human beings or creation as venial obscures the primal rejection of the claim of God as Lord of human life behind them. All sins arise out of the sinner's violation of the first commandment. Because human creatures are created in God's image and thus for a personal relationship with him, the least of offenses against the Creator still amounts to defiance of him, his word, and his will. Luther conceded that he had not outwardly committed murder, adultery, theft, and other sins in his relationships with other people. But his failure to fear and love God had brought him to inward violation of God's will for his life. He counted his sins as so numerous "that an ox's hide would not hold them." His failure to fear, love, and trust in God above all things was "so grave, so real, so great, so infinite, so horrible, and so invincible" that his most pious efforts were of no benefit, but only damaged his relationship to God. Only with that conclusion could he come to the depths of his trust in Christ and his gratitude for his sacrifice and his resurrection.[50] Thus, Luther observed that evil works do not condemn a person but are only symptoms of a fundamental alienation from God already present in the heart.

Luther placed failure to fear, love, and trust in God at the heart of his definition of sin, sins, and sinning. This resulted in his rejection of the teaching of some in previous generations that concupiscence, desire for what lies outside God's commands, is not in itself sinful but only the tinder from which sins spring when desire becomes action. Luther rejected this view on the basis of Isaiah's confession that "all our righteousnesses are like filthy rags" (64:6) and Paul's experience of his ongoing battle against the law of sin within him (Rom 7).[51] In 1532, Luther's sermons on the

48. WA 28: 349,15–35,26, LW 69: 230–231.
49. WA 42: 112,6–8, LW 1: 148.
50. WA 10.1: 87,19–89,18, LW 26: 35–36.
51. In *Contra Latomus* (1521), WA 8: 58–6–38, 118,10–126,14, LW 32: 158, 245–256.

Sermon on the Mount, specifically on Matthew 5:27–42, followed Jesus's admonitions from outward deeds—murder, adultery—back to inward thought—hatred, lust—that turned in upon the self. Such thoughts, Luther cited Jesus from the text, are evil in themselves as well as the wellsprings of sinful words and deeds.[52]

Every transgression of God's will flows from the failure to fear, love, and trust in God above all else. This failure is idolatry, denial of God's truth, the invention of new gods.[53] Although Luther railed against every kind of transgression of commandments two through ten, his treatment of the calling of Abram reveals his focus on the broken relationship with the Creator and the dependence on false gods. Lecturing on Genesis 12 in 1537, Luther suggested that the patriarch had lived an honorable life with all civic virtues: the pagan Abram had not let himself be governed by lust, greed, or other evil desires. He lived a life of moderation that conquered such desires. But through the Babylonian religion of Nimrod, Satan had held him captive until God grasped him through his word and reshaped him into a new person. God gave Abraham the faith in him that constituted a new relationship, the Edenic relationship of fear, love, and trust on Abraham's side. Abram had been, in other words, the prototype of all sinners, who cannot separate themselves from sin, death, and damnation apart from Christ.[54] God chose this idolater to be the ancestor of the Messiah "in order that the fainthearted and fearful, who are tempted to despair because of their sins, may find comfort and, encouraged by such examples, may learn to hope in such a merciful God."[55]

This emphasis on the broken relationship with God that fails to trust him did not distract, however, from Luther's frequent focus on both sins of commission and sins of omission in the daily practice of earthly relationships among his hearers and readers. In treating the topic "sin" in the Smalcald Articles, he enumerated sins as examples. The list began with ways in which the first commandment, and thus the relationship with God, is broken: "unbelief, false belief, idolatry, being without the fear of God, presumption, despair, blindness, and, in short, not knowing or honoring God." He then continued with sins against God that go beyond trust to specific actions: "lying, swearing [falsely] by God's name, not praying or calling on God's name, neglect of God's word." Commandments four

52. WA 32: 369,3–397,25, LW 21: 83–128.
53. WA 42:112, 20–22, LW1:149.
54. WA 42: 437, 15–19.
55. WA 42: 437,42–438,24.

through eight guided the list of ways that sinners break relationships with other human beings: "being disobedient to parents, murdering, behaving promiscuously, stealing, deceiving."[56]

Sin means, Luther observed, that we are turned in upon ourselves (*incurvatus in se*). The absence of God forces sinners to defend themselves with offenses against other creatures as well as God. Luther knew all too well what the British philosopher Mary Midgley described as living in a "mirror-lined box." She judges that any mode of conceiving of life that "insists on treating the universe as a mere projection screen for showing off human capacities, cripples and curtails humanity."[57] When life revolves around "me," it loses its true context and thus its proper fullness. To fill the hole left when God is kicked out, we turn to the one we know best, although we do not really know even ourselves. But we need a place to go when no one else will take us in. Entering our innermost, we find it cold and dark, with only a dim artificial life, with cardboard conversation partners who struggle to supply the hollow words we want to hear.[58] That has become the fallen human condition. This life trying to escape from God's presence, despite its loneliness, fashions barriers to his access.

As Steven Paulson notes, "God comes nearer to us than we would ever wish, precisely because sinners always want God at a proper distance." This can be for different reasons. Keeping God at a distance comfortably avoids his accusation, but it can also provide some sinners more space in which to create ever more formidable barriers to honest confrontation with the Creator. "Distance between us and deity falsely assures us that God grants mercy for the time being by staying away, withholding judgment, and providing time for the amendment of life."[59] God prefers to be close, in intimate and open conversation each day and hour, in our face with his expectations that pierce our hearts and with his love that melts them. The rhythm of dying to sinful instincts and renewal of life in Christ defined his view of the Christian life.

Thus, Luther's combat against sin did not stop with calling hypocrites and Pharisees to repentance, though that did occupy much of his time in the pulpit. Their pious lives had replaced God as the source of their comfort and security. He also strove to cultivate a rejection of the sinful habits which he encountered in the streets of Wittenberg. The Large Catechism's explanation of commandments four through ten reveals how

56. BSELK 746/747,21–26, BC 310.
57. *The Essential Mary Midgley* (London: Routledge, 2005), 377.
58. Cf. T. S. Eliot's poem, "The Hollow Men."
59. Steven Paulson, "Graspable God," *Word & World* 32 (2012): 52.

concrete and down to earth the reformer's perception of sinfulness and his commitment to nurturing the maturation of new obedience in the faithful were. These catechetical sermons aimed at effecting what the Small Catechism suggests: that believers "reflect on your place in life in light of the Ten Commandments: whether you are father, mother, son, daughter, master, mistress, servant; whether you have been disobedient, unfaithful, lazy,[60] whether you have harmed anyone by word or deed; whether you have stolen, neglected, wasted, or injured anything."[61] God's plan for human life directed actions according to the commands of the Decalogue within the framework of the callings of daily life. Believers practice virtues within their vocations.

Therefore, in his preaching and in his postils, designed to guide the preaching of his followers, Luther spent a good deal of time addressing human performance. From the pulpit he not only condemned the vices that plague the lives of believers. He also explained the form that their active righteousness should take as righteous people who practice their passively received identity in daily life. That passively received righteousness is to be lived out in active righteousness. Such preaching grew naturally out of the way that Luther had learned to confront his sins face to face in his own life, with Jesus at his side. Only in the shadow of the cross and the breeze blowing from a tomb with stone rolled away, could he then proceed to live in the light of faithful obedience. Mortification of the flesh and being turned to Christ's forgiveness convinces trusting believers that they are righteous according to God's judgment and thus must in fact be righteous. At the same time, Luther also repeatedly returned to the first commandment and the slivers of doubt that misshape decision-making. In repentance and trust in Christ, he then turned to the practice of righteousness in living within human society and God's creation.

LUTHER FACES THE LAW AND GOD'S WRATH

Viewing the law as a foe was for Luther a bit more ambiguous. Most of Luther's comments referring to the law and much of his proclamation of the law in the pulpit and in the lecture hall fall into his primary category of its usage: "Its foremost office [probably 'function' would be a better translation of the term] or power is that it reveals inherited sin and its fruits. It shows human beings into what utter depths their nature has fallen

60. The Book of Concord 1580 and the Wittenberg editions of 1535 and following omit: "ill-tempered, unruly, quarrelsome" after "lazy".
61. BSELK 886/887,6–9, BC 360.

and how completely corrupt it is. The law must say to them that they neither have nor respect any god or that they worship foreign gods. This is something that they would not have believed before or without the law."[62]

All theological musing is autobiographical. This appraisal reflects not only Luther's memory of the despair of his youth but also the honest evaluation of his failure to keep focus on his Lord too often in everyday life. As early as 1516 Luther contended, "The law makes sinners, the gospel comforts and saves them. The law is a word that humbles troubles, upsets, condemns: the gospel is a word that saves, exalts, comforts. The law is a ministry of death, condemnation, and unrighteousness: the gospel is a ministry of delight, joy, salvation."[63] He told students in 1532, on the basis of Psalm 45:2, that the teaching of the law curses and brings God's wrath as well as sin and death upon sinners. In this context he credited the law with "not a single blessing at all."[64] Two years later he observed, regarding Psalm 23:4, that the law has no ability to restore the soul. It gives commands. It follows up on God's creation of Adam and Eve to instruct on true human living. To be sure, it was never designed to originate or engender human life. Its evaluative standard crushes guilty consciences and informs liberated consciences. The law could only guide, as aid or corrective.[65] It was not by original intent designed as an expression of God's disappointment and anger over human doubt and defiance, but its evaluation expresses the wrath of the Creator when his will for human behavior collides with the honest introspection of the sinner.

The topic of the law as an expression of God's wrath and its place in Luther's body of doctrine set the stage for one of the grand debates at the beginning of modern Lutheran studies, between Albrecht Ritschl and Theodosius Harnack. Ritschl tried to blunt the effect of a doctrine of God's anger at sin while Harnack took it seriously as an integral part of Luther's doctrine of God. Egil Grislis was correct in suggesting that Harnack tried to answer more questions regarding God's anger with sinners based on Luther's writings than Luther actually did.[66] Nonetheless, Harnack rightly observed that Luther had no doubt that God was truly angered by human doubt and rebellion. He did, however, discuss this wrath in terms of the believer's experience of it and the devil's use of the believer's recognition

62. BSELK 750/751, 13-13-19, BC 312. See Robert Kolb, "Wittenberg Uses of Law and Gospel," *Lutheran Quarterly* 37 (2023): 249-267.
63. WA4: 567,5–9.
64. WA 40,2: 483,14–21.
65. WA 51: 282,34–283,13, LW12: 164–165.
66. Egil Grislis, "Luther's Understanding of the Wrath of God," *The Journal of Religion* 41 (1961): 278 (277–292).

of the justice of God's anger against this sinner to cause him to despair. He did not attempt an analysis of any of God's inner thought processes, including the origins of God's wrath or his mercy.

God's weapon of execution, however, is in and of itself good, according to Luther, when he assessed the law apart from his own existential situation. It remains in and of itself God's utterly beneficial plan and design for the truly human life. Luther reminded his students that the law produces blessings as an instrument of God, both in keeping political order and in leading sinners to the despair that turns their attention to Christ.[67] In teaching his barber Peter Beskendorf how to pray, Luther observed that the commandments are "instruction," that "that is really what [the law] is intended to be . . . what the Lord God in all seriousness demands of me."[68] Specifically, he regarded the Ten Commandments as "a summary of divine teaching on what we are to do in order to make our whole life pleasing to God. They are the true fountain from which all good works must spring . . ." The Ten Commandments enjoin a life of "gentleness, patience, love toward enemies, chastity, kindness, etc." But then his sensitive conscience looked inwardly while profoundly sensing the presence of his Creator, whose passion for the human enjoyment of the goodness that he had created for humanity, drove him to the cross. The reformer's conclusion to the Decalogue in the Large Catechism nonetheless insisted that "no one is able to keep even one of the Ten Commandments as it ought to be kept."[69] The law tells us what we need to know about the shape of truly human living, but only the gospel bestows the righteousness that allows us to lead a life corresponding to the Creator's design. Only the gospel re-creates children of God out of the nothingness of sin.

Luther used the law for the instruction of his people, more often by pointing out what practices they needed to abandon than by giving positive suggestions for carrying out God's plan for life. But positive instruction formed a significant part of his preaching. He did not speak of the "uses" of the law as a dogmatic category, as Melanchthon began to do, perhaps because he knew that however he intended to use it, it had the potential to crush people as honest with themselves as he was with himself. He certainly recognized that he was using the law with specific goals in mind, sometimes promoting societal order, sometimes instructing Christian consciences, and most importantly calling sinners to repentance. But he wrote of the function (in German *Amt*) and power (*Kraft*) of the

67. WA 40,1: 519,5–521,5.
68. WA 38: 365,1–3, LW 43: 200.
69. BSELK 1038/1038, 16–1040/1041, 17, BC 428.

law in the Smalcald Articles,[70] sensing the difference between the way Christians intend to use the law and its function in the hearer's life as well as the impact upon the hearer's actions. As James Nestingen has observed, like a very helpful tamed wolf that you have taken as a guide or service dog, "you never know when it will turn on you."[71] For honest sinners, it never loses the capacity to strike as "the thunderbolt of God, by means of which he destroys both the open sinner and false saints and allows no one to be right but drives the whole lot of them into terror and despair."[72]

However, Luther asserted that the law's accusations need no longer command the attention of those who recognize that the Holy Spirit has placed their sins in Christ's tomb. "The Christian who by faith takes hold of the benefits of Christ has no law at all but is free of it. . . . for those who believe in Christ the entire law, with all its terrors and troubles has been abrogated."[73] The mystery of the continuation of sin and evil in the lives of the baptized means that the terrors and despair that sin induces still lurk in the consciousness of believers. Nonetheless, the forgiveness of sins through Christ's death and resurrection gives them the confidence that there is no condemnation for those who are in Christ Jesus (Rom 8:1).[74]

Freed from the law, believers are free to exercise their humanity by bonding themselves to their neighbors and binding themselves to their neighbors' needs, as Luther argues in *On Christian Freedom*.[75] And for that life Luther found authoritative and helpful instruction in the law. He expected that the mortification of the flesh would defeat sinful desires and that the Holy Spirit would construct godly habits of mind and action, since sinners who wish to act in accord with God's judgment that they are righteous need the guide dog. But he was at the same time realistic about the nature of the mystery of the continuation of sin and evil in the lives of the baptized. The law's nagging, gnawing presence returns God's children each day to the repentance that effects anew the drowning of the Old Adam that doubts the word of the Lord even at our most pious moments. Repentance permeates the whole life of the Christian. The law always accuses, and it accuses those faithful believers who seek instruction in it for living a godly life with a special fury. For as they learn what God wants them to do, they recognize what they have not done as he wills.

70. BSELK 750/751,13–14, BC 312.
71. James A. Nestingen, *The Faith We Hold, The Living Witness of Luther and the Augsburg Confession* (Minneapolis: Augsburg, 1983), 38–39.
72. BSELK 750/751, 27–30, BC 312.
73. WA 40,1: 670, 19–22, LW 26: 445–446.
74. WA 40,1. 671, 13, LW 26:447.
75. WA 7:49,20–21, LW 31:344.

But Christ brings liberation from this condemnation by consuming it in his own person and letting it fulfill its fatal mission on himself.

LUTHER FACES THE DEVIL

Luther viewed the devil in an unambiguous manner. Jesus's description of the devil as a liar and a murderer (John 8:44), in whom the truth does not abide, determined Luther's view of Satan. Satan was possessed by his spite for God; God remains his God, but the one against whom he continually fights to establish his own identity. All he succeeds in doing is to establish more deeply his identity as liar and murder because the Author of life and truth rules as Creator. In his sermon on John 8:46–59 in the House Postil of 1544, a sermon originally preached in 1533, Luther identifies the devil at his worst as the one who presents himself as God and holy, claims not to do wrong, and listens to nothing.[76] The preacher protested against those who do not listen to God's word, regarding their "mouth, eyes, reason and everything else" not as gifts and creations of God but of the devil. They have become the devil's children, as Jesus said, in contrast to God's children, who listen to him and remain faithful to what he says.[77]

Heiko Oberman's estimate of Luther as a man caught between God and the devil is not only much more accurate than Marius's regarding him as caught between God and death.[78] It also reflects Luther's understanding of reality as grounded in the relationship of the personal and speaking Creator, in whom human beings were to have absolute trust. For Luther, the very personal nature of Satan as well as the nature of his challenge to what the Creator says, as the fomentation of doubt in God's word, demonstrated again that the foundation of reality lies in persons and personal relationships.

Significantly, the reformer's extant writings from the 1510s contain relatively few references to the devil.[79] This reflects a general attitude in scholastic theology; the devil played a role in the narrative, but the individual focus fell on the suffering he causes and the human need to

76. WA 52: 200,31–32.

77. WA 52: 200,33–201,36.

78. *Luther: Man Between God and the Devil*. Cf. Hans-Martin Barth, *Der Teufel und Jesus Christus in der Theologie Martin Luthers* (Göttingen: Vandenhoeck & Ruprecht, 1967) for a detailed discussion, and Volker Leppin, "Luther on the Devil," in Kirsi I. Stjerna and Brooks Schramm, *Encounters with Luther: New Directions for Critical Studies* (Louisville, KY: Westminster John Knox, 2016), 30–41.

79. Barth, *Der Teufel und Jesus*; Barth cites very few passages referring to the devil prior to 1521/1522.

resist sin and perform the proper actions. Even in popular piety, the devil did not assume as threatening a role as he did with Luther. Heiko Oberman observes, "The medieval poltergeist is virtually harmless" compared to the combatant with whom Luther struggled. He "is armed with fire and sword, spiritual temptations and clever arguments, he has risen up against God to prevent the preaching of the Gospel. . . . The reformation symbol of Christ's presence is not the halo of the saint, but the hatred to the Devil."[80] As Oberman ably demonstrates, Satan assumed a central place in Luther's combat against evil in subsequent years—but only after his excommunication and the imperial declaration of outlawry in 1521. By that time, he had experienced not only his own personal rebellion against God but also the broader activities of the devil. For the advance of Wittenberg thinking brought ever more challenges to its spread. In all this, speculation about the origins of Satan's rebellion lay outside the reformer's interest. Where and why Satan broke the relationship with God for which he had been made, commanded not a minute of Luther's time. The combat against his attempts to reassert his rule in the reformer's life defined his interest in the Evil One.

Particularly in his Table Talks, Luther sometimes reflected a host of medieval perceptions of demonic activities, including deceptive appearances, for instance, as a relative suffering in purgatory returning as a ghost.[81] Satan provoked storms, either directly or through witches.[82] Oberman comments,

> Luther's world of thought is wholly distorted and apologetically misconstrued if his conception of the Devil is dismissed as a medieval phenomenon and only his faith in Christ retained as relevant or as the only decisive factor. Christ and the Devil were equally real to him: one was the perpetual intercessor for Christianity, the other a menace to mankind till the end. To argue that Luther never overcame the medieval belief in the Devil says far too little; he even intensified it and lent to it additional urgency: Christ and Satan wage a cosmic war for mastery over Church and world.[83]

In his preaching and lecturing, the professor's language regarding the Evil One was usually somewhat spare and to the point. In the Large Catechism readers learned of the impact of the devil's attempt to exercise his rule in

80. Oberman, *Luther*, 155.
81. Cf. Vincent Evener, "Wittenberg's Wandering Spirits: Discipline and the Dead in the Reformation," *Church History* 84 (2015): 531–555.
82. WA TR 4:620, Nr. 5027, 2: 504, Nr. 2529b, 4: 31, Nr. 3953.
83. Oberman, *Luther*, 104.

this world, and that sufficed; Luther did not attempt to depict him, neither with common medieval motifs, nor through his own imaginations.

Thus, Luther recognized that Satan attacks not only through temptations to commit sin in the popular sense of offenses against public order but also by opening many battlefronts in human lives, and his assaults on believers' reliance on God alone come from many directions. The devil attacks human beings through

> poverty, disgrace, death, and, in short, all the tragic misery and heartache of which there is so incalculably much on earth. For because the devil is not only a liar but a murderer as well, he incessantly seeks our life and vents his anger by causing accidents and injury to our bodies. He crushes some and drives others to insanity; some he drowns in the water, and many he hounds to suicide or other dreadful catastrophes. Therefore, there is nothing for us to do on earth but to pray without ceasing against this archenemy. For if God did not support us, we would not be safe from him for a single hour.[84]

In lectures, Luther distinguished "the black devil" from "the white devil" for his students. Both were engaging them in persistent combat. The black devil disguises himself and hides his clever tricks. He forces human beings to act wickedly and suggests excuses for what they intend to do as well as what they do outwardly. The anger of the murderer of human beings blinds sinners with a deceptive excuse so that they do not take his temptations seriously as sin. Sexual exploiters, robbers, drunkards, those consumed with covetousness, and similar sinners know how to hide their sinfulness.

Worse than temptations to open transgressions of the other commandments, Satan appears as a "white devil," in a person's relationship to God either as one who encourages confidence in the person's own faith rather than in Christ or as one who models a humility (or another virtue) that contributes just a tiny bit to salvation. Luther had encountered that in the monastic piety of his cloister and especially in the helpful engagement with the "theology of humility" that aided him on his way to strong trust in Christ as the only source of salvation. In a person's relationship to other people, the "white" devil arouses confidence in personal performance of moral goods or creates seemingly pious activities beyond and contrary to the command of God. He appears not as an evil figure but rather disguised as an angel or as God, clothed in great concern for pious performance and religious appearance. He uses deceptive thoughts and marvelous ploys. He offers his fatal poison in the form of misapprehensions of the meaning

84. Large Catechism, Lord's Prayer, seventh petition, BSELK 1108/1109, 5–17, BC 455–456.

of the biblical text or with misapplications of the word of God in specific contexts. He is particularly skillful at persuading believers to abuse the doctrine of grace and the gospel of Christ.[85]

Or, instead of fostering heresy or works-righteous piety, he simply magnifies the sins of believers. He focuses their gaze on their "lack of faith, doubt, despair, contempt for God, hatred, ignorance, blasphemy, ingratitude, abuse of God's name, neglect, loathing, and contempt for God's Word and the like."[86] Preaching on Luke 15: 1–10, the lost sheep and the lost coin, Luther posited that the sheep gets lost when it senses the burden of sin and does not know where to turn. The sheep is filled with terror because of the satanic corruption of its perception so that it focuses narrowly on the fury of God's disgust and anger. This crushes those who listen to the devil's turning God's law against the troubled conscience by depicting Christ only as a wrathful judge. This constitutes the devil's worst treachery: he alters the perception of Christ and what he has done to rescue and restore sinners.[87]

In his attempt to demonstrate the necessity of total reliance on God's choosing his people for himself, Luther described the devil's power as super-human in *On Bound Choice*. To that end, he employed a not totally apt adaptation of the medieval illustration of the human creature being ridden like a beast of burden by God or the devil.[88] There was no middle ground, no riderless donkey. But more often Luther focused on the ability of the believer with the aid of the Holy Spirit to resist the Deceiver. He told the evening circle gathered in the Black Cloister, "when the devil comes by night to bother me, my answer is: Devil, now I have to sleep, for this is God's command: working by day and sleeping by night."[89] Believers are not to listen to Satan but instead to grasp the shield of faith when he tries to nurture their guilt for his own purposes. They are to tell him that Christ is their shield, and he has given them his own righteousness, upon which they rely.[90]

Throughout the entire life of a Christian, every day begins in facing squarely all enemies that still attempt to put God's people at a distance from their Lord, tempting them to turn their backs in fear or defiance on the Father who loves them and wants to gather them to himself. Each

85. WA 40,1: 108,17–109,13, LW 26: 49.
86. WA 40,1: 87,32–89,12, LW 26: 35–36; cf. WA 40,1: 50,24—51,20, LW 26: 10.
87. WA 36: 296,14–297,37, LW 78: 147.
88. WA 18: 635,17–22, LW 33: 65–66. At least since Origen was this metaphor used in some connection with questions regarding sin and grace.
89. WA TR 2: 132, Nr. 1557.
90. WA 34,2: 401,36–402,30.

believer personally is engaged in the fight against all the enemies that Satan ranges against God's people. That confrontation face to face takes place only when Christ gives believers the assurance and courage that flow from faith in his substitutionary sacrifice of his own life that consumes sin, and in the resurrection that he shares in baptism as he restores life with God and renews true human righteousness. With repentance and faith in Christ's winning for each believer the forgiveness of their sins, they confront these foes—but not alone. The person of Christ, who delivered them, makes his claim against Satan and compels the law to release sinners into his possession.

In October 1531, with the renewed threat of extermination by the forces of Charles V hanging over the Wittenberg reform, Luther preached on Ephesians 6 and reviewed in this sermon the weapons that the Holy Spirit gives the children of God to combat Satan.[91] The sermon combined a sober assessment of Satan's power with the preacher's absolute confidence that God ensures his people that Christ's victory over Satan's evil intent and desires belongs to them as well. Luther began by asking "What sort of armor can that be?" that Paul describes in the text. "Where are we supposed to find that armor or where is the armor maker who can forge such armor?" No earthly armor maker can create that kind of armor.[92] The residents of Wittenberg saw armor occasionally at the electoral castle before the Coswig Gate at the west end of their town. Luther's knowledge of armor sprang from conversations with Melanchthon, who had grown up in a household dedicated to fashioning armor. His father was among the most famous armor makers in the German lands, having served not only the electors of the Palatinate but Emperor Maximilian himself, before he died at a young age, perhaps poisoned by a foe of his Palatine lord.[93] Luther explained that Paul used this imagery to emphasize the seriousness of the conflict between God and the devil. Their combat necessarily drew everyone on their side into the clash of truth and lie, of the Creator and Satan. The devil intends to destroy God's rule. Therefore, Christians must be prepared to resist him.

Luther accentuated the comfort believers have, however, in knowing that the conflict into which they have been drawn is ultimately not

91. The following paragraphs reproduce significant sections of Robert Kolb, "'The Armor of God and the Might of His Strength.' Luther's Sermon on Ephesians 6 (1531/1533)," *Concordia Journal* 43 (2017): 59–73, and is used with the editor's permission. This sermon, found in WA 34,2: 371,21–406,26. Translations here are the author's own.

92. WA 34,2:379,28–380,6.

93. Heinz Scheible, *Melanchthon, Vermittler der Reformation: Eine Biographie* (Munich: Beck, 2016), 12–15.

their conflict, but God's, and that God will give them aid and support against the raging and fury of the Foe. The preacher told his hearers that God is out to trick "this proud and angry spirit" by throwing believers up against him as a bulwark. He compared them to a poor, weak shanty that the devil could blow away, a little spark against a mighty wind. But God triumphs through our weakness, Luther said without mentioning 2 Corinthians 12:9. His "theology of the cross" shaped his expression of the way in which God does battle against the old evil foe.

Paul had explained why putting on God's armor is important: "So that you are able to stand against the cunning assault of the devil" (6:11). The devil will not attack directly when he sees that you grasp the sword, Luther told the congregation, but he will find the gaps into which he can sneak. He has indeed raged against Christendom with his tyranny, using sword, fire, water, and other means to persecute the church. But that has not worked so well; the church grows under persecution. Luther repeated the ancient dictum that the apostles planted the church but the martyrs watered it.[94] His own view of martyrdom departed from the medieval view that focused on witness unto death as a meritorious act of Christian courage. Luther taught instead that it was God's gift to die for the faith, both to the individual so honored and to the church, which receives edification through the martyr's death.[95] The Wittenberg hearers were to be prepared, on the other hand, to combat the devil whenever he would appear to them as an angel of light (2 Cor 11:14), employing the world's reasoning, wisdom, and cleverness to deceive. He would confront them as a friend, not an enemy, a shining, snow-white devil, out to blind Christians as the serpent deceived Eve. His intrigues take a variety of forms to enchant believers.[96] Instead of watching out for a despicable devil, clothed in black, who would say, "I am Satan. Protect yourself from me," the residents of Wittenberg were to expect that he would slink like a snake and adorn himself in God's word and name; he would cite Scripture. Luther warned them that the devil appears as a faithful, pious preacher, who is seeking only God's honor and the salvation of souls. He does so to distract believers from God's revealed truth. For example, he speaks of Christ ascended to the right hand of the Father, with the logical conclusion that his body and blood could not possibly be present in the Lord's Supper.[97]

94. WA 34,2: 381,18–32.
95. Cf. Robert Kolb, "God's Gift of Martyrdom: The Early Reformation Understanding of Dying for the Faith," *Church History* 64 (1995): 399–411.
96. WA 34,2: 381,33–382,24.
97. WA 34,2: 382,25–383,7.

The threat of Zwinglianism lay in the air in 1531, and Luther countered its claims in case its message had penetrated to his own precincts. The preacher turned to this new threat to the faith of his hearers. Satan had forged similar arguments from reason through the Arians, who had denied Christ's divinity and drawn an emperor of his time and many bishops to his false teaching.[98] The first attempt of the Spanish physician Michael Servetus to argue against the divinity of Christ had appeared earlier in 1531; whether Luther was aware of this new challenge to the biblical message or was simply using an example from church history is unclear, but Luther's attack on the Arians may have had current relevance in Wittenberg.[99]

Scripture defines "girding the loins" as properly equipping yourself and getting your equipment in working order so that you are ready to run or to fight, without hindrance, as in Luke 12:35 and 2 Kings 4:29. False Christians ignore this admonition, Luther charged. He warned those in the congregation who were not taking the struggle against Satan and the power of God's word seriously to do so.[100]

The "breastplate of righteousness" Luther defined as "a good conscience, that a Christian live in such a manner that he offends no one and no other person may have a complaint against him." For Luther, conscience oriented all of life toward Christ, but he also interpreted the "breastplate of righteousness" as the believer's practice of the active righteousness of upright outward conduct toward all, harming no one but "diligently serving everyone and doing good for all." This breastplate protects believers from being stabbed by the devil in the heart, losing courage because of a terrified, despairing conscience. Peter had admonished, "dear brothers, be all the more diligent to make your calling and election firm" (2 Pet 1:10). Such conduct confirms the faith through the good fruit that a good tree produces. John had written that this love would accompany believers to the presence of God on the day of judgment (1 John 4:17).

"The boots of the righteousness of peace" meant that Christians defend themselves against Satan by living in peace with others, as Paul had commanded in Romans 12:1. Beyond living in an upright manner, doing good, and not being indifferent to others, God wants his people to be at peace with everyone (as Paul says in Romans 12), both for their own sake and to help others, provide for others, and promote their welfare through the gospel, so that these beleivers in this way can conduct themselves

98. WA 34,2: 383,8–25.
99. WA 34,2: 383,26–385,8.
100. WA 34,2: 398,11–400,4.

with readiness and properly and move through this evil world without hindrance even if the world in and of itself grumbles and causes friction, discord, and strife, and people provoke them to anger, impatience, revenge and the like.

Patience is a prime characteristic of the Christian life because the cross will not remain far from God's people. All of Scripture reveals that even when we do good to all, we must expect resistance, violence, evil attacks, contempt, ingratitude, and humiliation. Luther advised the congregation that revenge and refusing to suffer injustice will never produce peace. Patience and the willingness to accept suffering pave the way to peace.[101]

Luther noted that Paul had described three pieces of armor that combatted the devil through the proper conduct of daily life, and, beginning with verse 16, that three others did so through faith. The shield of faith wards off the devil's fiery missiles. The devil not only tries to lead Christians astray in their relationships to other people, but also attacks the conscience and seeks to weaken and destroy the believer's relationship to God by creating fear and worry about that relationship. The preacher did not mention guilt directly, although it certainly stands behind the terror and despair upon which he focused. Satan attempts to arouse the concern that the believer's life demonstrates alienation from God. In such a case the first three pieces of armor will not provide protection from God's anger, for the devil's assault is designed to end the bond between the Creator and the forgiven sinner. Believers are instead to grasp the shield of faith and answer Satan's accusations in this manner:

> If I am a sinner and have not lived properly or done too little, there is the man who is holy and has given himself for me, died for me, has been given to me by the Father, so that his holiness and righteousness and so forth belong to me, and so you must leave me alone, in peace. No accusations allowed! I will stick to that. My life and activities may be whatever they are. I want to do as much as I can in my obligation to others. But where that is lacking and is not present consistently in my life (which I cannot perform on my own apart from Christ), there may my Christ help me and preserve, and you cannot bring an accusation against him. On that I rely as I would rely on a shield, in which I have confidence and with it can stand against every power and gate of hell.[102]

Paul's mention of "flaming arrows" indicated to Luther that "he was speaking as a man who has faced temptation, who had often been in the

101. WA 34,2: 401,20–32.
102. WA 34,2: 401,36–402,30.

midst of the daily assaults of the devil and experienced that nothing else lasts and is effective in this sort of battle, when the devil attacks." Then godly conduct is not enough to fend off the flaming arrows of the devil. They pierce through the armor to the heart. Through all kinds of sects and false teachers the devil strives to deprive believers of Scripture, baptism, and the Lord's Supper, that is, the voice of the promising God. The shield of faith remains the only effective protection.[103]

Hearers and readers were given their side of the dialogue that they were to pursue with Satan over their worthiness. They were to answer the devil's challenge to that sense of worth:

> God grant that my life and all that I do remain where they are intended to be, whether it is truly proper and can stand before the world. For I have in all seriousness and faithfulness taught, lived, and fulfilled my calling. But because you want to shoot me in the heart, and say that none of this is valid and with that you want to afflict my conscience, I will just let that all go by me and grab my shield, which covers and protects me and my entire life, etc. . . . For Christ stands before me, takes my place, and says, "I have given my flesh and blood to this person, placed my life and holiness in his stead." Therefore, leave me in peace.

Satan must yield and vanish at that point, the preacher concluded. Believers can hold Christ in front of the devil's nose and repudiate his accusation. Peter's admonition, "be alert and on guard, for your foe, the devil, is going about like a roaring lion and seeks to devour whomever he can. Resist him, firm in the faith" (1 Peter 5:8), reminded Luther's readers that without the shield of faith they cannot be certain that "the devil will not strangle us and gobble us down." Readers must "at all times have Christ in our hearts and hold fast to him."[104]

Luther defined the "helmet of salvation" as the hope and expectation of life in heaven, which sustains believers in all their suffering: as Paul had noted, "if we only hope in Christ for this life, we are the most miserable people on earth" (1 Cor 15:19). Thus, believers can defy the devil, confident that all the misfortune that he can bring upon them in this world cannot deprive them of eternal life with Christ.[105]

"The final but absolutely strongest weapon, the right one for the war, with which we must strike back at the devil and conquer him," is God's word. The confrontation with Satan demands not only the power to

103. WA 34,2: 402,31–403,14.
104. WA 34,2: 403,15–404,10.
105. WA 34,2: 404,12–405,2.

protect oneself but also the power to attack the devil and set him to flight. No sword of steel or iron is appropriate or allowed in this conflict. It must be the sword of the Spirit.

> That takes place above all when the Word is publicly presented from the pulpit, but also every Christian individually or with others is to be hearing, reading, singing, speaking, and meditating on the Word. For it has the power when clearly and purely proclaimed and used, diligently learned, and earnestly meditated on. Then neither Satan nor any devil can remain. For the Word reveals his deception and roguery which deceive people, with the intention of building false trust or false faith, sadness, or despair. For the Word reveals the Lord Christ, whom he crucified, but he collided with Christ and got burned, for Christ trampled on his head. Therefore, he is afraid and flees from his presence. That did him tremendous harm, takes many souls back from him, and weakens and destroys his kingdom.[106]

His word is God's might and power.

Thus, the preacher admonished readers of the printed text to actively hear and learn God's word and not hide it away or let it remain in the books, as if one would keep the sword in its sheath or let it rust. Therefore, the pastoral ministry must have preachers worthy of their office, faithful workers, to resist the sects and papacy. The followers of the pope read and sang by rote "without heart or understanding," Luther's critique of the practice of the faith with which his generation had grown up. For God punishes those who have contempt for his word and ingratitude for what he has taught.[107]

Luther's hearers and readers had received the equipment for waging the eschatological battle that goes on in their lives each day from the Holy Spirit. They were to take the devil's attacks personally, for their person was the booty this marauder sought. The weapons supplied by the Holy Spirit could effectively defeat him because Christ had forged them in his death and resurrection.

Luther told his students in 1545 that in the execution of Christ the law had set itself on fire, death had piled excrement upon itself, and Satan, hell, and sin itself decimated themselves. He spoke of the indebtedness or blame that Christ's death and resurrection had imposed upon these foes because in satisfying the law's demand for the death of sinners he had

106. WA 34,2: 405,4–32.
107. WA 34,2: 405,33–406,26.

become God's own weapon against all who, and which, are hostile to him and his chosen people.[108]

Luther engaged in personal combat with Satan throughout his life. He had squarely faced what the Liar and Murderer had introduced into his life through the threat of death, the practice of sin, and its roots in his own failure to fear, love, and trust in God above all things. He recognized that the condemnation of God's law and the resultant wrath of God over his sinfulness were staring him in the face. Gradually in the 1510s, he came to realize that standing next to him against the threats of all of them was his risen Lord, still with holes in his hands, but hands that supported the Augustinian Brother and the mature professor in the battle. With confidence he joined the fight, struggling with the *Anfechtungen* that never ceased to come and that never stopped scaring and hurting. But these threats could be contained and defeated in the shadow of the cross and the empty tomb because Christ had already confronted them and conquered. His presence in his word of promise framed the reality that Luther experienced in his daily life.

108. WA 44: 697,21–698,6, cf. LW 8: 162–163.

3.

The Reformer Face to Face with the Person of God Revealed

Martin Luther coram Deo revelato

LUTHER'S ENGAGEMENT WITH THE GOD WHO IS

The nineteenth-century German philosopher Ludwig Feuerbach proposed that human beings make God in their own image. Despite his atheistic beliefs Feuerbach knew Luther well.[1] He undoubtedly was familiar with Luther's dictum in his explanation of the first commandment in the Large Catechism,

> to have a god is nothing else than to trust and believe in that one with your whole heart. As I have often said, it is the trust and faith of the heart alone that make both God and an idol. If your faith and trust are right, then your God is the true one. Conversely, where your trust is false and wrong, there you do not have the true God. For these two belong together, faith and God. Anything on which your heart relies and depends, I say, that is really your God.[2]

Luther's view of God never drifted into the purely theoretical consideration of Divinity in its essence. His medieval piety had cultivated a sense of the personal dimensions of his relationship with the ground of his being. That

1. Cf. Paulson, *Outlaw God*, 3: 207–223. Cf. Carter Lindberg, "Luther and Feuerbach," *The Sixteenth Century Journal* 1 (1970): 105–125.
2. BSELK 930/931,10–932/933,3, BC 386.

relationship always embraced his mind as it considers what the Bible says about the Creator, his emotions that felt the relationship that God had with him, and his will that responded to what his mind and emotions told him about God.

The dim light of his own experience gave the young Martin Luther the sense that lurking directly in front of him in the shadows of life, murkier than the streets of Wittenberg without a moon at night, loomed a massive figure, a person. It was his Creator. Even though his medieval piety shaped an image of a God far away, this distant deity was a person, a person with feelings. From his childhood on, Luther sensed that the divine person was angry with unworthy sinners. The impression that his manifold failures to behave as God wanted him to behave haunted him. He became ever more certain that his performance had justly earned him God's wrath and rage. This infuriated, mighty Maker could and would place him rightly in eternal suffering.

A reflection of his own personality perhaps, and certainly as comment on the biblical writers' depictions of God, Luther accentuated the Bible's presentation of the strong, deep emotions of God. The Creator was not only the Mover on the move, but he was also the Mover who was moved in his own inner self to emotional reactions toward his people. God mourned over his rebellious people. He became angry when his human creatures defied him and his plan for good human living, as any parent becomes angry when children are doing what is harmful to themselves. The Creator grieves over their straying from him and turning their backs on him. The rampant and atrocious sins of humankind at Noah's time caused God to forget the delight he had felt at creation, Luther observed to his students in 1536 as he treated Genesis 6:6. Those sins caused him to grieve, regretting that he had created this human creature.[3]

But much more, Luther accentuated God's delight in showing mercy and kindness to his faithful people. With the delight of a lover, he exults in doing good for them. Lecturing on Isaiah 63 in 1530, Luther noted, "God is afflicted when we are afflicted."[4] In his Large Catechism he commented on the prologue to the Decalogue in Exodus 20, which he had made into his conclusion of the commandments, as a transition from law to gospel, "Learn from these words, then, how angry God is with those who rely on anything but him, and again, how kind and gracious he is to those who trust and believe him alone with their whole heart. His wrath does not subside until the fourth generation, but, in contrast, his

3. WA 42: 298,12–17, LW 2: 51.
4. WA 31,2: 538,27–28, LW 17: 358.

kindness and goodness extend to many thousands."[5] Despite his turning his gaze to this God Revealed, Luther continued to the end of his life to struggle with God Hidden even though he could not and would not look into his face.

Luther slowly came to realize that this early impression of a wrathful Creator was not totally false. His reading of Scripture convinced him that human doubt of his Maker's word and defiance of his lordship had justly aroused God's jealousy and wrath. He continued to encounter the Creator who expresses his dissatisfaction and disappointment at his people's rebellious wandering from his circle. But when God identifies himself to his people in Scripture, he reminds them of his faithfulness to them throughout the history of his chosen family and his repeated deliverance of them from their foes.

In Exodus 3:6 Moses wanted to know with whom he was speaking as a voice came from a bush. He knew that bushes do not speak, people speak. God's elusive answer went no further than claiming to exist as the person he was, but he did identify himself as the person who had interacted with Abraham, Isaac, and Jacob. In giving the covenant (Exod 20:1–20, Deut 5:1–22) and in addressing Israel at Jeremiah's time (Jer 2:5–6), he reminded them that he was the person who had led them out of Egypt. But deeper aspects of his mysteries he did not disclose.

His lordship became clear as he revealed himself to Moses in the burning bush: he is who he is. He was telling Moses, "I am here in my person, not in a formula that captures me or my power." God was not about to give Moses a name with which Moses could manipulate him. The children of Israel remained dependent on God's self-revelation. Apart from his revelation of himself, their Lord refused to be analyzed or managed or captured and tamed. Preaching on Exodus 3 in 1524, Luther took the text literally and identified the person who confronted Moses from the burning bush first as an angel who was delivering God's voice, his words, as his representative. Then he followed the text in reporting on God's conversation with Moses. But the preacher continued by placing the identification of God in his own mouth. God labeled himself the God of Moses's ancestors, of Abraham, Isaac, and Jacob. Luther recognized that the Creator had grounded his identity on his personal role in human history, in relationship to his chosen people.[6]

5. BSELK 940/941,29–34, BC 354.
6. On Moses's hearkening to the Lord in his subsequent return to Egypt to assume leadership of the Israelites, counter to any rational calculation of the dangers and difficulties of the task, see Paulson, *Outlaw God*, 1, 9–24.

Luther did not speculate about this claim of God to be the one who he is and will be. He anchored his knowledge of God on what God says in his word and in God's involvement in the history of his people.[7] His identity or righteousness expressed itself, above all, in his steadfast loving kindness. It was the distinguishing characteristic he liked to claim. In the dark, dangerous days of 1530, while he was at the Castle Coburg, Luther composed a commentary on one of his favorite Psalms, the *Confitemini* of Psalm 118, with its refrain of confessing the enduring steadfast love of God. The tracing of the goodness of God to the Israelites through their history gave the reformer occasion to note how God provides and protects in the daily life of believers in his day. Luther experienced the God of Abraham, Isaac, and Jacob not only in Scripture but also in his daily life as almighty, all-knowing, good, and especially as trustworthy, faithful to his people and his promises to them.[8]

The reformer did not discount natural revelation as a place of encounter with the person of the Creator. Commenting on Ecclesiastes 6:9 in 1526, he noted that the experience of the faithful echoes God's delight in his creation (Gen 1:31): the goodness of God's gifts elicits the believer's reaction of pleasure and satisfaction at their goodness.[9] Obviously, only those who know that these gifts come from their gracious Creator through their faith in Christ can fully enjoy and appreciate these gifts in nature. Otherwise, those upon whom the rain falls, and sun shines find in nature signs and signals that are not only kind and friendly, but also often terrifying. In the Large Catechism's explanation of the Creed, Luther confessed with Paul in Romans 1:18–20 that "all who are outside this Christian people, whether heathen, Turks, Jews, or false Christians and hypocrites . . . believe in and worship only the one, true God." He did not allow for other options. However, such people have no personal relationship to him; they do not know his gracious disposition toward sinners. "They cannot be confident of his love and blessing, and therefore they remain in eternal wrath and condemnation. For they do not have the LORD Christ, and, besides, they are not illuminated and blessed by the gifts of the Holy Spirit."[10] In 1531 Luther repeated this in a sermon on John 6. All imaginable religions worship the Creator of heaven and earth, but they are not able to make true contact with him because they do not believe that Christ, true God, the Son of God, became human as the bread of life. They come out of their

7. WA 16: 41,29–46,10.
8. WA 31,1: 65–182, LW 14: 43–106.
9. WA 20:117,22–118,22, LW 15: 101; cf. WA 20: 112,17–33.
10. BSELK 1068/106916–23, BC 440.

worship of him with empty hands and heart. Only in Jesus Christ does God provide his human creatures with access to himself.[11]

God had, indeed, created humanity for a relationship of love and trust with himself and other human beings. Luther's encounters with the voice of God convinced him that his Creator had decisively dealt with human sin and his own wrath through the incarnation of the second person of the Trinity, who was born of the Virgin Mary, and who died bearing all human sin. His resurrection, Luther taught with Paul in Romans 4:25, restored his own integrity or righteousness—his personal identity as child of God—by burying all human sin in Christ's tomb and raising up his own to walk in faithfulness and trust in Christ's footsteps, as new, reborn creatures in a new life (Rom 6:3–11). God revealed the depths of his personality as one who loves without condition, categorically without reservation, and without any contribution from the creature. He re-creates sinners into his children, just as he created human beings in the beginning "without any merit or worthiness in me, out of pure, divine goodness and mercy," as Luther confessed in explaining God's creative activity in his Small Catechism.[12] That is God's nature; that is his righteousness.

LUTHER'S DOCTRINE OF THE TRINITY

Luther developed an abhorrence of the speculative nature of much of the scholastic theology his instructors had fed him. As he became more and more familiar with the biblical text, he tried to avoid letting his mind wander beyond that text into imaginative constructions of a god that reflected his own image. No reader of Scripture can avoid just such ventures of the fancy of one's own heart, but Luther strove to cope with what he could not understand about God, himself, and the Creator's world through his determination to let mysteries be mysteries. In so far as God was hiding, Luther did not go looking for him unless his hiding seemed to betray his promises. Luther wished and intended to concentrate on God's voice as the prophets and apostles conveyed it.

Therefore, his understanding of just who this God is as a living, speaking, and triune person of three *persona* remained bound to the tradition that the church had mined from Scripture. Luther strove to resist the temptation to piece together a glimpse inside the inner being of the Godhead out of what he wished God would be like. The gulf between the

11. WA 33:184,26–185,5, LW 23. 120.
12. BSELK 870/871,15–17, BC 354–355.

person of God in his inner reality and what the human mind could find as analogies defied all who wished to cross the line between what God hides of himself and what he reveals. Luther's confession of the "immanent" Trinity remained with the historical credal and conciliar decisions of the church in the early centuries of its history. His catechisms reflect Luther's normal practice in both sermons and lectures of not dealing with the "immanent" inner relationships of the Trinity. He commented in the doctoral disputation of Georg Major and Johannes Faber in 1544 that the essence and substance of the persons of the Trinity consist in their relationships.[13] His printed sermon on John 16:12 described these relationships in terms of the speaking God: the Father speaks, the Son is the word he speaks, and the Holy Spirit listens. Such conjecture presses at the outer limit of Luther's peering into the inner nature of the Creator.[14]

Instead, he treated the "economic" activities of Father, Son, and Holy Spirit in the activities of each within the world of the Creator that they had fashioned. He could, on the one hand, affirm Augustine's dictum, "the works of the Trinity toward the outside are not divisible," and that the creation of humankind was accomplished by Son and Holy Spirit just as much as by the Father. On the other hand, he spoke specifically of works of each as it seemed appropriate in individual biblical texts.

Luther employed traditional formulations in the Smalcald Articles in his effort to reproduce the faith that provided the foundation for all Christians. His concise formulation repeated the ancient credal foundation and did not go beyond it. He wrote that he and the entire church of Christ confessed

> the lofty articles of the divine majesty, namely: 1. That Father, Son, and Holy Spirit, three distinct persons in one divine essence and nature, is one God, who created heaven and earth, etc. 2. That the Father was begotten by no one, the Son was begotten by the Father, and the Holy Spirit proceeds from the Father and the Son. 3. That neither the Father nor the Holy Spirit, but the Son became a human being.[15]

Six years later, in 1543, he elaborated in his comments on 2 Samuel 23:

> The Father is a different and distinct being from the Son in the one indivisible and eternal Godhead. The difference is that he is the Father and does not derive his Godhead from the Son or anyone else. The son is a person distinct from the Father in the same, one paternal Godhead. The difference is that he is the Son and that he does not have the Godhead from himself,

13. WA 39,2: 287–336.
14. WA 39,2: 317,6–15, (287,1–336,29).
15. BSELK 726/727,5–12, BC 300.

> nor from anyone else but the Father since he was born of the Father from eternity. The Holy Spirit is a person distinct from the Father and the Son in the same, one Godhead. The difference is that he is the Holy Spirit, who eternally proceeds from both the Father and the Son and who does not have the Godhead from himself nor from anyone else but from both the Father and the Son, and all of this from eternity to eternity.[16]

Luther maintained this faith against all critics. He left to Melanchthon the public refutation of the infant anti-Trinitarian thinking, for instance, of a Michael Servetus,[17] but in 1538 his treatise on the ancient creeds ranged their teaching against deniers of the Trinity such as the Jews and the Turks. He challenged them to look carefully at the biblical text and join Christians in recognizing the "one God who, within, is Godhead in three distinct persons." Luther insisted that it would have been impossible for the church to dream up such an idea, and therefore it can rest only on the testimony of both New and Old Testaments. He asserted, "our belief that the three persons are one God takes nothing whatever away from the true single Godhead. Indeed, he remains one God and one Godhead." No human being has or could ever peer into the inner being of God, but "we have indications in Scripture that there are three persons in the divine substance." Reason cannot plumb the depths of God's being. For the creature to be able to grasp the entirety of the Creator defies the definition of being creature and Creator.[18] Luther emphasized that all three persons of the Godhead had created the humanity of Jesus and that only God the Son became this human being.

Luther concluded his treatise on the ancient creeds of 1538 with the admission that "in the Old Testament this is not so clearly underlined but is nevertheless powerfully demonstrated."[19] Nonetheless, many of his criticisms of "the Jews" were not aimed at all those who attended synagogue but specifically at one or more Jewish exegetes for their failure to understand certain passages as confessions of the Trinity and of the incarnate Son of God, the Messiah, Jesus.[20] Neither biblical texts nor attacks from his contemporary opponents imposed the necessity of elaborating a doctrine of the Trinity, and so for Luther the subject commanded relatively little

16. WA 54: 57,26–58,14, LW 15: 302–303.
17. Melanchthon criticized Servetus and other anti-trinitarian writers from time to time and summarized his views in an addition to his *Responsiones Scriptae ad impios articulos Bavaricae inquisitions* of 1558, cf. *Melanchthons Werke in Auswahl* [Studien-Ausgabe], ed. Robert Stupperich 6: (Gütersloh: Bertelsmann, 1955), 6: 365–377.
18. WA 50: 280,11–14, LW 34: 227.
19. WA 50. 282,11–14, LW 34: 229.
20. E.g., WA 54: 37,14–38,15, LW 15: 278–279, WA 54: 72,32–74,10, LW 15: 321–322.

attention. He took for granted that all that exists comes from the person of this one God, who is Father, Son, and Holy Spirit.

GOD REVEALED IN THE PERSON OF CHRIST

The Smalcald Articles continue the confession of the foundation of the faith in the person of the Triune God with the affirmation of the credal faith:

> That the Son became a human being in this way: he was conceived by the Holy Spirit without male participation and was born of the pure, holy Virgin Mary. After that, he suffered, died, was buried, descended into hell, rose from the dead, ascended into heaven, is seated at the right hand of God, in the future will come to judge the living and the dead, etc.[21]

The Small Catechism had affirmed faith simply in, "Jesus Christ, [God the Father's] only Son, our LORD, who was conceived by the Holy Spirit, born of the Virgin Mary."[22] The operative word in this description of Jesus's person is "Lord," for that embraces the person who has demonstrated his mastery of all by dying and rising for his people. What he has done and who he is are inseparable. As eternal God, Creator of all that exists, he preserves his creation and served as Israel's rock, according to Paul in 1 Corinthians 10:4, accompanying the chosen people out of Egypt and into the land of Canaan. He came into human flesh and blood as this Jesus of Nazareth, son of the Virgin Mary, who died on the cross and in his resurrection demonstrated that he remains Creator and Lord.[23] Luther turned to Paul's acclamation of Jesus as the one who bears the treasures of wisdom and knowledge (Col 2:3) to label him the believers' investment capital, the basis and total sum of what they possess. The whole fullness of deity dwells bodily in Jesus Christ, that is, what God is has become personally present in Jesus, "in such a way that whoever does not find or receive God in Christ shall never again and nowhere else have or find God outside of Christ."[24]

Speculation about the incarnation lay outside Luther's way of practicing theology. He urged his students to grasp God as Paul advised in 1 Corinthians 1:21, 24, "since in the wisdom of God the world did not know God through wisdom, it pleased God through the folly of what

21. BSELK 726/727,14–18, BC 300.
22. BSELK 872/873,2–4, BC 355.
23. WA 54: 66,10–68,20, LW 15: 312–314.
24. WA 50: 267,5–10, LW 34: 207.

we preach to save those who believe." For God's foolishness is wiser than human wisdom, and God's impotence is stronger than the powers exercised by his human creatures. Luther directed his students to get acquainted with Christ at the location where he came into the world, in Mary's womb, in the crib of Bethlehem, at his mother's breast. He came into human existence, suffered, went to the cross and died in order to introduce himself to sinners and attract their rapt attention. Because that is his way of operating, he clearly defies human analysis and forbids speculation based on human reasoning.[25]

Nonetheless, Luther held firm convictions about the person of Jesus and his two natures as God and this man from Nazareth. The reformer made much use of the concept of the "communication of attributes," formulated in rough form by the time of Ignatius of Antioch, confirmed by the council of Chalcedon in 451, and further refined in subsequent councils. Luther believed that this concept expressed the biblical affirmation that the divine and human natures of Christ were so intimately connected they completely share their divine and human characteristics. In the union of the two natures—his personal or hypostatic union—Jesus Christ became totally God and totally human. That meant that while his divine nature in and of itself never possessed human characteristics, such as mortality, this nature nevertheless shares these characteristics fully as the one person of Christ. Indeed, his human nature could never be said in and of itself to be able to be present everywhere or wherever God wills, but in the personal union with the divine nature, it exercises the characteristics of what Luther's disciple Martin Chemnitz called "multivolipresence."[26] This view met with sharp critique from Ulrich Zwingli, especially as Luther allowed that the communication of attributes between the two natures would be a possible way of speaking of the sacramental presence of Jesus's body and blood in the Lord's Supper. Zwingli had been trained in the "Realist" school of medieval thinking and accepted as an indisputable axiom the phrase that later became a standard Reformed principle: "the finite cannot convey (or deliver) the infinite." To protect Christ's divinity, he wanted to avoid a compromising association with his humanity.[27] Trained in the

25. WA 40,1: 77,3–6, 77,20–78,13, LW 26: 29.

26. On this development of the Christology of the Wittenberg school, see Robert Kolb, "The Person of Christ in Sixteenth-Century Lutheran Theology," in *Common Places in Christian Theology: A Curated Collection of Essays from Lutheran Quarterly*, ed. Mark C. Mattes (Irvine, CA: 1517 Publishing, 2023), 159–192.

27. On Zwingli's realist philosophical presuppositions, cf. Daniel Bolliger, *Infiniti contemplatio: Grundzüge der Scotus- und Scotismusrezeption im Werk Huldrych Zwinglis* (Leiden: Brill, 2003), esp. 460–493.

Ockhamist school that embraced the created order and held that with God nothing is impossible, Luther believed that God could have indeed created a special purpose and condition that enabled Christ's body and blood to be present in bread and wine. Even independent of that concern, he contended that holding the two natures of Christ together, distinct but inseparable, rightly conveyed the biblical teaching of the incarnation of the second person of the Holy Trinity.[28]

The fifth century patriarch of Constantinople, Nestorius, symbolized for the medieval church the heresy of separating the two natures of Christ and essentially dividing his person into two separate entities, one divine and the other human. Luther's reading of the reports in the chronicles of the early church led him to conclude that this analysis of Nestorius's teaching was probably not historically accurate. He concluded nonetheless that Nestorius's arrogance led him into stubborn defense of his desire not to contaminate the divine nature by letting it be too entangled with the human nature, or to maintain the integrity of the human nature by not letting it be overwhelmed by the divine. Thus, Nestorius could affirm that Mary was Christ's mother, but he rejected the affirmation that Mary gave birth to the divine nature of this one person who is both this human being and God, the second person of the Trinity. Nestorius's opponents used the expression, "Mary is the mother of God," to defend the unity of the person of Jesus Christ and his divinity against those who denied these teachings. In his *On the Councils and the Church* (1539) Luther identified Nestorius's mistake as not recognizing that the two natures share—even though they do not appropriate as their own—the characteristics of the other nature.[29] Luther found it no more strange to say that in his second person God had died on the cross than to say that God had become human in the birth of Jesus. "We Christians must ascribe all the characteristics of the two natures of Christ equally to him. Consequently, Christ is God and man in one person." Not God apart from the incarnation, but the incarnate God in the person of Jesus Christ gives comfort through his sacrifice of his own life on the cross.[30]

In the debates leading to the promulgation of the doctrine of the communication of attributes in the fifth century, a monastic archimandrite named Eutyches countered Nestorius by teaching that humanity is not

28. Marc Lienhard, *Luther: Witness to Jesus Christ, Stages and Themes of the Reformer's Christology*, trans. E. Robertson (Minneapolis: Augsburg, 1982), esp. 153–176, 306–346, 371–382. Cf. Marilyn McCord Adams, *What Sort of Human Nature? Medieval Philosophy and the Systematics of Christology* (Milwaukee: Marquette University Press, 1999), 97.
29. WA 50: 582,15–592,15, LW 41: 95–103.
30. WA 50: 589,15–592,15, LW 41:103.

capable of exercising divine characteristics. Essentially, Luther reported, based on reading the ancient histories of the church, that Eutyches held that the human nature could not do what the divine nature does and that therefore the person of Christ as a whole exercises only divine characteristics. Luther had some doubt as to the accuracy of his own papal opponents' summary of Eutyches's teaching, but in discussing Eutychus he affirmed again that Jesus Christ is totally divine, and since his incarnation at the same time, totally human.[31] Speculation about how this personal union could take place and how this sharing of divine and human characteristics functions found no footing in Luther's thought. He simply confessed that the personal union of God and this human being formed the basis of the salvation of sinners. What this incarnate Son of God had done for fallen humankind commanded Luther's attention above all else.

Luther admitted to the Wittenberg congregation that his illustration was crude, but he affirmed that Jesus, born of Mary, had hair and head, legs and arms, and all other characteristics that belong to a human body—the water, the bones, the flesh. But God added sugar to the humanity of the second person of the Trinity, and it permeates his human being. That means, Luther declared, that the Creator and governor of all things does not want to be found or encountered anywhere other than in Jesus Christ, the son of Mary as well as the Son of God.[32] Access to the Divine comes only through the incarnate second person of the Trinity.

THE WORK OF CHRIST

Election

Luther affirmed God's sole responsibility for the salvation of his people to his choice, or election, of them before the foundation of the world, on the basis of Ephesians 1: 3–11. He was certain that God wanted all to be saved and that Christ had died and risen for the world, the entire human race. But believers could be certain that the promise of eternal life that they had received in baptism arose out of God's plan for them formulated before creation. Thus, Philip Cary's observation that John Calvin's theology was "the first theology in the wake of Augustine to inculcate and systematically support the belief that Christians on earth are already saved for eternity"[33]

31. WA 50, 594,17–596,10, LW 41:108–110.
32. WA 33:184,20–185,5, LW 23. 120.
33. Cary, "Why Luther is Not Quite Protestant," 475.

ignores Luther's affirmation of a "broken" doctrine of predestination.[34] His firm belief that Christ died for all did not hold him back from affirming Paul's avowal that God chose his own children before the foundation of the world and "destined us for adoption as his children through Jesus Christ according to the good pleasure of his will" (Eph 1:4–5). At the same time, he rejected attempts to force predestination into logical form with the predestining reprobation of the unrighteous. Pastoral care, not rational consistency, governed his treatment of Scripture. Therefore, his encountering people who believed that they were predestined to hell led him to direct his hearers to their reception of God's promise of salvation in Christ the Word as they had received it in oral, written, and sacramental forms rather than to thoughts of predestination.[35]

Luther's presumption that the salvation of every individual sprang ultimately from God's eternal plan revealed itself in his use of the term "chosen" or "elect" for believers quite often. In the 1510s his mentor Johannes von Staupitz had used an Augustinian doctrine of predestination to help the young Brother Martin find rest in Christ.[36] However, Luther largely avoided talking about "predestination" because he sensed that discussion of God's choice before the foundation of the world often led to discouragement and despair in those who focused on their own weakness of faith or obedience. In dealing with Romans 9: 15–18 in his lectures of 1516, Luther had taught that God had hardened Pharaoh's heart in order to exhibit his power.[37] But he soon abandoned that view and focused on his own experience of the boundness of his will's ability to choose to turn to God. Thus, he expressed the necessity of a doctrine of election by emphasizing the bondage of the will, most famously in his *On Bound Choice* (1525).[38] It focused on the will's impotence in spiritual matters and largely avoided mention of predestination. His lecture on Genesis 26:9 in early 1542 warned students about the pastoral problems that reading *On Bound Choice* with false presuppositions could produce. He feared that his words about the absolute and necessary unfolding of everything could be

34. The term is Bengt Hägglund's, developed in Rune Söderlund, *Ex praevisa Fide: Zum Verständnis der Prädestinationslehre in der lutherischen Orthodoxie* (Hannover: Lutherisches Verlagshaus, 1983).
35. Robert Kolb, *Bound Choice, Election, and Wittenberg Theological Method: From Martin Luther to the Formula of Concord* (Grand Rapids, MI: Eerdmans, 2005), 40–42.
36. David C. Steinmetz, *Luther and Staupitz: An Essay in the Intellectual Origins of the Protestant Reformation* (Durham: Duke University Press, 1980).
37. WA 56: 403-23-404,19, LW 25: 393–394.
38. WA 18: 600–787, LW 33; 1–295. For an excellent discussion of the dispute between Desiderius Erasmus and Luther on the freedom and bondage of the will, cf. Paulson, *Luther's Outlaw God*, 1, 75–225, and volume 2, passim.

misinterpreted, and so he told his students to look only to Jesus Christ to understand God's will toward sinners. He countered both the despairing doubt and the defiant arrogance that a doctrine of double predestination can foster, so turned his students simply to trusting God's promise in Christ as they had experienced in receiving the Word in all its forms.[39]

This concern had haunted Luther for more than a decade. In 1533, conversing with those gathered in his presence in the Black Cloister, he noted that Romans 9:16 was intended only to repudiate any thought of salvation through human works.[40] In similar conversations at the end of the decade, his student Hieronymus Weller heard him say, "disputation about predestination [is] beyond the limits of Scripture. It is the most ungodly and dangerous business to abandon the certain and revealed will of God in order to search into the hidden mysteries of God."[41] Another student, Johannes Mathesius, recalled Luther's comments on his *On Bound Choice*. "I was troubled by the thought of what God would do with me, but at length I repudiated such a thought and threw myself entirely on his revealed will. We cannot do better than that. The hidden will of God cannot be searched out by the human mind." At this time, around 1540, Luther asserted that God did not hinder Pharaoh's ungodly plans but permitted him to go his own way. "Why God didn't hinder [these plans] is not for us to ask. This 'why?' destroys many souls when they search after that which is too lofty for us." Luther maintained, "God says, 'Why I am doing this to you, you do not know, but ponder my Word, believe in Christ, pray, and I will make everything turn out well.'"[42]

This reflects what he wrote in *Admonition to Prayer against the Turk* (1541):

> We must be guided according to our calling, not according to that which we may think is predestined and about which we are in the dark and know nothing for certain. We have to put this idea out of our minds and hearts and allow the future to be a hidden secret. We have to do what we know we ought to do according to God's Word and the light he has given us. That which God has decreed will come to pass without our doing.[43]

Believers are to turn to God's promise of new life in Christ, expressed in oral, written, and sacramental forms, and cling to that assurance from

39. WA 43:458,35–459,6 and 463,3–17, LW 5:45–46, 50.
40. WA TR 1: 226–228, Nr. 502, LW 54:87–88; cf. WA TR 1: 234–235, Nr. 514, LW 54: 90–91.
41. WA TR 3: 492, Nr. 3655b, LW 54: 249.
42. WA 4: 641–643, Nr. 5070, 5071, LW 54: 385
43. WA 51: 616,20–25, LW 43: 236.

God that they had personally received in his communicating through the human language of promise. Gerhard Forde noted that God has sent preachers to proclaim the promise of new life in Christ. "This sending forth of preachers to do the electing [through this proclamation] is the aim of the God of the Scriptures (the proclaimed God) as distinguished from all the gods of idealisms (the explained God). The explained God is the God not preached who does everything in general, and so in the end does nothing in particular." God has his act of election come to pass concretely when the Holy Spirit creates and sustains faith through delivery of Christ's benefits to faith as it takes place in oral, written, and sacramental forms.[44]

Atonement

Twentieth-century scholars have debated precisely how Luther explained the way in which God's mercy achieved the rescue and restoration of sinners to their life as his children. The Swedish theologian Gustaf Aulén argued that Luther returned to the theory of the ancient church, that Christ conquered all enemies of the sinner, sin itself, Satan, death, the accusation of the law, and God's anger with sin.[45] Aulén conceded that Luther also used elements of the theory of vicarious satisfaction. But in developing his argument for the motif of "Christus Victor," the Swedish systematician Aulén wrongly discounted the prominence of this motif in the Wittenberg professor's thinking. He paid too little attention to Luther's fairly frequent proclamation of the "Vicarious Satisfaction" motif. Luther indeed told hearers and readers that Christ satisfied the demands of the law with his death as an innocent sacrifice; this satisfaction compensated for the obligation of the sinner to obey God's commands and fulfill his law or suffer death. No partial payment can compensate for failure to meet that obligation. The sinner is thus obliged to receive sin's payment for the transgression of the law with the death it demands (Rom 6:23). Christ did this by becoming substitute for the transgressors and sacrificing himself in their behalf.

In fact, Luther expressed his dissatisfaction with the term "satisfaction" to his students in 1531; "satisfaction [is] too weak to fully express Christ's grace and does not adequately honor his suffering."[46] And yet he frequently spoke of Christ's death, as he wrote in *Confession Concerning Christ's*

44. Gerhard O. Forde, *Theology is for Proclamation* (Minneapolis: Fortress Press, 1990), 31.
45. Gustaf Aulen, *Christus Victor: An Historical Study of the Three Main Types of the Idea of Atonement*. Trans. A. G. Hebart (New York: Macmillan, 1961), esp. 101–122.
46. "Summer Postil," 1544, WA 21:264,21–35.

Supper (1528), as that which rendered the law's death sentence no longer valid. All would be condemned to eternal death "if Jesus Christ had not come to our aid and taken upon himself this guilt and sin as an innocent lamb, paid for us by his sufferings, and if he did not still intercede and plead for us as a faithful, merciful Mediator, Savior, and the only priest and bishop of our souls."[47]

Aulén correctly found much more evidence in Luther's writings that he accentuated Christ's conquering all that opposes God and separates human beings from him. But in trying to balance out Luther's full proclamation of Christ's saving work, Ian Siggins has more accurately assessed Luther's explanation—or refusal to "explain" or to "analyze" Christ's atoning work—with his appraisal that Luther provided no "coherent explanatory discourse about how the atonement works." Instead, his sermons and lectures "abound in the motifs which figure in the historic atonement theories—patristic, classic, dramatic, or Western, Latin, and penal; objective or subjective."[48] In this cornucopia of ways to express the good news of new life in Christ are several themes through which Luther introduced his hearers and readers to his Savior and proclaimed what he achieved for sinners. What "Christ alone" truly meant for Luther may be illustrated with a musing from his Galatians commentary of 1519 on his Lord's presence at the hour of death: that God reveals himself in the hours as death approaches. He expressed his delight when someone presents to a dying person nothing but Christ on the cross, while moving them to trust in Jesus and place their hope in him. This means that all thoughts of a freely exercised will and of a righteousness gained through performance of the law no longer come into view. Trust in God's unconditional mercy is all that is left.[49]

As early as his lectures on Psalm 69 in 1514, Luther had affirmed that Christ had assumed the filth of "lust of our flesh" and descended into "the slime of sin" on behalf of sinners.[50] In his commentary of 1535 on Galatians 3:13, Luther informed readers that Christ was the greatest thief, murderer, robber, vandalizer, blasphemer, of all human history—with the qualification that he was not acting out those activities in his own person but rather as the sinner who carries and has taken possession of the transgressions of the great biblical saints such as Paul, Peter, David.[51] Shortly

47. LW 37: 362.
48. Ian Siggins, *Martin Luther's Doctrine of Christ* (New Haven: Yale University Press, 1970), 109.
49. WA 2: 562,12–19, LW 27: 328.
50. WA 3: 418,38–419,9, LW 10: 355
51. WA 40,1: 433,26–434,20; LW 26: 277.

after this passage in his lecture, Luther repeated this idea, this time also in the form of the monologue, expressing what he labeled "the indescribable and inestimable mercy and love of God." Assessing the curse of the law upon sinners, the Father told the Son to assume the person or identity of Peter, who had denied Christ; Paul, who had persecuted Christ's people and blasphemed in his rejection of Christ; David as an adulterer and murderer; Adam as he defied God in Eden; and the thief on the cross. God the Father instructed the Son to make the satisfaction demanded by the law, death. In the scene that Luther painted for his students, the law then gives its word of judgment, stating that all the sins that it can see in the world rested in Christ. Therefore, the law announced its verdict of death on him.[52]

Preaching on John's passion account a few years earlier, Luther depicted Jesus in Gethsemane and in Pilate's palace, a criminal convicted for humanity's mass of sins.[53] At the foot of the cross, Luther's hearers were pointed to Christ hanging on the cross as the worst of all robbers, rogues, rebels, and murders. The preacher drove home the point that Christ had assumed the place of each of his hearers, for even if they had not committed the most horrible of sins against other people, they had nevertheless certainly transgressed God's law and deeply offended their Creator.[54] Luther delighted in piling up images that proclaim this struggle of Jesus against Satan's claim on sinners: the lamb of God as sacrifice, the high priest as the one who sacrifices in behalf of God's people, the payment of God's Son that blots out sin, stills God's anger, overcomes death, and opens heavenly life with God.[55] The reality and depth of every individual's criminality—no matter how pious they may try to live—becomes clear in thinking of the nature of the execution carried out on the cross as place and manner of Christ's substitution for them. Something had to be done with sin, and God's solution was to bury it, in Christ's tomb.

Indeed, God took sin seriously, and Luther was convinced that something serious had to be done with sin. His use of what he sometimes called "the joyous exchange" of Christ's righteousness for human sin illustrated one part of Christ's removal of sin from the identification of the sinner. Early in his career as reformer, the description of the relationship of Christ and sinners found expression in the bride/bridegroom metaphor. He had

52. WA 40,1: 437,18–438,13; LW 26: 280.
53. WA 28: 353,28–355,27, LW 69: 232–233; cf. WA 28: 351, LW 69: 231 and WA 28:391, LW 69: 256.
54. WA 28: 391,27–392,19, LW 69: 256.
55. WA 28. 406, LW 69.265.

learned to use this metaphor from the monastic strain of mysticism that he had encountered in the writings of Bernhard of Clairvaux and Johannes Tauler.[56] In Germanic common law, brides and bridegrooms shared their goods completely. What had belonged to the one belonged to both in marriage. The metaphor was not perfect, for Luther taught that sinners no longer have any claim on their sin: the bridegroom had taken full possession of their sin (as was the case for the bride's possessions in Roman law). They indeed did have full possession of Christ's righteousness in God's sight (which was not the case in Roman law in terms of the rights of the bride in relationship to the bridegroom). This marital depiction of the relationship between Christ and believers figured prominently in Luther's *On Christian Freedom* (1520).[57] As he lectured on Psalm 22:2 in early 1521, Luther described this delightful transaction in terms of the bridegroom's emptying himself formally of his own righteousness to claim the sins of the sinful bride, and while sinners are emptied of their sins and filled with his righteousness. Luther joined with Paul (Phil 3:8) in regarding the righteousness of his own performance as dung and damaged goods.[58]

Steven Paulson draws out the implications of this comparison in Luther-like fashion. It permits bride and bridegroom to demand "fidelity when one is afraid the promise is not being kept," whether by the believer in a glance toward other gods, or by the Savior, who, it may seem, has also looked away from the problems of the believer. The bride in this case may indeed say, "Jesus, what are you doing to me? . . . I'm baptized, so why are you letting me hang here?" Paulson comments, "Such pugnacious faith seems irreligious since it fails to treat Jesus in a holy fashion; but this is what Jesus wants from you—to use him until he is used up in the promise." "He doesn't want you to be a wallflower of faith, he wants you to come out moving mountains." One side benefit: the same "chutzpah" works with Satan. Confidence of our identity as children of God empowers us to repudiate any claims Satan makes on us.[59]

Later in his life Luther employed two other images of joyous or blessed exchange metaphors to explain to his students what the consequences of Christ's death were for them. As noted above, the innocent Jesus became the criminal, who sinners are, to suffer the just judgment of the law: the consequence of their sinning was his death. Jesus did not pay a ransom with

56. Volker Leppin, "Luther's Transformation of Medieval Thought: Continuity and Discontinuity," in OHMLT, 122–123; cf. Joest, *Ontologie*, 371.
57. : WA 7: 54,31–55,23, LW 31: 351–352.
58. WA 5: 608,6–22
59. Paulson, "Graspable God," 60.

silver and gold, as Luther quoted 1 Peter 1:18–19 in his Small Catechism. Instead, like the lamb that died on the altar, he paid with the sacrifice of his life.[60] The lamb did not donate a pint of blood and return to the field, it went to the grave. In the use of "paying the price" language, Christ's sacrifice unto death is often reduced to the metaphor of a commercial transaction. However, in a commercial transaction the benefit of the sale goes to the owner. Satan, who had possessed us, came up with nothing at the end of this transaction—except defeat. Jesus has not paid an entrance fee for access to his Father for his people; he has won that access by burying their sins through his suffering and death and by rising to restore their righteousness so that they may approach their Creator once again as his beloved children. He has not purchased a free ticket to heaven but freed sinners from Satan's slave camp to march freely into the presence of their Father as beloved children. Satan possessed the sinners, but Christ's blood drowned him; it was not being paid into his account. Every benefit of Christ's paying the price for sin goes to the sinner, who is freed from sin's captivity and the law's just judgment. Sinners receive what they deserve, death, albeit baptismal death and burial. Sinners receive just the opposite of what they had earned, release from the payment of the death that the law demanded from them. The proper metaphorical framework for what is more than a metaphor in our use of "paying the price" is to compare it to the death of a soldier on the battlefield. The soldier's death "pays the price" to win freedom for others just as Christ's death liberates sinners from their captivity by washing away Satan's power over them and drowning his claim to possess them in a flood mightier than Noah's. With his death Christ paid the price the law demanded, death, as Luther observed to his students in 1531.[61]

In a sermon on Colossians 1:9–20 in November 1537, Luther also spoke of the "rich and blessed exchange." In this exchange of residence into another lord's domain, Christ has transferred his people from the domain of darkness, the devil, and his rule, into the rule that Christ has established by combatting and defeating the rulers and powers, the lords of this world, the devil and all at his disposal. He has led his chosen people as refugees and asylum-seekers out of captivity in Satan's Egypt and bestowed a new citizenship with their baptismal certificate as a new passport upon them. The domain of darkness in which Satan operates has fallen to Christ's own rule of light and the knowledge of God. God's

60. BSELK 872/8733–7, BC 355.

61. WA 40,1: 434, 19–20, LW 26: 277.

Son won this deliverance for his people through his shedding his blood, giving up his life, for his people.[62]

Steven Paulson notes that as offensive as the idea of God suffering may be to human reason, modern theologians have found a variety of ways to make such a suffering God sympathetic, especially to those observing the suffering of others. But the fact that the second person of the Trinity deserved it is harder to swallow. His substitution for sinners did not merely carry a burden. Jesus became the burden, the obligation of sinners to die, the guilt: sin for us, as Paul says in 2 Corinthians 5:21. Good-hearted sinners stumble over the claim that

> Christ died a free and willing death *under the power of the law.* The law, after all, did not make a mistake when it accused Christ of its offense and laid upon him its curse. Nor was the cross merely a case of mistaken identity by hapless disciples or the abuse of unlawful men. Neither did Christ merely submit to the law in order to became an example, or hero, to others. Instead, Christ actually became hated for this very death. . . . The cross is the hatred of God himself.[63]

Luther did not underestimate God's displeasure with human transgression and trashing of his good creature, fashioned in his own image.

Whether in baptism or in some other form of the gospel of forgiveness and new life, the encounter with God's justifying word of absolution delivers his promise decisively. It establishes the believer's identity as God's child, a subject of his protective governance. In the mystery of sin and evil in the lives even of the baptized, believers repent daily. This is not a re-giving or re-establishment of the identity given by God in his initial act of re-creating this child of God. It is rather an effective renewal of the justified identity once given for as long as the promising God rules.[64]

Anglican Luther scholar Jonathan Trigg suggests that Luther's early perception of baptism as Paul presented it in Romans 6 may well have shaped the development of his understanding of justification as a burial of the sinner's sinful identity and the resurrection of a new creature in Christ, whose new identity God has fashioned through Christ's resurrection.[65] In a sermon on John 19:38 from 1529 that Luther's student Andreas Poach

62. WA 45: 267,6–273,38, LW 51: 279–285.

63. Paulson, *Outlaw God*, 2: 7–8.

64. Contrary to Philip Cary, "Why Luther is Not Quite Protestant: The Logic of Faith in a Sacramental Promise," *Pro Ecclesia* 14 (2005): 448.

65. Jonathan D. Trigg, *Baptism in the Theology of Martin Luther* (Leiden: Brill, 2001), 1–2, cf. in Luther's Romans commentary from 1515–1516, his comments on Romans 4:25, WA 56: 296,17–23, LW 25: 284; cf. on Romans 6:3, WA 56: 321,22–323,9, LW 25: 309–311.

prepared for his House Postil of 1559, Luther delivered a soliloquy that praised the tomb of Christ as the place where God had placed his sins, as reflected in Romans 6:4 and Colossians 2:12.[66] The believer addressed the tomb with a word of thanks for receiving along with Christ's body his own sin that now lies buried there.[67]

Luther occasionally spoke of the incarnation as that which brought the only one who could deal with sin, God, into the being of the one who had sinned, the human being. But generally, he then went on to explain this plan in a manner that departed from the explanation that is popularly attributed to Anselm. Luther did not regard it as "necessary" according to some eternal law existing apart from the order that God created, a law with the authority to place restrictions on God's freedom to act as he wishes. Every "necessity" that human beings recognize stems from God's saying that it is necessary. Instead, Luther viewed the atonement as the enactment of God's plan that had been put in place personally before he got around to creating the universe (Eph 1:3–11). This plan culminated in Christ's death and resurrection. This was God's choice for dealing with sin. God set forth this plan by speaking of Christ's power to conquer and abolish the tragic and fearsome reality of sin. God alone had the power to change the past of sinners and deliver them from their sinful identities. He alone could personally join humanity to the One with the muscle and clout to wipe sin from the historical record of the sinner.[68] Focusing on the just accusation of the law against the sinner, Luther told his students that Christ, as a person both divine and human, begotten of God in eternity and born of the Virgin within human history, had come to place himself under the law. Submitting to the law, he employed his divine power to abolish its accusing force that constantly confronts sinners. This meant that Jesus experienced agony on the cross that exceeded the terror that any human being has ever felt as he found himself under the wrath of the Father. His sweating blood, the need for angelic consolation, his anguished prayer in Gethsemane, all demonstrate the depths of this terror as the law pronounced its judgment, and Jesus cried out, "My God, my God, why have you forsaken me?" In this way Christ rescued those under the law and freed them from their sin.[69] For, as Paul taught the Corinthians (1 Cor 1 and 2), God exercises power in what seems to sinners to be impotence, and he exercises wisdom in what they regard as foolishness.

66. WA 28: 418,36–419,5, 19–26, LW 69: 275–276.
67. WA 28: 420, 14–22, LW 69: 277.
68. WA 40,1: 65,10–18, 439,28–440,35, LW 26: 21–22, 281; WA 45: 271,21–34, LW 57: 283.
69. E.g., WA 49: 357,30–37.

More often, however, Luther did indeed speak of Christ as the victor over sin, death, and Satan and the liberator of sinners as Aulén had argued. The reformer called his programmatic explanation of the doctrine of justification published in 1520 *The Freedom of the Christian*, or in its Latin version, *On Christian Freedom*. This treatise spoke little of the atonement but focused rather on the experience of liberation that God's word delivers through the gift of the freedom he won in his death and resurrection. That experience arises out of the Holy Spirit's cultivating trust in him and his sacrifice and resurrection.[70] In his preaching, Luther's theology of liberation presented Christ's emancipating action with dramatic metaphors. His sermon on Mark 16 in his Summer Postil of 1526 depicted the resurrection of Christ in terms of his strangling the serpent and tramping on his head, recalling Genesis 3:15. Like Christ, believers take the gospel of Easter seriously and like him "overcome death, the devil, sin, and every misfortune." Christ had taken sin from the sinner upon himself and smothered it, killing each and every sin.[71] Death had gobbled him down, but he gobbled death down.[72]

In his Large Catechism Luther explained what it means that Jesus is Lord:

> He is the one who has liberated and released me from sin, from the devil, from death, and from all misfortune. Before this I had no lord or king, but was captive under the power of the devil. I was condemned to death and entangled in sin and blindness . . . under God's wrath and displeasure, sentenced to eternal damnation, as we had merited it and deserved it. There was no source of strength, no help, no comfort for us until this only and eternal Son of God, in his unfathomable goodness, had mercy on us because of our misery and distress and came from heaven to help us.

Luther continued with the theme of Christ the conqueror:

> Those tyrants and jailers have now been routed, and their place has been taken by Jesus Christ, the Lord of life, righteousness, and every good and blessing. He has snatched us, poor lost creatures, from the jaws of hell, won us, made us free, and restored us to the Father's favor and grace. As his own possession he has taken us under his protection and shelter, in order that he may rule us by his righteousness, wisdom, power, life, and blessedness.

70. WA 7: 50,32–51,11, LW 31: 345–346.
71. WA10,1: 220,19–221,30; cf. Uwe Rieske-Braun, *Duellum mirabile: Studien zum Kampfmotiv in Martin Luthers Theologie* (Göttingen: Vandenhoeck & Ruprecht, 1999).
72. Robert Kolb, "Das Kreuz – die wirkliche Befreiungstheologie," *CA Confessio Augustana* 2016, 4: 43–54.

This liberator

> has brought us back from the devil to God, from death to life, from sin to righteousness, and keeps us there. . . . he became a human creature, conceived and born without sin, of the Holy Spirit and the Virgin, so that he might become Lord over sin; moreover, he suffered, died, and was buried so that he might make satisfaction for me and pay what I owed, not with silver and gold but with his own precious blood. And he did all this so that he might become my LORD. For he did none of these things for himself, nor had he any need of them. Afterward he rose again from the dead, swallowed up and devoured death, and finally ascended into heaven and assumed dominion at the right hand of the Father. The devil and all his powers must be subject to him and lie beneath his feet until finally, at the Last Day, he will completely divide and separate us from the wicked world, the devil, death, sin, etc.[73]

As the liberator of sinners and the one who satisfied the law's demand for their death, Christ thus appropriated or acquired sinners as his own possession. So, Luther looked him in the eye as his Lord to whom he belonged—which meant that this Lord belonged to him. In Luther's explanation of the second article of the creed in his Small Catechism, the German word *erworben* is usually translated as "purchased," but frequently it indicates not just a purchase but any acquiring of possession: as Luther says, Christ "acquired possession and won me" so that "I may be his own." The term *gewonnen* may refer to a victory that has been won, but it is also a word for "gaining" in the sense of acquiring possession. Both these words explain that this change of ownership took place through Christ's blood—not a gold and silver kind of transaction—as his means of his "redeeming" sinners. The German word *erlösen,* usually translated as "redeem," has a much broader meaning than only "purchase" or "ransom." Its root lies in loosing the bonds, and like the redemption of Israel from Egypt, the kidnapper receives no ransom payment—though in Christ's case he paid the soldier's price as he fulfilled the law's demand for the death of the sinner. For Christ died "that I might belong to him, live under him in his kingdom and serve him in everlasting righteousness, innocence, and blessedness."[74] Luther was confessing in the Small Catechism that he belonged to Christ because of Christ's death and resurrection. Jesus Christ had brought him into the family of God.

His baptismal new birth, however, did not mean the end of the conflict. In his Galatians lectures of 1531 Luther spoke of the "magnificent duel"

73. BSELK 1056/1057,10–17, BC 434–435.
74. BSELK 872/873,2–10, BC 355.

between Christ and all the foes of his people. Their duel continues even if Christ has already mortally wounded Satan. It takes place on the battlefield of believers' lives. Christ took the field as the devil of death, hell, and the devil in order to slay them on behalf of his people.[75] At the beginning and in the end, reality rests in the person of Christ conquering this personal challenger, Satan, and all the tools the Evil One uses to imprison human beings under his rule. Like their Savior, believers are bitten, bound, and beset by the law and the devil, but Christ addresses them and announces the end of their tyranny.[76] In 1530 Luther had explained to hearers while at the Coburg,

> The two heroes meet, each giving his best effort. The devil brews one calamity after another, for he is a mighty, malicious and turbulent spirit. So it is time that our dear God be concerned about his honor, for the Word which we wield is a weak and miserable Word, and we who have and wield it are also weak and miserable. We bear the treasure as Paul says in earthen vessels, which can easily be shattered and broken. Therefore, the evil spirit spares no effort and confidently lashes out to see if he can smash the little vessel, for there it is under his nose and he cannot stand it. So, the battle really begins in earnest, with water and fire to dampen and quench the little spark [of faith in the believer]. Then our Lord God looks on for a while and lets us get into a tight place so that we may learn from our own experience that the small, weak, miserable Word is stronger than the devil and the gates of hell. . . . let them storm. [The devil and his cohorts] will encounter something there that makes them sweat, and still they will not conquer it, for it is a rock, as Christ calls it, which cannot be conquered.[77]

Luther also loved the analogy that compares the new creature in Christ with the original creation. The Wittenberg professor frequently drew the parallel between God's original creation of the world out of nothing by speaking and his re-creating the sinner out of the nothingness and chaos of sin through the word of absolution. In lecturing on Genesis 15:13–16 Luther described God in his essence as the "savior and liberator from death." With an application of his distinction of law and gospel, Luther continued by noting that before he rescues, he destroys; before he makes alive, he immerses people in death, "for he is accustomed to making everything out of nothing."[78] Preaching on John 3:16, he noted that "thieves, adulterers, and murderers" lose their old identity when,

75. WA 40,1: 279,14–29, LW 26: 164. Cf. Paulson, *Outlaw God*, 104–106.
76. WA 40,1: 279,23–281,20, LW 26: 164–165, WA 40,1:439,2–440,14, LW 26: 281.
77. WA 32: 36,28–37,28, LW 51:206–207.
78. WA 42: 572,21–23, LW 3: 33.

face to face with Christ, they trust in him: "you became a new person, for you have the light in your heart."[79] Repeatedly, readers and listeners encountered the reformer's assertion of this parallel between the original creation, justification of sinners, and the final resurrection of the dead.[80]

Luther had been born again, a new creature. At Christmas 1522 he had told his hearers that the gospel is God's womb in which he conceives, bears, and gives birth to his own people.[81] Nearly twenty years later he again called God's word "the divine womb" in which he had been born anew: "it is the birth through which I have become who I am. He created me and made me his child. We are his heirs and have the forgiveness of sins. We are safe from the devil because we have received salvation since we have been created as new creatures."[82] This new identity reminded Luther of the life that springs from a germinating seed.[83] In 1536 Luther preached on James 1:18 and explained the phrase "firstborn of his creation" as "a new creature and created work at its initial stage." This act of creation of the new person in Christ, like God's initial creation, is accomplished without human contribution.[84]

This new birth as a new creature in Christ parallels God's initial creation as an act of God's speaking or pronouncing sinners righteous, newborn children in his family. Because Luther believed that God actually accomplishes forgiveness and new creation through human language, his understanding of justification defined the renewal of the conversation broken off in Eden as a verbal—or forensic—action of God. This word from the Creator changes the reality, the identity, of the person restored to righteousness by God's forgiving re-creative word of absolution. Mark Mattes notes that Luther parted with his scholastic instructors over the nature of justification because they had appropriated Ockham's and Biel's definition of justification as "something that God does in order to initiate

79. WA 47: 97,26–27, LW 22:374.

80. WA 1: 13,39, WA 39,1: 48,23, WA 10,1,1: 232,7–8, WA 5: 544,1–2f, 6–9, WA 17,2: 317,2–8, WA 5: 672,7–10, WA 36: 327,22–328,11; WA 37: 536,35–537,11; WA 49: 399,1–400,2, 399,38–400,27; WA 49: 436,32–39, WA 49: 402,36–41. Cf. WA 49: 405,39–41, 406,29–30, 408,29–31, 412,29; 433,16–35, WA 1: 10,2427, WA 5: 162,29–32, WA 5: 544,9–10, WA 18: 754,1–4, WA 38: 36,29–34, WA 45: 80,26, WA TR 6: 148. WA 21: 521,21–22, WA 7: 337,15–19, WA 41: 159,9–11, WA 45: 80,31, WA41: 581,4–8, WA 2: 430,9–13, WA 1: 477,3–4. Cf. Johannes Haar, *Initium creaturae Dei. Untersuchung über Luthers Begriff der „neuen Creatur" im Zusammenhang mit seinem Verständnis von Jakobus I,18 und mit seinem „Zeit"-Denken* (Gütersloh: Bertelsmann, 1939), 36–44.

81. WA 10,1,1: 232,13–14.

82. WA 40,1: 597,6–7 (student notes on the lecture on Gal. 4,7, not in the printed commentary, cf. WA 40,1; 597,23–28 and LW 26:392).

83. WA 17,1: 189, 18–35.

84. WA 41: 587,20–33.

a process on the ladder of ontological, moral, and mystical fulfillment." This understanding defined faith as a theological virtue, exercised by the sinner to serve as a basis for efforts to attain grace through doing one's best and to claim heaven by using grace to fulfill God's law. This sanative view of justification stood in sharp contrast to Luther's comprehending the verbal nature of the actions of God and the relational view of reality that guided Luther's thinking.[85]

Scholars have debated for more than a century whether Luther's understanding of justification was "forensic"—a verbal act—or "effective"—actually transforming a person from sinner into one who obeys God's command. The flaw in this debate is twofold. Trying to settle on one or the other fails to take into account that God's forensic actions establish reality; his regarding sinners as righteous actually redefines the reality of their identity because this new identity—their righteousness—is established by the Creator's regard for them. This failure to appreciate Luther's understanding of the gospel as God's operative Word also ignores the fact that the trust that responds to his promise of new life agrees with his judgment that this sinner is righteous, and with the logic of trust it acts out that appraisal of the Creator. Gerhard Forde noted that God's justifying word is not only a verbal expression; it creates a new reality. He commented, "the more forensic it is, the more effective it is!" Forde insisted that since God is speaking and since the faith it creates seeks to follow through on God's declaration with its own corresponding righteous behavior, absolution leads believers to act out actively the righteous identity that they have received passively.[86]

By renewing the conversation with sinners through forgiveness, God does not focus on space inside the person first, but rather, on the space between himself and his new creature. Thus, Luther defines the heart of being this new creature as trust in the performance of Christ rather than relying on the believer's own performance of the righteous actions that the new status as God's child produces. Nonetheless, righteous actions flow forth as the fruits of faith. Contrary to those who have accused Luther of creating a legal fiction by defining the justification of sinners as a verbal action of the Creator, Luther affirmed the biblical use of the

85. Mark Mattes, "The History, Shape, and Significance of Justification for Preaching," in *Justification is for Preaching*, ed. Vergil Thompson (Eugene: Pickwick, 2012), 53–56; Bernd Hamm, *The Early Luther: Stages in a Reformation Reorientation*, trans Martin J. Lohrmann (Grand Rapids, MI: Eerdmans, [Minneapolis: Fortress Press], 2020), 233–257.

86. Forde, *Justification by Faith Justification by Faith, a Matter of Death and Life* (1982; Mifflintown, PA: Sigler, 1991), 30; cf. Oswald Bayer, *Living by Faith: Justification and Sanctification*, trans. Geoffrey Bromiley (Grand Rapids, MI: Eerdmans, 2003), 42–73.

word as a re-creative pronouncement by the Creator that establishes the reality of his people's righteousness against satanic deception that tries to preserve their primary identity as sinners.[87] His pronouncement of re-creation effects active righteousness by bestowing passive righteousness, both because God's regard and pronouncement create reality and because, psychologically, faith that absorbs God's definition of believers also acts out that new definition of themselves.

This address of God through those who proclaim his promise of new life in Christ breaks through human jabbering of excuses for sin, and even the use of Christ's death as an excuse. For God does not excuse; he executes sinners, on Golgotha, and at the baptismal font, as Paul assured Roman (6:3–4) and Colossian (2:12–20) believers. God delivers his decision to choose those who are hearing the promise from one who delivers it to them, whether in oral, written, or sacramental form. The proclamation of the promise liberates; it re-creates, with all the certainty that a decree of the Creator from before the creation can carry.[88] That assurance was lacking in Luther's early life, so he treasured it all the more. Because God is reliable, what he says is reliable. Therefore, Luther proclaimed his word with the assurance that he set forth as his method of practicing theology against that of Erasmus.[89] Steven Paulson highlights what Erasmus knew five hundred years ago. Despite the fact that Luther "adhered to the platonic, apophatic (negative) sense that God—at the core, in his oneness—is mostly unknown, especially concerning the terms that Scholastics liked to explore, . . . the very little that Luther actually does know about God he knows too well and too confidently" for some theologians to be comfortable with the reformer's bold assertion of faith.[90] He pronounced the forgiveness of sin without hesitation.

It was the Almighty, the Creator—Father, Son, and Holy Spirit—who had the right to demand obedience, and even more, the entirety of his person, from Luther, who terrified him out of wit and wisdom. It was this same Almighty Creator who had the disposition and the power to re-create him, through the work of the Second Person of the Trinity, who had assumed human nature as Jesus of Nazareth. God dealt with Luther's sin in fatal fashion in Christ's death. God's disposition of mercy and love led him to raise Martin with Christ from the death of sin to be

87. Mattes, "The History, Shape, and Significance of Justification for Preaching," 58.
88. Cf. Steven Paulson's development of this in *Outlaw God*, 3: 52–69 and passim.
89. WA 18: 601,1–605,34, LW 33: 19–24; cf. Kolb, *Bound Choice, Election, and Wittenberg Theological Method*, 16–18.
90. Paulson, *Outlaw God*, 1: xx.

a living child in his family, under his rule, in everlasting righteousness, innocence, and blessedness.

Face to face with this God, Luther relaxed, with God, with himself, and with his worries about relating to other human beings and God's creation. Relaxed, he could perceive how to serve them all and find therein the joy and peace that the radiance of the bloodied face of Jesus gave him. Even in the face of despicable evil, in his own sins and in the machinations of his foes, Luther held onto the God who, even when he seemed absent and unconcerned, continued to be Lord of all, in control, and present despite his seeming absence, speaking his person into Luther's conscience and consciousness.

4.

The Reformer Face to Face in Conversation with the Person of God Revealed

Martin Luther coram Deo dicendo

THE PERSONALIZATION OF GOD'S PRESENCE WITH BELIEVERS IN DIALOGUE AND MONOLOGUE

Martin Luther is generally recognized as something of a linguistic genius, the "inventor" of the modern German language (a claim that scholars now recognize as simplistic and exaggerated), and above all a translator without peer.[1] His student Johannes Mathesius described his speaking ability with a paraphrase of Proverbs 25:11, comparing his mentor's words to a golden apple or a beautiful pomegranate or lemon in a silver bowl.[2] Luther had mastered the rhetorical tools that the medieval and humanistic learning of his day had placed at his disposal.[3] But his skill at putting the languages he normally spoke, Latin and German, to use pedagogically, has not been

1. Gordon A. Jensen, *Experiencing Gospel: Martin Luther's 1534 Bible Project* (Minneapolis: Fortress Press, 2023); Heinz Bluhm, *Martin Luther, Creative Translator* (St. Louis: Concordia, 1965), and *Luther, Translator of Paul: Studies in Romans and Galatians* (New York: Peter Lang, 1984).
2. Johannes Mathesius, *Historien/Von des Ehrwirdigen in Gott Seligen thewren Manns Gottes, Doctoris Martini Luthers/anfang/lehr/leben vnd sterben . . .* (Nuremberg: Johann vom Berg's heirs and Ulrich Neuber, 1566), CLVIa.
3. Ulrich Nembach, *Predigt des Evangeliums: Luther als Prediger, Pädagoge und Rhetor* (Neukirchen: Neukirchener Verlag, 1972).

as extensively studied.[4] Not only his much-heralded exploitation of the printing press,[5] but also his use of the discipline of rhetoric served as a medium for spreading his message. His own modeling of oral communication in lecture hall and parish pulpit provided instruction and inspiration for the students who left his university to minister across Germany and much of Europe beyond.[6] The rhetorical aspect of his linguistic gifts also contributed to his proclamation of the word of God in many different ways, for instance, as he went about creating staged scenes for pedagogical purposes in his lectures and his preaching at the church of Saint Mary in Wittenberg.[7] In these conversations, he showed how God revealed himself as a conversation partner of sinners in the experience of daily life as they lived out of their encounter with him in Scripture.

LUTHER'S USE OF DIALOGUE AND MONOLOGUE

Among the cornerstones of Luther's theology underlying this interplay of God's address and human trust was the reformer's conviction that God had created his human creatures in his own image as conversation partners for himself and each other. He was convinced that the Creator had put the widest range of material blessings, including human language, at the disposal of his church and all his human creatures for their use. He also believed that ordinary human language—its words, expressions, rhetorical devices—serves as God's means of conveying the transforming power of his re-creating word. Therefore, it was natural for him to capitalize on the contemporary humanist movement's use of rhetoric, including its employment of the forms of dialogue and monologue. These tools aided the Wittenberg reformer in engaging the people of God with the word of God. His skillful practice of the rhetorical arts as he interacted with his students, both in lectures, and in sermons at the town church, embodies one contributing factor to his success in spreading the biblical message,

4. Along with Nembach, *Predigt des Evangeliums*, the work of Birgit Stolt is an exception: *Martin Luthers Rhetorik des Herzens* (Tübingen: Mohr Siebeck, 2000) and *Wortkampf. Frühneuhochdeutsche Beispiele zur rhetorischen Praxis* (Frankfurt/M: Athenäum, 1974).
5. Cf., for example, Andrew Pettegree, *Brand Luther: 1517, Printing, and the Making of the Reformation* (New York: Penguin, 2015).
6. Mark U. Edwards, Jr., *Printing, Propaganda, and Martin Luther* (Berkeley: University of California Press, 1994), 11, 37.
7. I am grateful for permission granted by Erik Rottmann of Wild Boar Press, publisher and editor of *Teach These Things: Essays in Honor of Wallace Schulz*, ed. Erik Rottmann (Versailles, MO: Wild Boar Books, 2008), to use sections of my essay in that volume, "'This is My Customary Procedure,' Says God: Martin Luther's Use of Dialogue and Monologue in his Lectures and Sermons," pp. 25–40. Much of what follows immediately has appeared in that essay.

both in his time, and in his enduring contribution to the church of later centuries.

Luther frequently used dialogues and monologues in his sermons and lectures, as well as written works. He often cast God and his hearers in the roles of conversation partners; in his preaching and teaching, God and Adam, Jesus and his disciples, God and Satan, his students and Satan, believers and Jesus, met each other in friendly engagement or hostile confrontation. He recalled conversations that he had had with the devil, in which he had put the Evil One in his place by observing, "devil, you lie." He sang his report on the battle, "one little word can fell him," as part of his explanation for the everlasting endurance of God's rule of his people.[8] On occasion, the reformer could also bring personifications of "sin and righteousness, life and death, and heaven and hell" into a tête-à-tête.[9]

Ulrich Nembach anchored Luther's use of dramatic scenes in the rhetorical theory of Quintilian (35–95), the first century master of Roman rhetoric, whose works guided Luther's generation, like many before and after, in the study of good oral communication. What Quintilian called *prosopopoeia* created for hearers a sense of the presence of the individual who was speaking, thus making alive, in Luther's case, the biblical message or theological concept he was trying to convey.[10] This practice coincides with Gerhard Forde's argument that the biblical message is naturally at home in "first order discourse," the "I and you" language of face-to-face conversation.[11] God planted the ability and desire for such conversation deep in the nature of his human creature, created in his image. It belongs to, and expresses, his nature and human nature as personal.

Luther firmly believed that the pronouncement of the forgiveness of sins, the absolution, is God's most important word for sinners and that it is designed to be spoken directly to them. Therefore, it was natural that Luther should echo what he regarded as the normal form of connection between God and the creatures created in his image, the conversational exchange. It was also natural, given his understanding of the sermon as the place where God's side of the conversation was most decisively delivered, that the reformer would turn to first person expressions to model the conversation he believed that God wants to have with his people. Even while he was speaking of faith as the product of illumination in his lectures

8. WA 51: 469,32–470,11, LW 41:185–186.
9. Fred Meuser, *Luther the Preacher* (Minneapolis: Augsburg, 1983), 50.
10. Nembach, *Predigt des Evangeliums*, 154–155.
11. Gerhard O. Forde, *Theology is for Proclamation* (Minneapolis: Fortress Press, 1990), esp. 13–37, 135–190.

on the psalms at the beginning of his career as professor of Bible, Luther confessed to his students, "faith comes by hearing, not by seeing. It is a golden word: we are to learn to have ears . . . we have two ears. Therefore, we should first be more ready at all times to learn than to teach, to hear than to let our voices be heard, to yield to the person speaking rather than to be speaking ourselves. For we have only one tongue, which is tucked away behind twenty-eight teeth, among them four sharp teeth, in our mouths while both of our ears are open."[12]

Perhaps Luther's most famous use of dialog appeared in his Small Catechism. Until Luther's time the word "catechism," a designation of a general program for instruction, usually referred to something oral. The word itself contains the Greek root "ēch" [ἠχή] which refers to "sound."[13] While Luther employed the homiletical form of catechetical instruction, which had been its typical means of delivery in the Middle Ages,[14] in his Large Catechism, the instructional method in the Small Catechism took the form of the answers to be given by the children to the questions posed by the parents and teachers in the school as well as pastors. Luther envisioned parents as the primary teachers of young Christians.

In his sermons, Luther could also put the "Q and A" system to use. In the sermon for the festival of Saint Stephen reprinted in his "church postil," the book of model sermons on the pericopes for Sundays and festivals that the reformer prepared as a kind of continuing education program for the priests of his time, Luther created a series of four questions to guide hearers through their review of the text. The sermon treated the gospel lesson appointed for the festival, Matthew 23:34–39. After treating the conflict between faith and reason that leads to the persecution of the prophets, the preacher turned to a closer examination of the reading itself. Luther anticipated questions that might come to the mind of his contemporaries. "Why does Christ say that all the righteous blood from Abel on shall come upon all the Jews since they all did not shed it all?" a person might wonder. Luther explained that Christ was directing these words to the entire band of persecutors throughout the ages. "But why does he cite only two, Abel and Zachariah?" Luther's interlocutor wants to know. The preacher explains that Abel is the first martyr, and Zachariah is the first prophet to be martyred. But they serve only as representatives of all those whose blood was shed because they proclaimed the word of the

12. WA 3: 227,30–228,3, LW 10: 188.
13. Charles P. Arand, *That I May Be His Own* (St. Louis: Concordia, 2000), 58–63.
14. See Paul W. Robinson, "Lord, Teach Us to Pray. Preaching the Pater Noster in Germany and Austria, 1100–1500," Ph.D. dissertation, University of Chicago, 2001.

Lord, Luther explained. "Why does Christ mention the son of Barachiah since the Scriptures call him the son of Jehoiada?" (2 Chr 24:20–21), the imaginary parishioner asks. Luther explains that Barachiah and Jehoiada could be two different names for the same person, the former being a descriptive epithet for Jehoiada since it means "blessed." Luther called attention to Jerome's explanation that also builds upon that definition.[15]

The first three questions the parishioners ask regarding this lesson addressed textual matters that might cause hearers or readers to stumble over the precise meaning or significance of its words. The final question posed turned to the theological import of the text: "No one can withstand God's will. Why then does he say, 'How often would I have gathered your children together, and you did not want to be gathered!'?" Luther conceded that these words could be used as a defense of the ability of the free will to choose God. He rejected as a forced interpretation Augustine's explanation that Jesus was telling Jerusalem that he had gathered those whom he had gathered against their will. Instead, Luther reflected his conviction that in the mystery of what it means to be a human creature of God, Jesus was presenting the tension between the total responsibility of God, which Scripture teaches in presenting God as creator and also as savior, and the total responsibility of his human creatures, which his law demands.[16] For, "Christ speaks here as a human being. He has taken all human care upon himself." Because he was speaking here as that human being who ate, drank, slept, walked, wept, suffered, and died, he was expressing the emotions he felt as a human being. Luther barred all speculation about the hidden will of God: such thoughts "are uttered in harmony with our feelings and fancy, and not according to the real state of the divine nature. Therefore, they are not to be perverted by lofty speculation as utterances of the divine nature, but they should be understood as spoken to common people here upon earth according to our human understanding."[17] Luther put the form of question and answer to use to help hearers concentrate first on the simple understanding of the text itself and then on one larger idea found in it. This use of the catechetical method helped implant both the message that Luther found in the text for his hearers and an approach to reading Scripture and explaining it properly in its native intent and content.

In preaching on lessons from the gospel, Luther occasionally found dialog already in the text itself, and sometimes he elaborated the conversation.

15. WA 10,1,1: 276,3–278,9, Lenker, *Sermons*, 1: 229–230.
16. Cf. pp. 16–17, on the responsibilities of God and human beings
17. WA 10,1,1: 275,5–279,11, Lenker, *Sermons*, 1: 228–231.

For instance, in preaching on John 3 for Trinity Sunday, he paraphrased Christ's words in verse 3 regarding being born anew within the exchange between Jesus and Nicodemus: "No my dear Nicodemus, I am not moved by your beautiful words. You must give up your old life and become a new person. You have not the faith which you say you have; you are still afraid." Sinners can enjoy hearing God's word before it pierces their hearts, Luther observed. He insisted that his hearers must put their own way of thinking to death and receive new life, the message that Jesus was delivering to Nicodemus and the preacher was delivering to the Germans of his own day.[18] The dialogue in the text continued, and when Nicodemus challenged Jesus on his insistence that the older rabbi be born again, in verse 4, Luther expanded Jesus's reply in conversational tone,

> Don't tell me how to express myself. I know very well what I have said, and so that you may know that a person does not enter the kingdom of God by his own ability, I repeat that he must be born in a different manner, or he cannot enter God's kingdom. However, I do not mean natural birth, from father and mother, which you imagine because you know of no other birth. I am speaking of a different birth, a new birth, of water and the Spirit . . . .[19]

This expansion of the text added no vital ideas to Luther's presentation, but it surely did give his hearers a deeper understanding of its significance.

The preacher could also construct a conversation between himself and the congregation. Lecturing on Genesis to the Wittenberg students, Luther meandered, as he often did, from the blessing of Jacob, or Israel, found in Genesis 48:20, into God's blessing the people of his own day. God did not promise physical abundance, he noted, but his promise orders our seeking: first the kingdom of God, then other things as well (Matt 6:33). Luther dialoged with his students by posing a question that led to an outburst of thanksgiving. In his exchange with them, he had them protest that they did not notice God behind their blessings, and Luther urged them to believe since they had the sacraments and the sermon.[20] Luther continued the conversation by proclaiming the power of God's word to work all good.

Luther's belief that God is a speaking God who enjoys talking with, and to, his people led him to turn from time to time to the form of the monologue to present God addressing the hearers before him in the lecture hall or the church. The third gospel sermon in his "church postil" for

18. WA 10,1,2: 299,3–5, Lenker, *Sermons*, 3:412–413.
19. EA 12: 306, Lenker, *Sermons*, 3:335; cf. *Sermons of Martin Luther*, 3:430; EA 12: 405.
20. WA 44: 713,19–39, LW 8: 184.

Pentecost, on John 14:23–31, contained two such brief monologues. In interpreting John 14:28, "if you had loved me, you would have rejoiced because I go to the Father," Luther had God confront his hearers and readers by paraphrasing the verse with an expansion of what Jesus meant to say to his disciples here:

> I have told you, and it is true, that I must leave you. You do not like to hear this, for you know that, as long as I am with you, you have nothing but joy in me. But, my dear disciples, if you have heard the one message, then hear the other, and listen to what is said, that I will again come to you with better and greater comfort and joy than you have had in me up to this point. If you loved me truly, as you think you do, you should be glad that I am leaving you, for it is truly in your best interest, and you should be very pleased, both for your sake and mine, and you should not want to see it otherwise. For my going away does not mean that you are losing me, or that either I or you will suffer any hurt. It is only for your sake that I enter into my glory, in my Father's kingdom, and sitting at the right hand of the Father, should become a mighty Lord over everything in heaven and upon earth, where I can protect and help you against everything that seeks to injure you. This I cannot do now upon earth in my humility and lowliness, where I have been sent to suffer and die.[21]

Shortly after this passage, Luther hammered home this message of comfort, returning to the same conversation, this time extended explicitly from first century Judea into Saxony: Jesus reports to Luther's hearers,

> Dear Christians, do believe me, it will not be to your harm but for your good. My departure does not mean that I am forsaking you, but that I, through my departure, will conquer so that you may experience my power and might as I, seated at the right hand of the Father, rule over your sin and over your enemies, the devil, death and hell. Then none of them shall touch you even a hair's breadth, except at my will. They shall not hurt you but rather serve and benefit you. Therefore, listen to my Word more than your feelings.[22]

This face of God and such words from him carried Martin Luther through life, into death, and beyond into the full enjoyment of gazing at the divine Lover. He constantly returned to engaging his Savior by listening to his words and responding in prayer, "as a dear child turns to a beloved father."[23] Using passages such as Ephesians 5:25–27 and 2 Corinthians 11:2, Luther affirmed that Christ alone has the right to occupy the bridal

21. EA 12: 306, *Sermons of Martin Luther*, 3:335.
22. EA 12: 308–309, *Sermons of Martin Luther*, 3:337.
23. BSELK 874/875,5–7, BC 356.

chamber of the believer's conscience and address his people's concerns. There Christ reigns, "who does not terrify sinners and afflict them, but who comforts them, forgives their sins, and saves them. Therefore, let the afflicted conscience think nothing, know nothing, and use nothing else against God's wrath and judgment except Christ's Word, which is a word of grace, forgiveness of sins, salvation, and life everlasting."[24] Christ's conversations with Luther framed and grounded his life.

EXPERIENCING GOD IN CONVERSATION AS PERSONALLY PRESENT

People communicate; they create community with others by conversing with them. For Luther, being Christian meant listening to God speaking and replying in prayer and praise. Luther encountered God not in the inner reaches of his own soul or by communing with nature. The reformer's belief that God does not mind getting down and in the dirt with his earthly creation led to his belief that this God of conversation and community used normal human language to convey what his entering into human flesh and blood had accomplished, to restore his people to himself. He believed that the word of promise becomes concrete in oral, written, and sacramental forms. The faith was inextricably tied into human language, human speaking. To be sure, what the eyes see feeds faith with images that make God's message to them concrete—in Luther's day in altar pieces and woodcuts. But what they see always depends for its communicative power on what the ear has heard, from the voice of God in Scripture and from all the means by which his words there find their way into human consciousness.[25] He presumed that this speaking God accompanies his people through the unfolding of history, as he created time and its passage to usher humankind through life. This turned the professor of Bible to careful listening to his Lord in the context of the human authors whom he had taken as his vehicles for conveying his message.

Luther presupposed that God had chosen to be talking to him from the pages of Scripture. God was there not only to point readers to a heavenly reality. He was there with the power that had created the world, the verbal power that could bring judgment and salvation through human language to those with whom he came in conversation. Some of his contemporaries, such as Ulrich Zwingli and Andreas Bodenstein von Karlstadt, reflected

24. WA 40,2: 214,15–21, LW 26: 120.

25. Joest, *Ontologie*, 280–298.

their training in the Realist school of scholastic theology. Together with those influenced by the revival of Platonism and Neo-Platonism at their time, they regarded reality as existing in the heavenly forms, in the mind of God. They believed that material elements of God's creation, including human language, could only reflect that reality above. As an Ockhamist, Luther was convinced that God indeed could and did order such an earthly existence that selected elements of the created order served as his instruments of accomplishing his saving will.

GOD SPEAKS IN THE CONTEXT OF HUMAN HISTORY

Every other use of human language as God's instrument proceeds from his selecting the written word of certain prophets, evangelists, and apostles to serve as the source and standard for all contemporary preaching and mutual sharing of God's word as well as the delivery of his promise of forgiveness, life, and salvation in sacramental forms. Their reports are anchored in human history and tell of God's mighty acts in history and the words he addressed to his people at specific times. Israel's God had often employed object lessons to reinforce his words in Israel's history, Luther pointed out. God had revealed his will to Gideon through a fleece (Judges 6:37). He confirmed kings in office by anointing them with oil. David recognized God's guidance in the rustling of the breeze under the pear tree (2 Sam 5:24). "Christ gave all such signs not only for the sake of love but also to confirm people in the faith, that they might believe in him and through him in God. The whole of salvation history unfolds through the external signs: Mary's virginity, Pilate's administration, the church, the Word."[26]

Luther recognized that history consists of human and divine experiences, in which both are present, God sometimes revealed in his actions, sometimes hidden in the way he deals with his human creatures and all of creation. Stones, trees, and even frogs do not process their experiences of the passage of time in the way that the human creatures fashioned in God's image do. Our experiences of encountering stones, trees, and frogs impose human analyses on the subjects. The reality of the history of human beings moves with its unfolding, and this movement reveals itself in human experiences. Because human beings are more complex creatures than stones, trees, and even frogs, interpretation of what God is doing with them and for them in the flow of history is more elusive. Framing

26. WA 27:57,6–29.

the passages of time is the fact that all history is God's history—even if it is not all the history of salvation.

"Doctrine"—the topics of public teaching, the themes that are to guide proclamation and instruction that foster the believer's understanding of what God is saying in Scripture—arise not only out of the dicta of biblical writers but also out of the narratives that they report. The narratives of the experiences of long-departed people of God whom he chose to write for him lead into doctrine, the teaching of Scripture summarized and synthesized for use among and by God's people. Doctrine informs the perception that believers have of their own personal experiences. Their experiences in turn shape their formulation of the biblical teaching regarding God and what it means to be human. God has endowed the dynamic flow between narrative, doctrine, historical events, and experience as it is proclaimed and taught with the power to kill and to make alive in Christ.

Stanley Fish notes that Aristotle's ideal plots tell of the intersection of character and choice with circumstance to produce a result. "But a Christian plot, in the sense that there is one, is haphazard, random in its order," with events both reversible and interchangeable. "Divine fiat" determines the unfolding story of life, and its results are the result of God's choice rather than that of the individual. Human choice flows from God's choice, and from his redeeming, liberating action in Christ. The price paid for being created and redeemed is the loss of "self-sufficiency and independence, the illusion of moving toward a truth rather than moving by virtue of it and with it . . ."[27] Christian experience of history leads to the conviction that God is in charge and that this is a good thing because God is, in essence, gracious. This reflects Luther's understanding of how God has spoken and speaks in the world's history.[28]

GOD SELECTED ELEMENTS OF HIS CREATED ORDER AS HIS SAVING INSTRUMENTS

Luther exulted in God's grace, which he shows by addressing the five senses of the human creature. Through the hand and tongue of the minister of the gospel, God is at work.[29] "In baptism there is an oral word and a pourer, in the sacrament an oral word and a feeder, in preaching an oral word and

27. Stanley Fish, "Structuralist Homiletics," in *Is There a Test in this Class: The Authority of Interpretive Communities* (Cambridge: Harvard University Press, 1980), 195.
28. John M. Headley, *Luther's View of Church History* (New Haven: Yale University Press, 1963); Mark Thompson, "Luther on God and History," in OHMLT, 127–142.
29. WA 46:148,16–21.

a speaker, as in absolution." If God had delivered our justification through an angel instead of through those who pour, feed, and speak, he would not have done it any other way. The angel, too, would have had to pour, feed, and speak. For God himself is pouring, feeding, and absolving. The angel would be no more than his instrument.[30] God has so structured his world that the reality of salvation which his word effects is delivered and brought into being through selected elements of the created order.

As Bernd Hamm has argued, many in fifteenth-century German-speaking lands sought the nearness of God.[31] Luther moved beyond his dread at God's being present in his life as the psalmists and then the apostle Paul engaged him in such a way that God's speaking to him conveyed the strong sense of his nearness, his presence, as a person standing by him in every time of trouble. Luther encountered that presence fundamentally in God's engaging him in conversation, in the intimate connection of presence and words. The philosopher George Steiner argues that "any coherent account of the capacity of human speech to communicate meaning and feeling is, in the final analysis, underwritten by the assumption of God's presence."[32] Luther presumed that any coherent account of God's interaction with his creation expressed who God is and what he does in language, intelligible even if mysterious in part, beyond rational explanation. When the Creator, in his second person, became a human being, his disciple John labeled him "the Word made flesh" (John 1:14), and the writer to the Hebrews acclaimed him as God's way of communicating with his human creatures (Heb 1:2). The concepts of personhood and communication in one form of language or another fit together inextricably, and Luther affirmed both the bodily presence of Jesus as the incarnation of the second person of the Trinity and the spoken presence of the Trinity in oral, written, and sacramental forms of conveying the promise of new life in Christ.

Luther's sense of the importance of personal presence informed his view of Scripture. Already in 1519 at the Leipzig Disputation he argued on the basis of the sole authority of the Bible in determining the message of the church.[33] "The Holy Spirit is nowhere more present than in the Holy

30. WA 46:149,23–150,30.

31. Hamm, *Religiosität im späten Mittelalter: Spannungspole, Neuaufbrüche, Normierungen*, ed. Reinhold Friedrich and Wolfgang Simon (Tübingen: Mohr/Siebeck, 2011); cf. also the essays in *Gottes Nähe unmittelbar erfahren. Mystik im Mittelalter und bei Martin Luther*, ed. Bernd Hamm and Volker Leppin (Tübingen: Mohr/Siebeck, 2007).

32. George Steiner, *Real Presences* (Chicago: University of Chicago Press, 1989), 3.

33. Scott H. Hendrix, *Martin Luther, Visionary Reformer* (New Haven: Yale University Press, 2015), 79, Martin Brecht, *Martin Luther: His Road to Reformation, 1483–1521*, trans. James L. Schaaf (Minneapolis: Fortress, 1985), 317–322.

Scriptures," he wrote the next year.[34] His translation of 2 Timothy 3:16 used the word for "infuse" or "pour into" for what in English is translated as "inspired" as the description of the Holy Spirit's role in creating the Scriptures.[35] It is essential also to note that Luther took the human authors of the biblical books very seriously as authors, paid attention to their style, and noted discrepancies in some accounts in the gospels, for instance on the calling of the apostle Andrew, without dismissing the presence of the Holy Spirit with each author as he wrote and without any apparent need to solve the problem.[36]

Luther confidently asserted against Erasmus that Scripture is clear,[37] but it is clear in context. God speaks from its pages to those who wrestle with guilt or shame, whose fears of deprivation or death overpower them. It does not communicate effectively with those whose false gods function well, but it delivers life and salvation to those who read it out of their trust that Jesus Christ delivers them from evil and restores them to true human life. The Holy Spirit uses normal human languages but with his own grammar that becomes clear through extensive conversation with him from the whole of the Bible.

Luther certainly did not discount using the ancient church fathers, medieval theologians, and contemporary authors in presenting the biblical message. He treasured some traditional hymns of the medieval liturgy and other devotional and theological writings. But he judged them all according to Scripture. In Scott Hendrix's terms, he "deparentified" the ancient church fathers and made them colleagues, with whom he gladly exchanged views of the biblical word and from whom he gladly gained insights.[38] For example, his evaluation of Augustine turned from his general positive attitude to a specific critique of his failure to understand the justification of the sinner in terms of the distinction of two kinds of righteousness.[39] This critique did not keep him from making copious use of Augustine in his exegesis and argumentation.

34. WA 7: 97,2–3.
35. WA DB 7: 280/281.
36. Robert Kolb, *Martin Luther and the Enduring Word of God: The Wittenberg School and its Scripture-Centered Proclamation* (Grand Rapids, MI: Baker Academic, 2016), 86–88.
37. WA 18: 606,1–609,14, LW 33: 24–28.
38. "Deparentifying the Fathers: the Reformers and Patristic Authority," in *Auctoritas Patrum. Zum Rezeption der Kirchenväter im 15, und 16. Jahrhundert,* ed. Leif Grane, Alfred Schindler, Markus Wriedt (Mainz: von Zabern, 1993), 1: 55–68.
39. Wolfgang Bienert, "'Im Zweifel näher bei Augustin?' Zum patristischen Hintergrund der Theologie Luthers," in *Oecumenica et Patristica*, ed. Damaskinos Papendreou et al. (Stuttgart; Kohlhammer, 1989), 281–294.

Although he employed oral transmission of the message as the most basic form of conversation, he viewed written and printed words also as suitable tools for the Holy Spirit. He believed that oral communication forms the foundation of personal exchange, but he also experienced the voice of God as he read the printed text of the Bible and in other writings that faithfully repeated the biblical content. Through printed texts other than the Bible itself, he and others were able to bring the gospel of Jesus Christ to thousands of readers and to those who heard public readings of texts. The printing press with movable type made it possible for Luther to address a much larger audience more directly and more easily than it had ever been possible in the history of Christianity. He saw this invention as a great blessing and made use of it himself, also encouraging others, to convey the benefits of Scripture to others.

God spoke to Luther out of the psalms as he began to probe Scripture in exchange with his students in 1513, but he soon found in Genesis the plot for God's entire narrative within human history. He found that the Old Testament creation accounts are more about God than about his human creatures. In Genesis 1 God comes out of nowhere, and he creates the world *ex nihilo*, instead of organizing previously existing something, as was the case in many Ancient Near Eastern religions and in traditional religions around the world. What distinguished the Hebrews from their neighbors is their recognition that God is totally free, not subject to forces and fates of any kind. The God who engages his human creatures from Scripture, and in the historical events it reports, stands wholly outside time and space while being directly present within the flow of history and the lives of his human creatures.

God's presence is never passive; he is always active in preserving and directing his creation, doing, shaping, directing all that we experience. His voice conveys his presence from beyond the limits of human ability to grasp. He acts in human history by guiding the course of events, but his physical and historical manifestations always need the prophetic word to engage his human creatures. He creates community with and among them through conversation set in motion as he speaks through the prophets and apostles. There may be long stretches of silence in his film, but it is not a silent film. He explains his intentions for sinners and his disposition toward them. He does not intend to leave them guessing but instead to give them what they need to know about himself and themselves. Only in their sinful curiosity do human beings feel compelled to venture further into speculation about him and his creation in their efforts to establish the mastery of their own minds over their situation and their future.

God's presence with his human creatures presumes their presence with him. Luther sensed that God notices the absence of those whom he created, as he did in Genesis 3, and goes on the hunt for them. He finds something lacking when someone is not present among his own people. He longs for the returning of the prodigal, the missing, the lost.

In the Smalcald Articles Luther described how God engages sinners in a life-transforming conversation. Luther labeled as "gospel" the ways in which God "gives guidance and help against sin." He does so in several ways "because God is extravagantly rich in his grace." Luther began with the preached word, "the spoken word, in which the forgiveness of sins is preached to the whole world (which is the proper function of the gospel)." His illiterate contemporaries, the majority of the population of Europe at the time, could not deal with written works. But Luther presumed the presence of Scripture in every sermon, so he did not mention the Bible or other printed media that conveyed the biblical message. He did, however, include the visible signs that bore the promise, "second, through Baptism; third, through the holy sacrament of the altar; fourth, through the power of the keys," that is, formal pronouncement of absolution. He added, either as an extension of that formal activity or as a fifth form of the word, again in oral form, "and also through the mutual conversation and consolation of brothers and sisters. Matthew 18 [:20]: 'Where two or three are gathered together in my name, I am there in their midst.'"[40] Luther regarded God as a multimedia communicator.

Oral pronouncement of the gospel outperforms the performative speech of modern linguistic theory. This theory posits that certain "speech-acts" actually accomplish things and determines reality on the basis of legal or social agreement, such as the words of umpires and referees, of judges in courtrooms, of those who pronounce a woman and a man husband and wife. God's pronouncements with his creative speech determine reality simply according to the will of God. God's speaking did so in the beginning, and, Luther believed, it does so as it delivers the promise to those who hear it. In 1523, preaching on Genesis 1, he equated God's speaking and his acting: "to speak and to make are the same for God."[41] A sermon on Matthew 24 in 1539 echoed this insight:

> The re-creative promise of the gospel not only creates the individual but also the church. The church cannot be recognized by its having outward

40. BSELK 764/765,33–766/767,5, BC 319. On Luther's analysis of the various forms of Word, see Joest, *Ontologie*, 355–365.
41. WA 14: 306,10–11.

peace but by its having Word and sacrament. Where you see the remnant that has the gospel and the sacraments in proper form, there is the church. If only the pulpit and baptismal font are right! The church's existence rests not on the holiness of a person but on the holiness and righteousness of the Lord Christ. He has sanctified the church through Word and sacrament.[42]

PROCLAMATION OF THE PROMISE IN THE SERMON

Most Christians, Luther believed, most often encountered God speaking to them in the sermon addressed to the entire congregation of God's people in one place.[43] God's voice echoes out of the pages of Scripture through the spoken words of his people, Luther taught, primarily in the sermon in the congregation's worship service. In contrast to many late medieval sermons that treated the lives and benefits of the saints on the basis of the fourteenth-century *Legenda aurea* (Golden Things that Must be Read), Wittenberg preaching arose only out of the text of Scripture and was dedicated to expositing what God says there within the proper distinction of law and gospel. In 1520 Luther's advice to a nearby pastor discouraged "verbose introductions" and counseled beginning every sermon with prayer in the heart. Then the preacher was to read the text, explicate it with an exposition of its significance for the hearers, and conclude with, "That is enough," or "more another time," or "Enough said; we will call on God and his grace, that we may do it," or "God help us." He then suggested closing words: "Let us commend [to God] our spiritual and temporal situation, in particular, etc. For these and all else for which we are obligated, we will pray the Lord's Prayer together." After this, preachers should say, "the blessings of God the Father, etc. Amen."[44]

The "Instructions for the Visitors of Parish Pastors" that Melanchthon drafted with significant input from Luther[45] advised village pastors to select the biblical books on which they preached during the week carefully "so that they are useful and not too difficult and that faith be proclaimed, so that true Christian repentance, God's judgment, the fear of God, and good works" not be forgotten.[46] Luther's sermons reflected his serious textual

42. WA 47, 556, 27–33.
43. For a fuller exposition, see Kolb, *Enduring Word*, 174–208.
44. WA Br2:124, §300.
45. According to the latest scholarship, cf. *Der "Unterricht der Visitatoren" und die Durchsetzung der Reformation in Kursachsen*, ed. Joachim Bauer and Stefan Michel (Leipzig: Evangelische Verlagsanstalt, 2017).
46. WA 26: 195–240, LW 53: 214–309.

study and his sensitivity to the rhythms of life in Wittenberg's homes, shops, and marketplace. He understood his task in the pulpit as that of a messenger, who brings vital news to his hearers. For behind and distinct from the preacher's voice God is speaking, and the Holy Spirit is present to drive the proclaimed word into hearers' hearts and minds.

In the worship service Luther's concept of the living voice of the gospel, the Scripture's report on the work of Christ, takes active, dynamic form in address to, and application for, the lives of others. Without this preaching, sinners still stand peering in the direction of the dim outline of a divine figure or into utter darkness. Particularly where the events of daily life do not match what God says he is feeling toward, and doing with, his people is the voice of the preacher vital. The preacher repeats the words of the Lord, coming as they do from outside human attempts to package him. For in these words his person emerges amid the darkness. In the person of the preacher and in the sometimes rather ill-prepared rhetoric of the preacher's best efforts, God is hiding in words that convey the power to save, as Paul noted in Romans 1:17 (and not in the human being whose words he is using).[47]

Particularly when faced with difficult passages of Scripture or difficult incidents in daily life, Luther wanted a preacher who "knows where the rabbit holes are when one is devoid of the theological distinction between clothed and unclothed God. He knew how near to grace and death these questions came, and he felt how tragically different life is without a preacher than it is with one."[48] Steven Paulson follows Gerhard Forde in accentuating God's presence in the congregation of his people as "God preached," the God whose mercy displays itself in daily life. In contrast, where "God not preached" is sensed, his true self remains buried under human speculation and fear or under false confidence in someone or something other than God. The preacher who leads people to the cross and empty tomb executes God's decree of election. That task functions in the proclamation of the person and work of Christ whenever the gospel speaks itself through human agents into the lives of sinners.[49]

As noted in the introduction of this volume, Luther categorized God's messages for his human creatures as either words about how he designed human creatures to live, or words about his rescue of his people from their alienation from him. The first word proceeds out of an indicative description of the divine design for human life, and it turns into an imperative

47. Paulson, *Outlaw God*, 3: 177–205.
48. Paulson, *Outlaw God*, 1: x.
49. Paulson, *Outlaw God*, 2: 45–62.

as it bids the individual to respond to what God says with obedience. The gospel proceeds out of the view of creation's Maker, a gaze filled with love and, after his human creatures ran away from him, with longing for their return. It remains in the indicative.

The Creator's view of human life certainly included his law that, by revealing God's planned shape for human life, killed Luther's pursuit of the false gods of his own efforts to please the true God. The law had smothered him in his own guilt, shame, and fear. God also addressed him with a word that repeated his creative activity at the beginning. God spoke his absolution, and the new Martin took place. He took his place in the circle of God's family. Luther carried this experience into the pulpit. He believed that all people face a similar encounter with God in some form or other and that preachers facilitate these encounters in their preaching. He published two sermons on the distinction of law and gospel that he had preached in Wittenberg as instruction for readers, especially for pastors. This distinction gains its strength from its use in first order discourse. The law can deliver its message with the second order observation that God wants people in general not to harm each other in body or reputation, but it strikes home when I hear the words, "you are not to kill." The gospel can convey the promise by stating that on a hill far away, on an old rugged cross, the man who claimed to be God died for all sinners. But God wants me to hear "given and shed *for you*." The reality of what God has to say to his people, Luther believed, pierces hearts in his personal conversation with each of his chosen children.[50]

In 1532 Luther told his hearers in Wittenberg, "Whoever knows well how to distinguish the gospel from the law should give thanks to God and know that he is a real theologian."[51] Making this distinction properly is "the noblest skill in the Christian church," for both are the word of God, but both can be lost if they are mixed together and not correctly distinguished from each other.[52] The law preached from the pulpit sketches God's good design for human life, but when it evaluates such life gone off track, "it imprisons, it crushes, it kills."[53] The proclaimed law presents "what he commands us to do, what we should do. It demands works from

50. Forde, *Theology is for Proclamation*, esp. 135–158.
51. WA 40,1: 207,3–4; LW 26: 115. The following material is taken in part from Robert Kolb, "'The Noblest Skill in the Christian Church': Luther's Sermons on the Proper Distinction of Law and Gospel," *Concordia Theological Quarterly* 71 (2007): 301–318.
52. WA 36:8,14–10,18, 25,1–34. Cf. WA 36: 28,12–16, 33–38.
53. WA 40,1:517,10–518,6. Cf. on the crushing power of the law, Smalcald Articles, III:iii: 2, BSELK 750/751,28–33, BC 312. On Luther's use of the baptismal language of killing and making alive in the development of his doctrine of justification in these lectures, see Robert

us." Luther presumed that external compliance could be accomplished without difficulty (he labeled this compliance *in causa formali*) but with great difficulty *in causa finali*—in truly fulfilling the commands with a faithful disposition.[54]

In a sermon of 1537, Luther elaborated: The law reveals "what the human being is, what he was, and what he will become once more." Its first prescriptive is "'You shall love God with your whole heart.' . . . You had this treasure in paradise and were created so that you could love God with your whole heart. You have lost that and must return to it. Otherwise, you cannot come into God's kingdom." With this understanding of the law, Luther confronted libertine tendencies that he detected in his former student Johann Agricola and his supporters at that time. It is false and cannot be tolerated that someone preaches that even if you love neither God nor neighbor and are an adulterer, "it does not harm you if you just believe." Sin brings condemnation. That is clear, the preacher argued, from Galatians 5:19–21, Matthew 5:17–18, 12:36, Romans 8:3–4, and Romans 3:31.[55]

> Adam lived before the Fall in perfect love toward God and pure love for the neighbor, in total obedience, without evil desires. Had he remained in that state, we would not be in the state we are. Because he fell into sin, fell from this command, we lie in the same misery as he, full of sin and disobedience, under God's wrath and curse, and we tumble from one sin into another. The law stands there at all times, regards us as guilty, drive us and demands that we should be upright and obedient to God.

The law sets my conscience against me, Luther pointed out, "because I am to love God with my whole heart and my neighbor as myself, and I do not do it. So I must be condemned."[56]

When the law hits the sinner's conscience head-on and the conscience senses the significance of its sin—when the pressures of death mount, with war, pestilence, poverty, shame, and the like—then the law speaks, Luther explained to his hearers in 1532:

> "You are lost. I demand this and that from you, but you have not done it and cannot do it." When it comes to this, it terrifies people to death, stomps on them, and they must despair. Whoever can make the distinction [of law and

Kolb, "God Kills to Make Alive: Romans 6 and Luther's Understanding of Justification (1535)," *Lutheran Quarterly* 12 (1998): 33–56.

54. WA 36:13,25–27; cf. 36:30,19–35.
55. WA 15:146,25–147,33. On Agricola's troubled relationship with Luther, see p. 249.
56. WA 45:147,37–148,19.

> gospel] in this situation, make it! For here this distinguishing is absolutely necessary![57]

Lutheran theologians have often interpreted Luther's understanding of the hostile function of the law in terms of Melanchthon's description of its accusing power.[58] This passage conforms to Luther's broader understanding of the law's power not only to accuse of specific sins but also to analyze the deeper impact of original sin and the power of the law to crush and terrify, as he expressed it in the Smalcald Articles, for example.[59] "War, pestilence, poverty, and shame" along with guilt inform sinners that they are lost apart from fear, love, and trust in God. All forms of evil, those which sinners perpetrate and those of which they are victims, terrify them to death and stomp them into despair. To be sure, Luther also could emphasize the obligation that fell as guilt—debt or burden—upon the sinner. The editor of the first printing of his sermon of 1536 on the distinction of law and gospel had Luther say, "The law lays guilt upon me. I have not done this or that, I am unrighteous and a sinner in God's record of guilt. It is a word which puts my guilt on my account."[60] Rörer described this function of the law as pointing to Christ by "terrifying the unrepentant with God's wrath and displeasure."[61]

As the sermon came to a close, Luther spoke of the terrified conscience facing the demands of the law.

> Performance is very difficult, particularly when the law wants to puts its claim on the conscience. Then a person must grasp the promise, and so that you do not fall under his justice, do not leave it with the law, for whoever denies the gospel must thrash about in the hope that God does have a gospel, that he will not play with me according to the standards of justice, but rather will deal with me on the basis of grace for Christ's sake, that he forgives you all that you have failed to do out of grace, and what he will give you what you cannot do.[62]

Rörer paraphrased the text, "See to it that you grasp the promise and not let the law gain the upper hand and rule in your conscience. That will

57. WA 36:15,30–16,25.
58. E.g. Ap IV, 38, 103, 179, BSELK 750/751,23–752/753,25, BC 312–313.
59. SA III:iii,1–9, BSELK, 436–438, BC, 312–313.
60. WA 36:17,23–24, cf. 36:1–35.
61. WA 36:26,19–20.
62. WA 36:22,30–23,12.

bring you under judgment if you deny the gospel. You must cast yourself upon and grasp the word of grace or the gospel of the forgiveness of sins."[63]

Luther challenged the conclusion of many that because God's law commands human beings to do certain things and forbids them to do others, it must even after the fall into sin necessarily be possible even for sinners to keep the law. Such people did not understand the nature of sin, Luther concluded. In an extensive argument in *On Bound Choice*, Luther demonstrated that after the fall into sin, human incapability did not alter God's design for humanity, but it prevented obedience to the law from providing help, much less a way, for reaching out to God. With the presence and aid of the Holy Spirit, believers do indeed search God's law for information on the good life. The more seriously they take what they learn there, the easier it is for them to hear the law's continuing accusation as they take seriously that the "law of sin," as Paul calls it in Romans 7, is asserting its vicious presence in the lives of God's own people.[64] The initial task of the preacher brings hearers and God's law face to face.

Luther usually restricted his use of the term "gospel" in the pulpit, as elsewhere, to its referring to the work of Christ in the atonement and the Holy Spirit's delivery of the benefits of that atoning work to believers in every age. This definition unfolded out of his doctrine of the freely formulated plan of God to create. He created without any conditions, out of pure love for his creatures. He made all of creation to be in an open and binding relationship to him. His person, majestic as it is, reaches out to his human creatures. They are designed to respond with trust, and their very existence depends on this trust that grasps life by grasping the Creator of life himself. God is by nature a person who makes promises and who invites the response of trust rather than a person who offers proof and demands our testing his offer. Oswald Bayer identified Luther's discovery of the significance of God's promising in oral, written, and sacramental experiences of the gospel of Christ as the critical point in his development of his thinking about God and his way of delivering his people from sin.[65]

As Luther pursued the deconstruction of medieval piety in 1520, he placed the promise of forgiveness and life at the heart of his understanding of the sacramental action of the Holy Spirit, as outlined in his *Prelude, On the Babylonian Captivity of the Church*. This title pointed to the scholastic theologians' "extinguishing" of the promise that creates trust as the heart

63. WA 36:41,37–42,21.
64. Paulson, *Outlaw God*, 2:149–184.
65. Oswald Bayer, *Promissio. Geschichte der reformatorischen Wende in Luthers Theologie*, 2nd ed. (Darmstadt: Wissenschaftliche Buchgesellschaft, 1989).

of the believer's reborn identity in Christ. Driven by the failure to teach properly of the faith that clings to God, the hierarchy had fostered "the most godless superstition of works." Without trust in Christ at the center of life, Christians were "despoiled of our precious possessions" and chained to the church's prescribed works.[66] Luther claimed, "God does not make connections with human beings in any other way than through a word of promise." Good works do not make the connection since he does not need them. God needs people who consider him faithful in his promises and who, framing life within his promises, live a life of faith, hope, and love. The promise is not a magical incantation or a disconnected thunderbolt. It is part of the personal conversation for which God created his people. The only response to a promise is faith. "These two, promise and faith, most necessarily go together. For without the promise there is nothing to be believed while without faith the promise is useless since it is established and fulfilled through faith."[67]

His completion of the argument of the *Babylonian Captivity* came a few months later with the construction of an evangelical theology and piety in *On Christian Freedom*. This treatise defined God's promises and his promising as that which faith honors by trusting what he says. Luther characterized God's promises as "holy, true, righteous, free, and words of peace, full of goodness." In clinging to these promises, believers so identify with God's description of them as his righteous people that his promise shapes who they are and how they live. Turning to language learned from the mystical devotion of the fourteenth century, Luther described the activity of God's active word of promise. It *absorbs* believers, and their very identity and personhood are now determined by the defining action of the promiser as delivered in preaching. The promise *saturates* their being and *intoxicates* them, taking possession of their thinking and acting. This restores believers to their righteousness as his children, their identity as new creatures in Christ.[68] "Promise" is the form that the re-creative, justifying speaking of God takes. The forensic action of God's pronouncement of forgiveness and new life restores righteousness; it justifies.[69]

> The gospel or faith is something that does not demand our works or tell us what to do, but tells us to receive, to accept a gift, so that we are passive, that is, that God promises and says to you: "this and that I impart to you. You can do nothing for it; you have done nothing for it, but it is my doing." Just

66. WA 6: 520,10–14, LW 36: 47.
67. WA 6: 517,8–21, LW 36:42.
68. WA 7: 24,22–29 (German), 53,15–23 (Latin), LW 31: 349.
69. Joest, *Ontologie*, 371–394.

> as in baptism, I did nothing; it is not of my doing in any way. It is God's doing, and he says to me, "Pay attention. I baptize you and wash you of all your sins. Accept it, it is yours." That is what it means to receive a gift. This is the distinction of law and gospel. Through the law a demand is made for what we should do. It presses for our activity for God and the neighbor. In the gospel we are required to receive a gift. . . . The gospel is pure gift, freely bestowed, salvation.[70]

Therefore, Luther could say in the *German Mass* of 1526 that the "preaching and teaching of God's Word" is "the most important part of the divine service."[71]

PROCLAMATION OF THE PROMISE IN ABSOLUTION

God engages his people in conversation in the midst of their daily struggles with temptation and their desires to fashion their own reality instead of God's. He asserts his presence amid their struggles with Satan, with the systems of the world that Satan has perverted, and with their own willfulness to "do it my way." Luther did not use the phrase "the mystery of the continuation of sin and evil in the lives of the baptized," but he wrestled with this mystery. The medieval sacrament of penance had offered him a solution, in a form that he transformed. Luther had grown up with the practice of penance in three parts: contrition—sorrow for sin (different theologians defined differently the degree of sorrow necessary to be worthy for the next part)—followed by confession of sins to the priest, whose absolution took away the sinner's eternal guilt before God. Third, however, the performance of satisfactions to satisfy the judgment of temporal punishment on sin was necessary to complete the sacrament and ensure passage through purgatory to heaven.[72] Luther focused on absolution, without abandoning concern for contrition and confession of sins.[73] Contrition and confession did not, however, earn any merit before God. Absolution bestowed righteousness before God upon all whom the Holy Spirit moved to trust in Christ. That righteousness produced—and was in no way caused by—the fruits of faith. Luther recognized times when God remains hidden and sinners with most repentant hearts still quake and quiver in his presence. But in those moments, he proclaimed, they have

70. WA 36:14,22–32, cf. 36:311–32,25.
71. *The German Mass*, 1526, WA19: 78,26–27, LW53: 68.
72. Thomas N. Tentler, *Sin and Confession on the Eve of the Reformation* (Princeton: Princeton University Press, 1977).
73. Bayer, *Promissio*.

faith to flee to the cross and find God Revealed there. Absolution brings the individual into hearing range of Christ's personal pronouncement of forgiveness for the beleaguered, bedraggled sinner.

Alongside preaching, the hearing of confessions and the absolving of sinners formed the heart of the pastoral ministry, reflecting Luther's own service as an Augustinian brother in and around Wittenberg. The Small Catechism taught readers to believe firmly that through absolution "our sins are forgiven before God in heaven." Children learned that they should go to their pastor and before him they were to "reflect on your walk of life in the light of the Ten Commandments," combining God's structure for life in the callings of daily life and his commands to practice virtue as a means of reviewing life. Appropriate Bible verses for the distress of this particular person should supplement the simple formula, "I forgive you in the name of the Father, Son, and Holy Spirit."[74] Formal confession and absolution actualizes the rhythm of law and gospel, repentance and trust along with its fruits, for believers in a special manner.

In the 1530s a controversy broke out within the church of Nuremberg over whether absolution might be pronounced upon the entire congregation in public worship or whether absolution might be given only after private confession to the pastor. Luther and Melanchthon supported their long-time friend Lazarus Spengler, administrative secretary of the city council; their former student Veit Dietrich, who had become pastor in Saint Sebald in the city; and other pastors against their colleague in Nuremberg, Andreas Osiander, by arguing that while private confession and absolution is preferred, the word of absolution pronounced to the general congregation carries the power of the promise and delivers the benefits of Christ.[75] God establishes his relationship with his chosen people through his word, not through the office or the person who speaks the word.

PROCLAMATION OF THE PROMISE IN THE MUTUAL CONVERSATION AND CONSOLATION OF BELIEVERS

The Holy Spirit used preachers as first instances of delivering law and gospel to the community, in preaching and in formal confession and absolution. However, Luther also insisted that God calls every Christian,

74. BSELK, 884/885,23–888/889,9; BC, 360–62.
75. Ronald K. Rittgers, *The Reformation of the Keys* (Cambridge, MA: Harvard University Press, 2004), esp. 158–164.

by virtue of being made his child in baptism, to communicate his message to others as his spokespersons. This word took command of their lives and mouths in order to convey forgiveness won by Christ as he died and rose. In so doing, all believers are to function as the Holy Spirit's instruments to forgive, reconcile, and empower others as their trust moves from reliance on Christ and confidence in him, to love and services to others.

In 1522, preaching on 1 Peter, Luther explained that God places believers on earth to be of aid to others, and that nothing is more important than bringing them to trust in Christ.[76] Coming to 1 Peter 2:9, he translated Peter's words "you are a royal priesthood" with "you are Christians." He explicated what it meant that God had called the people of Wittenberg and appointed them to be his priests, so that they could declare the mighty, liberating, illuminating acts of God as he rescued them in the face of every kind of evil. Their most important activity he identified as the presentation of God's word in order to call others into the light in which God longs to place them.[77]

The Lord's commission of his people to speak his word extended to all of them on the basis of their baptism, Luther was convinced. In his Church Postil of 1526 for the nineteenth Sunday after Trinity he wrote that

> all who are Christians and have been baptized have this power [to forgive one another's sins]. For with this they praise Christ, and the word is put into their mouth, so that they may and are able to say, if they wish, and as often as it is necessary: "Look! God offers you his grace, forgives you all your sins. Be comforted; your sins are forgiven. Only believe, and you will surely have forgiveness." This word of consolation shall not cease among Christians until the last day: "Your sins are forgiven, be of good cheer." Such language a Christian always uses and openly declares the forgiveness of sins. For this reason and in this manner a Christian has power to forgive sins.[78]

Luther resituated the power of penance—precisely, its absolution—from the priest to God's word itself. He continued to admonish his congregation to practice the mutual forgiveness of sins in the family and community in which they lived. The reformer elaborated on this "mutual conversation and consolation" of believers in his Large Catechism. Believers are to express remorse for their sin and desire comfort, restoration, and forgiveness "through the Word placed on the lips of another person."[79] When

76. WA 12: 267,3–7, LW 30: 11.
77. WA 12: 318,26–319,6, LW 30: 64–65.
78. WA 10,1:412–414, Lenker, *Sermons*, 5: 209.
79. Large Catechism, 1529, Confession BSELK, 1158,1–1162,18; BC 477–478.

"some particular issue weighs on us or attacks us, eating away at us until we can have no peace" or when we "find ourselves insufficiently strong in faith," Luther counseled setting those burdens before another believer "at any time and as often as we wish." From fellow Christians, believers receive "advice, comfort, and strength." For, "by divine ordinance Christ himself has placed absolution in the mouths of his Christian community and commanded us to absolve one another from sins. So, if there is a heart that feels its sin and desires comfort, it has here a sure refuge where it finds and hears God's Word because through a human being God looses and absolves from sin."[80]

In 1537, preaching on John 14:13–14, Luther explained that all Christians naturally want to help others receive deliverance and life in Christ as they have.[81] He also said that all sinners long for this deliverance and that when "your neighbor absolves you in God's stead, it is just as if God himself were speaking."[82] The reformer provided concrete details about his vision of Christians sharing the gospel with each other individually or in small groups when he was preaching to the Wittenberg congregation on Matthew 18:15–20 a few months later:

> Here Jesus is saying that he does not only want [the condemnation of sin and proclamation of the forgiveness of sins] to take place in the church, but he also gives this right and freedom where two or three are gathered together, so that among them the comfort and the forgiveness of sins may be proclaimed and pronounced. He pours out [his forgiveness] even more richly and places the forgiveness of sins for them in every corner, so that they not only find the forgiveness of sins in the formal assembly of God's people but also at home in their houses, in the fields and gardens, wherever one of them comes to another in search of comfort and deliverance. It shall be at my disposal when I am troubled and sorry, in tribulation and vulnerable, when I need something, at whatever hour and time it may be. There is not always a sermon being given publicly in the church, so when my brother or neighbor comes to me, I am to lay my troubles before my neighbor and ask for comfort . . . . Again, I should comfort others, and say, "dear friend, dear brother, why don't you lay aside your burdens. It is certainly not God's will that you experience this suffering. God had his Son die for you so that you do not sorrow but rejoice."[83]

80. Large Catechism, 1529, Confession, BSELK, 1159,2–1160,4, BC 477–478.
81. WA 45: 540,14–23, LW 24:87–88. Cf. WA 19: 482–523, LW 36: 359.
82. *The Sacrament of the Body and Blood of Christ—Against the Fanatics*, 1526, WA 19: 321,13–17, 320,320,17–19, LW 36: 359.
83. WA 47: 297,36–298,14, author's translation.

Professor Luther told his students in 1542, "If you want to be absolved from your sins in this manner, go to your pastor, or to your brother or neighbor if your pastor cannot hear you; [the neighbor] has the command to absolve you and comfort you."[84] Luther repeated this idea in a sermon of 1544 on Matthew 3:1, expressing his gratitude that God had given his people the gift of both bestowing and receiving forgiveness of sins from one another. He preferred to receive absolution from his pastor, but if he found himself in despair, he knew that God could send "even a woman or a child" to lay a hand upon him and pronounce him free from sin. They, too, are members of Christ and have been given this power. He rejected the idea that this practice diminishes the pastoral office. His concern for upholding the pastoral office did not invalidate recognizing that the power of absolution lies in God's promise, and it is given to all.[85]

The reality of the believer's life amid the continuation of sin and evil arose from the re-creative word of forgiveness that was to take its place in daily life, when believers speak the promise to one another. The gospel of Christ did indeed saturate the lives of believers, providing comfort and sending them to others with that comfort that Christ has given them. This spirit of forgiveness and forgiving determines the relationship between God and his people and among his people with each other.

PROCLAMATION OF THE PROMISE IN BAPTISM AND THE LORD'S SUPPER

Luther redefined the term "sacrament" to be an expression of the promise of forgiveness and new life ordained by Christ and accompanied by an external sign. Some would say, "how odd of God to choose just plain old water and bread and wine placed together with Christ's body and blood to convey the promise he conveys effectively in human language." Steven Paulson admitted that the "irresistible quality of water . . . tempts us to speculate endlessly about it, trying to peek into the hidden God's choice of water as the thing of salvation." The answer eludes us, but the Creator uses this water that is connected with his promise as he wills, even as his own hiding place from which he effects a new creation.[86] As previously discussed, God is a multimedia communicator, Luther believed, so he chose sacramental signs to serve as vehicles of his promise.

84. WA 44; 95,41–96,1; LW 6: 128. Cf. WA 44: 712,33–36; LW 8: 183.
85. WA 49: 312,26–313,23, cf. LW 58: 75.
86. Paulson, "Graspable God," 53–54.

Luther developed his concept of the sacraments as forms of God's promise of forgiveness of sins, life, and salvation against the backdrop of his rejection of the use of sacramental ritual to bestow God's grace *ex opere operato*. This medieval pillar of sacramental theology posited that the performance of the ritual accomplishes what it aims to effect simply through the participation of the Christian in the ritual action. Popularly understood as the activity of being present for the performance of the mass, for example, this made attendance at mass a possible way to acquire grace apart from faith through human activity. Luther's concept of God's active bestowal through the promise in oral or sacramental form met objections from other reformers, however, as well. They came at him from the opposite direction from the medieval sacramental doctrine and practice, for they were reacting to the association of God's power with material objects and with human effort in the medieval view.

Ulrich Zwingli and Johannes Oecolampadius represent this point of view.[87] Amy Nelson Burnett traces their views in part back to the humanist network that stood under the influence of Erasmus. She notes that the differences between Luther and Erasmus regarding God's use of material elements of his creation as instruments of his saving power are not as easy to detect as is what separated them in the frontal confrontation over the freedom or bondage of the will. Nonetheless, she concludes that these differences in sacramental theology made a greater impact on the German humanists who were flocking to the banner of reform than even the latter, much more public, clash between the two. Their differences on the sacraments arose out of "metaphysical assumptions about the relationship between the material world and spiritual reality." Erasmus and those who followed him, such as Zwingi and Oecolampadius, stood under the influence of the revival of platonic and neo-platonic thought, whereas Luther's rootage in Ockhamism gave him a different approach to the created, material world. His own experience with spiritual searching inside himself or in the heavens had led to despair. He concluded that "God worked only through those external things he had established: his Word and the sacraments." For Erasmus, externals were, in Burnett's words, "'training wheels' that could help believers rise to higher spiritual things." Furthermore, Burnett points to a difference in the way that they

87. Andreas Bodenstein von Karlstadt, Luther's Wittenberg colleague, developed similar views out of his sense of the medieval reform movements that had objected to viewing ritual action as salvific apart from following Jesus with proper moral performance. Cf. Amy Nelson Burnett, *Karlstadt and the Origins of the Eucharistic Controversy: A Study in the Circulation of Ideas* (New York: Oxford University Press, 2011). See pp. 248–249.

applied the philological insights of the linguistic studies of the time. Erasmus sought ultimate meaning beyond the trivialities of the text, whereas Luther found God at work in history and human language as reported in sometimes baffling detail in the text.[88]

Luther had experienced a monastic tendency to look inward. He had gained much from certain mystical writers who encouraged such introspection as the path to higher spiritual accomplishment. Such experiences may have been the cause of his commitment to finding solace and peace in Christ only through the external forms in which his word takes place. In his Smalcald Articles he confessed,

> God gives no one his Spirit or grace apart from the external Word which comes first [and thus produces faith]. . . . God does not want to deal with us human beings except by means of his external Word and sacrament. Everything that boasts of being from the Spirit apart from such a Word and sacrament is of the devil. For God even desired to appear to Moses first in the burning bush and by means of the spoken word; no prophet—not even Elijah or Elisha—received the Spirit outside of or without the Ten Commandments; John the Baptist was not conceived without Gabriel's preceding word, nor did he leap in his mother's womb without Mary's voice; and St. Peter says: the prophets did not prophesy "by human will" but "by the Holy Spirit," indeed, as "holy people of God." However, without the external Word, they were not holy—much less would the Holy Spirit have moved them to speak while they were still unholy. Peter says they were holy because the Holy Spirit speaks through them.[89]

Baptism

Baptism invades sinners' lives with the gospel as new birth in Christ; the Lord's Supper offers sustenance for living out life in Christ. The significance of both lies in the promise of new life through forgiveness wrought by Christ. To the Anabaptist rejoinder, "How can water do such great things?"[90] Luther taught children to reply, "Clearly the water does not do it, but the Word of God, which is with and alongside the water, and faith, which trusts this Word of God in the water. For without the Word

88. Amy Nelson Burnett, "Revisiting Humanism and the Urban Reformation," *Lutheran Quarterly* 35 (2021): 191–193 (173–400); Amy Nelson Burnett, *Debating the Sacraments: Print and Authority in the Early Reformation* (New York: Oxford University Press, 2019).
89. BSELK 770/771,10–14, 772/773,17–30 BC 322, 323
90. John S. Oyer, *Lutheran Reformers against Anabaptists: Luther, Melanchthon and Menius and the Anabaptists of Central Germany* (The Hague: Nijhoff, 1964), 114–139.

of God the water is plain water and not a baptism, but with the Word of God it is a baptism, that is, a grace-filled water of life and a 'bath of the new birth in the Holy Spirit,' as St. Paul says to Titus in chapter 3" [:5-8].[91] With one eye on medieval ritualistic practice, Luther taught the children that the eating and drinking in the Lord's Supper is not what delivered the benefits of Christ's death and resurrection. Instead, they received these benefits through "the words that are recorded: 'given for you' and 'shed for you for the forgiveness of sins.' These words, when accompanying the physical eating and drinking, are the essential thing in the sacrament, and whoever believes these very words has what they declare and state, namely, forgiveness of sins."[92] The physicality of the sacraments is vital to Luther even if the promise is what is effective. God communicates with the sacrament as a semiotic conversational act that communicates what it accomplishes as a re-creative expression of God's saving will through "sign" and pronouncement.[93]

Luther understood baptism as God at work with his promise, in a special form of reinforcing the words with the illustrative water. God's omnipotence itself is in baptism. He does not give a simple bath but rather a bath for the soul, "through which he cleanses us from all sins and sludge."[94] Alluding to 1 Peter 3:21, he commented, "The Lord causes a new deluge, but it is the deluge of salvation. He gives a new water, a new spirit. Baptism is this deluge."[95] In 1539 he began the last sermon of his last series on baptism, according to Johann Stoltz's notes, with the words, "Baptism is the water of regeneration through the Holy Spirit in this life for life eternal. This is the proper definition of baptism."[96] A year earlier he had observed, "The word may not look like much, and the water either, but let nothing else sway you. Rather, look to him who is giving the command."[97] Later in this sermon series, the preacher reinforced this point: "Christ ordained this baptism. God and the Holy Spirit confirmed

91. Small Catechism, Baptism, question three, BSELK 884/885,2–11, BC 359.
92. Small Catechism, Lord's Supper, question three, BSELK 890/891,3–8, BC 362.
93. Joest, *Ontologie*, 406–421.
94. WA 46:169,10–25, 27–170,31. Material in this section is taken in part from Robert Kolb, "'What Benefit Does the Soul Receive from a Handful of Water?' Luther's Preaching on Baptism, 1528–1539," *Concordia Journal* 25 (1999), 346–363, used with the permission of the editor.
95. WA 31,1: 553, 8–10.
96. WA 47: 653,21–22. See Robert Kolb, "'What Benefit Does the Soul Receive from a Handful of Water?' Luther's Preaching on Baptism, 1528-1539," *Concordia Journal* 25 (1999), 346–363, from which elements of what follows are taken.
97. WA 46:168,5–6. On this association, see Jonathan D. Trigg, *Baptism in the Theology of Martin Luther* (Leiden: Brill, 2001), 67–75. Cf. Lorenz Grönvik, *Die Taufe in der Theologie Martin Luthers* (Åbo, Åbo Akademi, 1968), 55–93.

it. God gave his testimony with his voice, the Holy Spirit with his presence. Those who want to be saved shall hold to it, to him who here was baptized (Christ) [by John the Baptist at the Jordan, the text of the sermon] and confirmed by the Father's voice. If we do not listen to him, we will lack everything. If we listen to him, the Father will be pleased with us and we will have his favor, his heart, and everything that he has."[98]

Early on, Luther followed Augustine in saying that the sacrament saves because it is believed, not because it takes place, but he did not mean that faith is a work that makes the sacrament valid as forgiveness and salvation. God is always at work, but in the conversational mode that creates relationship between God and his chosen.[99] Philip Cary notes that the grounding of the sacramental promise in Christ's words in Scripture forms the basis of the delivery of the promise in the celebration of the sacrament in the twenty-first century. "[Luther] originally worked out the correlation between faith and promise in the context of a sacramental theology, where he sees a double structure of God's word: first a scriptural promise of Christ that institutes the sacrament, then an oral word that is part of the sacramental action itself."[100] Cary notes that in contrast to Calvin, who separated the outward sign from its spiritual impact, Luther held to the unity of God's communication of the promise and the delivery of it with its benefits.[101] As Luther wrote, "faith clings to the water and believes it to be Baptism in which there is sheer salvation and life, not through the water . . . but through its incorporation with God's Word."[102] In a sermon in 1539, Luther made it clear that water apart from God's baptismal command does nothing. "There is no baptism, but merely water, if the command of God is not present. Holy water [not baptismal water in Luther's usage, but the water consecrated for use as protection or blessing, a practice Luther regarded as superstitious] remains water because God has not commanded it. Attention must be paid to the institution. The authority and command of God must be present, or there is no real institution."[103]

This promise delivered in baptism demands the same faith that other forms of the promise demand:

98. WA 46: 185,12–29. Luther repeated these ideas at the beginning of the next sermon, WA 46: 194,15–195,9, 194,22–196,31. He had treated the baptism of Jesus perhaps most extensively in the third of the 1534 sermons, WA 37: 270–273.
99. Joest, *Ontologie*, 395–399.
100. Cary, "Why Luther is Not Quite Protestant," 450.
101. Cary, "Why Luther is Not Quite Protestant," 461–462.
102. BSELK 1116/1117,34–36, BC 460.
103. WA 47:646,23–29.

> In Baptism, therefore, every Christian has enough to study and practice all his or her life. Christians always have enough to do to believe firmly what Baptism promises and delivers—victory over death and the devil, forgiveness of sin, God's grace, the entire Christ, and the Holy Spirit with his gifts. In short, the blessings of Baptism are so boundless that if our timid nature considers them, it may well doubt whether they could all be true. . . . Now, here in Baptism there is brought, free of charge, to every person's door . . . a treasure and medicine that swallows up death and keeps all people alive. Thus, we must regard Baptism and put it to use in such a way that we may draw strength and comfort from it when our sins or conscience oppress us and say: "But I am baptized! And if I have been baptized, I have the promise that I shall be saved and have eternal life, both in soul and body."[104]

Luther drew the specific parallel between God's creative action in the sacrament, baptism along with absolution, and his creation of heaven, earth and all creatures through his Word.[105] Paul's words in Romans 6:4–5 and Colossians 2: 11–15 described what actually happens when the promise is given to sinners at the baptismal font, according to Luther in 1519: "a blessed dying unto sin and a resurrection in the grace of God."[106] In Steven Paulson's words, in baptism "God does double work, first by putting to death the old sinner, and then by raising up a new creature without sin. God chooses the water of baptism as the place where he executes the old Adam or Eve so that he can finally be found on your side—not as a judge but as the creator of a new you."[107] Baptism associates the baptized person with God's name, and "God's name is nothing other than God's power. It is eternal salvation, life, purity. Does it not sanctify, vivify, and purify not only the body but also the soul? It does this not because it is water but because God's power is in it."[108]

Luther explained to his hearers in 1538 that the human agents who perform the baptismal rite serve as God's tools. "The priest who baptizes is an instrument that carries out the baptism. He lends God his hands and tongue, but the words are God's, not the person's. 'I baptize you' is not said by the one who is performing the baptism but by the Trinity. The Trinity is baptizing through this tool."[109] God's personal presence in Scripture's words flows into believers' lives. Also, in the promise concretized in the sacraments, he is Immanuel, God with us. Luther reminded users of his

104. BSELK 1120/1121,24–1122/1123,4, BC 461–462.
105. WA 37: 278,15–22.
106. WA 2: 727,30–31; LW 35:30.
107. Paulson, "Graspable God," 52.
108. WA 37: 264,34–265,5.
109. WA 46: 148,36–149,27. Luther repeated the point in 1539, WA 47: 648,2–3, 23–25.

Small Catechism to think on their baptismal identity by giving them a pattern for morning and evening meditation that included making the sign of the cross, as they had received it in baptism, while they placed themselves under God's care by calling on the name of Father, Son, and Holy Spirit.[110]

The prominent use of the concept of *signum* for the elements of water or bread and wine (albeit an effective sign, not merely a symbol) found in Luther's earlier treatments of the sacraments had largely disappeared from his theology by the late 1520s. This vocabulary occurred in passing in one of the sermons of 1528 on baptism, but thereafter occurs very rarely in his published works.[111] He rejected the belief that baptism was "a mere sign," as the Anabaptists said in slandering baptism.[112] Instead, he argued, God has always used physical signs of various kinds, including the form of a dove and of fire to bestow his presence in the midst of his people. Therefore, God can certainly come through the use of water when he uses it in connection with his word.[113] This baptismal sign pronounces upon believers the forgiveness of sins and gives assurance that he wishes to preserve them, as he preserved Noah and his family in the ark (1 Peter 3:20).[114] When Luther did use the term, baptism functioned not only as a sign of God's grace, however; it was also to serve as a *signum* of their common identity among Christians as well, according to the reformer.[115]

The way in which God connected external means with the promise of new life remained a mystery for Luther, but he did know how some medieval teachers had confused their connection. Luther asserted that Thomas Aquinas had focused on a "secret divine power, which the Holy Spirit had placed in the water, which bathes the soul." Luther found that an obscure way of speaking. Likewise, he ascribed to Duns Scotus a dismissal of the external means of water, concentrating baptismal effectiveness in the will of God. Luther urged his readers to be content with God's word, with its omnipotence, which purifies us from all sins and death and bestows new birth, through the power of the Father, Son, and Holy Spirit in the baptismal promise.[116]

110. BSELK 890/891,18–20, 892/893,2–4, BC 363.

111. WA 46:148,18; 149,5; 150,15–16.

112. WA 27: 55,24–56,10. See Grönvik, 101–126 on Luther's concept of *signum* as he used it in connection with baptism.

113. WA 27: 60,9–21.

114. WA 27: 59, 10–12.

115. WA 27: 57,30–58,1.

116. WA 46: 168,8–24, 168,30–169,169,29. Cf. Smalcald Articles, III.v., BSELK 766/767,9–15, BC 320; here his interpretation of Duns Scotus rejects Scotus's attributing the power of the sacrament to God's will apart from water and word.

Luther began his final series of baptismal homilies in 1539 by emphasizing once again that the sacrament was not a human invention; God had instituted it. Along with other forms of God's word, it is the vehicle of the Holy Spirit's presence, through which he bestows holiness upon God's saints, upon his church.[117] With a series of illustrations, including marriage and ordination, Luther showed that abuse of an ordinance of God does not invalidate what God establishes.[118] Whores may have men with whom they live and by whom they bear children, but similarity to marriage is not marriage: their way of life lacks God's support and command. Thieves and robbers acquire homes, goods, and money just as those who work for them do, but those who live by theft stand under God's wrath because they have constructed a way of life against God's command, following the devil's instruction. Criminals and magistrates both use the sword, the former against God's will, the latter under his institution. Judges and bandits both hang and torture, but God is at work through the one, not the other.[119] So it is with the use of water, even in sacral ways. Apart from God's command there is no blessing. That word of command that his people baptize creates the reality of God's execution of his will on earth. True prophets, Peter wrote, do not operate on the basis of human will but rather God's word (2 Peter 1:21). God rules his church and does so through his word.[120]

Baptism plunges the child into the eschatological battle with the devil. What God has done in baptism provokes the opposition and attacks of Satan. Luther's comments in his Sexagesima sermon, the fifth on baptism in 1538, are reminiscent of his observation in his 1523 order for baptism that baptizing a child makes a lasting enemy for that baby.[121] "The devil does not stay asleep but is always getting up to make people forget the fruits of their baptisms." That is why Paul warned against such deceit that "seduces us away from Christ our head, whose members we are" (Col 2:8). Baptism is a handful of water and therefore is the object of contempt. All the acts of medieval monastic piety had been preferred to it, but God had placed the promise of salvation in baptism.[122] Baptism will always remain an

117. WA 47: 640,7–643,10/29. Cf WA 47: 644,11/31–646:5/10.
118. WA 27: 34,28–36,2. Cf. the further development of the point, WA 27: 36,2–38,22.
119. WA 47: 647,2–15, 646,31–647,32.
120. WA 47: 647,22–23, 37–38.
121. In his 1523 order for baptism, WA 12: 47,11–20; LW 53: 102.
122. WA 46: 179,6–8; the entire thought is developed, pp. 179–183.

effective weapon in the battle against Satan, Luther claimed, on the basis of his own experience.[123]

Luther reaffirmed the objective nature of God's performative promise in baptism by labeling the baptismal word a covenant. The Ockhamist concept of covenant as an agreement in which human beings also played a contributing role made Luther shy about using the word, but in the case of baptism his qualms disappeared. He experienced very few baptisms of adults in his life. Therefore, he found it natural to see this promise of God as a covenant bestowed by the suzerain as a gift to the receiver of the covenant. "No one can say [of baptism], 'I did this myself.' This covenant proceeds from God without our input."[124] Just as God had established his covenant with the Jews through circumcision, so his pact, treaty, covenant between himself and his people is a promise that he will be our God and that he takes the infant who was circumcised or who is being baptized into his people as his own child. This covenant regards the baptized as God's children and as innocent. Christ functions as chief priest, that is, mediator, of the new covenant just as Abraham did of the old. With the new covenant in baptism "God has established a covenant not just with one people but with the whole world," linking all Christians with one another in the family of God's reclaimed children.[125]

Luther affirmed that baptism cleanses us from sins and numbers the baptized among God's beloved children. In 1538 he made the nature of the baptismal covenant clear once again: "Baptism is an eternal covenant which does not lapse when we fall but raises us up again. If we fall out of the ship, God helps us on board once again. When Christians fall, they always remain in their baptisms, and God binds himself to them so that he will help them when the baptized call upon him." There is no satisfaction that merits baptism before or after the sacrament is administered. There is only the lamb of God, sacrificed from the beginning of the world. He has the power to initiate life and to bring us into death.[126]

In contrast to the medieval church's leaving baptism at the beginning of life in the memory of an initiation that did not cover the sins of today,[127] Luther insisted that believers live each day under the impact of their baptisms. "Christian life is nothing else than a daily baptism. . . . For

123. WA 27: 33,3–14. On baptism as God's work in Luther's baptismal preaching, see Martin Ferel, *Gepredigte Taufe, eine homiletische Untersuchung zur Taufpredigt bei Luther* (Tübingen: Mohr Siebeck, 1969), 128–149.

124. WA 27: 33,27–29.

125. WA 27: 50,16–52,25.

126. WA 46: 172,29–35, 12–17.

127. *Prelude, On the Babylonian Captivity of the Church,* WA 6: 527,9–12, LW 36:57–58.

we must keep at it without ceasing, always purging whatever pertains to the old Adam so that whatever belongs to the new creature may come forth." That means that the old creature's sinful habits must be reduced and set aside while gentleness, patience, and other virtues grow. "This is the right use of baptism . . . Where this does not take place but rather the old creature is given free rein and continually grows stronger, baptism is not being used but resisted." Loss of faith renders baptism "a mere unfruitful sign." In its rhythm of dying and rising with Christ, baptism continues to "snatch us from the jaws of the devil and makes us God's own. It overcomes and takes away sin and daily strengthens the new person." It is "the daily garment" (Gal 3:27) that Christians wear continually as they produce the fruits of faith. [128]

Luther did not prescribe a mode of baptism, but a casual observation in the *Large Catechism* suggests that "this act or ceremony consists of being dipped into the water, which covers us completely, and being drawn out again." He had experienced the immersion of infants in the larger baptismal fonts of the Middle Ages and treasured the value of immersion for illustrating Romans 6 and Colossians 2, with the burial of sinful identities and the raising up of the new life in Christ.[129] Whatever its mode, however, this water combined with the promise of death to sinful identity and new life in the identity that Christ bestows and enables had become the focal point and abiding lodestar of Luther's life.

The Lord's Supper

Luther's teaching on the Lord's Supper evolved quickly once the implications of his growing concept of God's word, and especially his concept of "promise," became clear. Luther's initial published writing on the Lord's Supper, his *Sermon on the Blessed Sacrament of the Holy, True Body of Christ* (1519), emphasized the communion or community that believers experience as they partake of Christ's body and blood together, in contrast to the concentration of believers' attention on the spiritual benefits they hoped to accrue for themselves through their individual participation in the ritual of the mass. The focus of later treatments of the sacrament of the altar paid less attention to this emphasis on the communion of the believers who received Christ's body and blood, but the human community remained essential to his teaching on the sacrament. This treatise did also view the

128. BSELK 1120/1129,20 1132/1133,30, BC 465–467.
129. BSELK 1126/1127,24–1128/1129,19, BC 464–465.

Lord's Supper as a "ford, bridge, door, ship, or stretcher, by and in which we pass from this world into eternal life," through faith.[130]

The next summer, Luther's *Sermon on the New Testament* appeared in print, reflecting his maturing understanding of the power of God's word as promise to which saving trust responds and grasps. This insistence on trust in the promise of forgiveness "for you" rejected any use of the Lord's Supper that sought to make human participation in it effective apart from faith.[131]

Luther's *Prelude, On the Babylonian Captivity of the Church*, appearing in October 1520, recapitulated and deepened the ideas of the *Sermon on the Blessed Sacrament*. It did so as a result of the redefinition of the church as the "communion of saints" in his *On the Papacy of Rome* of late June 1520,[132] as further developed in his *Open Letter to the Christian Nobility* of about the same time.[133] This redefinition of the church restructured the power relationships within the church by placing ultimate power of God's word in this word itself rather than in its administration by the hierarchy of the church. It assessed the entire sacramental-sacerdotal system of the medieval church and presented Luther's revised definition of the word "sacrament." That resulted in discarding four of the medieval sacraments, with only baptism, the Lord's Supper, and confession and absolution remaining.

The *Prelude, On the Babylonian Captivity of the Church* found three serious faults in the medieval church's teaching and practice of the Lord's Supper. His critique grew out of the context of Luther's pastoral concerns, his reading of Scripture, and his deeper understanding of God's word of gospel as promise and its power to deliver forgiveness and life. First, his critique of the refusal of the chalice to the laity labeled it an oppressive tyranny over God's word in Christ's institution of the sacrament and over the laity, contradicting Christ's command. He found no reason for refusing lay people the blood of Christ. This prohibition was designed only to exalt the power and position of the priest.[134] Second, he called into question any use of the Aristotelian concept of "substance" to try to explain the presence of Christ's body and blood in the Supper. He knew

130. WA2: 742,5–747,3; LW35: 49–56.

131. WA 2: 751,18–752,24, LW 35: 63–65; WA 6: 364,14–373,8, LW 35: 93–106. Luther repeated this critique often, cf. *The Misuse of the Mass*, 1521, WA 8: 506–537; LW 36: 162–198, and *The Adoration of the Sacrament*, 1523, WA 11: 431–56; LW 36: 275–305.

132. WA 6: 285–328, LW 32: 55–104. Cf. Denis Janz, *Martin Luther's* The Church Held Captive in Babylon: *Latin-English Edition with a New Translation and Introduction* (Oxford: Oxford University Press, 2019), 19–28.

133. WA 6: 404–469, LW 44: 115–217.

134. WA 6: 502,1–507,34, LW 36: 19–28.

that the fifteenth-century theologian Pierre d'Ailly, following arguments of Duns Scotus and William of Ockham,[135] had suggested that apart from the church's having labeled what happens in the sacrament as "transubstantiation," "consubstantiation" could just as well explain that presence. Luther found all such talk of substance unacceptable as an attempt to break through the mystery of God's delivering forgiveness and life in the sacrament.[136] As time went on, Luther's objections to transubstantiation became ever sharper because this theory seemed to reinforce a superstitious dependence on the material elements that that was quite contrary to God's use of these selected external elements to communicate his promise.[137]

Luther's chief concern regarding medieval understanding and practice of the Lord's Supper in what was popularly called "the mass" focused on the interpretation of the sacrament as the repetition of Christ's sacrifice for sin. With all other Protestant reformers, he recognized that on the popular level attendance at the mass and witnessing the ritual actions of the priest was regarded as meritorious, able to attain God's favor and power for benefits temporal and eternal. Luther had learned the sacramental teaching of his scholastic instructors. He knew that their teaching, though more refined than popular belief, also held the celebration of the mass and participation in its liturgy to be a vital means of gaining grace, whether one partook of the Lord's body or not. Luther repudiated this fundamental element of the ritualistic-hierarchical system of the medieval church, especially in its popular form, as a denial of the sole efficacy of Christ's work in dying and rising for sinners. Furthermore, in addition to dependence on ritual performance, he abhorred the commercialization of the liturgy of the mass, the sale of it as a commodity to support the priesthood.[138]

His own sacramental teaching centered, in the case of the Lord's Supper, on its nature as a last will and testament, "a promise made by one about to die, in which he designates his bequest and appoints his heirs . . . what we call the mass is a promise of the forgiveness of sins made to us by God and . . . confirmed by the death of the Son of God."[139] Thus, he avoided the term "covenant" in the case of the Lord's Supper because it does not express

135. Marilyn McCord Adams, *Some Later Medieval Theories of the Eucharist: Thomas Aquinas, Giles of Rome, Duns Scotus, and William Ockham* (Oxford: Oxford University Press, 2010), 126–127, 164.
136. WA 6: 508,1–512,6, LW 36: 28–35.
137. Carl F. Wisløff, *The Gift of Communion: Luther's Controversy with Rome on Eucharistic Sacrifice*, trans. Joseph M. Shaw (Minneapolis: Augsburg, 1964); Wolfgang Simon, *Die Messopfertheologie Martin Luther. Voraussetzungen, Genese, Gestalt und Rezeption* (Tübingen: Mohr/Siebeck, 2003).
138. WA 6: 512,7–536,33, LW 36: 35–57.
139. WA 6: 513,24–36, LW 36: 38.

the concept of testament, the intended meaning of the Greek διαθήκη in this case. The bequest of a person's treasure to another person establishes the special relationship of benefactor and heir. God's action and gift elicit faith: "where there is the Word of the promising God, there must necessarily be the faith of the accepting human being." This faith produces a life of love for others that fulfills God's law.[140] Luther also advocated in *Babylonian Captivity* for the abolition of several abuses, including private masses and masses for the dead.[141] Seventeen years later, in the Smalcald Articles, he repeated his withering critique of these ritual practices, including purgatory, pilgrimages, fraternities for paying for masses for deceased members, veneration of relics, indulgences, and invocation of the saints.[142] In the five years following 1520 Luther developed his teaching on the Lord's Supper as a bestowal of the promise of forgiveness, life and salvation with treatises including *The Misuse of the Mass* (1521),[143] *Receiving Both Kinds in the Sacrament* (1522),[144] *The Adoration of the Sacrament* (1523),[145] and *The Abomination of the Secret Mass* (1525).[146]

By 1524, however, the focus of his public teaching was shifting from the power of the sacrament as an expression of God's promise to the nature of the presence of Christ in the Supper. Luther saw no reason to doubt that Christ's body and blood are truly present and received in, and with, the consecrated bread and wine of the Lord's Supper. He refused to define how that could take place since he did not wish to go beyond what Scripture states. He was able to understand Christ's words instituting the Lord's Supper literally. His linguistic and epistemological framework acknowledged that biblical writers had often employed metaphor, and he explained at length why the words of Christ, "this is my body," and "this is my blood" should not be interpreted as metaphor.[147] His Ockhamistic understanding of God's power to order the world and thus create the ways in which his universe functions freed him from metaphysical hedges against such a joining of the spiritual and the material elements of God's creation. Familiarity with Platonic and Aristotelian distinctions or separations of the material and spiritual had not convinced him that they applied in every case. All things material and spiritual existed in relationship to

140. WA 6: 514,13–25, LW 36: 39.
141. WA 6: 525,13–526,4, LW 36: 55–56.
142. BSELK 728/729,15–738/739,14, 14, BC 301–306.
143. WA 8: 482–563, LW 36: 133–230.
144. WA 10,2: 11–41, LW 36: 237–267.
145. WA 11: 431–456, LW 36: 275–305.
146. WA 18: 22–36, LW 36: 311–328.
147. WA 26: 379,16–418,25, LW 37: esp. 252–278.

the Creator, and his decisions on their use determined what they did and how they served divine purposes.

Critiques of Luther's understanding of the presence of Christ in the Lord's Supper came first from his colleague Andreas Bodenstein von Karlstadt. His views sprang from his training in the Realist school of thinking that placed reality in the divine ideas in heaven and from a traditional popular call for reform that had diminished the role of the sacraments.[148] Soon criticism also appeared in the writings of the reformer of Zurich, Ulrich Zwingli, a product of both Scotist Aristotelianism and Platonic and Neo-Platonic streams within biblical humanism.[149] Basel's reformer, Johannes Oecolampadius, had been closer to the Wittenberg circle, but his humanist training led him to share Zwingli's fear that Luther's teaching upheld a superstitious, quasi-magical understanding of the sacraments' visible elements. Luther argued that their teaching that saw the sacramental bread and wine as merely symbolic disregarded the Holy Spirit's ability to comfort and forgive through the promise when communicated with outward means. Luther expressed himself at length in 1525–1528, demonstrating how seriously he regarded the external instruments of the Holy Spirit's work.[150]

In *The Sacrament of the Body and Blood of Christ* Luther argued that God uses material elements, including Christ's flesh and blood, human language, and the sacramental elements, to convey the benefits of Christ's death and resurrection to his people. Beyond human reason, God's use of human tools of communication provides an anchor for believers in their experience of hearing and learning to trust God's promise in the several ways in which he conveys it. Luther argued that God's way of accomplishing his will consistently defies human reason. God's Word, the institution by Christ himself, trumps those who cannot understand and thus deny how this is possible.[151] Luther's "theology of the cross" held that faith born of hearkening to what God says eclipses reason in the matters of God's operation on earth. Therefore, Luther judged that Karlstadt, Zwingli, and Oecolampadius were "mak[ing] God's glory an altogether earthly and carnal thing, just as it would be inglorious for a worldly king to be

148. See pp. 248–249.

149. On the Scotist influence on Zwingli, see Daniel Bolliger, *Infiniti contemplatio: Grundzüge der Scotus- und Scotismusrezeption im Werk Huldrych Zwinglis* (Leiden: Brill, 2003).

150. The course of arguments over power and presence in the sacraments is carefully traced in Burnett, *Debating the Sacraments*. The classic treatment of these disputes is Walter Köhler, *Zwingli und Luther*, 2 vols. (Leipzig, Heinsius, 1924, Gütersloh, Bertelsmann, 1953). See also Hermann Sasse, *This is My Body* (Minneapolis, Augsburg, 1959).

151. WA 19: 482–523, LW 36: 335–361.

hanged or crucified. But the glory of our God is precisely that for our sakes he comes down to the very depths, into human flesh, into bread, into our mouth, our heart, our bosom; moreover, for our sakes he allows himself to be treated ingloriously both on the cross and on the altar."[152]

In the early course of Luther's call for reform, the university disputation had gone public. In these very public exchanges, arguments were direct and sharp, both from his foes,[153] and from Luther, especially in *That These Words of Christ, "This Is My Body," etc., Still Stand Firm against the Ravers*[154] (1527),[155] and *Confession concerning Christ's Supper* (1528).[156] Zwingli thought Luther's language of "in" and "under" to describe the relationship of bread and body revealed his use of contradictory definitions. Luther more clearly and precisely compared Zwingli's contention that the bread represents the body with Oecolampadius's position that the bread is a sign of the body and Karlstadt's argument that Jesus said the "this" in the words of institution while pointing to his own body at the table.[157] Luther provided extensive grammatical and syntactical support for his position[158] and carefully reviewed the relevant Scripture texts[159] of his opponents. They replied in kind. Both parties cited patristic evidence extensively as well.[160] Luther believed that his opponents' interpretations had Christological implications of the most serious kinds, leading them into a kind of latter-day Nestorianism. Zwingli held that Jesus's ascension to the "right hand of the Father" eliminated any possibility that his body and blood could be on many altars since that is impossible for human beings. His human nature must remain in heaven. Luther replied, "The Scriptures teach us that God's right hand is not a specific place in which a body must or may be . . . but is God's almighty power, which at one and the same time can be nowhere and yet must be everywhere. It cannot be

152. WA 23:156,28–34, LW 37: 72.
153. Köhler, *Luther und Zwingli*, 1:619–729; cf. Zwingli's *Amica Exegesis*, 1527, CR 92: 548–758, *Klare Unterricht*, 1526, CR 91:773–862, *Das diese Worte*, 1527, CR 92: 795–977.
154. Luther coined the term "Schwärmer," here translated "Raver," often translated "Enthusiast," from the cognate of the English "swarm" referring to those who, he believed, ignored Scripture and used reason to spin their own ideas. He applied it to Anabaptists and spiritualists first but then also to those who differed from him regarding Christ's presence in the Lord's Supper. Cf. Amy Nelson Burnett, "Luther and the *Schwärmer*," in OHMLT, 511–524.
155. WA 23: 64–283, LW 37: 13–159.
156. WA 26: 261–509, LW 37: 161–372.
157. WA 23: 88,33–124,25, LW 37 :30–51.
158. WA 26: 437,30–445,17, LW 37: 294–303.
159. WA 26: 445,18–498,30, LW 37: 303–360.
160. Gottfried Hoffmann, *Kirchenväterzitate in der Abendmahlskontroverse zwischen Oekolampad, Zwingli, Luther und Melanchthon* (Göttingen: Edition Ruprecht, 2011).

[restricted to] any one place."[161] Because the human nature could share the divine nature's characteristic of being present wherever God wills to be present in whatever form, Christ's body and blood could be present in the Lord's Supper. Luther explained that Scripture reveals that Christ has several ways of being present, including in the "circumscribed corporeal mode of his Incarnation" and in the "incomprehensible, spiritual mode" of presence that enabled him to move through the locked door on Easter evening (John 10:19). Luther did not venture an explanation of a mode that would clarify his presence in the Supper but instead simply held to what Christ said in instituting the Supper.[162]

The rising necessity of establishing harmony among those opposing the papacy within the German Empire created political pressure for the reformers of Basel and Zurich to reconcile with Luther and those who agreed with him. They met in a colloquy at Marburg in October 1529. They came to agreement on fourteen articles of doctrine but could not agree on the nature of Christ's presence in the sacrament.[163] This exchange marked a temporary end to mutual public criticism though trust broke down with public utterances from both sides until Zwingli died on the battlefield on October 11, 1531.

Martin Bucer, reformer in Strasbourg, struggled to find common ground after creating suspicion of his views by translating portions of a sacramental treatise of Luther's Wittenberg colleague Johannes Bugenhagen on the Lord's Supper in such a way as to make them seem Zwinglian. Philip Melanchthon strove to reconcile Luther with Bucer, and this led to the formulation of the "Wittenberg Concord" of 1536. Both sides agreed that "with the bread and wine the body and blood of Christ are truly and essentially present, distributed, and received. . . . and the body and blood of Christ are truly distributed even to the unworthy; the unworthy truly receive the body and blood when the sacrament is conducted according to Christ's command." Three points of compromise mark this wording. Bucer affirmed that Christ's body and blood are received "with" but not "in" or "under" the elements; Luther held the three prepositions to be synonymous in significance in this case, no more than attempts to confess the mystery of the presence. Luther's definition of "reception of the body and blood through the mouth" (*manducatio oralis*) was missing in the "Concord." Instead of Luther's "reception by the impious" (*manducatio impiorum*), designed to give assurance that God's Word alone effects

161. WA 23: 133,19–134,11, LW 37: 57.
162. WA 26: 326,12–338,17, LW 37: 214–220.
163. See reports on the colloquy in WA30,3:160–171, LW38:15–89.

Christ's presence, an almost synonymous expression, "partaking by the unworthy" (*manducatio indignorum*), was adopted since Bucer found it acceptable.[164] The next year in his *Smalcald Articles*, Luther defined Christ's presence simply: "the bread and the wine in the Supper are the true body and blood of Christ and they are not only offered to and received by upright Christians but also by evil people."[165]

Two factors, determinative of Luther's theology throughout, explain his fiercely determined stand on the presence of Christ's body and blood and the power of the promise in sacramental form to bestow forgiveness, life, and salvation. He wished to remain faithful to the Scripture and found no metaphysical reason to abandon a literal interpretation of this text in this case. Furthermore, he did not wish to lose the comfort that he found the promise in sacramental form gives to troubled consciences. His *Large Catechism* taught that the Supper "is appropriately called food of the soul, for it nourishes and strengthens the new creature. . . . [It] is given as a daily food and sustenance so that our faith may be refreshed and strengthened and that it may not succumb in the struggle but become stronger and stronger."[166] Indeed, "because he offers and promises forgiveness of sins, it can be received in no other way than by faith. This faith he himself demands in the Word when he says, 'given FOR YOU' and 'shed FOR YOU'. . . . The treasure is opened and placed at everyone's door, yes upon the table, but it also falls to you to take it and confidently believe that it is just as the words tell you."[167]

Ockhamist presuppositions permitted Luther to be comfortable with the possibility of God's using the material elements of his creation in executing his saving will and sustaining God's relationship with his children through a dramatic form of his promise of new life in Christ. Pastoral concerns focused his attention on finding the comfort of the gospel of Christ's death and resurrection in God's address in Scripture and the various forms of communication that arise out of it. His doctrine of creation and his understanding of human nature pointed him to God's desire to engage his people with all the senses. Thus, Luther processed the medieval heritage of sacramental practice with a sharp critique. He

164. Gordon A. Jensen, *The Wittenberg Concord: Creating Space for Dialogue* (Minneapolis: Fortress Press, 2018). Bucer is often placed in the Reformed camp, but following the Wittenberg Concord, he sent students to Wittenberg and engaged some in Strassburg (e.g., Johann Marbach, Bucer's successor as superintendent in Strasbourg, and Ludwig Rabus, as well as Cunman Flinsbach, who became superintendent in Zweibrücken).

165. BSELK 766/767,19–23, BC 320.

166. BSELK 1138/1139,23–30, BC 469.

167. BSELK 1142/1143,11–18, BC 470.

rejected the stream of thought that made what he regarded as a magical use of sacramental words and elements possible, for it disregarded the necessity of faith and thus failed to support the relationship of believers to Christ. Equally vehemently, he rejected all views that spiritualized God's sacramental approach to his chosen people. He found in baptism and the Lord's Supper, as in the oral and written word of God, the created, material means by which God gives the forgiveness of sins, life, and salvation.

AS A DEAR CHILD ASKS A DEAR FATHER

In whatever form God spoke to him with his law or his promise, Luther responded in prayer. His Small Catechism prescribed boldness and confidence to those who pray, the kind of audacity and assurance that children have when approaching a loving parent.[168] The Creator built conversation with himself into the nature of his human creatures. He designed them to be in conversation and in the community to which it leads, just as conversation and community characterize what he reveals of himself from Genesis 1 on. He speaks, and he longs for response. That is why he sought out Adam and Eve when they tried to avoid continuing the conversation with him.

Believers pray, Luther postulated, because God commands prayer as an integral part of their lives. Furthermore, he promises to hear prayer and to respond appropriately, in his wisdom and concern. He also places the words of the Lord's Prayer in their mouths, Luther observed. The reformer praised the Lord's Prayer as a model prayer, a sufficient expression of all that Christians can want from their providing Father.[169] His exposition of the Lord's Prayer in the Small Catechism drew believers into the sanctified use of God's name, the delivery of his providing and protecting rule, and the carrying out of his will in the world around them in the first three petitions. Without our requesting it, God's name is holy, his reign is active, and his will takes place, but Jesus offered the prayer so that these activities take place in the midst of his people and with their participation as instruments of the Holy Spirit. Each case—the hallowing of his name, coming of his kingdom, and the execution of his will—comes to pass because the Holy Spirit is working through God's word. In response to that word, its hearers plunge into the tasks God has appointed for them in bringing his name, his rule, and his will to those around them. The

168. BSELK 874/875,5–13, BC 356.
169. BSELK 1070/1071,18 1080/1081,20, BC 441–443.

final four petitions call upon God to support those who pray actively by providing temporal blessings, spiritual restoration, and protection against the devil, the world, and their own rebellious desires.[170]

Alongside the Lord's Prayer, the psalms provided Luther models for his praying. His active conversation with God had taken on text in the cloister above all through the psalms that were sung daily in the seven hours of devotion. Luther commented, "the psalter is a practice field of faith and the spirit. Whoever reads the psalms without faith, reads them perceiving nothing but darkness and coldness in them. Such a person continues living without light and warmth. Faith, however, lives and grows only in suffering. The harder it is, the more beautifully it blossoms."[171] The psalms accompanied Luther from his days in the cloister to his dying moments. They taught him to praise and to demand, to lament and to call down curses upon God's foes.

Luther knew that some people felt fearful that they might pray in false fashion. He responded,

> Imagine that the richest and most powerful emperor commanded a poor beggar to ask for whatever he might desire and was prepared to give lavish, royal gifts, and the fool asked only for a dish of beggar's broth. He would rightly be considered a rogue and a scoundrel who had made a mockery of the imperial majesty's command and was unworthy to come into his presence. Just so, it is a great reproach and dishonor to God if we, to whom he offers and pledges so many inexpressible blessings, despise them or lack confidence that we shall receive them and scarcely venture to ask for a morsel of bread.[172]

The reformer rebuked such doubt of God's generous care with indignation.

Luther prayed for everything. Initially, he had followed the stream of medieval interpretation of the fourth petition that identified the bread as spiritual bread, Christ himself, also as he gives himself in the Lord's Supper. As his appreciation for the goodness of God's presence and providence in daily life grew, he embraced the interpretation of this petition as a request for a continuation of all the temporal blessings God gives, with a list that includes environmental factors including good weather and protection from storms, hail, fire, and flood along with health in the face of plagues and illness and air that is not poisoned, an act of Satan. He expressed a plea for God's help in preserving good family life, ensuring prosperous practice

170. BSELK 874/875,1–882/883,6, BC 356–358.
171. WA 5: 351,26–28.
172. BSELK 1088/1089,3–20, BC 447.

of occupation, good neighbors, and good friends.[173] He was certain that God desired to have his input regarded in the course of Luther's daily life.

The reformer used the Lord's Prayer particularly as a weapon against the three sources of temptation, the devil, the world, and the desires of the rebellious flesh. As noted in chapter 2, he viewed the temptation to commit acts contrary to God's law as tools of these foes. The evils from which believers pray to be delivered include "poverty, disgrace, death, and in short, all the tragic misery and heartache, of which there is so incalculably much on earth." The devil "vents his anger by causing accidents and injury to our bodies. He crushes some and drives others to insanity; some he drowns in water, and many he hounds to suicide or other dreadful catastrophes." Prayer remains as the weapon against all the devices of the archenemy.[174] The entire Lord's Prayer pleads for deliverance from "all kinds of evil—affecting body or soul, property or reputations" and asks God "when our final hour comes, . . . grant us a blessed end and take us by grace from this valley of tears to himself in heaven."[175]

There Luther planned to continue the conversation forever. That was the nature of the relationship that God had practiced in Eden before the fall and died and rose to renew as the heart of the reality of our humanness.

173. BSELK 1096/1097,26–1098/1099,23, BC 451.
174. BSELK 1106/1107,28–1110/1111.5, BC 455–456.
175. BSELK 880/881,15–30, BC 358.

5.

The Reformer Face to Face with Himself

Luther coram seipso

I LISTEN, THEREFORE I LEARN WHO I AM

Attention to one's self, self-awareness, is part of being human. Posing the question "How do I appear in other people's eyes?" is part of being human in community. Often sinners arrogantly overestimate their own capacity and significance. On the other hand, they may also shrink in desperation and despair from the fullness of God's gift of life because they underestimate what God has enabled them to be and do as they look into their own hearts. Robert Burns's gift of seeing ourselves as others see us contributes significantly to how we see ourselves, how we conduct ourselves, and how we find balance and peace in daily life.

Human beings evaluate themselves according to some standard, perhaps a standard they set for themselves but almost always with criteria set by others. Thus, we assess who we are, *coram seipso* ("evaluating myself"), in the contexts of the other *coram* relationships. Luther did not conceive of this kind of formal introspection, although he did record times when his thoughts turned to examination of his relationship with God. Preaching to the congregation in Kemberg, near Wittenberg, in 1531, Luther referred to his hearers' relationships with God, other people, and themselves,[1] but he had no concept of "self" in the modern sense.

1. WA 34,2: 108,24–109,5.

Nonetheless, Gerhard Ebeling was correct when he spoke of the reformer face to face with himself.[2]

In assessing my own identity and integrity, the most important question is, "Who does God say that I am?"[3] The young Brother Martin had a despairing answer to that question. Quite parallel to his fear of facing God was his fear of facing himself. The young frater and theology student was trapped in the Ockhamist solution to the Bible's twin assertions: first, God is Almighty Creator and thus completely responsible for everything that is and happens in all creation; second, God holds human beings responsible for all for which they have been given to do. Following Gabriel Biel, the source of much of Luther's teachers' thinking and whose ideas found their foundation in the thought of William of Ockham, Luther struggled with what his teachers taught him: that in his grace Almighty God had so structured human life that in their sinfulness human beings were to "do their best" "out of their purely natural powers." The young Augustinian brother wrestled to believe that if he were to be able to offer God whatever meager good works he was able to perform, his "incongruent" or "insufficient" merit would earn the divine grace that he needed to produce truly God-pleasing works. With the assistance of these works, believers then gained "condignent" or "worthy" merit—God's favor and eternal life.[4] Unlike most of his contemporaries, Luther faced his own thoughts and deeds with a brutal honesty that recognized how flawed his best efforts to please God were.

Luther came to terms with the tension between God's responsibility for all that he had made and his holding human beings responsible for being all that they can be as his creatures by not resolving that tension. Instead, he addressed specific situations in which hearers and readers might find themselves by addressing them with appropriate words of either law or gospel, focusing on their own actions or Christ's actions on their behalf. For him, the tension between sin and life as a forgiven sinner, between law and gospel, remained throughout life on earth. This provided proof that not only is the nature of God as Trinity a profound mystery. Being a responsible human creature, created in God's image, as the creation of

2. Gerhard Ebeling's masterful treatment of Luther's understanding of what it means to be human is found in his *Lutherstudien*, volume 2, *Disputatio de Homine*, issued in three separate parts (Tübingen: Mohr/Siebeck, 1977, 1982, 1989).

3. Cf. the title of William W. Schumacher's *Who Do I Say That You Are? Anthropology and the Theology of the Theosis in the Finnish School of Tuoma Mannermaa* (Eugene, OR: Wipf & Stock, 2010).

4. Heiko Augustinus Oberman, *The Harvest of Medieval Theology* (Cambridge, MA: Harvard University Press, 1963), 131–184.

an Almighty Creator, is also a profound mystery. This mystery of our humanity is compounded by the mystery of sin and evil, and especially by its continuation in the daily life of the baptized believer.

This tension forms the context in which to understand Luther's affirmation of human "passivity." His use of this word asserts the creaturely nature of the human being. God is ultimately responsible for each human being's existence and the continuation of that existence. God alone is responsible for the believer's reborn status as child of God. But the creatures that are human—and thus shaped in the image of God—have their own full responsibility to be the creatures whom God made and called them to be. Every human being is created and called to be as an active, thinking, willing, feeling creature because every human person is fashioned in the Creator's image. Precisely what that means in its fullest dimensions remains hidden in mystery. But God communicates both his affirmation of his love for the faithful—love is received, a passive "act"—and his expectations for their active behavior.

LUTHER'S FOUNDATION OF BEING HUMAN AND ARISTOTLE'S

In the analysis of the Wittenberg reformer's reactions to Aristotle and to the medieval use of Aristotle in its German context, it is apparently easy to ignore two fundamental factors essential for assessing the relationship between Luther and Aristotle. First, some scholars have failed to recognize the fact that Luther's extensive use of Aristotle's categories of analysis occurred within the framework of his presupposition that God created, and remains in relationship with, all creation that these categories describe. Second, some ascribe to Aristotle's "ontology" a primary claim on the term "reality" that outside the heritage of Graeco-Roman thinking often has little or no validity.[5]

Wilfried Joest posed the question whether Luther might have accepted another "ontology" than Aristotle's that did not proceed from God's revelation of himself but from human observation and experience.[6] Aristotle had devised an analysis of reality that had no place for a lively, communicating personal God. It is not totally clear whether his Unmoved Mover, operating in an already existing something, had personal characteristics. This Ultimate Mover did not communicate with human beings, in any

5. Joest, *Ontologie*, 14–15.
6. Joest, *Ontologie*, 130–136.

case. Thus, the answer to Joest's rhetorical question is clear: the basis of reality lies in the person of the God of Abraham, Isaac, and Jacob, who came into human form and flesh as Jesus of Nazareth. Real humanness centers in fearing, loving, and trusting in the God who promises new life and restoration from sin in Jesus Christ. Therefore, the root of the problem with Aristotle lay for Luther not in any peculiar formulation of the Stagarite or any particular flaw in his mode of analysis.

The Creator's word not only brought everything into existence. His continuing to speak in his creation sustains its forward movement in the phenomena of time and history that God also built into the structure of his universe. In contrast to some streams of thought in mystical traditions and others in the Renaissance revival of Neo-platonic ideas, both scholastic Realism and scholastic Ockhamism had strictly distinguished Creator and creature. That the second person of the Holy Trinity could cross that line and become God and human being in one person remained the singular exception. His incarnation remained a mystery beyond speculative powers of the creatures. Luther followed his Western theological forbearers in this regard. He drew a strict boundary between the Creator and everything created, including the creature created in his own image and likeness.[7] He constructed his worlds, Luther believed, in six days, and rested. That sabbath rest continues in his governance of its operation on the long eighth day.

As Joest points out, all attempts to answer questions regarding the ultimate origin of reality, and its goal and purpose apart from God's address in his Word made flesh and in the proclamation of the prophets and apostles, inevitably miss the mark. God determines what reality is because he created it and because creatures, especially sinful creatures, simply cannot command and fully comprehend the fullness of what reality is. Luther's perception of what it means to be human centered on the intensely personal relationship with the Creator who identified himself to Moses as "the one who is what he is," the God who made pledges to Abraham, who preserved Isaac and rescued Jacob, who came into human flesh as Jesus of Nazareth as he revealed who he is as Trinity.

Nonetheless, Luther had learned to use his rationality within the system set in place by Aristotle. He never abandoned much of the understanding of the makeup of human beings that Aristotle had bequeathed his heirs over the centuries. Aristotle's logic made sense to Luther except when it tried to invade the person of God himself and the fullness of what it is to be

7. Joest, *Ontologie*, 61–68.

his human creature. Therefore, Aristotle could do no better than to define the human creature as an *animal rationalis*, a living being. This human *animal* operated with reason to figure out the eternal law that governed the proper existence of all things. This law determined the proper ways for human beings to deal with the form and material, the potential and the activity, the substance and accidents or individual characteristics of all that they encountered in this world and life.[8]

Luther used much of Aristotle's terminology in speaking of human creatures, but he defined being human with more depth than had Aristotle. Being human is at its very center fearing, loving, and trusting in God above everything else in God's creation. Turned toward God with their entire beings, people cannot fathom with the gift of reason the nature of God or the core of their own humanity. They simply listen to his voice and accept his limits to human knowledge.

As noted above, Luther never abandoned Aristotle's means of analyzing the physical universe, composed of substances and accidents, and he sensed divine forms or patterns for everything. But those divine ideas did not constitute the ultimate reality of every item in creation. God's active speaking did. Behind whatever human research could ascertain about the reality around us stands the relationship of the Creator to his creation. Luther enjoyed his colleagues' probing of the world here and now, as they launched into dissection to learn more about the human body, as they introduced field trips into the forest to find out more about plants, as they adapted Copernicus's mathematical description of the stars.[9] For Luther, nature did not possess an independent integrity of his own, as something alongside human beings and God. Each element of the natural world has life as God's noun and continues to exist only in and through his action. This observation expresses, for Luther, what his being creator and almighty really means. His personal relationship to human hairs and to sparrows sustains them as his creatures (Matt 10:29–31). In commenting on Ecclesiastes 3:20 the professor observed that human beings and animals share the same dust and the same breath as products of their common Creator. Both die, and Luther ventured no ultimate explanation

8. Generally supportive of this narrowly focused assessment of Luther's use of the terms "Aristotle," "philosophy," and "reason" as enemies of the truth is Rudolf Malter, "Luther und die Geschichte der Metaphysik," in *Thesaurus Lutheri. Auf der Suche nach neuen Paradigmen der Luther-Forschung*, ed. Tuomo Mannermaa, Anja Ghiselli, and Simo Peura (Helsinki: Luther-Agricola Gesellschaft, 1987), 37–62.

9. Robert Kolb, "The Wittenberg Impact on University Education and the Christian Liberal Arts," in *My Savior's Guest: A Festschrift in Honor of Erling Teigen*, ed. Thomas Rank (New York: Lulu Press, 2021), 91–108; see chapter 6, pp. XX.

for the visitation of death in God's good creation, human or animal. What differentiates them is that God gave his spirit to his human creatures.[10] In the final analysis Luther sensed that even in the nature that God had given into human care and investigation, there is more than meets the eye, namely the presence of God. He is there in every thing there is.

Without conceiving of a personal Creator who continues to be present and active in the ongoing history of his creatures, Aristotle posited that eternal law and human compliance with it hold life together. He therefore presumed that change and variation threaten that order. He could not grasp the biblical sense that historical movement and the passage of time take place—take their place in God's unfolding of his plan for his universe—under the watchful eye of the Creator. Luther recognized that God wrote such development and change into the very nature of his world and his human creatures. Such development and movement do not by their very nature contain elements of disruption. Aristotle's perception of decay and destruction in his estimate of life around him arose from the fact that he was judging reality in its fallen state. Because the philosopher constructed his view of change in the creation apart from the presence of a personal Creator who preserves his creation and provides for it in the midst of history, with its rises and declines of empires and personal fortunes, he desired to the extent possible a static universe.

Luther agreed that there are essential elements of God's creation that remain as he made them. For example, what constitutes humanity does not change. Human nature and experience remain safe and guaranteed in the midst of the constant change that human experience enjoys and suffers in every culture.[11] God had so constituted the character and essence of human life. Philosopher George Steiner observes that while the Judaic sense of the Creation and of the Mosaic reception of the transmission of the Law has "no temporal singularity, no enigmatic historicity," "there is a strict, utterly mysterious temporality in the coming and ministry of Christ. Being so naturally, if inexplicably, immersed in actual time, the meaning of that coming, the normative consequences of the sayings of Christ and of the writings of the Apostles, must, as it were, be stabilized in eternity."[12] Luther saw specific historical roots in the Torah, to be sure, but he would have agreed that the historical intervention of the second person of the Trinity, as the human Jesus Christ, shared with human beings not

10. WA 20:70,19–71,21, LW 15: 59–60.
11. Cf. Mark Thompson, "Luther on God and History," in OHMLT, 127–142; and John M. Headley, *Luther's View of Church History* (New Haven: Yale University Press, 1963).
12. George Steiner, *Real Presences* (Chicago: University of Chicago Press, 1989), 44.

only flesh and blood but also place and time, specific years in the domain of Caesar Augustus, Quirinius, and Pontius Pilate. So, with every human creature. Try as they may, creatures cannot avoid the passage of time and the flow of history. At the same time, they cannot alter what God has deemed them to be, what remains constant in their makeup and what is designed to undergo alteration. No creatures can "self-actualize" or invent personal sets of laws for themselves since all remains in the hands of God, and they find their true existence within his design of human life. He has placed them where they find themselves in the course of history's flow. He remains their constant companion in its further course.

Within the framework of this sensitivity to the historical nature of creation and of Luther's Ockhamist perception of God's being at home in the created world and the ongoing passage of time, Luther became aware of flaws in the medieval perception that placed God's realm above, rather than in the midst of, the created order. Medieval theology and piety had constructed an interpretation of God's modus operandi that Volker Leppin has identified as embracing the re-presentation of the biblical story that made its actual place in human history secondary to its being re-presented in sacramental form, most essentially in the mass. According to this view, God breaks down the distance between Christ's crucifixion in Palestine fifteen hundred years earlier and the Germans' being able to grasp its benefits through participation in the mass in Luther's day.[13] This perception fed—and fed on—the allegorical method of biblical interpretation, for this method too often quickly abandoned the concrete historical reports of Scripture for the realm of philosophical principles and doctrinal formulations derived from them that floated above actual concrete human life as experienced by individuals.

Luther exulted in the Holy Spirit's preoccupation with the small, even trivial, details of the lives of the patriarchs and the particularities of daily life in the historical contexts of both the ancient world and of his own central European milieu.[14] Especially the Old Testament presented him with a "mirror of daily life."[15] The biblical narratives make concrete the hope and confidence that believers can have on the basis of the experiences of the patriarchs, the prophets, and the apostles both as they endured and enjoyed the daily grind and as they faced beatings, imprisonment,

13. Volker Leppin, *Repräsentation und Reenactment: Spätermittelalterliche Frömmigkeit verstehen* (Tübingen: Mohr Siebeck, 2021).
14. WA 43: 332,10–16, LW 4: 274.
15. Heinrich Bornkamm, *Luther and the Old Testament*, trans. Eric W. and Ruth C. Gritsch (Philadelphia: Fortress, 1969), 11–44.

and execution for their faith. Much more powerful than abstractions and allegories of some grand truth from biblical reports of God's presence and interaction with his people, the real-life stories of Abraham and Sarah, of David and Jeremiah, of Paul and Silas, depicted the kind of help that God provides by exhibiting his presence as biblical words rise from the page and invade daily life. Luther delighted in them and therefore did not try to transport his hearers across time into Abraham's and Sarah's age, nor did he believe that John or Paul had become his contemporaries. He believed that the word of God was bridging the historical gap by promising and, through the promise, delivering the actualization of what God had done in Christ. Not ritual transportation of the actors but verbal conveyance of the benefits and lessons of God's acting in history made his practice of the faith work as God meets his people face to face—voice to ear—through the several forms of his word. In that meeting, trust develops at the heart of the relationship with the loving God.

Thus, place and time are intertwined for Luther because both are elements in the personal engagement of God with his human creatures. Amid the rolling waves of historical passing, God rules. In commenting on Psalm 33:12, "blessed is the people, whose God is the Lord, the people whom he has chosen as his heirs," Luther observed that God is "merciful and faithful, he intends to give aid and gives it gladly, as he has promised in the first commandment." Luther had God say to the congregation, "I intend to be your God, that is, I intend to be your comfort, help, blessing, life and every good thing against all that is trying to harm you." Luther comments, "that is what it means to be God. Especially [the psalmist] thanks and praises the mighty goodness of God, that he steers the hearts of the entire world, of every king and prince—their thoughts, plans, their wrath and raving. They go where he wants them to go, not where they want to go."[16]

Time and place are inextricably interwoven, Luther recognized. Events "take place." God missed meeting Adam and Eve because they had fled from their accustomed place at the normal time and could not meet him face to face in their flight. He came after them and asked the place question, "Where are you?" Luther commented on Genesis 3:9 that Adam's consciousness that he had sinned brought terror to his heart, so he tried to remove himself from any place in God's sight and inaugurate a new usage of time. Such an effort, of course, is in vain, for no place or time escapes the presence of God. In anguish-driven haste, Adam was so foolish as to try to flee from God, but his problem lay precisely in the distancing and

16. WA 38: 29,2–8.

withdrawal from God that he had already attempted. Sin hurls sinners into an ever more vain attempt to put time and space between themselves and Eden, with it the presence of the omnipresent Creator. Luther viewed "Where are you?" as a word of law, for it shows Adam clearly that he had abandoned his God-given place in relationship to his Creator.[17] Despite the loss of this relationship, human creatures remained their Creator's creatures with God-given components and characteristics that determine who they are throughout their entire life. Failing to accord every human being worth and dignity insults their Creator.

LUTHER'S ANTHROPOLOGY AND THE MAKEUP OF THE HUMAN BEING

What Aristotle had regarded as the unitary structure for analyzing every individual person and thing, a structure of substance and accidents, Luther regarded as a largely helpful tool for explaining that which God had created and sustained. Some logical principles from Aristotle served him in theological formulations, as well; they dared not, however, dominate and determine God's revelation of himself and the true nature of his creatures found in Scripture.[18] Already in 1513, lecturing on Psalm 32, Luther drew a sharp line between "celestial, eternal, spiritual and invisible" knowledge that comes alone through faith and the knowledge gained through rational probing and observation.[19] This line remained firmly in place throughout his subsequent career.[20] Joest notes that the reformer designated the things of faith and the matters of the realm of reason more abstractly or categorically—visible/invisible, future/present, etc.—before 1521; thereafter, he contrasted concrete elements of God's saving intervention in human and individual history, as Scripture reported and his experience noted, against that which reason could master in the earthly realm.[21] Human reason easily retreated into abstractions that led to reading accepted philosophical and cultural opinions into Scripture through the allegorical method and other appeals to principle. Luther preferred

17. WA 42: 129,10–130,7, LW 1: 173–174.
18. Brian Gerrish, *Grace and Reason, a Study in the Theology of Luther* (Oxford: Clarendon, 1962), 57–137; Theodor Dieter, *Der junge Luther und Aristoteles: Historisch-systematische Untersuchungen zum Verhältnis von Theologie und Philosophie* (Berlin/New York: de Gruyter, 2001), 627–642.
19. WA 3: 172,20–19,29.
20. Joest, *Ontologie*, 89–93, provides select citations tracing the presence of this distinction.
21. Joest, *Ontologie*, 95–102.

dealing with the Scripture's concrete reports of events that demonstrate the nature of God's interactions with his human creatures and their actions among themselves.

Luther found that God deals in Scripture with individual human beings and groups of human beings whose identity and essence proceeds from their relationship to him. Beyond that core relationship defined in the Small Catechism, Luther assumed the common wisdom of his time that reflected the medieval blending of biblical understandings of humanity with the analyses of ancient Greek and Latin thinkers. He could speak of the human being as having soul and body or as having body, soul, and spirit without feeling compelled to define soul or spirit in terms that placed them within reason's analytical domain.[22] He used the parallel distinction of "spirit" and "flesh" from Paul (e.g., Gal 5:16–26) without trying to define the terms precisely. This usage employed these terms not as an analysis of the constitutive parts of the human being but as a description of the godly mindset and direction of a person's conduct of life, the "spirit," and the rebellious stance and movement of a person in opposition to God, labeled the "flesh." This contrast predominated in Luther's usage of the terms, although in *On Christian Freedom* he also denoted the eternal aspects or relationship with God as "spirit," whereas at times in this treatise "flesh" referred to godly actions in the sphere of relationships with other creatures.[23] The former sense dominated Luther's usage because he experienced Christian existence in the midst of the conflict between God and Satan, between his own trust in God—his "spirit"—and his sinful tendencies—his "flesh."[24]

The setting for this understanding of human experience lies in the Christianized use of Aristotle's anthropology. From his university instructors Luther had absorbed certain presuppositions from the traditions implanted in Western thought by Plato and Aristotle. Like his instructors, Luther used terminology from each rather freely, speaking at times of three parts of the human person—reason, will, and emotions—but also using Aristotle's distinction of vegetative, emotional, and cognitive elements and functions of a person (embracing both principles and aspects along with their practical application and activities).[25] Medieval scholastic thinkers employed these categories in varying forms and with varying

22. Joest, *Ontologie*, 163–193.
23. In 1520 Luther was still polishing his terminology and seeking standard usages that he would continue to use for another quarter century; cf. Robert Kolb, *Luther's Treatise* On Christian Freedom *and Its Legacy* (Lanham, MD: Fortress Academic/Lexington, 2019), 39–41, 58–60.
24. Joest, *Ontologie*, 192.
25. Joest, *Ontologie*, 139–142.

terminology. Gabriel Biel spoke of reason and will as the cognition of the mind (*cognitio intellectiva*) and the desire of the mind (*appetitus intellectivus*). He ascribed to the human sinful will a power to choose, also in choosing to obey God and live a life pleasing to him.[26] Luther had experienced the rebellious nature of both his reason and his will; while he treasured both as gifts of God, he recognized that his rejection of God's terms for their relationship in favor of counting on his own efforts to please God had also twisted the capabilities of both reason and will. Encountering the person of the Creator in Scripture led Luther to rethink the relationship between Aristotle's anthropology and the biblical view of being human while continuing to use elements of it.

LUTHER'S DEFINITION OF SELF AS SINNER

From his childhood, others—parents, priests, teachers, monastic superiors, university instructors—had reminded him of his missing the mark that God (and they) had set for him. His sensitive personality had no trouble recognizing the transgressions of God's will for his life that plagued him day in and day out. That all went back to what the church labeled "original sin." Based on years of experience Luther took that term, affirmed the existence of what it designated, and then deepened its meaning. As set forth in chapter 2, medieval theologians all attributed sinfulness in the human race to the fall of Adam and Eve from God's favor into rebellion against him. Passed from generation to generation, it either damaged or destroyed—depending on which theologian was talking—the human ability to hearken to the Lord, to obey him. Luther viewed the "root sin," as he often called the "inherited sin"—the usual German translation of the Latin *peccatum originale/originis*—as not only the ultimate historical cause of human sin but also the cause of every sin he committed and every failure to do the right thing each day.[27] He spoke of original sin as *peccatum radicale*—root sin—because all other sins sprang from it.[28] This root no longer determined the identity of the child of God, but its infection still continued to flare up as his children battle against Satan's temptations.

Though all people have some sense of sin (in others if not in themselves), the Holy Spirit must show sinners what original sin is, according to Luther, because only those who recognize the true God can adequately grasp and digest what it means to have doubted and defied him and his

26. Joest, *Ontologie*, 139–211.
27. Cf. chapter 2, pp. 68–71.
28. WA 40,2; 363–26–364,27, LW 12: 350–351.

word. Since trusting constitutes the very core of being human, as Luther came to recognize, removal of trust from the Creator compels human beings to replace him with substitute gods of their own fashioning.[29] The devil gladly cooperates in this manufacture of idols without sinners even realizing it. He lends his aid to the process since changing or corrupting God's word results inevitably in finding substitutes for the Ultimate and Absolute in life. Luther quoted the song of Moses to his students: when we exile God, then foreign gods of our own fashioning, not the God whom the patriarchs had worshiped [Deut 32:17,] invade our lives.[30] This echoed the conclusion of Luther's Large Catechism on the first commandment: trust in anyone or anything other than God himself is the root of all sin.[31] Misplaced trust in any substitute for the Creator perverts and poisons human existence itself. It also blinds sinners to the fact they have made the wrong choice in selecting a god, and only the true God can correct that perverted vision of reality.

In the Smalcald Articles Luther stated that "this inherited sin has caused such a deep, evil corruption of nature that reason does not comprehend it; rather it must be believed on the basis of the revelation in the Scriptures," citing Psalm 51:5, Romans 5:12, Exodus 33:20, and Genesis 3:1–13 as passages which testify to the reality of this corruption.[32] In 1532 he commented on Psalm 51 that the world cannot perceive original sin, for human power and speculation cannot discern it. Sinners hide it and hide from it; they defend their idolatries and excuse themselves through them. Thus, sinners depend on God's word to show them their impurity, the fundamental flaw in their nature.[33] The reformer's lectures on Psalm 90 delivered in 1534 repeated the point that humankind fell completely away from the Creator and became totally blinded by original sin. Thus, sinners do not understand who God is, who they themselves are, and in what a deplorable condition they exist, although they have some sense of it. But they recognize neither whence it has come nor whither it leads. Luther found the terrible situation that Adam and Eve had initiated beyond description.[34]

Because Luther believed that trust in God constitutes the very heart of humanity, he viewed the doubt of God's word expressed by Eve and then

29. Smalcald Articles, III.i, BSELK 930/931,12–934/935,32, BC 386–387.
30. WA 42: 112,6–8, LW 1: 148.
31. BSELK 930/931,12–934/935,32, BC 386–387.
32. BSELK 746/747,21–27, BC 311.
33. WA 40,2: 385,22–27, LW 12: 351.
34. WA 40,3: 485,9–15, LW 13: 76. Cf. Dennis Ngien, *Fruit for the Soul: Luther on the Lament Psalms* (Minneapolis: Fortress Press, 2016), 25–83.

Adam in the Garden of Eden as the historical origin and the paradigm for his own broken relationship with God. The serpent attacked the very will of God itself and God's image in the human being by attacking his word, Luther explained in his lectures on Genesis 3.[35] Satan invented a new god for Adam and Eve, as stated in Deuteronomy 32:17.[36] Luther noted that Eve had not only rejected God's command but also distorted it by adding to it (Gen 3:3).[37] Treating Psalm 51:5 in 1532, Luther insisted that David was not talking about his mother's sinful actions, about procreation and sexuality, but simply stating the truth that all human beings since Adam and Eve have been conceived and born seeking always to fashion false gods as substitutes for him.[38] They had learned to rely on their own judgment, a fatal mistake. They rely on their own wisdom, wealth, and possessions, presuming that they can satisfy every desire. By relying on such substitutes for the true God, they repeat that initial sin of wanting to be God, the worst and most serious of all sins, the root or source of every other sin.[39]

Especially those who live outwardly good, pious lives have trouble recognizing this condition, unless, like Luther, they are honest enough to note their own refusals to fear, love, and trust in God above all else in unexpected corners of daily life. The evaluation of God's law crushes their presumption that they can make themselves even partially worthy of God's blessings. In order that people who have turned in upon themselves recognize their own misery and condemnation, the law must come, as it had for this Augustinian friar in the earliest decade of the sixteenth century, in his case in the form of lightning and thunder, as the divine trumpet blast, the hammer of Jeremiah 23:39, to break the hardness of heart that held God with his mercy and forgiveness at bay.[40] Luther told his students in 1531 that the conviction that a person is righteous through his own deeds breeds pride and presumption, a sense of self-assurance that leads to hating God, disdain for his grace and mercy, and disregard for Christ and what he has promised. This creates a blockage of monumental proportions that prevents a sinner from receiving God's gifts of his favor and pardon. Presuming the possession of righteousness through one's own efforts is a huge and horrible monster, Luther commented. He advised that the law alone could function as the hammer that can crush rocks like

35. WA 42: 110,7–17, LW 1: 146; WA 42: 111,2–4, LW 1: 147. Cf. chapter 2, pp. 68–72.
36. WA 42: 112,6–8, LW 1: 148. Cf: chapter 2, pp. 70–71.
37. WA 42: 116,40–117,14, LW 1: 154–155.
38. WA 40,2: 380,26–36, LW 12: 348.
39. WA 28: 349,15–35,26, LW 69: 230–231.
40. BSELK 750/751,18–34, BC 312.

fire, wind, and earthquake.[41] Luther gained this perspective when facing himself and scrutinizing his own person and performance.

Luther had experienced assaults on his conscience from both Satan and other people, for his own sins had laid the basis for such accusation. In his Church Postil treating 1 John 4:16–21, his autobiographical description depicts the state of sinners when they come before God's judgment throne. Luther drew on his own experience by using physical terms: the voices of the world and the sinner's own consciences convinced him that he had lived an impure life, bringing a blush to his cheeks and palpitations to his heart. This judgment tastes sour and evokes the sweat to break out. He urged his readers and hearers to place their confidence in Christ as they confront all that they have failed to do and all that they have done wrong since these sins continue to weaken them. The pain of God's punishment will thrust a thorn into their heart and conscience and terrify them. Their anxiety and fear, however, blocks their trust. This eschatological battle weighs heavily on believers as they struggle to become free of the thunderbolts that Satan continues to hurl at them. They fight a two-front war against God's anger and against the accusations of those around them, who bring their charges against the believer to God's court.[42]

Luther depicted the alternatives of arrogant presumption and despairing terror frequently, often in terms like these. In a sermon on John 20:19 from April 4, 1540, based on the apostle Thomas's example, he pointed out that in this text the Holy Spirit was demonstrating that apart from trust in Christ, all are completely blind, hard of heart, and amount to nothing spiritually. Zechariah (7:12) called the sinful heart harder than steel and diamond, and yet this rebellious heart becomes as feeble as water or oil in its despair. Pharaoh's heart became hard as diamond, and Luther confessed that he and his hearers also managed to ignore the threats of hell despite the fact that God's ominous fury stands behind those threats. But this hardened heart turns to putty when a leaf rustles or the rafters in a bedroom creak. Such noises sound like thunder and lightning and banish comfort from the heart. That was the state in which the disciples found themselves on Easter evening. Luther then turned back to the arrogance of his contemporaries, criticizing greed, and noting that people find it easy to ignore God's condemnation of it. But from his own experience he also noted how the law reduces sinners to death. From his pastoral

41. WA 40,1: 481,26–485,31 LW 26: 310–312,
42. WA 36: 471,15–32, LW 78: 400–401.

experience, he observed that preaching to the proud is like preaching to a corpse or a stone pillar, but in another sense preaching to the terrified also resembles preaching to the dead. His mission was to bring consolation to the terrorized who were conscious of their own sin and death and the threat of hell.[43]

Luther faced himself as one whom the Lord had humbled, made miserable, afflicted, oppressed. His lectures on Galatians in 1531 offer another spiritual autobiographical reflection. He had been reduced to despair, to nothing, by the law. The actions of law and gospel in the believer's daily life repeat the action of the original *creatio ex nihilo*. The Lord exalts the humble, gives the hungry nourishment, restores the sight of the blind, comforts the afflicted, restores the identity of the sinner as child of God, raises the dead, and rescues the despairing from their condemnation. Luther observed that God goes about this act of re-creating sinners without regard for "this most poisonous plague" of self-righteousness, or the claim that the sinner is really righteous and not sinful. His law crushes and eliminates the vain lack of faith of sinners, or their counterfeit faiths, by bestowing on them his own wisdom, righteousness, and might.[44]

Luther described his self-perception in those times when he focused on his sinfulness. He had known that he was dressed in Adam's attire, the garb of sin and death. He, like Adam, had been sold into slavery to sin, blindness, ignorance of God, and even contempt and hatred for his maker. He confessed that evil desires, impurity, and greed had trapped him in the human nature that Adam had bequeathed his descendants.[45] "Thick, dark clouds" had enveloped him because he had failed to cling to Jesus. In the continuing battle between God and Satan that was being waged in his life, he felt the footing of faith uncertain under him since God's law continued to point out his sin and unworthiness. The majesty of Sinai recorded in Exodus 19, and, for that matter, any single Scripture passage, could shake the confidence of the believer in this on-going battle.[46] Luther never forgot this action that engenders terror and despair, even after the Holy Spirit had changed his fundamental self-perception to that of being a child of God, chosen without condition by his Creator.

43. WA 49: 136, 3–38, LW 69: 426–427.
44. WA 40,1: 488,15–32, LW 26:314–315.
45. WA 40,1: 540,19–25, LW 26: 352.
46. WA 40,1: 129,13–26, LW 26: 64.

LUTHER'S REDEFINITION OF HUMANITY IN TWO MODES

As often as he was tempted to dwell on his sinfulness, even in later years, Luther's fundamental view of himself changed in the late 1510s. Instead of seeing himself as a Sisyphus condemned at least to long-term striving on earth and in purgatory (in fact, he considered himself condemned to never-ending wrath), Luther came to see himself as totally righteousness in God's sight even though he continued to note that sin completely infected his actions. This view of the believer as "at the same time sinner and saint" arose in part out of his finding in Scripture a strikingly different definition of what it means to be human than his scholastic instructors and monastic mentors had given him. As noted above, he designated as "our theology" the concept of a two-fold human righteousness.[47] He defined the righteousness of human creatures in both the vertical and horizontal dimensions of life in terms that were grounded in personal relationships. Both kinds of righteousness proceeded from the Creator's design for human life, and both involved trusting and loving first God, with heart, soul, mind, and strength, and second, loving and serving other human beings, just as people are to love themselves as creatures worthy of God's love (Matt 22:34–39).

With this term he did not mean that human beings find their integrity and true identity in two stages or two manners of the exercise of righteousness—first believing the biblical account of salvation and then completing it with obedience in love—as this language was used by sixteenth-century Roman Catholic theologians to express the initial righteousness of faith and the completed righteousness attained by human works.[48] Instead, Luther used the phrase to assert that the single righteous person is first of all righteous in God's sight because of God's coming face to face or voice to ear with sinners, pronouncing his re-creative word of forgiveness. That conversation takes the poison of their sinfulness away; it performs the re-creative act that forgives sins and gives new birth. This twofold human righteousness emerges from the Holy Spirit's creation of a new person through Christ's death and resurrection. This new person joyfully acts out the righteous nature that God's forgiveness has bestowed.

47. WA 40,1: 45,24–26, LW 26: 7. See *The Alien and the Proper: Luther's Two-Fold Righteousness in Controversy, Ministry, and Citizenship*, ed. Robert Kolb (Irvine, CA: 1517 Publishing, 2023).
48. On the role of this view in attempts to reconcile Rome and Wittenberg in the 1530s and 1540s, see Anthony N. S. Lane, *Regensburg Article 5 on Justification: Inconsistent Patchwork or Substance of True Doctrine* (Oxford: Oxford University Press, 2020), 89–145.

The constitutive element of that new person on the human side is trust in God and his unconditional love.

As noted in the introduction of this volume, Luther's first attempt to define human righteousness in a treatise appeared in 1518 under the title, "Three-fold Righteousness."[49] First, he contrasted open sins and criminal acts with outward conformity to God's plan for human life, with the appearance of godliness, but apart from faith. This kind of righteousness brings benefits to societal life and the neighbor but has no value for the person's relationship with God. It is exercised in external conformity to God's law but does not proceed from fearing, loving, and trusting in God.[50]

The second kind of righteousness has its opposite in the broken relationship of original sin (*peccatum essenciale, natale, originale, alienum*), which permeates the entire person and is the core of sinful existence. In contrast to this defining sin, Luther set the righteousness which Christ bestows through baptism (*natalis, essencialis, originalis, aliena*). This righteousness is the "determining judgment [of God], the head, the foundation, the cornerstone [of human existence] and our entire substance." (*sors, capitale, fundamentum, petra nostra et tota substancia nostra*; John 3:5, John 1,12, 1 John 3:9, Rom 5:18–19). A person acquires this righteousness through faith, and God confers it upon the sinner through baptism. Luther concluded that this righteousness places believers under God's mercy even when they sin. Believers become "lords of all things," because their righteousness rests on what God thinks of them and is constituted by their trust in his word that applies Christ's death and resurrection to their persons.[51] This understanding of righteousness as alien—coming from outside oneself and one's own efforts (*extra nos*)—departs quite totally from a medieval understanding of righteousness grounded in sacramental, ritual practice. It rests alone on God's forensic—speech-act—pronouncement that has determined reality and given everything its existence and identity since the beginning.[52]

The third kind of righteousness is the opposite of the unrighteous deeds of daily life, the sinful acts that typify the defensive behavior of those apart from faith (*peccata actuales*). This righteousness flows from faith and the essential righteousness that God bestows out of his unconditional grace into the godly actions commanded by God. The good works of service and love to others, or praise and prayer to God, earn no merit in

49. *Sermo de triplici iustita*, WA 1: 43–47.
50. WA 2:43,12–44,13.
51. WA 2: 44,32–45,33.
52. Contrary to Philip Cary, "Why Luther is Not Quite Protestant," 471.

God's sight. They are rather the product of God's grace and the power of the Holy Spirit, who dwells in the believer. This form of righteousness resembles the first externally, but this righteousness arises from the faith that actualizes the godly conduct of life of the baptized.

Luther's treatise *Two Kinds of Righteousness*, composed in early 1519, abandoned the "civil righteousness" of the earlier treatise, perhaps because he presumed that all his readers were baptized and thus were called in faith to practice the righteous way of life prescribed by God's plan, or because he regarded outward performance of godly deeds as no more than a spurious righteousness since Paul wrote in Romans 14:23 that everything done apart from faith is sinful. True righteousness can exist only as God's gift and is present through trust in Christ, whether it be that of the human core, righteousness in God's sight, or that of the deeds, words, and thoughts on behalf of other creatures generated by the Holy Spirit through faith.

"The righteousness of Christians is two-sided," Luther began. The first "comes from outside the self and is poured into us from outside ourselves" (*aliena, et ab extra infusa*). This righteousness is Christ's righteousness, which is given to sinners through faith (1 Cor 1:30, John 11:25, 14:6). Bestowed in baptism and renewed through true repentance, which Christians practice their entire lives, this righteousness becomes the possession and property of believers in a manner which Luther illustrated with the analogy of the relationship of bride and bridegroom, applying passages from Paul speaking of the church to the individual believer (e.g., Eph 5:25–30). The mutual sharing of all possessions paralleled Luther's use of Paul's statement in Romans 6:3–11 that in baptism Christ buries the sins of believers in his tomb and raises them up to new life, walking in the Savior's footsteps. Thus, believers receive Christ's innocence in the Father's sight as their own.[53]

The acquisition of this gift takes place because faith accepts and shares God's estimate of the self. The faithful are still fully aware of their own sin, but despite that they agree with God's perception of them as possessing the identity of his own child. They realize that because of Christ's death and resurrection, God has accepted sinners as his own children. Their sins are buried in Christ's grave, into which God the Father no longer looks; with Christ believers are raised to enjoy God's regarding them as his own and to follow in Christ's footsteps that lead from the cross through his empty tomb to life everlasting. On the way they demonstrate the integrity which God sees them as possessing. They actualize their God-given

53. WA 2: 145,7–147,6.

righteousness in thoughts, words, and deeds fitting for members of God's family (Rom 6:3–11) as God converses with them from the pages of Scripture on the shape of the humanity he created. The German word for "obey" is *gehorchen*, closely associated in the ear's mind with *hören*, to hear, parallel to the Hebrew שלום [shalom], which can mean either "hear" or "obey," depending on the context, and the Greek association of ἀκούω [akouo] and ὑπακούω [hupakouo] ("hear" and "obey") and the Latin *audire* and *obedire*. Luther's obedience sprang from listening to what God says, hearkening to the word of the Lord. That placed the focus for him on the one giving the instructions for the true human life, not on his own performance.

THE RIGHTEOUSNESS OF FAITH

From his instructors Luther had learned that faith, in Latin *fides*, is "an infused intellectual virtue or habit from which the 'act of faith' proceeds." His instructors had defined *fides* essentially as the assent of the intellect to propositional truths, a "merely" historical recognition of the facts of Christ's life. For many medieval thinkers, this faith formed the basis for the acts of love that constituted the righteousness that God demands from his human creatures. Luther rejected the definition that "faith is only the outline but love provides the living colors and fills out the picture." He contended that "faith is not an inactive quality or empty husk in the heart, which can coexist with mortal sin until love joins it and gives it life."[54] Instead, he turned to the word *fiducia*, "trust," which, Desiderius Erasmus and Philip Melanchthon had convinced him, is the better translation of the Greek πίστις of the New Testament writers which had normally been rendered, by Jerome and others, as *fides*. Luther's definition of faith combined the recognition of the historical interaction of God in human history and the necessity of assent that Christ's death and resurrection made the life-changing, life-giving recreation of "me" and "us." This assent flows into the absolute reliance and ultimate confidence that is unrestrained trust in Jesus as deliverer from all ills and restorer of true life.[55]

54. Denis Janz, "What Did Luther Understand by 'Faith'," in *Reforming the Reformation: Essays in Honour of Principal Peter Matheson*, ed. Ian Breward (Melbourne: Scholarly Publishing, 2004), 71 (69–80).
55. On Luther's development of faith or trust as the core of his anthropology, see Bernd Hamm, *The Early Luther: Stages in a Reformation Reorientation*, trans Martin J. Lohrmann (Grand Rapids, MI: Eerdmans, [Minneapolis: Fortress], 2020), 59–84.

Thus, Luther concluded, true faith is "a certain trust in the heart and a firm assent through which Christ is grasped." In his Large Catechism Luther defined humanity as trusting an Ultimate and Absolute object: "a 'god' is the term for that to which we are to look for all good and in which we are to find refuge in all need. Therefore, to have a god is nothing else than to trust and believe in that one with your whole heart." Luther heard God saying to him,

> see to it that you let me alone be your God, and never search for another. . . . Whatever good thing you lack, look to me for it and seek it from me, and whenever you suffer misfortune and distress, crawl to me and cling to me. I, I myself, will give you what you need and help you out of every danger. Only do not let your heart cling to or rest in anyone else.[56]

This passage and countless others demonstrate how ill-informed is the judgment that Luther's person-centered view of reality did not take the divine design of human psychological structures seriously. His presentation of the concept of faith and his address to his hearers and readers that appealed to their emotions and will, as well as their mind, show how well he understood the Creator's construction of human feeling, willing, and reasoning.[57]

Luther perceived that faith determined and defined who and what he was; it defined his worth and integrity through God's gift of the psychological action of trusting him and God's certain promise intertwined with this trust. He had this worth and integrity not because he possessed it as an accomplishment or achievement credited to himself or because it possessed him as something in and of itself. That is not the nature of trust. It is not self-manufactured, not homemade, nor an object distinct from the person who is trusting. Luther knew that his worth and integrity existed only because he trusted the promise and person of God in Christ. His own identity came as a gift from the identity of his Crucified and Risen Lord. God's faithfulness invites and creates the response of confidence and reliance on his person and his word. Weaker or stronger, trust bound Luther to God and permitted him to go face to face and even toe to toe with his Creator. Philip Cary aptly observes of Luther's view of faith,

> Luther makes Christian faith profoundly unreflective: faith does not include knowing one has faith. It does not even require *believing* one has faith; for 'he who doesn't think he believes, but is in despair, has the greatest faith.'

56. BSELK 930/931,14–932/933,3, BC 386–387.
57. Joest, *Ontologie*, 21–27; Janz, "What Did Luther Understand."

> Christian faith puts no faith in faith, precisely because it is faith in God's word alone. . . . Faith does not rely on itself but only on the promise of God.[58]

Trust creates not only its "god," as Luther said in the Large Catechism, but it also creates the identity of the person who is trusting another person in whom it places itself. Trust or faith in Jesus creates the identity as children of God.[59] This emphasis on trust echoes the entire Scripture in its presentation of the relationship of the human being to the Creator.

Abraham served Luther as a prime example of promise and the trust that abides despite the patriarch's doubts and disobedience. Paul directed Luther's eyes to Abraham already in Romans 4 and 5, as the professor noted in 1515. On Romans 4:1, he explained that the apostle's simple statement "Abraham believed God" referred to their relationship from the time of God's first approach and promise to him.[60] Although Luther regarded Abram as a noble pagan when he lectured on Genesis twenty years later, in 1515 he had labeled the patriarch a "nothing." He had nothing to offer God, but precisely from nothing God created this key to his plan for salvation.[61] Abram simply trusted the promise that God had made, not without doubting at times, not without occasionally trying to devise an alternative plan to help God keep his plan going, and not without his sins of lying about Sarah's identity and treating Hagar and Ishmael as objects under his control in a variety of ways.

But the patriarch was always brought back to trusting God to carry out his plan faithfully even in the face of the command to kill Isaac on the altar of sacrifice. Luther described the inner struggle of Abraham as he weighed command of God against promise of God, as he followed the command of God while trusting in the promise. This battle of God against God conducted in Abraham's mind and heart shook Abraham to his core. God worked his will, and Abraham trusted against trust in the person who was speaking, even when he was speaking in contradiction to himself.[62] In the midst of this probing of God's way of dealing with his chosen people, Luther assured his students that they could hold fast to the comfort of a reliable God. His baptismal promise is his unchangeable word.[63] For Luther, trust ultimately rests only in the person, the person who is speaking to his people in and through Jesus Christ.

58. Cary, "Why Luther is Not Quite Protestant," 452.
59. WA 10,1,1:228,3–4.
60. WA 56: 267,9–28, LW 25: 255.
61. WA 42: 437,10–439,14, LW 2: 246–249.
62. WA 43: 200,25–203,34, LW 4. 91–98, cf. Paulson, *Outlaw God*, 3: 215–268.
63. WA 43: 204,34–205,2, LW 4: 96.

Luther's emphasis on trust anticipated the insight of the twentieth-century psychologist Erik Erikson, whose anthropological dogma placed trust in the central role of determining human personality and sense of personhood.[64] Erikson further identified the quest for identity and concern for the integrity of that identity as a key to human well-being. His concept of identity somewhat paralleled the heart of Luther's understanding of righteousness. Human beings' righteousness is their sense of who they are. Trust looks to an Ultimate and Absolute object and receives from that "god" a sense of identity.

Just as Erikson viewed the mother as the most important factor in cultivating trust and thus a sense of identity in the infant, so Luther regarded God as the source of his own identity. Alongside supplying identity, this haven in time of need provides a sense of safety or security. Human beings also long for some feeling of worth and meaning for their persons. They desire not only an internal appraisal that their lives have meaning, but they also crave the respect of others. To feel safe and secure, they treasure having a place where everybody knows their name, a place that has to take them in when they have no other place to go.[65] This ultimate apprehension of our place, respect, identity, security, and meaning comes through trusting in whomever or whatever it is that functions as our god—whether it be the true God or some created person or thing which we have chosen as a substitute for God.

Trust reacts to a person rather than to proof. Trust responds to a promise, which is the substance of things not yet seen or experienced. Like the origins of love, the origins and essential characteristics of trust elude even psychologists. Luther's deepened concept of promise took form alongside his deepened concept of faith. "Faith in Christ is thus always faith in a divine promise."[66] The Holy Spirit creates trust in Christ and in his promise of new life. Thus, trust empowers living the godly life through his word. In his *Prelude, On the Babylonian Captivity of the Church* Luther wrote that God deals with human beings only through a word of promise, leading to the conclusion that they can deal with him only through trusting his promise. "He does not desire works, nor has he need of them. We deal with others and with ourselves on the basis of works. But God

64. Though burdened by his Freudian orientation, Erik H. Erikson has helpfully accentuated the role of trust in the forming of human personality, for example, in *Childhood and Society* 2nd ed. (New York: Norton, 1963), 247–251, and *Identity: Youth and Crisis* (New York: Norton, 1968), 82, 102–104,

65. Cf. Robert Frost's poem, "The Death of the Hired Man."

66. Cary, "Why Luther is Not Quite Protestant," 449.

needs this: that we consider him faithful to his promises and patiently persist in this belief."[67]

Steven Paulson comments, "To find God without a promise is to find death, wrath, sin, and the devil all wrapped up in a single package. So for sinners who are in flight from God, these things of creation are threats," as God observed in Leviticus 26:36, noting that even the rustling of a leaf puts fear into sinners' hearts. "God is not healthy for a sinner unless God comes to give himself wholly and completely in his Son—the Christ—and in the Holy Spirit, in whose baptism a promise is made for the forgiveness of sins."[68] Despite all contrary challenges to God's reliability that believers experience, as Timothy Saleska reports from Israel's experience in the Old Testament, God has created the believer's reality by promising life and salvation in Christ.

> Can God be trusted to keep his promises? When the visible evidence is all against it, is God able to do what he said? The Scriptures tell us that surely the answer is, "Yes." God always showed Israel that he was faithful. He raised a seed from Abraham when he was as good as dead. He raised a dead nation, first from Egypt and then from Babylon. . . . Now, in these last days, Scripture tells us that God also raised his own Son.[69]

The promise provides steady ground under the feet of believers in the midst of daily life. In 1526 Luther preached in Halle on Acts 9. He stated,

> Faith takes away all misfortune, sin, death, hell, and the wrath of God and makes us heirs of God and of eternal life. That is right: that alone accomplishes this. If you wish to participate in the blessings of heaven, such as forgiveness of sins and eternal life, you have to let go of your silly works in which you trust, listen to God's Word that proclaims faith in Christ, accept it, and believe. In this way you will experience salvation. For being saved and having eternal life is nothing else but being free of sin. When sin is gone, nothing but God's grace and mercy, eternal righteousness and blessedness pour down upon us. That is eternal life.[70]

God's pledge that Christ has freed his people from the tyranny of sin, death, and Satan and is present with them in the midst of daily life sustains believers. The Christian life unfolds in the midst of cross and tribulation,

67. WA 6: 516,20–517,7, LW 36: 42.
68. Paulson, "Graspable God," 51–52.
69. Tim Saleska, "The Clarity of Paradox: A Meditation on Exodus 34:6–7," in *Simul: Inquiries into Luther's Expression of the Christian Life*, ed. Robert Kolb, Torbjörn Johansson, and Daniel Johansson (Göttingen: Vandenhoeck & Ruprecht, 2021), 210.
70. WA 51: 147, 3–11.

Luther told his students, commenting on Jeremiah 27:9 in 1528, under the shadow of his own illness and an outbreak of plague in Wittenberg; it is in the midst of such testing that faith becomes stronger.[71] Faith grows under the cross as the flesh is mortified, Luther told students as he lectured on Isaiah 27 in late 1528 or early 1529.[72]

He explained to hearers at Coburg in 1530 that "In our suffering we should so act that we give our greatest attention to the promise, in order that our cross and affliction may be turned to good," contrary to human reasoning. Others, who cannot rely on the promise, find no comfort in tribulations. Those who trust the promise have "the assurance that God will help them to bear the affliction" and that he will "turn their affliction and suffering to good."[73] Christ's promise in John 16:33 applied to them when he said that they would have tribulation but in him they would have peace. He put words into Jesus's mouth, "Danger and terror will surely hit you if you accept my Word, but let it come. This will happen to you because of me. So be of good cheer; I will not forsake you. I will be with you and will help you. No matter how great the affliction may be, it will be small and light for you, if you are able to draw such thoughts from the Word of God."[74]

Luther came to understand that his Creator wanted him to find his righteousness and identity alone in Christ. He perceived that God was inviting and empowering him to trust in Jesus Christ, the incarnation of the second person of the Trinity. Christ's promise offered the change of identity from sinner to child of God for which Luther longed. Trust in Christ overcame his fears and despair and gave the Wittenberg reformer the courage to confront his sin out of his perspective of relying on the saving work of Jesus. Recognizing his continuing sinfulness yet confident that nothing could separate him from the love of God in Christ Jesus (Rom 8:39), he confronted and dismissed what would have been justified trepidation and terror apart from Christ. Christ's affirmation of the Father's choice of Martin as his own permitted him to be honest about his failures and his new doubts and defiance because he knew that Christ would claim them as his own, bury them in his tomb, and set the professor on the trail left by the Lord's own footsteps.

Although Luther himself seldom talked in this specific language about believers face to face with themselves, his reflections on his trust in Christ

71. WA 25: 179,27–180,9, LW 16: 215.
72. WA 31,2: 153,28–154,3; LW 16: 216.
73. WA 32:31, 29–32, LW 51: 201.
74. WA 32:35,30–36,10, LW 51: 205.

and what it enabled him to do justify our looking at Luther in the mirror of his own self-perceptions. He explained the relationship of believers to their Savior to his students by associating Christ with the Aristotelian concept of form, the plan that gives purpose and goal to its object. The point of his analogy of Christ's being painted on the walls of his people is that the paint becomes the "form," the identifying mark, of the wall; the analogy is incomplete in that Christ is much more than simply an outer coating of the believer. His identity as the innocent one who has taken the sinner's place under death's condemnation and then risen to new life permeates the entire life of the believer. As his thought was developing in the Romans lectures in 1515 and 1516, Luther explained that just as the Word made flesh assumed the form of a servant (John 1:14, Phil 2:7), so believers assume "the form of the Word"; that is, the identity of Christ as the righteous One determines the righteousness of the human creature who trusts in him.[75] By 1531, in his lectures on Galatians, Luther was emphasizing faith as the "form" or "formal factor" in believers as it grasps what Christ has done for them and conforms their lives to him.[76] His disputations on Romans 3:28 and Matthew 22:1–14, held in 1537, clarify his transformation of the definition of the "substantial form" of true faith as the recognition and acceptance of the *pro me* of the rescuing love of God. This faith grasps the imputation of what Christ accomplished in dying and rising for sinners, and it exercises Christ-like love for others through good works.[77] Angela Michael concludes that the believer's personal unity with Christ took its *forma* from the crediting or imputation of Christ's righteousness and from the transformed life that results. God alone destroys sin and creates the righteousness of believers. This *forma extrinsica*, formation from outside the individual believer, creates a new constitution for existence, embracing what scholars have labeled both the forensic and the effective nature of justification.[78] Thus, Christ therefore bestows identity upon believers and gives them their appearance, as paint does for a wall. In Philip Cary's words, "in effect an Aristotelian theory of perception (receiving the form of Christ in our ears by hearing his word) replaces the Aristotelian theory of habituation (developing the form of righteousness in our souls by doing good works)." This transformed "formal righteousness" from the medieval concept of created grace indwelling

75. WA 56: 330,1–8, LW 25: 317; cf. Angela Michael, "'Quod Christus sit mea forma': Zur Bedeutung des Wortfeldes *forma / formari* in der Rechtfertigungslehre Martin Luthers," *Lutherjahrbuch* 89 (2022): 22–23.
76. Michael, "Quod Christus," 30–33.
77. Michael, "Quod Christus," 35–47.
78. Michael, "Quod Christus, 44–45.

in believers to the presence of Christ with us by faith.[79] By determining who we are, God's word of forgiveness forms a new identity for his chosen people. Because trust in an Ultimate and Absolute constitutes the identity of a human being at its core, trust in Christ conforms us to him as the image of God placed in human form.

Faith takes hold of Christ in a way that makes him truly present in their lives. Faith pierces the unpierced darkness and takes the presence of Christ in hand. Luther compared this presence to God's presence on Sinai or in the temple: no doubt that he is there even if he remains beyond human comprehension and capture. Faith defines human righteousness before God because it places sinners in an intimate relationship with Christ, a relationship that lies beyond human power to grasp fully and to create. In this sense Luther used the term "form of righteousness" to designate that this personal relationship of trust constitutes the righteousness of God's children rather than, as medieval theologians had contended, acts of love.[80]

With this righteousness centered in trust in Christ, a new identity based on the presence of the dead and risen Christ, Luther viewed himself as a person restored to the proper and healthy, Edenic, relationship God intended for human creatures to have with their Creator. Such people, convinced that they are truly restored to righteousness by faith, then naturally practice this righteousness in a life of love and service, as God designed human beings to live. Luther reminded his students of Abram's situation. He left behind the security of an established home and property, a family network extending to his clan, as well as friends. He left all that without hesitation to search for a new place to dwell that he did not know since God had not yet revealed precisely where he was to land. He trusted only in the Lord and in his promise of blessing.[81] He did not follow a dream into Canaan. He followed a person whom he trusted.

By defining his new existence in Christ around the concept of trust in God's promise, Luther rejected the mystical view of someone like Meister Eckhart that repeated ancient gnostic metaphysics with its goal of having the human soul lose its bodily materiality and its individuality as it was absorbed into the Divine. He saw himself instead as bride of the bridegroom Jesus Christ, whose presence in his life did not absorb or abolish his humanity but enhanced it, as does the marital union for both wife and husband. Christ's presence brought the joyous exchange of his being regarded by God as rebel and lost child for God's counting him

79. Cary, "Why Luther is Not Quite Protestant," 468.
80. WA 40,1: 228,28–229,30, LW 26: 129–130.
81. WA 42: 453,16–23, LW 2: 268.

as a prodigal returned and a pardoned rebel. Indeed, he had become the child of grace, born again in the forgiveness of his sins.[82] The description of his relationship with his Creator and Deliverer as that of parent and child dominated the language of Luther in the last two decades of his life. Birgit Stolt has noted that Luther's perception of himself as God's child, whom God encourages to come to him in prayer "as truly his child, boldly and with complete confidence," grew after he became a father.[83] Thus, in his Galatians lectures of 1531 Luther could cry out, as Paul had, "abba, Father," because that meant the end of slavery to sin and Satan. It brought true liberation, adoption, acceptance as God's child. Luther noted the necessity of letting this father be truly father by responding as children who embrace what the father gives and promises. That was for Luther the significance of the Aramaic word "abba" (Gal 4: 6). Luther then mixed the metaphor by concluding that the father and the child seal a marriage contract.[84]

A new family relationship, indeed, a new creation or new birth, gave Luther peace and joy. He found this new contentment and delight by taking refuge in Christ's dying to dispose of sinner's doubt and defiance and in his rising to restore righteousness or the identity of God's human creatures as his children (Rom 4:25). Galatians 2:20 placed Paul's conviction about himself in Luther's mouth and heart. Because he knew that Christ was living in or with him, he viewed himself as crucified with Christ, dead to sin, having come alive with Christ through the liberation accomplished by Christ's resurrection. Christ lived within him, having set aside the law, placing judgment upon sin, and murdering death, banishing all three. For Christ liberates from terror and despair and bestows peace, comfort, righteousness, and life. God's claim upon his children removed the sense of terror and despair that comes from sin, hell, death, and the accusation of the law.[85]

SINNER AND RIGHTEOUS AT THE SAME TIME

Yet Luther never lost his awareness of the daily struggle between God and Satan, between the truth of Christ and the deceit of the devil, that he was experiencing. Joest notes that the paradox of the continuation of sinfulness in those whom Christ has forgiven of sin and made his own

82. WA 40,1: 272,19–20, LW 26:159.
83. BSELK 874/875,5–12, BC 356.
84. WA 40,1: 10–19, LW 26: 389–390.
85. WA 40,1: 283,33–284,19, LW 26: 167.

does not lie in an understanding of forgiveness as a sort of legal fiction that essentially leaves the sinner intact as sinner. Luther understood God's word of forgiveness as an act of re-creation that renders sinners truly, ontologically, righteous. The paradox lies in the fact that this reality encounters the power of sin and Satan day in and day out. These evil powers strive to label God's change in the reality of the faithful a falsehood.[86] Luther rested in the presence of his Creator in his life, and therefore he was able to live with the tension that exists because of the law of sin that challenges God's word and his place in the believer's life.

Faith's confidence in God's unshakable love and the resulting honesty it produced gave Luther the courage to confront the continuation of sin and evil in his life. To reduce guilt and guilty feelings, most people reduce the standards which they set for themselves and think that God has set for them. Luther did not need to do that since confession of guilt no longer posed a risk for him. Christ's death had liberated him from shyness about being open with God about his sin. His trust in Christ clung to his baptismal promise that his sins had been banished to the utmost depths of Christ's tomb. His faith shared God's view of the self. In his Heidelberg Theses, he laid down a foundation or guiding principle for his practice of theology, "being able to tell it like it is." He received that courage only by finding refuge at the foot of Christ's cross, by nestling in his new home on God's lap. This courage, this trust, can think and act against our experience. Luther noted two contradictory perspectives: God sees sinners as his righteous children while they perceive the abiding presence of sin in their lives. Luther took both perspectives seriously but found that God's perspective ultimately trumps that of his sin-sensitive chosen, faithful people.

Therefore, he concluded that "a Christian is not a person who has no sin or never senses sin, but rather is someone to whom, because of faith in Christ, God does not reckon sin. This teaching delivers unshakable consolation to consciences struggling with genuine fears."[87] Luther's

86. Joest, *Ontologie*, 265–270.

87. WA 40,1: 235,15–18, LW 26:133. Bernd Wannenwitsch argues that this *simul* cannot literally mean "at the same time" since righteousness and sin cannot exist together. But that is precisely Luther's point: the simultaneity of God's re-creative reckoning his people righteous while they are still experiencing their sinfulness is, as Paul laments in Romans 7, for believers the only true comfort because they can cry with Paul, "who shall deliver me from the body of death? Thanks be to God through Jesus Christ our Lord! . . . Therefore, there is now no condemnation for those who are in Christ Jesus because through Christ Jesus the law of the Spirit of life set me from the law of sin and death" (Rom 7:24–8:1); cf. Wannenwitsch, "The Simultaneity of Two Citizenships. A Theological Reappraisal of Luther's Account of the 'Two Regiments' for our Times," *Simul*, 178.

occasional use of the axiom "righteous and sinful at the same time" reflects his oft-repeated conviction that Christians never lose their sense of their own failure to fear, love, and trust in God above all things but that they also recognize that God's regard for them as his innocent children on the basis of Christ's death and resurrection constitutes the superior reality in the face of the mystery of continuing sin and evil in the believer's life. His perception of the tension between God's pronouncement that his people are his righteous children and their own continuing experience of the brokenness of their relationship to him also forms the basis for the confidence of believers that they are capable of performing good works for the sake of those whom God has placed within their reach, whether from Judea, Samaria, or the ends of the earth. The Holy Spirit empowers that kind of life. For those who trust in what God says about them have confidence that he has pronounced them forgiven, giving them the identity of his children. They do endeavor to reflect this identity, this righteousness, in acting like his children in the world.[88]

Romans 7 became for Luther, as it had for no theologian before him, a key hermeneutical passage, as he strove to insist that believers do struggle and triumph over sinful habits while still acknowledging that their "desire to live according to God's law and to obey it in the most holy way possible" is often interrupted. Every pious person "wishes to be free from those vexations and difficulties which engulf him [*sic*] here, and never to be taken captive and harassed by those things which offend God the Father. But this cannot happen in this life; we are flesh."[89] Nonetheless, Luther concludes that believers are not solely sinners, even amid the struggles. God's pronouncement of righteousness convinces faith that it can live as God's righteous child. Despite "feeling many sins and desires," believers acknowledge that "with the Lord helping we do not permit them to rule."[90]

Luther did not shy away from the tensions and paradoxes imposed by the mystery of the continuation of sin and evil in God's good world. Thus, as Jonathan Linebaugh notes on Galatians 2:20:

> the persistence of the person . . . is not grounded in the person: I am not me but, by grace, in Christ. But it is exactly this grace and this Christ—the one who loved me and gave himself for me—that establish a kind of continuity, what might be called the passive persistence of the person. The cross is, at once, a death that breaks the story of the self into two even as it is a gift

88. Robert Kolb, "Old Adam, New Martin: The Fatal and Resurrecting Consequences of Baptism in Luther's Use of Romans 7," in *Simul*, 63–78.
89. WA 39,1: 512,6–513,1.
90. WA 39,1: 505,17-19.

and love that has a way of holding it together. I may no longer live, but, in the dative and accusative cases if you will—in the cases of the creature and receiver—there is and was and will be a me who is persistently loved and graced by God.[91]

Luther placed his experience of the disruptions and tensions of sin and Satan in the context of his *theologia crucis*. That phrase formed a hermeneutical key with openings to several questions: that of the Hidden and Revealed God, that of faith's superiority in spiritual matters to reason, that of the manner of God's atoning for sin, that of the weight of the neighbor who needs the believer's help. But it also explained the sufferings of the cross from attacks of Satan, locked as he is in combat with God, on the battlefields of the lives of God's people. That is the form of Christian living.

Therefore, suffering should not surprise believers. Satan is concentrating his forces on them to regain lost territory. In the end, the individual believer as well as the church are caught up in the personal eschatological struggle of God and Satan. The people of God go face to face each day in this battle between truth and lie, righteousness and unrighteousness, faithful humanity and perverted humanity.[92] "Saint and sinner" also means "saint and sufferer." As sinners encounter the attacks of all their foes in faith, they plunge into the battle that uses their suffering as a weapon against these foes of God. Faith alone in Christ sustains Christ's followers in this fight. Believers experience this battle in what Luther called *Anfechtungen*, defined by Denis Janz as "an untranslatable word which connoted for him a combination of doubt, fear, dread, the temptation to despair, the suspicion that God is not good, and that human destiny is death and eternal nothingness thereafter."[93]

The Wittenberg reformer took all the attacks of Satan, the world, and the sinful desires from within seriously. Since faith is key to human personality, his reaction to the temptations to doubt surrounding impending death provides a good illustration from early in his reforming career for his way of contending with such afflictions. This passage reflects his regarding brooding over one's sins as a view of the self through Satan's eyes. In his *On Preparing to Die* he wrote:

sin also grows large and formidable when we dwell on it and brood over it too much. This is increased by the fearfulness of our conscience, which is

91. Jonathan A. Linebaugh, "'The Speech of the Dead:' Identifying No Longer and Now Christ Living 'I' of Galatians 2:20," *New Testament Studies* 66 (2020): 104–105.
92. Joest, *Ontologie*, 320–353.
93. Janz, "What Did Luther Understand," 75.

> ashamed before God and accuses itself terribly. That is the water that the devil has been seeking for his mill. He makes our sins seem large and numerous. He reminds us of all who have sinned and of the many who were damned for lesser sins than ours so as to make us despair or die reluctantly, thus forgetting God and being found disobedient in the hour of death. This is true especially since human beings feel that they should think of their sins at that time and that is right and useful for them to engage in such contemplation. But they find themselves so unprepared and unfit that now even all their good works are turned into sins. As a result, this must lead to an unwillingness to die, disobedience to the will of God, and eternal damnation. That is not the fitting time to meditate on sin. That must be done during one's lifetime. . . . In the hour of death when our eyes should see only life, grace, and salvation, [the devil] at once opens our eyes and frightens us with these untimely images so that we shall not see the true ones.[94]

Eyes and ears on Christ—this was the stance that Luther strove to take. Scripture gave him the words and images to describe himself. In 1533 he told the Wittenberg gathering in the Black Cloister,

> We can truly say with confidence: My Lord Jesus Christ is truly the only Shepherd, and I, alas, the lost sheep, which has strayed into the wilderness. I am anxious and fearful and would gladly be good and have a gracious God and peace of conscience, but here I am told that he is as anxious for me as I am for him. I am anxious and in pain about how I shall come to him to secure help. But he is in anxiety and worry, and he desires nothing else than to bring me again to himself.

God's "gushing desire, anxiety, and longing for us" take away our dread and fear and enable us to "joyfully run up to him and stay with him alone, and hear no other teaching or teacher." For he is the one who has said, "Come unto me, all you who labor and are heavy laden, and I will give you rest."[95]

Luther found it sinfully natural as a sinner to live without this rest and quiet. He found this feeling came when he was not able to see himself correctly. He was not seeing God correctly and not listening to him. He was looking at God's back turned to him, not in God's face. It is a twenty-first century problem—though certainly not restricted to our time—that people do not want to get personal with God and often find themselves unable to get personal with other human beings. Many problems contribute to our wanting to hold God at bay. Family abuse deprives us of

94. WA 2: 687,18–36, LW 42: 102.
95. In the text of Poach's Hauspostille, EA^2 5: 285–294; Lenker, *Sermons*, 4:86.

our learning trust as children. Competition and rivalries, at school, at home, at work, as well as all forms of selfishness and self-seeking, serve as warnings against relying on personal relationships. The *incurvatus in se* that results from a breakdown of trust and the love which trust creates binds us, imprisons us, smothers us. The restoration of our ability to turn outward and seek relationships with others takes place through trusting that Christ has covered us from behind, stands guards at our sides, goes before us into battle against all forms of selfishness in others. For trusting in Christ brings contentment, satisfaction.

The presence of Christ ultimately gave Luther a contented life, satisfied with what God had done to him and what he continued to provide each day. The English word satisfaction comes from two Latin words, "making enough." The German word used as the equivalent of this contentment means literally "at peace-ness." Luther could also view his circumstances as he presumed God saw them—sufficient or satisfactory. Christ had freed him from the necessity of securing life, and he could rely on the goodness of God to take care of all this needs, to be the source of all the good his life required. This confidence in the Creator sets aside self-indulgence that must find pleasure in self-filling rather than in meeting others' needs and enjoying the neighbor's successes. That confidence stops us short before the black hole of our discontent, insatiable because self-reliance is the capacity and compulsion to want ever more.

Since Christ could live with him, Luther came to live comfortably with himself, *simul justus et peccator*, at the same time confident in God's love and acknowledging his sinfulness. For Luther, the phrase meant that he was righteous, God's child. But he also recognized that he had a defiant, disbelieving streak left in him. His spiritual-genetic identity, anchored in his new birth, secured his conviction regarding his own person, determined by God's eternal plan to claim him as one of the family. But he encountered the dissonance of ongoing desires to live apart from God's law. He "blessed himself" each morning with the sign of the cross to remind him of his newborn identity, and he then prayed that the wicked foe would have no power over him during the day[96] because he knew that the struggle of God and Satan would continue to take place in his life. He also faced each day confidently because he knew that at the end Christ would deliver him into life everlasting. This relationship with his Creator and Liberator laid the basis of his relating to the person he was as righteous child of God caught in the battle with sin.

96. BSELK 890/891, 26–27, 892/893, 10–11, BC 363,364.

6.

The Reformer Face to Face with the World

Martin Luther coram Mundo

THE WORLD—AT THE SAME TIME GIFT AND FOE

Reformation scholars speak of Luther's concept of the Christian in relationship to other human creatures with two phrases, *coram hominibus* or *coram vicino*—face to face with other human beings, with those whom God has placed within our reach—and *coram mundo*—face to face with "the world." In this volume we are distinguishing the two phrases in order to discuss the relationship Luther perceived and practiced in relationship to other individuals distinct from the relationships he had to the communities he encountered in society, in the systems and institutions of his culture.

Luther's attempt at retreating from the world by embracing the monastic way of life failed in part because he sought that refuge in the nearest cloister to his student residence in Erfurt, and it belonged to the Augustinian Eremites, a mendicant order. Its members lived together as brothers, but they actively served outside the cloister in the world. Luther began preaching while in Erfurt, and when his superiors sent him to the cloister in Wittenberg, he began aiding the priests of the Wittenberg congregation and those in nearby villages by hearing confessions and preaching.[1] Luther rose to being district vicar for his order and traveled to more than a dozen cloisters under his supervision, dealing with local officials as well

1. Roland M. Lehmann, *Reformation auf der Kanzel: Luther als Reiseprediger* (Tübingen: Mohr Siebeck, 2021), 35–91.

as the Augustinian brothers. In the small town of Wittenberg, with some four hundred buildings and less than 2,500 people when he arrived there in 1508, his effectiveness in the pulpit quickly brought him into contact with leaders in the town. Though he left little record of early conversations with prominent citizens such as the court painter and town apothecary, Lukas Cranach, they apparently became friends early on. Luther became acquainted with members of the court who resided in Wittenberg and undoubtedly heard their conversations. While his thoughts in the cloister and at the universities in Erfurt and Wittenberg often turned to Aristotle, William of Ockham, Gabriel Biel, and others whose materials he used in lectures, he was immersed in the society surrounding him.[2] In the marketplace and cloister he was discussing threats from the Turks, prospects for harvest, and rising prices.

Yale professor H. Richard Niebuhr set forth an analysis of Luther's stance toward "the world" in his study of the relationship between church and society, *Christ and Culture*. This study arose from five lectures delivered in 1950 on the topic of the church and the world. Niebuhr's description of Luther's view of this relationship—which, according to Niebuhr, Luther shared with the apostle Paul and the heretic Marcion, as well as Niebuhr's brother Reinhold—is summarized with the phrase "Christ and Culture in Paradox." In fact, it is the existence of sin and evil in the presence of a good and almighty God that is truly paradoxical. Luther's understanding of the believer's stance within that paradox is not paradoxical since it simply distinguishes the vertical dimension of human life, the sphere in which believers relate to God, from the horizontal dimension, the sphere in which believers relate to the rest of God's creation. It is not paradoxical to observe that children have a different kind of relationship to their parents than they have toward their siblings. Furthermore, it is not paradoxical to be critical of that which is dear to us when we see flaws damaging or detracting from its quality or beauty. Love cultivates a critical spirit with the intent of improving its object. Luther exemplified this critical love and appreciation for his culture and its people.

Therefore, Luther contended, believers are called by God to recognize the goodness of his continued activity and blessings in this world and its culture and societal organization. However, they are also called to be sharply critical of the abuses of their Father's property, which he

2. Biographical details are taken from Martin Brecht, *Martin Luther*. Vol. 1: *His Road to Reformation, 1483–1521*; vol. 2: *Shaping and Defining the Reformation, 1521–1532*, trans. James Schaaf (Philadelphia: Fortress Press, 1983), and Scott Hendrix, *Martin Luther, Visionary Reformer* (New Haven: Yale University Press, 2016).

created, when such abuses arise. They do so not for their own sakes, for their criticism often invites rejection, exclusion, and even persecution. Their criticism always is to aim for the improvement of life in this world for all people, according to Luther. Despite his conviction that sinners as individuals and as groups are deeply infected by their doubt of God's word and defiance of his lordship, Luther insisted that Christians work for justice for all in this world. He believed that it was possible to attain more justice rather than less even if the abuses of power and the temptations to exploit others would assert themselves again. This is simply part of the context imposed by the paradox of the continuing sin and evil in the world and in the baptized lives. Only with the recognition of this tension of God as Creator and Satan as invader and deceiver (John 8:44) can believers properly cope with daily life. Only by seeing life in two dimensions can Christ's people live with delight in the world, in society and culture, and also be their lovingly sharpest critics.[3]

Luther presumed that the world belongs to God and that God makes himself at home in the world, even when the world does not recognize him. Although he stressed the need to hear God's direct address to sinners in Scripture, he also asserted that God reveals himself in his creation. It serves as "our Bible in the fullest sense, this our house, home, field, garden and all things, where God does not only preach by using his wonderful works, but also taps on our eyes, stirs up our senses, and enlightens our heart at the same time."[4] And yet this multi-sensual approach from God trying to communicate in nature with his human creatures is understandable only when faith, "which we have already established previously on the basis of Scripture," provides the key for seeing the Creator and the creation through Christ. With the knowledge of the Creator provided also through the incarnation, "Christians can talk with the trees and everything that grows on the earth, and those plants can answer back."[5]

Luther fully appreciated how much good God introduces and preserves in this world that too often becomes chaotic or oppressive. In temporal blessings of all kinds, in his exercise of lordship over human history, and in sinners' external conformity to "the law of nature," as he called it, expressed in "civil righteousness," Luther recognized the hand of the providing God at work in the world that he created. In his lectures on

3. Niebuhr, *Christ and Culture* (New York: Harper, 1951); cf. Robert Kolb, "Niebuhr's 'Christ and Culture in Paradox' Revisited," *Lutheran Quarterly* 10 (1996): 259–279.

4. WA 49:434,16–18.

5. WA 36:646,15–20; see the presentation of this material in Oswald Bayer, *Martin Luther's Theology. A Contemporary Interpretation*, trans. Thomas H. Trapp (Grand Rapids, MI: Eerdmans, 2008), 111–112.

Genesis the professor mused on the material blessings that the patriarchs had enjoyed, for example in the "rich and sumptuous" gifts that God enabled Isaac to give Jacob (Gen 27:39–40).[6] Jacob modeled the kind of life Luther expected would come in reaction to this kind of faithfulness to God: his contentment in serving the Lord in the lowliest of earthly tasks served as an example for the Wittenberg students and their future hearers.[7]

THE WORLD AS GOD'S CREATION AND HIS WORKSHOP

Luther often employed the word "world" to refer to the place, the earth, or to the contingent earthly existence of human beings. Following New Testament usage, the reformer spoke of the "world" both as God's good creation and domain as well as his rebellious creation which had fallen under the devil's domination. This world appeared to him as a personal collection of individuals placed by God into responsible positions and governed by God-given standards. His high appreciation of cultural gifts in the musical and graphic arts combined with his belief that all uses of learning can function for the benefit of others, of all. Thus, God's good gifts of nature and culture sparked wonder, interest, and enthusiasm in him that led to praise and thanksgiving to the Creator, who has kept this world moving in the history the Maker had planned for it.

Luther gave few details of the human relationship to the world of plants, animals, and inanimate objects, but he recognized that, as he taught the children in his Small Catechism, God made human beings "together with" all the rest of creation.[8] He taught responsibility for the care and proper use of creation. The "dominion" given to human beings in his world (Gen 1: 28) lay beyond Luther's imagination, he confessed in 1535. He could not envision what use could have been made of livestock, fish, and other animals in Eden, for Adam would have eaten far better fruits. He would have used creatures of all kinds "only to express awe and wonder for God and a holy pleasure" beyond sinful imagination.[9] When creation performs in an imperfect way, the devil is at fault, Luther believed,[10] so

6. WA 43:523,16–524,31, LW 5:138–140.
7. WA 43: 617,36–619,4, LW 5: 274–276; cf. WA 43:642,33–39, LW 5:310–311. Cf. Robert Kolb, "Luther's Providential God," in *The Interface of Science, Theology, and Religion: Essays in Honor of Alister E. McGrath*, ed. Dennis Ngien (Eugene: Pickwick, 2019), 48–65.
8. BSELK870/871,9, BC 354.
9. WA 42: 54,18–30, LW 1: 71.
10. BSELK 1098/1099,1–2, BC 451.

that we may conclude that those human beings who pollute the air and contaminate the soil act in the service of the Evil One.

Luther is well-known for his pessimistic view of human performance as individuals sought a relationship with God. As mentioned above, he perceives the miseries of a world in which violence, illness, and all manner of ill treatment from fellow human beings seem constant. His comments often present a dour, dreary mien. However, with his high appreciation of the blessings God regularly bestows, Luther recognized God's providential hand in daily life. Both maternal and paternal grandparents, townsfolk in the first case, peasants in the second, had enjoyed relative prosperity. His own parental household, while experiencing the ups and downs of every beginning entrepreneur, had furnished the young Martin a materially comfortable life for Mansfeld circumstances. He recognized that this world belongs to its Creator. His high appreciation of the created order and material blessings expressed itself in thankfulness for the provision of daily bread and for "good weather, peace, health, faithful neighbors," and much more.[11] He reflected that experience of blessing in his thankful explanation of both the first article of the Creed and the fourth petition of the Lord's Prayer. The former notes that

> God has given me and still preserves my body and soul: eyes, ears and all limbs and senses; reason and all mental faculties. In addition, God daily and abundantly provides shoes and clothing, food and drink, house and farm, spouse and children, fields, livestock and all property—along with all the necessities and nourishment for this body and life.[12]

In explaining the fourth petition, he expanded on this last phrase:

> the necessities and nourishment for our bodies, such as food, drink, clothing, shoes, house, farm, fields, livestock, money, property, an upright spouse, upright children, upright members of the household, upright and faithful rulers, good government, good weather, peace, health, decency, honor, good friends, faithful neighbors, and the like.[13]

In this way the reformers described the world as God's cornucopia of blessings.

The narrative of the disciples' great catch of fishes moved Luther to treat the connection between God's provision of temporal blessings and faith. He expressed high appreciation of the gratitude and contentment

11. BSELK 878/879,8–20, BC 357.
12. BSELK 870/871,9–17, BC 354–355.
13. BSELK 878/879,8–20, BC 357.

that emerges from trusting in Christ. The reformer models the proper expression of joy at receiving temporal blessings while offering at the same time a sober analysis of the ways in which the temptation to sinful interruption of God's gifts damages the shared life in society. "All who believe will have enough for their temporal needs, but those who do not believe can never get enough and have no rest in scheming how to secure riches, by which they fall into all kinds of vice."[14] The faithful remain constant even in times of want.

> Peter might well have thought since he had fished so long and caught nothing, "now God will let the stomach languish." But he does not despair. He continues to work; he stands and hopes that God would give it to him although he might delay. . . . even if God should delay a little and let you toil in your sweat, so that you imagine that your labor is now lost, you must be wise and learned to know your God and to trust in him.[15]

Luther connected the bounty of God's gifts with his hearers' conduct of daily life. He told the Wittenberg congregation that Christians must learn to deal with the evils perpetrated in his world and to strive against its way of doing things. They were to engage in this battle because God has given plenteously, reminding his hearers that they had rich supply from which to share the plenty and aid the neighbor.[16] Discontent with what God has provided causes love to cease, "so that a person does good for no one but scratches together everything only onto his own pile."[17] But "if a person believes, God gives him so much that he is able to help all people, outwardly with his property and gifts, from within by breaking forth, teaching others, and making them inwardly rich also, for such a person cannot keep silent but must declare to others what he experienced."[18]

God gives his blessings in the midst of the challenges and misfortunes of life in a sinful world. He serves not only as provider but also as protector amid all kinds of perils and threats. Scripture offered many examples of his care for his people. The case of God's protection of Jacob as he returned home and met Esau (Gen 32), the brother whom he had cheated out of his inheritance, reminded Luther that the whole course of nature and human life reveals more good than evil. Believers must acknowledge that his example demonstrates that Satan controls very little in believers'

14. WA 10,3: 228,13–19, Lenker, *Sermons*, 4: 133.
15. WA 10,3: 231,8–17, Lenker, *Sermons* 4:136.
16. WA 45: 700, 10–15, LW 24: 261.
17. WA 10,3: 229,16–18, Lenker, *Sermons* 4:134.
18. WA 10,3: 233,25–234,5, Lenker, *Sermons* 4: 139.

lives.[19] God rules. Even when the ungodly forget God and their obligations to him, he is leading and governing them as well as the godly in all their actions.[20]

In 1521 Luther had been sitting in the Wartburg, and as Fred Meuser has speculated, was watching how God presented a parable of his providential care for both the spiritual and the physical needs of his people in the courtyard below his window, where chickens had free run. His sermon for the festival of Saint Stephen at the end of 1521 treated Matthew 23:37, "O Jerusalem, how often have I longed to gather your children together, as a hen gathers her chicks under her wings . . .". Christ depicted God's providential protection of believers by comparing it to a hen sheltering her chicks from attack. Luther may indeed have been considering how to treat the text while looking into the courtyard below.[21] His sermon set forth descriptions of the actors in the drama: the mother-hen is Christ, the chicks play his faithful people, and the hawks take the role of the devils and evil spirits out to feast on their prey, the faithful. The chicks are none too clever but know enough to rely on the mother-hen, that is, Christ's righteousness, as their shelter and shield. They creep, snuggle, and crouch in the protective love of Christ in confidence that he will shelter them. The mother-hen searches and scratches for food and tries to coax her chicks into eating. Christ, like this mother-hen, with the concern showing in his voice, spreads wings of his merit over his people, warms them with his natural heat, that is, the Holy Spirit, and defends them against the devil. The hawks—Luther enriched the story by adding wild boars to their throng—want to devour and pursue the chicks and tear apart their victims, but God indeed protects and provides.[22]

In preaching on John 14:11 in 1537, not many weeks after suffering mightily from urinary tract stones in Smalcald, Luther observed that Jesus's reference to his works in this passage reminds believers to recognize all that God does to help and save his people. Luther commented that God is at work daily to keep his creatures going while conceding that God also does visit punishment upon those who do evil and puts limits on their ability to harm. Nonetheless, his hearers had experienced physical or earthly blessings more than they had felt his anger and resulting punishment. Without revealing the sources of his statistics, he suggested that the

19. WA 44: 67,9–10, LW 6: 90.
20. WA 44: 68,1–27, LW 6: 92.
21. Fred Meuser, *Luther as Preacher* (Minneapolis: Augsburg, 1983), 62.
22. WA 10,1,1:280,5–282,3, LW 52:96–97; this passage reproduces material in Robert Kolb, *Luther and the Stories of God, Biblical Narratives as a Foundation for Christian Living* (Grand Rapids, MI: Baker, 2012), 79.

healthy people outnumber the ill, blind, deaf, paralyzed, or leprous people one hundred thousand to one. Even when they have one body part that does not function well, the entire person, body and soul, exhibits nothing other than the goodness of the Creator.[23]

Luther echoed these thoughts commenting on the next verse. God's providence for his rebellious world reveals itself in his directing the course of history even through the wicked but also through his judgment upon them. Twelve years had passed since the confrontation of tyrannous rulers and their rebellious subjects had occurred in the Peasants' Revolt. At that time, in 1537, Luther spared none, but referred to discontent and resentment among all social groups of people. Speaking directly to his Wittenberg hearers, he noted that the riffraff among the middle class did not differ from peasants and noble families. They all submit to the rules of society reluctantly and unwillingly. They resent the rule of law. With a note of sarcasm directed at the courtiers among his hearers, he noted that it is clear that rulers are not the ones responsible for upholding public order; another power subdues the wickedness and rebellious spirit of the crowd. If God were not doing that, society would fall apart. Luther criticized both rulers who act tyrannously and the common people, for both reject and oppress the word of God and the people of God, killing them and putting an end to their prayers. God's patience with these ways of the world runs out. He shuts his eyes and gives free rein to princes and civic leaders, as well as the common people, with the result that they bring about their own ruin like a building that collapses in upon itself. The world cannot govern itself. It goes its own way to its own ruin.[24] But this negative form of providence is intended to call sinners to repentance even as it gives protection to the people of God.

Luther's understanding of human righteousness envisions an external performance of God's law that constitutes what he labeled "civil righteousness." It provides some degree of order in society and thus preserves the outward semblance of peace in the world. Though arising from other than God-pleasing motivations, anchored in some kind of system of rewards and punishments, even the actions that only externally conform to God's plan for human life benefit society and make life with other people possible. In the Smalcald Articles Luther noted that the "political" or "societal" use of the law, with its threats of punishment and promise of rewards, diminishes sins and restricts evil.[25]

23. WA 45: 527, 27–37, LW 24: 73.
24. WA 45: 534,21–535,2, LW 24: 81.
25. BSELK 750/751,1–12, BC 311–312.

In other contexts, he was even more positive regarding what he could call the "law of nature" and the "civil" righteousness it produces. He took for granted that all people have this "law of nature" written in their hearts and conform to it for a variety of false reasons instead of because of their trust in Christ. Both Jews and the heathen performed works conforming to God's law outwardly because of this law of nature.[26] In defending his view of justification by God's unconditional grace through faith in Christ against the critique of Jacob Latomus in 1521, he wrote that

> those things which seem good offer no benefit [for justification], as, for example, skills, talents, prudence, courage, chastity, and whatever natural, moral, and impressive goods there are. . . . It must be added that God himself does not deny that these [good things] are good . . . he rewards and covers them with temporal benefits, such as power, wealth, glory, fame, dignity, honor, enjoyment, and similar things.[27]

Most importantly, God does not view them as grounds for granting human beings the favor he gives freely quite apart from and preceding their feeble performance that can only truly arise from faith. Nonetheless, the reformer affirmed the goodness of these temporal gifts from God.

In his Galatians lectures of 1531, in the context of a discussion of the works produced by faith, Luther acknowledged that apart from God's justifying actions in Christ, good people who do not trust in Christ nonetheless served the public order and achieved significant accomplishments. He mentioned, as examples, names his students knew from their education in ancient literature: Xenophon, Aristides, Fabius, Cicero, Pomponius Atticus, and others. He cited Cicero's courageous death as he pursued a good, righteous goal for Rome.[28] He praised the integrity of Pomponius, who exhibited outstanding virtues and produced works that corresponded to God's law. These noble accomplishments did not justify those who did them in relationship to God, but they conformed outwardly to God's expectations for humanity.[29] Luther's comments on Psalm 51 in 1532 echoed this judgment. He noted that the civic virtues of many served the public good but also observed that this virtue was flawed. His list of ancient models of virtue included again Pomponius Atticus, Aristides, and Socrates. With a hint of wonder in his voice, he found that it was

26. See the marginal note to Romans 2:14–15, WA DB 7:35; cf. also WA 18:80,28–81,3; WA 14: 638,2–8.
27. WA 8:104,30–105,2, LW 32:225.
28. Cf. Carl P. E. Springer, *Cicero in Heaven: The Roman Rhetor and Luther's Reformation* (Leiden: Brill, 2018).
29. WA 40,1: 219,22–33, LW 26: 123–124.

even possible to find an honest merchant. God demands this honesty in the public arena, he commented, and yet it will always be blemished. Nonetheless, this honesty, as an expression of trust and trustworthiness, the basis of all human sound relationships, holds society together.[30] It does not give God the honor of trusting in Christ, which restores our humanity, but God nevertheless honors uprightness in society and rewards it so that society can continue to exist under the maintenance of public order,

LUTHER'S APPRECIATION OF TECHNOLOGY, ART, AND LEARNING

Luther basked in the many temporal gifts that God had showered upon him and upon the German and wider European culture of his time. He demonstrated imaginative openness to innovation combined with his application of a wide range of aspects of his culture.

Luther's appreciation of the cutting-edge technology of movable type took advantage of the infant printing industry. Andrew Pettegree describes his relationships with the several printers in Wittenberg and many beyond the town as cordial, professional, and demanding. The professor showed sensitivity to their economic needs as well as the artful form of efficient presentation in the medium of print. His aesthetic sensibilities led him to insist on the highest quality type and typesetting. He also complained about how rich the printers were getting. (He did not personally receive the equivalent of royalties on his publications although patrons of various kinds helped make his life comfortable). In Luther, printers found a cooperative author, who delivered manuscripts by the page if the printer was eager to get a product to market. In him some printers found a family friend, who shared their joys and sorrows.[31]

With Lukas Cranach's imaginative help, the author and the printers invented what Pettegree labels "Brand Luther," a new approach to the title page that sold copies by exploiting Luther's name, Wittenberg as location, and special attractive borders sketched in the Cranach workshop. With Cranach's innovative invention of a title page framing illustration and the local printers' adding to the typical medieval title page the place of publication and the author's name (which had generally not graced title pages of incunabula), the Wittenberg team carried book publication into

30. WA 40,2: 389,32–390,6, LW 12: 354.

31. Andrew Pettegree, *Brand Luther: 1517, Printing, and the Making of the Reformation* (New York: Penguin, 2015), 267–280.

a new phase.[32] Luther titles offered many printers a path to prosperity and success. Their success is reflected in the bitter notation of papal legate Girolamo Aleandro that in Worms in 1521 the bookstands were filled with Luther's works, and they were selling like hotcakes.[33]

Luther's own musical gifts opened another avenue for spreading the Reformation while it provided him with relaxation and enjoyment with family and friends. His well-known judgment, "after theology I accord to music the highest place,"[34] does not exhaust his belief in the intimate relationship of God's word in Scripture and musical tone and rhythm. But this appraisal of music as worthiest of highest praise after theology itself indicates the place of music in his personal experience and his apprehension of one element of the created order.[35] With musical gifts himself, and with a profound sense of the interconnection of melody and mood in human beings, Luther exploited God's gift of music with his own compositions. He promoted music with his own hymns;[36] with prefaces to six hymnals, such as the printer Georg Rhau's;[37] and with his defense of cantors such as Johann Walther.[38] In addition to Walther, he employed others, including the Bavarian composer Ludwig Senfl.[39]

His extensive use of liturgical music and hymnody in his understanding of worship indicates how he tied music closely into the proclamation of God's word. Joseph Herl demonstrates that Luther's promotion of popular hymns in no way excluded the continuation of choral singing; his appreciation for the potential of musical genres embraced a full range of his own musical experiences.[40] Robin Leaver's masterful survey of Luther's theology and practice of music played key roles in the reformer's practical, pastoral application of the gospel to the lives of people. As a gift of God, music creates joyful hearts, drives away the devil, creates innocent delight, and reigns in times of peace.[41]

32. *Brand Luther*, 147–163.
33. Hendrix, *Visionary Reformer*, 100–101.
34. WA 30,2: 695–696 Cf. WA TR 3:636, Nr. 3815.
35. Cf. examples in WA TR, Nr. 3815, Nr 7034, and in is preface to Georg Rhau's *Symphonia Iucundae* of 1538, WA 50:370, LW 53: 323.
36. WA 35:411–473, LW 53: 211–309.
37. WA 50: 368–374 (Rhau), and 331–333, 474–475, 478–483, LW 53: 315–334.
38. Walter Blankenburg, *Johann Walter: Leben und Werk* (Tützing: Schneider, 1991), Martin Bender, *Allein auf Gottes Wort, Johann Walter, Kantor der Reformation* (Berlin: Evangelische Verlagsanstalt, 1971).
39. Cf. Leaver's comprehensive overview in *Luther's Liturgical Music: Principles and Implications* (Grand Rapids, MI: Eerdmans, 2007).
40. Joseph Herl, *Worship Wars in Early Lutheranism: Choir, Congregation, and Three Centuries of Conflict* (Oxford: Oxford University Press, 2004) 3–22.
41. Leaver, *Luther's Liturgical Music*, 89–97.

Dietrich Korsch describes Luther's connecting music in its effect on emotions to human physiology and psychology, on the one hand, and to the deepest theological thinking.[42] "Just as the law is ruled by the gospel, so the b fa b mi governs the other degrees. And just as the gospel is the sweetest doctrine, so the mi and fa are the sweetest of tones. The second tone is a poor sinner, who in b fa bi permits both mi and fa to be sung."[43]

Equally significant as his engagement with the musical arts, his contacts to Lukas Cranach and other graphic artists led to his employing not only hymnody and other forms of music—including his fascination with polyphony—but also the woodcuts and paintings of the Cranach studio and other graphic artists for promoting his program of reform. His enjoyment of the graphic arts also provided him and his family, colleagues, and friends enjoyment. He often expressed his own confidence in the power of the visual, always against the background of biblical explanation, to cultivate the faith and aid learning.[44] The Cranach workshop's proclamation of Luther's distinction of law and gospel in several forms illustrates how both the Elder and the Younger Cranach digested Luther's thinking and placed it in the spread of Luther's message. Luther probably also influenced Cranach's practice of his trade. Hanne Kolind Poulsen concludes that "Luther's thoughts on images partly legitimized the process in Cranach's portraits toward an iconic quality, which contrasted sharply with the humanists' idea of mimesis, and partly reinforced it. The portraits became 'masks'" of the reformers and others.[45]

Wittenberg university not only pioneered theological thinking, but also promoted advances in a number of other fields of learning intrinsic to the medieval university curriculum while expanding its offerings.[46]

42. "The Word of God and Music in Luther: Re-Reading Luther's 1538 Rhau Preface," in *Lutheran Music Culture: Ideals and Practices*, ed. Mattias Lundberg, Maria Schildt, and Jonas Lundblad (Berlin: de Gruyter, 2022), 21–33, esp. 24–28; cf. Joyce Irwin, "Luther, Mattheson, and the Joy of Music," in *Lutheran Music Culture*, esp. 115–122, in which Irwin shows that Luther's joy is not merely happiness but a joy in the midst of *Anfechtungen* because it springs from the gospel and expresses itself in praise of God. See also, Mikka E. Antilla, *Luther's Theology of Music: Spiritual Beauty and Pleasure* (Berlin: de Gruyter, 2013).

43. WA TR 1: 396, Nr. 816, cited in Eyolf Østrem, "'Musicam semper amavi': What is Remarkable about Luther's Views on Music?" in *Lutheran Music Culture*, 40.

44. Mark M. Mattes, *Martin Luther's Theology of Beauty, a Reappraisal* (Grand Rapids, MI: Baker Academic, 2017).

45. Hanne Kolind Poulsen, "Between Convention, Likeness and Iconicity: Cranach's Portraits and Luther's Thoughts on Images," in *Lucas Cranach 1553/2003: Wittenberger Tagungsbeiträge anlässlich des 450. Todesjahres Lucas Cranachs des Älteren*, ed. Andreas Tacke (Leipzig: Evangelische Verlagsanstalt, 2007), 215, 205–216.

46. Robert Kolb, "The Wittenberg Impact on University Education and the Christian Liberal Arts," in *My Savior's Guest: A Festschrift in Honor of Erling Teigen*, ed. Thomas Rank (New

In his Genesis lectures of 1535, Luther praised the mathematical disciplines alongside rhetoric and dialectic.[47] Fundamental to all learning, the language arts practiced by Luther—and developed into advanced theory in grammar, dialectic or logic, and rhetoric by Melanchthon and their disciples—advanced the understanding and use of linguistic principles across the confessional spectrum of later sixteenth and seventeenth century Europe.[48] Wittenberg students continued their work in cultivating proper understanding and use of language, producing major works in neo-Latin poetry, for instance.[49]

Melanchthon and Luther shared a common perception of history, both sacred and secular, as an important tool in cultivating the mind. Under Melanchthon's leadership it edged its way into the university curriculum. Their students established foundations for the writing of church history in the modern era, particularly under the direction of Matthias Flacius, Johannes Wigand, and Matthäus Judex.[50] Others produced chronicles and other historical-cultural studies for instruction in secular history.[51]

York: Lulu Press, 2021), 91–108; Robert Kolb, "Melanchthon as Model of Scholarly Practice," forthcoming.

47. WA 42: 34, 37–35,7, LW 1: 46.
48. Brian Cummings, *The Literary Culture of the Reformation: Grammar and Grace* (Oxford: Oxford University Press, 2002), 88–101, treats Luther's contribution of "the reformation of grammar." On Melanchthon's contributions to the linguistic arts, see William P. Weaver, "Volume Introduction," in *Philipp Melanchthon: Schriften zur Dialektik und Rhetorik/ Principal Writings on Dialectic and Rhetoric. Principal Writings on Rhetoric*, ed. William P. Weaver, Stefan Strohm and Volkhard Weis, in *Philipp Melanchthon—Opera Omnia: Opera Philosophica* 2/2 (Berlin: de Gruyter, 2017), XXXIII–LIV; William P. Weaver, "Melanchthon's Rhetorics and the Order of Learning: A Case Study in Library Database Research," *Reformation* 22 (2017): 120–146, here pp. 121–124; "Triplex est Copia: Philip Melanchthon's Invention of the Rhetorical Figures," *Journal of the History of Rhetoric* 29 (2011), 367–402, https://www.jstor.org/stable/10.1525/rh.2022.29.4.367.
49. Georg Elliger, *Die neulateinische Lyrik Deutschlands in der ersten Hälfte des sechzehnten Jahrhunderts* (Berlin: de Gruyter, 1929).
50. Harald Bollbuck, *Wahrheitszeugnis, Gottes Auftrag und Zeitkritik: die Kirchengeschichte der Magdeburger Zenturien und ihre Arbeitstechniken* (Wiesbaden: Harrassowitz, 2014); Martina Hartmann, *Humanismus und Kirchenkritik. Matthias Flacius Illyricus als Erforscher des Mittelalters* (Stuttgart: Thorbecke, 2001); Arno Mentzel-Reuters and Martina Hartmann, eds., *Catalogus und Centurien: Interdisziplinäre Studien zu Matthias Flacius und den Magdeburger Centurien* (Tübingen: Mohr/Siebeck, 2008).
51. On Caspar Peucer's historical work, cf. Mark A. Lotito, *Reformation of Historical Thought* (Leiden: Brill, 2019), 84–280, 337–469; on Paul Eber's work, see Hans-Peter Hasse, "Paul Ebers Calendarium historicum (1550)," in *Paul Eber (1511–1569): Humanist und Theologe der zweiten Generation der Wittenberger Reformation*, ed. Daniel Gehrt and Volker Leppin (Leipzig: Evangelische Verlagsanstalt, 2014), 288–219, and Christoph Bultmann, "Paul Ebers Gelehrsamkeit," in *Paul Eber (1511–1569)*, 258–287; on Cyriakus Spangenberg's work, see Susan R. Boettcher, "Cyriakus Spangenberg als Geschichtsschreiber," in *Reformatoren im Mansfelder Land. Erasmus Sarcerius und Cyriakus Spangenberg*, ed. Stefan Rhein and Günther Wartenberg (Leipzig: Evangelische Verlagsanstalt, 2006), 155–170, and Siegfried Bräuer, "Cyriakus Spangenberg

At Luther's time Wittenberg pioneered in introducing the discipline of botany with practical methods when Valerius Cordus took students on field trips into the lands surrounding Wittenberg.[52] Luther's and Melanchthon's colleagues provided critical support for the propagation and use of the mathematical calculations and theory of Nikolaus Copernicus and thus served as a center point of astronomical discussion.[53] A pastor in the Wittenberg vicinity and later professor of mathematics at the University of Jena, Luther's disciple Michael Stifel, made contributions to the study and theory of mathematics.[54] Luther believed that God's creation lay completely in the Creator's hands and that its functioning should command dedicated interest and exploration from all human beings, especially Christians. The Wittenberg reformer's encouragement and support for the broad spectrum of learning reflects his conviction that believers are to praise God also through reason and research.

THE WORLD AS PERVERTED BY SATAN

Luther's experience had convinced him that God's holy world had been seriously disrupted. He had felt the impact of temptation and trial from the devil, the world, and his own desires. The biblical description of the roots of this triad of foes ranged against God's human creatures lies at least in part in Luther's favorite gospel, John. It seems that John's usage posits two perspectives on the "world," a created world and a sinful world. For John, it is precisely the sinful world that is the created world for which God gave his only begotten Son (John 3:16). This vision of a fallen, yet good, world shaped Luther's view of society and the life of believers in society. He preached the regular sermons on John in the absence of the Wittenberg pastor Johannes Bugenhagen when Bugenhagen traveled to

als mansfeldisch-sächsischer Reformationshistoriker," in *Reformatoren in Mansfelder Land*, 171–189.

52. Karl H. Dannenfeldt, "Wittenberg Botanists during the Sixteenth Century," in *The Social History of the Reformation*, ed. Lawrence P. Buck and Jonathan W. Zophy (Columbus: Ohio State University Press, 1972), 223–248.
53. Among many studies, see Dennis Danielson, *The First Copernican: Georg Joachim Rheticus and the Rise of the Copernican Revolution* (New York: Walker, 2006); Robert S. Westman, *The Copernican Question: Prognostication, Skepticism, and Celestial Order* (Los Angeles: University of California Press, 2011). Some Wittenberg colleagues followed Melanchthon in the employment of astrology despite Luther's bemused doubting; cf. Claudia Brosseder, *Im Bann der Sterne: Caspar Peucer, Philipp Melanchthon, and andere Wittenberger Astrologen* (Berlin: Akademie-Verlag, 2004).
54. Matthias Aubel, *Michel Stifel, ein Mathematiker im Zeitalter des Humanismus und der Reformation* (Augsburg: Rauner, 2008).

aid in the formulation of church ordinances in other towns or territories. Both in the early 1530s and at the end of the decade his Johannine perception of the "world" in need of its Creator's salvation guided the text.

Thus, Luther's reputation as one soberly realistic about the negative side of human experience is justified. Luther acknowledged that God gives rain and sun to the ungodly as well as the godly, and that often the world cannot grasp the fact that it is under judgment because life seems to be going well. Those who reject God and live apart from his plan for life also experience blessing and good in this world. The reformer called attention to the foolishness of the world; in its blindness it counts on a little good fortune lasting forever. It rejects the possibility that bad times could follow good. It ignores the existence of Satan and misery. Thus, the world is unable to cope with disaster since it loses heart, hope, and courage in its despair. On the contrary, believers know that in this world peace and tranquility will be interrupted by sin and thus that they must depend solely on God and his word of comfort.[55]

Luther observed in preaching on John 14 that it is in the world that the devil continues to enjoy causing misery and suffering among human beings. He was, after all, the one who shoved human nature into sin and death.[56] The "world" could simply be so "blind and foolish" that it seeks other ways to live than God's ways,[57] and thus it could be a place of temptation, of wrongdoing under Satan's direction.[58] The world is a place of temptation for believers because it opposes God. In this sense, "the world" is the condition of human thinking apart from an understanding of what is correct and proper in human behavior; thus, it is subject to futility (Rom 8:20). Above all, it is the enemy of their faith in Christ. Neither foreswearing proper use of God's gifts in this world nor indulgence of desires fostered by loving "the world" serve God and express trust in Christ.[59] The opponents of Jesus exemplified the "world" that vents its anger against the gospel and adds to its pagan sinfulness and wickedness with assaults on the gospel.[60]

Luther recognized that every society or culture operates on behalf of those who serve false gods as well as believers in God himself. Therefore, these systems and the institutions that they govern inevitably exercise self-defense in their efforts to preserve themselves as systems. They

55. WA 45: 470,31–471,40, LW 24: 11–12.
56. WA 45: 527,38–529,2, LW 24: 73–74.
57. WA 45: 496,27–37, LW 24:40.
58. WA 20: 799,19–39, LW 30:326.
59. WA 20: 660,33–663,20, LW 30:218–219.
60. WA 45: 582,3–585,3, LW 24: 133–134, WA 45: 722–723, LW 24 :287.

provide services for their inhabitants according to their own standards of value and order. They operate to benefit, first, the institutions of their own systems, and second, the people of the society, perhaps aiming for the good of all, perhaps designed to secure and profit a small group that possesses power. Some of these structures and standards, though serving broad human interests in theory, can be perverted by people turned in upon themselves. Others of these structures and standards more directly entice and ensnare individuals and groups in transgressions of God's will. This world is filled with temptations for people to sin, either through its allurements or through its persecution of those who trust in Christ. This world is a place where broken identities and lamed self-consciousnesses may gather together to lose their own disappointed dealings with themselves and place their core identity into the hands of the group, which means the hands of its leaders.

Therefore, as a model for his students, Luther continually admonished his hearers to avoid both "the subtle darkness" of perversion of God's word as well as public sins. As Christ said in the text on which he was preaching, "people love darkness more than the light'" [John 3:19]. Therefore, thanklessness, contempt for God's word, sexual sins, larceny, and coveting thrive in the world. Vices of all kinds proliferate in the world, in society, but no one wants to listen to criticism, Luther complained. He admitted that in his younger years he, too, had lived in this darkness, hostile to Christ while relying on the Virgin Mary and Saint George, the patron of the church of his Mansfeld childhood. In this way, in its blindness the world plunges toward its destruction, which gives way to even thicker darkness after death, piling up its own destruction with its desires, gluttony, drunkenness, showing off, avarice, jealousy, and the like. Luther concluded his critique by repeating his protest that the world hates and persecutes the servants of God's word and the Creator himself.[61]

It is not surprising that Luther placed those who proclaim God's word in the center of the attack on abuses of God's good creation. For, at the heart of the matter, the world's problem lies in its rejection of God's word. When the world repudiates Christ and pursues its own pleasures and material blessings, or becomes prideful, and when it dedicates itself to accumulating for self and exceeding other people in honor or power, it gains only the loss of grace, Christ, and salvation. It closes the door to heaven, and it earns God's eternal anger and displeasure. It throws itself into the company of the devil in hell.[62]

61. WA 47: 110,38–111,5, 111,26–35, LW 22: 390.
62. WA 45: 610,33–612,3, LW 24: 164–165.

Preaching to the Wittenberg congregation on John 1:47 in 1537, Luther described the sins that characterized the madness and foolishness of the wild and wicked world: he labeled its wickedness an infection and an infestation. Believers are tempted to conform to public expectations, even when those expectations contradict society's legal regulations. He singled out sexual sins, drunkenness, and the desire for revenge. He complained that the people of his time had no sense of shame, that all claimed to be good Christians. He labeled that simply self-deception.[63] Earlier, Luther had depicted the world as living carefree, self-assured, and with arrogant carelessness, without any fright. It ignores its need to be conscious of God's anger and his grace as well as its need to gain his comfort.[64] Thus, his hearers needed to know that the world already was standing under God's judgement because of original sin and was condemned by the law of Moses. Its inhabitants should know what their conscience (*Gewissen*), and heart was telling them, as Paul observed in Romans 1:32. The devil had led it astray, and it was filled with the results of judgment and death, no longer worthy of being loved. However, Christ had come to call his people to abandon their own fashioning of rules for life, putting them to death.[65]

Nonetheless, it was precisely this world that God had loved enough to send his only Son for the salvation of those who trust in him. In a sermon on John 3 in 1539, Luther noted that God loved the world so inexpressibly much that he gave his only begotten son, the ultimate expression of his mercy and compassion for the lost and condemned world. His hearers found the message that the world had been lost disgusting, Luther observed. Instead, they should recognize that the worth of the world in God's sight is measured in his giving a gift more unimaginable than the gift of a kingdom or a thousand angels. Nothing was more precious to God the Father than God the Son, God come now in human flesh. The world offers no merit to deserve this salvation, but those who were doomed and damned have become recipients of God's love and deliverance. So, the preacher appealed to his hearers to trust in Christ and cling to him and, as a consequence of this faith, to overflow with good works.[66]

Thus, Luther's relationship to "the world" in this sense took place in the context of what he viewed as the eschatological battle with this world, under Satan's direction, with aid of humans' own flesh. This "world" had gone awry through its governance by systems and institutions that are

63. WA 46: 708,21–25, LW 22:198.
64. WA 45: 561,3–8, LW 24: 110.
65. WA 47: 99,21–31, LW 22: 376.
66. WA 47: 96,40–98,40, LW 22: 373–375.

necessary for the smooth running of society. It had accepted the lies of the Deceiver regarding how to find and maintain the good life. This world seeks the pleasures that appeal to those who have lost vision of truly good life. It craves the security of an order based on some humanly devised ideology rather than fearing, loving, and trusting in God above all else. The world lives by its own wisdom, derived from its own way of reasoning. Therefore, it spitefully attacks the proclamation of God's word.[67] Luther asserted that Christ's call to his people to set aside its own wisdom does not appeal to the denizens of the world. But Christ demands that they abandon the world's conceptions about who God is, how he created and governs the world, and does what he does in it.[68] That is simply the way it is. Thus, to preserve its own systems and principles the world often must persecute believers. Against the fury of rulers and church leaders who persecute the gospel, Luther defiantly observed that this is God's way of dealing with the contempt of the world. He was relying on the power of God himself to preserve the gospel.[69]

Luther believed that God sometimes used such evils to the benefit of his people. "If all the devils, the world, our neighbors, and our own people are hostile to us, revile and slander us, hurt and torment us, we should regard this as no different from applying a shovelful of manure to the vine to fertilize it well, cutting away the useless wild branches, or removing a little of the excessive and hampering foliage."[70] Such persecution and harassment dare not arouse in believers feelings of vengeance or resentment. Preaching on John 17, Luther noted that Jesus urged prayer for the entire world for the sake of the believers in it. He noted that Jesus prayed for forgiveness for the world and the overcoming of its hostility to God. Prayer for the transformation of the attitudes of the persecutors of the church sought both their welfare and the welfare of those whom they were persecuting.[71]

In such passages modern readers sense that Luther defined the world in this negative sense as the perversion of God-structured relationships, which took place in daily life and formed the institutions and culture that he did not treat as entities in themselves extensively. The world in this sense had become the realm of Satan, whose temporary occupation of God's territory had had its certain end announced and sealed in the death and resurrection of Christ. The three enemies of believers, the devil, the world,

67. WA 33: 329, 26–330,29, LW 23: 208–209.
68. WA 33: 185,6–25, LW 23: 120.
69. WA 33: 247,27–248,21, LW 23: 158.
70. WA 45: 641,7–19, LW 24:198.
71. WA 28.130, LW 69:63.

and the flesh, were closely allied. Luther defined the "lust of the flesh" as the typical sinful search for whatever makes sinners "in the flesh," that is, in their sinful condition, comfortable and prosperous. The disposition of the sinner wants to avoid tribulation. This means that the world seeks and strives solely for things that serve the comfort and well-being of the flesh, which is loath to undergo any toil, distress, or disquiet, striving to escape the judgment of God in Genesis 3:19. All sinners seek a life without burdens or bonds.[72]

While the "world" unsettled Luther because of its attacks on the church, his awareness of social ills and evils led him to call for reform in civil society even while admitting that such issues lay outside his calling and competence as theologian. His *Open Letter to the German Nobility* (1520) had focused on reform of ecclesiastical life but also called for five improvements in civic life. He criticized "extravagant and costly dress," the spice traffic, usury, excessive eating and drinking, and brothels.[73] His preface written for the publication of the Smalcald Articles in 1538 focused on the theological and ecclesiastical questions that the reformer wished to have raised at the papally called council that was scheduled to meet that year. But he also called attention to concerns in society:

> There is disunity among the princes and the estates. Greed and usury have burst in like a great flood and have attained a semblance of legality. Wantonness, lewdness, extravagant dress, gluttony, gambling, conspicuous consumption with all kinds of vice and wickedness, disobedience—of subjects, servants, laborers—extortion by all the artisans and the peasants (who can list everything!) have so gained the upper hand that a person could not set things right again with ten councils and twenty imperial diets.[74]

God had called others to execute reforms in society and government, but Luther felt bound by his calling as a professor of theology to admonish governmental leaders to undertake such civil correctives as part of God's assignment for them.

POLITICAL AND ECONOMIC SYSTEMS OF EVIL

Luther had some sense that power structures bestowed a special kind of ability to wreak evil. He defined "the world" that persecuted Jesus's first disciples not as common folk at the societal level of these disciples but

72. WA 45: 608, 13–28, LW 24: 161.
73. WA 6: 465,25–467,26, LW 44:212–215.
74. BSELK 722/723,20–27, BC 299.

rather as the establishment, the ruling power-holders, nobility, wealthy, important, learned, who had repeatedly attempted to suppress and eliminate those who proclaimed God's word.[75] The solutions for these larger institutional problems lay, the reformer believed, in the responsible exercise of callings of leaders of commerce and government. He regarded them as having more burdens than privileges, and more threat of damnation, than did the ordinary people. That arose from the fact that the "world" in which they had been given responsibility and power in institutional form functioned as a tool of Satan when it failed to exercise its God-given responsibilities in proper godly fashion.

His observations of the political system of his time often did not identify clearly the still rather amorphous development of structure of the modern state. His fundamental perceptions of the ways in which the world works were set in his childhood. He grew up in the village of Mansfeld, among peasants engaged in the mining and smelting industry. At his parents' supper table, he heard much talk about the local counts and the elector of Saxony, who supervised mining in that area. His paternal grandparents lived in a part of the Saxon domains, in Möhra, south of Eisenach, where peasants had a good deal of independence but nonetheless lived well aware of the jurisdiction of their princes and nobles over them. Through his father's business dealings, he encountered the bankers with their developing capitalist structures and modus operandi. He met courtiers and merchants on the streets of Wittenberg daily. Thus, Luther had experienced political and economic institutions as well as individual actors in society.

At age 13, in early 1497, young Martin left Mansfeld for Magdeburg and his introduction to secondary education. Magdeburg was one of the six largest cities in Germany, with some twenty-five thousand inhabitants. After a year he went to much smaller Eisenach, where his mother's family and a circle of friends from the merchant class certainly gave him a picture of the changing political, social, and economic circumstances of the time. In 1501 he matriculated at the University of Erfurt, in a city with an independent municipal spirit even though it was technically ruled by the Archbishop of Mainz. Its nearly twenty thousand inhabitants also had a lively tradition of citizens' participation in the municipal government.

But despite these exposures to the more republican way of life in Magdeburg and Erfurt and the increasingly sophisticated aspects of the economic system of his time, Luther's view of good government and the proper functioning of the economy remained framed by the experiences

75. WA 46: 34,39–36,36, LW 24: 336–338.

of his childhood, reinforced by the nature of life in the shadow of the electoral court at the other end of Wittenberg's main street. For instance, commenting on Erfurt, he once mentioned the city's prominence and power but called its government directionless, "feet without a head." It possessed four counties, five castles, seventy-two villages on the best soil in Thuringia, but its government did not function well.[76] Commenting on another occasion on the four forms of secular government, monarchy, aristocracy, democracy, and oligarchy, Luther ranked aristocracy the best because it took care of the needs of the population with understanding, respect, and virtue. He recalled that Erfurt, in contrast, was subject to an oligarchy, which permitted only an exploitative few to possess power.[77] However, attempts to introduce new leadership through revolt brought no good results, Luther informed his students, lecturing on Isaiah 3:6 in 1527.[78] In 1509/10 bloodshed had accompanied tensions between artisans and merchants, respectively allied with the city's legal overlord, the archbishop of Mainz, and its neighbor, electoral Saxony. Luther told his table companions that he had gone to Johannes Staupitz with his despair at the way in which God governed his world and that Staupitz had explained that God calls people to repentance and teaches them righteousness through such a collapse of order.[79] Luther criticized lower class uprising with the example of what he considered the unjust execution of the Erfurt city counselor Heinrich Kellner in 1514, after Luther had left the city.[80]

It must be noted that based on his experience, Luther often railed against princely courtiers, merchants, and bankers, but the development of the impersonal nature of corporate entities had not progressed far enough for him to grasp their significance. He had experienced capitalistic practices and quite accurately imagined the kind of greed, seeking security in money, that stood behind them.[81] Thus, his discussion of economic issues called for personal obedience, particularly to the seventh commandment, but his judgments only skimmed the edges of the deeper systemic problems

76. WA TR 5:638–639, Nr. 6392, 6393.
77. WA TR: 4:238,12–15, 240,39–45, Nr. 4342.
78. WA 31,2:30,10–15, LW 16: 42.
79. WA TR 1:35–36, Nr. 94, see Brecht, *Luther*, 1: 33–36; cf. WA TR 1: 213–214, Nr. 487. Luther recalled the political maneuvering between Saxony and Mainz, cf. WA TR 2:669, Nr. 2800.
80. WA TR 2:487–488, Nr. 2494a and 2: 609, Nr. 2709b. On these Erfurt experiences, see Robert Kolb, "Luther's Recollections of Erfurt: The Use of Anecdotes for the Edification of His Hearers," *Luther-Bulletin, Tijdschrift voor interconfessioneel Lutheronderzoek* 10 (2010): 6–16, from which much of this section is directly derived.
81. Ricardo Rieth, *"Habsucht" bei Martin Luther: Ökonomisches und theologisches Denken, Tradition und soziale Wirklichkeit im Zeitalter der Reformation* (Weimar: Böhlau, 1996); Ricardo Rieth, "Luther's Treatment of Economic Life," in OHMLT, 383–396.

arising out of the development of capitalism and its replacement of the feudal system. He had experienced intrigues at the electoral court in the castle at the other end of Wittenberg's main street, but he still regarded them on a personal level. He sought solutions to injustice and maladministration in the personal repentance of the individuals within the systems, not in the alteration of the systems themselves[82]

Luther lived in another age. His thinking is therefore only partially helpful as a model for ours since he lacked a clear conception of institutions and how they function in a supra-personal, systemic fashion. His experience gave him a limited—medieval peasant's—perspective on the larger social structure and issues of his time. The Wittenberg professor knew that the Creator had designed the structures and institutions he encountered, and he thought of them in terms of the medieval understanding of "estates" (Latin: *status*, German: *Stand*), a network of mutual responsibilities for which God holds individuals responsible. The de-relationalized world of twenty-first century North America, Western Europe, and Australia removes the *corams*, with their face-to-face nature, in many cases. Individuals live within environments determined by forces set in motion a long way off, on Wall Street or in Washington, Berlin or Frankfurt, Beijing or Shanghai; seemingly impersonal powers pull the strings of lives half a nation or half a world away. Luther's personal world has diminished into a world in which most experience actions that affect their lives for which no one person takes responsibility.

John Nunes argues that Luther did indeed have some sense of the nature of institutions and systems that use the web of laws to practice exploitation and manipulation that harm the less powerful and privileged. Nunes points out that in his explanation of the ninth and tenth commandments in the Small Catechism, the reformer comments that the fear and love of God prevents believers from "try[ing] to trick our neighbors out of their inheritance or property or try to get it for ourselves by claiming to have a legal right to it and the like."[83] He had observed and experienced that some have the knowledge and the evil imagination to manipulate the legal system and its specific mandates as instruments for self-aggrandizement and exploitation of others, particularly the weaker in society. They used legal as well as illegal means to take advantage of the common people and

82. W. D. J. Cargill Thompson. *The Political Thought of Martin Luther*, ed. Philip Broadhead (Sussex: Harvester, 1984), 62–111; Eike Wolgast, "Luther's Treatment of Political and Societal Life," OHMLT, 398–420.

83. BSELK 868/869,4–7, BC 353. Nunes has laid out his analysis to me in personal conversation as he prepares a monograph on institutional evil.

deprive them of gifts from the Lord that these individuals with economic power coveted. Furthermore, in his Smalcald Articles, Luther recognized that individuals elected to the office of bishop of Rome were caught in the requirements of the papacy, indicating some vague sense of how evil is woven into an institution.[84]

Similarly, Luther clearly recognized that courtiers and capitalists conspired with each other for their own gain. This points to some sense that more was at work in the higher-placed sinners in society than individual responsibilities that belonged to their callings. After his admonishing servants, artisans, and merchants to repentance for their sins in the workplace and marketplace, he addressed "the great, powerful archthieves" in his Large Catechism, treating them as a type but nonetheless as individuals conspiring sinfully. He did not analyze the systems and institutional frameworks within which they were already operating.

> Yes, we might well keep quiet here about individual petty thieves since we ought to be attacking the great, powerful archthieves [with whom lords and princes consort and] who daily plunder not just a city or two, but all of Germany. Indeed, what would become of the head and chief protector of all thieves, the Holy See at Rome, and all its retinue, which has plundered and stolen the treasures of the whole world and holds them to this day?
>
> In short, this is the way of the world. Those who can steal and rob openly are safe and free, unpunished by anyone, even desiring to be honored. Meanwhile, the petty, sneak-thieves who have committed one offense must bear disgrace and punishment to make the others look respectable and honorable. But they should know that God considers them the greatest thieves, and that he will punish them as they deserve.[85]

Luther called those who exercise power in the world to repentance, but he perceived only dimly how others are simply caught in their web, serving those exercise leadership and control in society's systems and institutions and dependent on them for their standing in society and economic livelihood.

The example of the reformer's advice to the mercenary soldier, Assa von Kram, that he obey God rather than any human power (Acts 5:29)[86] is of little help to those employees of big banks and bureaucratic systems who are called to serve others precisely in capacities that do provide services to the public but often involve exploitative means. Luther directed

84. BSELK 742/743,10–20, BC 308
85. BSELK 1010/1011,15–30, BC 417.
86. WA 19: 656,22–657,10, LW 46: 130.

von Kram to do God's will when his calling as soldier imposed crises of conscience upon him. Von Kram was able to do that more freely as a mercenary than those drafted into a national army can do today. Nor do all those with significant responsibilities in multi-national corporations or the complex web of modern governments always have power or wisdom to decide how best to carry out God's will in specific situations when decisions are reached in equally multiple and complex processes of determining governmental or corporate policy. But believers in Christ dare never hide behind the complexities in doing what they should or must in such specific situations, Luther maintained.

It was at this personal level of perception that Luther described just, godly exercise of governmental responsibilities so vital in the world of God's order and Satan's corruption of it. The professor's experience with the courtiers at the other end of Wittenberg from the Black Cloister—and in other princely courts with which he dealt—convinced him to tell those officials of Saxony who heard his sermons in the town, or castle church in Wittenberg, that they dare not govern according to their whims. They dare not, like many, strive to attain only benefits for themselves. They should not be concerned simply about their own reputations and power, for that is not the task to which God had called them. They needed to seek the best interests of their lands, not their own honor or material benefit. Their calling would necessarily involve danger, and it would provoke reactions of thanklessness, contempt, and dishonor. They dare not react to such rejection in anger and seek vengeance. That brings good government to an end. Those who carry out their callings as public servants are to ignore their own reputation and well-being, ignore ingratitude and evil intent, and seek only the welfare of their subjects.[87] Luther endeavored to cultivate a sense of personal responsibility in all his hearers, and he recognized that those given authority to govern and lead a political entity of any kind bore intensified, increased responsibility for the welfare of neighbors who were subject to their governing.

Luther is often labeled a "toady of the princes," but in fact few theologians have been so openly critical of government structures as he. It was not particularly daring for him, once excommunicated and outlawed, to enter into public criticism of the theology and ecclesiastical policy of King Henry VIII of England, Duke Georg of the other Saxony, or Duke Heinrich of Braunschweig-Wolfenbüttel, all ardent partisans of Rome, from the safe ground of electoral Saxony. But his criticism very close to

87. WA 45: 582,25–583,3, LW 24: 133–134.

home in electoral Saxony does reveal his concern for justice in society and for the spiritual welfare of those who had responsibility for ruling. He called injustice against other human beings what it was, an offense against God that brings judgment upon its perpetrators.

Luther's condemnation of the revolting peasants in 1525 overshadows what he said of the princes and nobles at the same time. In that year he repeated his call to those with secular authority to repent of their injustices and of their excessive use of force in suppressing the revolt, reprimanding them sharply as "furious, raving, senseless tyrants," bloodthirsty dogs who belonged to the devil and were bound for hell.[88] Only when peasant violence threatened to reduce society to chaos did he urge the full force of government responsibility for order and the safety of all subjects be turned against the peasant rebels. Almost two decades later, Luther's lectures on Genesis held up Joseph's example as a framework for sharp criticism of princely tyranny and negligence in office. The ambition and arrogance of rulers enflame them against God and their people.[89] These rulers do not listen to the proclamation of God's Word, and they fail to exercise their rule properly. They ignore crime.[90] They fail to support the church and its pastors.[91] They raise taxes unreasonably.[92] God's judgment rested upon such misuse of God-given responsibilities.

Worse than the princes were their counselors. Those who were efficient in the exercise of their duties too often administered their responsibilities to their own benefit rather than the benefit of their princes' subjects, for whom they were supposed to be ruling. They resembled wolves, foxes, vultures, and other birds of prey in their striving for their own advantage.[93] In front of his students, Luther directly criticized Johann Friedrich's court for its wastefulness in the context of his exposition of the story of Joseph.[94] In so doing he addressed the decision-makers, not those who carried out their orders. In treating John 14:19 in the pulpit, he pointed out, with government officials among his hearers, that administration of a government office dare not be done simply by letting one's own mind lead and dictate. The world has many who are using such positions for their advantage,

88. WA18: 384–401, LW46: 63–85. Behind this treatise lies a sermon preached on June 4, 1525, "Verantwortung D. Martin Luthers auff das Büchlein wider die Reüberischen und mörderischen Bawren," WA 17,1: 264–268.
89. WA 44: 665, 3–7, 436, 27–31, LW 8: 117.
90. WA 44: 667, 32–35, LW 8: 121.
91. WA 44: 670, 28, 671, 18, LW 8: 125–126.
92. WA 44: 417, 33, 418,6, LW 7: 160.
93. WA 44: 416, 13–17, LW 7: 158.
94. WA 44: 451, 40, 452, 5, LW 8: 206.

to enhance their own reputation or power. That betrays their office and their nation. They avoid danger, contempt, and disgrace, unwilling to face anger. They should not have governmental responsibilities.[95]

God's word takes precedence over the word of the ruler, Luther consistently insisted. Rambling off from Rebecca's breaking the rules to deceive her husband and win the blessing for Jacob (Gen 27), he reminded his students that a civil government that permits the teaching of God's word deserves to be honored and respected as God's instrument for peace and order. But if civil government commands Christians to deny God's word, it should not be recognized as a proper government, as if its officials were carrying out their callings properly.[96] That led the professor to the conclusion in commenting on Psalm 82 that preachers of God's word are also obligated to call governing officials to repentance. Preachers who do not do so will be held accountable for the revolts of the oppressed and discontented.[97]

Luther expressed his deep concerns about the lack of faith and piety among not only courtiers, but also merchants and tradesman. He also criticized the peasantry—perhaps thinking of his relatives in the ancestral village of Möhra as well as those he encountered in the market in Wittenberg—for their contempt for God's word.[98] The peasantry, too, could embody the world in opposition to God. Luther objected to the way they often treated village pastors. He complained about peasants who had told the governmental visitors who came to inspect their congregations that they should not have to pay their pastors since they had to pay those who tended the sheep that supplied their physical needs, "and we must have shepherds."[99] He told of the pastor in Holsdorf, Saxony, who refused to admit some peasants to the Lord's Supper because they did not know the catechism and could not pray. When this pastor admonished them, they replied that they did not have to know how to pray because they were paying the pastor to pray for them.[100] However, Luther grouped peasants with townspeople and nobles who also objected to their pastors' denunciation of their pride and godlessness.[101] He could also attribute the peasants' faults to misgovernment and lack of proper discipline from

95. WA 45:582,25–583,3, LW 24: 133–134.
96. WA 43: 507,6–42, LW 5:114–115.
97. WA 31,1: 196, 19, 198, 18, esp. 197, 3–198, 2 and 198, 12–13.
98. WA TR 1: 43–44, Nr. 115; 1:146, Nr. 352: 3: 292–293, Nr. 3366. Cf. Robert Kolb, "Luther on Peasants and Princes," *Lutheran Quarterly* 23 (2009): 125–146.
99. WA TR 4: 68, Nr. 4002; cf. 2: 260–261, Nr. 1909; 2: 252, Nr. 2622.
100. WA TR 6: 163, Nr. 6752.
101. WA TR 4: 73, Nr. 4007.

the nobility;[102] the princes and nobles had provoked them to rebellion. He concluded that the Peasants' Revolt of 1524–1526 was only a primer on rebellion, an introduction to revolt before the catastrophe which the misgovernment of the princes and nobles would bring upon Germany.[103]

His experiences with rebellious violence, coupled with the general mood current among established people of the time, formed the context of Luther's reaction to the Peasants' Revolt. Thirty-four peasant revolts took place in German lands between 1509 and 1517 and 112 in the following six years. These breakdowns in order triggered widespread fear of social chaos and shaped Luther's beliefs that stable and just government was absolutely necessary, and that rebellion against established authority never brought a good solution, but rather often worsened the general state of society. Because his grandparents had lived as peasants without heavy restrictions or extremely burdensome obligations, his view of the peasantry contrasted with some colleagues who lived in areas where serfdom imposed poverty and suffering upon the population.

The revolts of peasants in several areas of the German-speaking lands in 1524 to 1525 placed Luther in a dilemma. Some peasant groups had appealed to him as an arbiter in disputes with their lords, who had taken possession of what had formerly been village lands under the newly introduced Roman law. His response had criticized their appeal to Scripture in matters of civil law but had also severely censured the nobility and princes for oppressive practices.[104] When, only a short time later, order was breaking down because peasants resorted to violence, he urged swift measures of repression of the rebels in order to ensure the safety of other peasants as well as town dwellers. He recognized that some peasants had been forced to join the rebel forces, but he still insisted on their personal responsibility for violent acts.[105] He had no grasp of the phenomenon of the "crowd,"[106] which swept individuals into group thinking as they surrendered control of their own decision-making.

Luther not only criticized the peasantry with the freedom of a person who arose out of a peasant background. He also held before his students the peasants as praiseworthy models of robust trust in God. He attributed this trust to their reliance on God's direct care and provision of the soil

102. WA TR 2: 371, Nr. 2230.
103. WA TR 5: 284, 285, Nr. 5835.
104. *Admonition to Peace,* 1525, WA 18: 291–334, LW 46: 17–33.
105. *Against the Robbing, Murdering Hordes of Peasants*, 1525, WA 18: 361,7–14; LW 46: 54 *Open Letter on the Harsh Book against the Peasants*, 1525, WA 18: 394,14–27; , LW 45: 76.
106. Cf. the analysis of Gustave LeBon, *The Crowd, a Study of the Popular Mind* (French original, 1895; New York: Greenpoint, 2022).

and weather that gave them directly the fruits of their labors.[107] He did not examine the institution of serfdom in any of his censures of principle mistreatment of peasants. Nor did his support of their pleas for justice address the system-based flaws as well as the individual offense against God's law that inevitably led to what Luther perceived as a sin-ridden world, to injustice.

Whether speaking of God's governance of nature, or of history, or expressing appreciation of civil righteousness, or human culture and learning, whether warning of Satan's domination of many aspects of life in this world, or attacking the vices or viciousness of the world as Satan's instrument and ally, Luther insisted that the world ultimately belongs to its Creator, the Father of the children he has gathered through Christ into his family. In the enjoyment of its goodness and in the battle against its pernicious perversities, God remains Lord, ever-present with his people in the world. In that certainty Luther lived at peace face to face with this world and with other human beings, indeed, face to face with himself. He enjoyed and reveled in the blessings of both a temporal and an eternal nature as he relished the prospect of peace eternal in his continuing face-to-face relationship with God.

107. WA TR 1:193, Nr. 443.

7.

The Reformer Face to Face with Other Human Beings

Luther coram hominibus

FREED TO SERVE THE NEIGHBOR

In 1526 Luther used lectures on Ecclesiastes to follow up on his critique of Desiderius Erasmus's defense of the free will in *De servo arbitrio.* Erasmus's treatise, cast in the genre of the university disputation, treated the impact of a doctrine of somewhat free human choice on the believer's understanding of the relationship given by God between himself and his chosen children. The professor's lectures on Ecclesiastes a few months later, in 1526, offered a realistic appraisal of the sense of futility and frustration depicted by "the Preacher." The lectures were dedicated to showing his students why belief in the freedom of the will to choose God over sin led to selfish exploitation of others for one's own spiritual gain. For Luther, "the Preacher's" words called attention to the powerlessness of people to counteract or manage the effects of sin and evil.[1] If the believer's own will is responsible in any way for salvation, its decisions will always be self-centered, focused on gaining merit by pleasing God rather than truly aiding others.

1. Robert L. Rosin, *Reformers, the Preacher and Scepticism: Luther, Brenz, Melanchthon and Ecclesiastes* (Mainz: von Zabern, 1997), 89–150.

Luther's recognition of how little human willing can accomplish nonetheless led him, like "the Preacher," to confess that believers should simply "fear God and keep his commandments" (Eccl 12:13). For, only those who fear God, who recognize that he exercises lordship over the course of human history, are able to cope with evil times and the temptation to be turned in upon oneself. Wise, noble individuals live well until tribulation comes, but then they act haughtily (presumably Luther meant that they try to exercise control, to their inevitable disappointment). This brings suffering upon them. Those who know that God is lord, on the other hand, can mock and show contempt for such afflictions while they show gratitude to God when evil stays away.[2] Luther recognized that his past lay buried in Christ's tomb and his future lay in God's hands, so he felt free to live out his identity as God's child in the present, praising God and serving other creatures in the callings that God had given him. Since the past lies in God's hands, it can teach his people but can no longer accuse or shame them. Because the future lies in God's hands, his people plan and prepare for it as they can according to his will, but they do not become obsessed with it or let fears of any kind overshadow it.

Despite the experience of doubt and despair in the course of daily activities, believers live in God's present and in his presence, counting on the Holy Spirit's aid in carrying out the full responsibilities that the Spirit has written into human existence. Christians are created and called to live out what they recognize in faith as their unconditionally granted righteousness in God's sight. They actively claim their new identity as members of his family, and they project that identity in righteous—God-designed and God-pleasing—thoughts, words, and deeds. They do that in the world into which God has placed his human creatures. Believers receive not only the forgiveness and new life of Christ's death and resurrection, but also the "mind of Christ" that took the form of a servant and led him to the cross for the benefit of those who had deserved only an angry rejection from him. In his treatise *On Christian Freedom* (1520), Luther set forth this truth with his two—only apparently conflicting—axioms: "the Christian is a free lord over all things and subject to no one; the Christian is a dutiful servant of all things and subject to everyone."[3] The Latin version of this treatise places the adjectives "free" and "dutiful" in the superlative.[4] Human freedom is quite complete as created (as it is)

2. WA 20: 202, 19–25, LW 15: 186.
3. WA 7: 21,1–4, LW 31: 344. Cf. Robert Kolb, *Luther's Treatise* On Christian Freedom *and Its Legacy* (Lanham, MD: Fortress Academic/Lexington, 2019).
4. WA 7: 49, 22–25.

by God's totally unconditional love and mercy. It is not the freedom to do what we please but the freedom to risk doing only what pleases God. Thus, inevitably generating the spirit of service to God's creation, this freedom is ready to push itself to its limits in self-sacrifice and self-giving.

Luther might have phrased the second axiom, "Christians are free to be once again completely human and thus to subject themselves to every other creature's needs, in love and service." For God created human beings not to be alone but to be in community as those who help and provide for each other (Gen 2:18). Real life unfolds in interpersonal relationships, Luther, like all medieval people, knew. The mutual accusations of Adam and Eve in the garden (Gen 3:12–13) are not the identifying marks of the original humanity that God created. Instead, delight at mutual assistance and cooperation, being the helper God had in mind in the first place, express our being in the image of God. Liberated from being, as Luther was wont to say, "turned in upon oneself" (*incurvatus in se*), people who are trusting in Jesus Christ for life itself give themselves freely and joyfully to others. In this way they are able to experience through these believers the love and concern of God himself. God's love, as embodied in Jesus, bonds them to those within their reach. Risks on behalf of others pose no ultimate threat or danger for those who believe that nothing can separate them from Christ's love. Difficult as some sacrifices for others may be, the fears of losing oneself if one takes risks to aid and heal the neighbor no longer need to cramp the style of loving and assisting without return. That is simply human nature as God designed it and as he has restored it through Christ. Confidence in the God who hung on the cross fashions the trust that such sacrifices will ultimately bring the benefit of discipline and strength to the believer.

Luther's own maturing understanding of his concept of the Christian's freedom emerged from challenges that the developing institutionalization of his reform created. He increasingly took note of the complex of relationships in which God's callings place believers, sometimes in the service of, and with responsibilities toward, other individuals, and sometimes with responsibilities toward groups of people to serve and care for them. Australian Luther scholar Brett Muhlhan places *On Christian Freedom* in the context of Luther's subsequent use of its axioms in the years immediately following its publication. Muhlan calls attention to the reformer's differentiation of two ways in which the love and service that flow from trusting in Christ express themselves in practice. Muhlhan recognizes that the nature of God's word, including his pronouncement of the liberating forgiveness of sins, creates reality in Luther's thinking.

He took for granted that this reality is the product of God's speaking. It is, above all, relational, between creator and creature and among God's creatures. This leads Muhlhan to summarize the treatise: "The modeling of freedom, for Luther, consists of the ontological (forensic) freedom of imputed lordship that is bound and compelled to bear the fruit of love, which will, in turn, resist the fleshly nature with good works and work for the neighbor."[5] Essential for understanding Luther's intention and modus operandi in *On Christian Freedom* is this identification of Luther's ontology as an affirmation of the creative power of God's word and a recognition that God as Creator grounds all reality in his relationship with every person and thing he has made.

Muhlhan perceptively distinguishes two forms of the imperative of love and service that give concrete form to the bonds of believers to other people. The "personal-social" command to love the individual neighbor, the imperative *coram vicino* (face to face with the neighbor) takes different paths of action than the "official-social" command to practice love within society and for benefit and blessing of groups of people, love *coram mundo*. The disposition of trust leads inevitably to action in both fields of relationship, Muhlhan demonstrates, within the framework of the distinction of law and gospel and the theology of the cross.

The understanding of the Christian life outlined in *On Christian Freedom* served the reformer well during the tumult provoked by the rush to reform led by Karlstadt in Wittenberg in 1521 to 1522 and during the Peasants' Revolt of 1524 to 1525, Muhlhan demonstrates. In the first context, the offense to individual believers caused by rapid changes in ecclesiastical practices concerned him. In the second, his worries concerned the welfare of society in general as the chaos of rebellion threatened everyone. The reformer's conduct during these events "reveals the profound theological and practical consistency Luther maintained throughout an extremely difficult stage of the reformation and reveals that the character of Luther during this intense conflict is consistent with the genius of his concept of Christian freedom."[6] Luther's concrete engagement with the daily human experience shaped in him a flexibility and inventiveness that let him come to grips honestly with the pressures and the potentials of life. The confidence to do that rested on his trust that in the concrete commands and promises that God gave him in Scripture, there are to be found the form and the motivation for truly human living. This enabled

5. Brett Muhlhan, *Being Shaped by Freedom: An Examination of Luther's Development of Christian Liberty, 1520–1525* (Eugene, OR: Pickwick, 2012), 20.
6. Muhlhan, *Being Shaped*, 246.

him to approach difficult situations within the distinction of the plans and design God delivers in his law and the renewing power God offers in the gospel.

GOD IS CALLING

Two elements constituted Luther's understanding of how God designed human nature to function in this earthly community of reciprocal communal life: the callings by which God structures human life and the commands which specify how people are to act. These vocations are the "places" or paths, or situations where love for other human beings and all creation is practiced. The virtues which God has written into human nature are the proper way to enjoy life, living for the Lord of life and the rest of his creation. God provides for his creation through human "masks," behind whom and through whom he actively cares for all that he has made as they carry out his commands in the context of their callings. Luther insisted that human beings are God's co-workers, not co-creators.[7]

Medieval social theory had identified three "estates" (Latin: *status*, German: *Stand*)—better translated as "walks of life" or "situations"—that structured society. The teaching estate (*Lehrstand*), the church (*ecclesia*), taught the truth to the society. Priests, monks, and nuns comprised this walk of life, which was also labeled an "order." The status of "calling" (*vocatio*) was accorded only to those in this estate. The protecting estate (*Wehrstand*) preserved the orderly and ordinary structures of society, especially those of public governance (*politia*), maintained public order, administered justice, and provided defense against external enemies. The nourishment-supplying estate (*Nährstand*), or household (*oeconomia*), the bulk of the population, lived in families that made services and products available for the entire society. Each individual was placed in one of these situations for the benefit of the whole society. These individuals exercised specific responsibilities or "offices" (Latin: *officium*, German: *Amt*) which embraced both the role or societal position and the functions of these offices. God is indeed responsible for everything and every movement in his creation, but as part of his image in his human creatures he has made them responsible for being the agents of his providing care in the warp and woof of daily life.

Luther appropriated this theory but transformed it into a tool for cultivating the practice of the Christian life within the framework of his own

7. WA 47: 857, 35.

understanding of God's will for individuals and society. The medieval definition of these walks of life limited the concept of having a call from God, "vocation," or having the privileged status of being in an "order," to the clerical walk of life. Luther broadened the use of these two terms to explain how all Christians should view the responsibilities to which God had *called* them, universalizing the understanding of what had been reserved for priests, monks, and nuns. He was convinced that God had designed each of the callings that shape human participation in his care of others as part of divine providence. Timothy Wengert has shown that Luther's desacralizing of the clerical estate ran parallel to this "monasticizing" of all of life.[8] In addition, the church was no longer the most important of the walks of life. The family became the foundation and cornerstone of society; if the family does not function well, Luther reasoned, the other societal elements will fail to function properly, as well.[9]

In addition, the Wittenberg professor came to maintain that all individuals have responsibilities in all three walks of life. When he wrote his Small Catechism in 1529, his thinking remained with the medieval model, and he provided biblical instruction for rulers but not for subjects, for pastors but not for the laity. The role of subjects and laity in their respective walks of life had no place in the societal schema that Luther had learned. By 1540, revisions in the text reflected his maturing view of the Christian life: the walks of life then included the members of the congregation and the subjects of a ruler.[10] Luther also departed from (or amplified) the general concept of this societal analysis with a distinction within the societal situation which embraced both family life and economic activities. For example, in the Table of Christian Callings in his Small Catechism, he addressed parents as father or mother and as employers, thus as master or mistress. He addressed the young as children and as servants. God calls individuals to serve others and care for creation in all four societal situations: family, occupation, society, church. Human life takes place in relationships so structured and so designed.

These structures function according to Luther within two interposed frameworks, both of which he designated with the term *Reich*

8. Wengert, "'Per mutuum colloquium et consolationem fratrum': Monastische Züge in Luthers ökumenische Theologie," in *Luther und das Monastische Erbe*, ed. Christoph Bultmann, Volker Leppin, and Andreas Lindner (Tübingen: Mohr/Siebeck, 2007), 253–258. It must be noted that Luther here was adapting and deepening medieval theological terminology; he was not using the biblical word "calling" in the sense in which the New Testament writers used it as God's call through the word to faith.

9. LC, Fourth Commandment, BSELK 968/969,11–13, BC 400.

10. BSELK 895/896,25–897/898,14, BC 365.

or "kingdom." In fact, he used this term in three ways. He had no idea that his words would be fashioned into dogmatic categories and be in use a half millennium later since he thought that the return of Christ was near in his time. So, he spoke or wrote for the people of his time, without much care for the precision needed by those who come later and could not understand him as easily in his own context. Occasionally in his writings and preaching, the word *Reich* referred to the political authorities and the ecclesiastical authorities, much in the fashion of some interpreters of Augustine's "two cities" in the Middle Ages. Much more often his usage of *Reich* designated the reign of God in contrast and opposition to Satan's attempts to rule over God's creation. Luther applied the term also, however, to two dimensions of human life, the vertical in relationship with God and the horizontal, in relationship to God's other creatures. In each of these *Reiche* in the Christian's life, the *Reich* of God is battling daily against the *Reich* of Satan. The three or four walks of life exist in the horizontal dimension of life even though family and church have responsibilities to present God's word in private and public domains. Luther designated these two dimensions of life as *Regimenten* as well. It is best to use distinct terms for the *kingdoms* of God and Satan, which do battle on the fields of both *realms*, vertical and horizontal. The danger of not distinguishing these two uses of *Reich*, even though the distinction is usually clear from context, lies in the false association of the horizontal realm with Satan's kingdom. Luther did not equate the horizontal realm with a more formidable presence of evil and temptation. If anything, the opposite was true. It is precisely in the vertical realm of life that the most severe temptations and the root of all sin, doubt of God's word, occur. So, "kingdom" of Christ does not mean "church of Christ" when considered in its institutional form despite the fact that the institutional church is designed by God to be, along with family, the vehicle for proclamation of the word that introduces and maintains Christ's rule.

God's commands give specific instruction for proper human behavior within the structure of callings. Sinners encounter the commands of God as a standard of evaluation. Honest appraisal of their actions and orientation always leads to negative conclusions. In a commentary on Psalm 23:3–4, Luther called the law a teaching that curses and condemns under God's wrath. The law sets the parameters of humanity, and thus it describes a system in which sin and death have come to reign. The law in and of itself bestows neither blessing nor benefit. Benefit and blessing come from God himself.[11] Indeed, his law reveals the shape of life as the

11. WA 51: 282,34–283,13, LW 12: 164–165.

Creator designed it and as the Holy Spirit moves people toward living according to it. It is intended to instill fear and humility in them so that they flee to a proper relationship with God. The law kills so that God can resurrect and restore life.[12]

Believers do encounter these commands not only as an evaluation of the sin that still invades their lives but also as God's plan for living the good, God-designed life. Concluding his exposition of the Ten Commandments in his Large Catechism, Luther stated that these commands are "a summary of divine teaching on what we are to do to make our whole life pleasing to God. They are the true fountain from which all good works must spring, the true channel through which all good works must flow. Apart from these Ten Commandments no action or life can be good or pleasing to God . . ."[13]

Luther's understanding of God's commands and the benefits of following them flows from his focus on the Creator as the source of all good and a haven in every time of need. Fearing, loving, and trusting in God above all things formed the basis of the truly human life. Each of his explanations of the other ten commandments begins with this foundation in faith in the Creator that issues in a desire to obey him; nine times Luther repeated the phrase "we are to fear and love God so that . . ."[14] as the basis for the thanks and praise of God and all service and obedience that mark the believer's life. For, only by finding the ultimate good and absolute security in him is the human being free to leave self-interest and self-protection behind and reverse the inward turn into oneself. It is hard to believe that every little aspect of the service we render to others is praise and service to God. But God has enlisted every human being in his structures of mutual support and care, and he thereby provides for the welfare of all his human creatures.

The obedience of believers, taken for granted as a natural product flowing from trust in Christ's pronouncement of forgiveness, finds as its object the neighbor in need. Its goal is that person's welfare. Luther recognized that if good works contribute in any way to salvation, then they will be first calculated by their value for the doer rather than the one for whom they are done. Because of this, even pious good deeds, when self-selected, often exploit the neighbor. When trust in God's securing life for believers stands behind their relationships with others, those relationships are unencumbered, emancipated from the compulsion to protect or glorify

12. WA 40,1: 517,19–23, LW 26: 335
13. BSELK 1038/1039,16–21, BC 428.
14. BSELK 862/863,4–868/869,2, BC 351–354.

the doer. This is the result of Christ's liberation of his people from the condemnation of the law, from their sinfulness and the tyranny of Satan, from the cloud that death casts across every human horizon. Christ frees his people to serve freely.

Luther spent much of his time in the pulpit setting forth God's plan for the proper enjoyment and practice of humanity. He addressed parishioners both with the call to repentance that the accusing or crushing force of the law generates and with positive and negative instruction for daily life. His succinct explanations of the Ten Commandments in his Small Catechism summarize what God wants human beings to do and what they have done wrong. The command, "you are not to kill," means that we are "not to endanger nor harm the lives of our neighbors but instead help and support them in all of life's needs."[15] These words could be interpreted as the condemnation of endangering and harming others and the positive admonition to help and support them, or they could be heard as a confrontation with sins of active commission, acts of endangering and harming, and of sins of omission, or neglect of the neighbor, failing to help and support them. The reformer sensed that the commands do both, depending on the mindset of the hearer. Luther seems to have realized that however we may intend to use the law as we address it to others, its actual function or impact in hearers may be quite different than the impact we intended it to have.

James Nestingen's observation that the law is like a tamed wild wolf and "never knows its limits" rings true. As helpful as the law can be for believers in their faithful decision-making, they never know when it will turn on them and ravage their conscience.[16] The law by any other name is still the law: it is designed to put the burden on the human creature, just as the gospel puts the burden on Christ. The burden on us can be light, as in the "he ain't heavy, he's my brother" principle, if borne by the reborn child of God. The more people believe the gospel that they have been re-created as a righteous child of God, the more they will strive to act out that righteousness. In consulting the law to ascertain the pattern of his design for human life, they will again see their own bowing to the practice of sin. No matter how helpful the law is, it is still the law, and it reflects the fact that from my our perspective we are not a pretty sight. That God sees us differently is pure bonus. Thus, in his Large Catechism, Luther treated the seventh commandment, for instance, presenting what

15. BSELK 864/865,15–34, BC 352.
16. *The Faith We Hold, The Living Witness of Luther and the Augsburg Confession* (Minneapolis: Augsburg, 1983), 38–39.

the will of God is for human conduct in callings that meet the economic needs of other people. He knew that it would impact individual readers and hearers in different ways. Some would be forced against their own wishes to behave publicly in a responsible manner; others would feel accused and crushed by the commandment's prescription; and others among the faithful would take seriously this presentation of God's will for dealing with goods and services.

In 1529 the level of the knowledge and practice of God's word that Luther encountered while a visitor examining local congregations for the Saxon leadership disturbed him profoundly. The people's knowledge of God's word and their adherence to God's commands after nearly a decade of their hearing the gospel moved him to write,

> The deplorable, wretched deprivation that I recently encountered while I was a visitor has constrained and compelled me to prepare this catechism . . . Dear God, what misery I beheld! The ordinary person, especially in the villages, knows absolutely nothing about the Christian faith, and unfortunately many pastors are completely unskilled and incompetent teachers. Yet supposedly they all bear the name Christian, are baptized, and receive the holy Sacrament, even though they do not know the Lord's Prayer, the Creed, or the Ten Commandments! As a result, they live like simple cattle or irrational pigs and, despite the fact that the gospel has returned, have mastered the fine art of misusing all their freedom.[17]

The seriousness with which Luther had hoped for the gospel's changing civic life became clear as he grew older and protested against the failure of his hearers and fellow residents to live the Christian life. In July 1545 he wrote Katharina that he would not return to Wittenberg since no one there listened to his message. He complained bitterly over sexual mores and indifference to God's word.[18] Luther wanted to see the fruits of the gospel in the lives of the people.

AN EXAMPLE: LUTHER'S VIEW OF HUMAN RESPONSIBILITY IN ECONOMIC CALLINGS

Economic life had attracted the Wittenberg professor's attention in part because of his family's experiences in establishing and maintaining the smelting operation in Mansfeld, and in part because German theologians were debating issues around the charging of interest in the 1510s. The

17. BSELK 852/853,6–18, BC 347.
18. WA Br 11: 149–150, LW 50:273–281.

colleague who would become his leading foe in the Roman Catholic camp, Johann Eck, defended at least some modification and relaxation of the strict prohibitions of usurious practices in the ethics of his time. It was said, especially among opponents of his position within the Roman Catholic circles, that he did this in the pay of the Fugger banking family in Augsburg, with which he was associated.

In 1524 a dispute developed within electoral Saxony between Elector Frederick's court and pastors in Eisenach over usury; this provoked Luther to write *On Trade and Usury*.[19] This treatise sketched the rule of the law as God's plan for human life and its impact as the crushing weight of humanness on those who violate the natural, created shape of life with materialistic idolatry, and its resulting disobedience. Luther took for granted that human community has its essential economic elements: "buying and selling are necessary. They cannot be dispensed with, and can be practiced in a Christian manner, especially when the commodities serve a necessary and honorable purpose." People need "cattle, wool, grain, butter, milk, and other goods." However, it is necessary to recognize abuses of God's gifts because of the search for self-gratification and self-indulgence. "Foreign trade, which brings from Calcutta and India and such places wares like costly silks, articles of gold, and spices—which serve only for ostentation and no useful purpose and drain away the money of the land and people—would not be permitted if we had proper government and princes."[20] In general, he advised merchants, "where the price of goods is not fixed either by law or custom, and you must establish it yourself, one can truly give you no instructions but only lay it on your conscience to be careful not to overcharge your neighbor, and to seek a modest living, not the goals of greed." Luther recognized that price controls would only have a limited effect and therefore suggested that only the conscience can bring justice to the marketplace.[21] Luther regarded God's law as his framework for life to which human legal formulations and regulations give only limited access; human wisdom is necessary to find our way through the tiny cracks in life.

When Luther addressed behavior in the economic sphere in his Large Catechism, no reader went unscathed. Luther began with a call for repentance from servants:

19. WA 15: 293–313, 321–22, with WA 6:36–60 appended, LW 45: 245–310. Cf. Ricardo Rieth, "Luther's Treatment of Economic Life," in OHMLT, 383–396.
20. WA 15: 293,29–294,7, LW 45. 246.
21. WA 15: 296,25–36, LW 45: 250.

> Suppose, for example, that a manservant or a maidservant is unfaithful in his or her domestic duties and does damage or permits damage to be done when it could have been avoided. Or suppose that through laziness, carelessness, or malice a servant wastes things or is negligent with them in order to vex and annoy the master or mistress. When this is done deliberately—for I am not speaking about what happens accidently or unintentionally—you can cheat your employer out of thirty or forty or more gulden a year. If someone else had filched or stolen that much, he would have been hung on the gallows, but here you become defiant and insolent, and no one dare call you a thief![22]

But Luther did not simply address the servants, most of whom were young and many from poorer circumstances. He also addressed "artisans, workers, and day laborers." They act

> highhandedly and never know enough ways to overcharge people and yet are careless and unreliable in their work. These are all far worse than sneak thieves, against whom we can guard with lock and bolt. If we catch the sneak thieves, we can deal with them so that they will not do it anymore. But no one can guard against these others. No one even dares to give them a harsh look or accuse them of theft. People would ten times rather lose money from their purse. For these are my neighbors, my good friends, my own servants—from whom I expect good—who are the first to defraud me.[23]

Economic activity in Wittenberg had an important focal point in the market. Luther continued in the Catechism with words for the merchants:

> Furthermore, at the market and in everyday business the same fraud prevails in full power and force. One person openly cheats another with defective merchandise, false weights and measures, and counterfeit coins, and takes advantage of the other by deception and sharp practices and crafty dealings. Or again, one swindles another in a trade and deliberately fleeces, skins, and torments him. Who can even describe or imagine it all? In short, thievery is the most common craft and the largest guild on earth. If we look at the whole world in all its situations, it is nothing but a big, wide stable full of great thieves. This is why these people are also called armchair bandits and highway robbers. Far from being picklocks and sneak thieves who pilfer the cashbox, they sit in their chairs and are known as great lords and honorable, upstanding citizens, while they rob and steal under the cloak of legality.[24]

Sermons behind the text of the Large Catechism did not only call for repentance from Luther's neighbors and friends. He recognized something

22. BSELK 1008/1009,11–22, BC 416.
23. BSELK 1008/1009,21–1010/1011,17, BC 416.
24. BSELK 1010/1011,3–17, BC 417.

of the larger problems involved in German economic life, though he still viewed these problems in personal terms rather than recognizing the institutional dimensions that commandeer and deaden individual responsibility.[25] Luther's vision of society regarded it as the God-ordained interconnected network of situations in which individuals exercise their God-given responsibilities.

OTHER CALLINGS AND COMMANDS

Underlying the commands of God is the fundamental disposition of human creatures that being created in his image has determined. Reflecting God's nature, the command to love the neighbor as oneself undergirds and informs every other command (Matt 23: 39). Callings focus the carrying out of God's will in daily life, but callings do not limit the practice of love. Love is not restrained by the boundaries of specific normal, or regular, areas of responsibility but goes beyond these boundaries of responsibility determined by these callings when the opportunity arises.[26] Believers are always alert to God's luring them into the adventure of loving the abandoned and the lonely, doing good to aggressive rebels even as their threat to society is being tamed. Believers seek opportunities to engage in conversation with those who have lost all orientation and fallen into apathy and ennui, or open hostility against Creator and creatures. Luther's entire ethical system flows from this fundamental disposition of love for the neighbor as God defined love in Christ, obedient to the Father, open to self-sacrifice for others.

The treatment of the eighth commandment in the Large Catechism illustrates this point. According to Luther, the commandment not to bear false witness does not compel one to publicly speak out with the truth in every case. The commandment "forbids all sins of the tongue by which we may injure or offend our neighbor." "It is a common, pernicious plague that everyone would rather hear evil than good about their neighbors." Luther continued by restricting public repetition of even the truth that might damage the other person if such public judgment is not part of the Christian's calling, for instance, in the administration of justice and the preservation of public order. Otherwise, "when you become aware of a sin, . . . do nothing but turn your ears into a tomb and bury it until you

25. See chapter 6, pp. 213–218.
26. Reinhard Schwarz, *Martin Luther: Lehrer der Christlichen Religion* (Tübingen: Mohr Siebeck, 2015), 407–442, esp. 430–442.

are . . . authorized to administer punishment by virtue of your office."[27] In a sinful world Luther knew that he and those around him needed to be reminded of the very concrete limits and possibilities for hearing God's call to live as Christ-like loving siblings of all other human beings and careful caretakers of all God's natural creation.

Luther placed special emphasis on the need for obedience to superiors because of the threat of revolt that hung over sixteenth century society. Both the sense of injustice in the populace and the sense of fear of chaos at every social level lent urgency to his exposition of the fourth commandment. Luther called for obedience to parents, employers, pastors, and teachers, as well as to governing officials. He also stressed the burden of responsibility placed upon them. When Emperor Charles V threatened to send troops to suppress the Wittenberg reforms and those princes and towns that had introduced them, Luther reluctantly gave up his opposition to the use of armed force against the emperor, at first by conceding that the constitution of the German empire gave "lesser magistrates" that power, and finally forging a theory to justify such resistance on the basis of the emperor's abandoning his calling, which included defense of true religion.[28]

The reformer's comments on his expectation for the exercise of civic leaders' God-given responsibilities in their calling as government officials illustrates the concreteness with which the reformer described specific callings. To his words of reproof of government officials who abused their office, Luther added instruction for carrying out their duties for the benefit of the population in general and for the pastors who were charged with their spiritual welfare. In 1530 he composed a "mirror of the prince" in a commentary on Psalm 82. It differed from Niccolo Machiavelli's *Il Principio* (1531/32) more than from Erasmus's *Institutio principis christiani* (1516/18), but in contrast to both it reveals his own unique understanding of the relationship between God and prince, prince and subjects. Luther labeled princes "saviors, fathers, and deliverers" of their subjects. God placed them in public office to give aid to these subjects, to provide for them and protect them, and to support the church without interfering in its conduct of the preaching of God's word.[29]

27. BSELK 1022/1023,6–30, BC 421.

28. Cf. Mark U. Edwards, *Luther's Last Battles: Politics and Polemics, 1531–46* (Ithaca, NY: Cornell University Press, 1983), 20–37; Eike Wolgast, "Luther's Treatment of Political and Societal Life, in OHMLT, 397–423; and W. D. J. Cargill Thompson, *The Political Thought of Martin Luther*, ed. Philip Broadhead (Sussel; Harvester, 1984), 91–111

29. WA 31 I, 189–218; cf. James M. Estes, *Peace, Order and the Glory of God: Secular Authority and the Church in the Thought of Luther and Melanchthon, 1518–1559* (Leiden: Brill, 2005), 181–188.

Scholars distinguish advice given to princes for knowing what is right, or virtuous, in their personal conduct from instruction on how to carry out their office wisely, with the proper practical activities.[30] Luther's treatment of Psalm 82 in 1530 concentrated on the concrete daily operations of the ruler. They consist of "doing justice to the God-fearing and thwarting the wicked," or promoting the preaching of God's word and the salvation of many people; aiding and supporting the poor, suffering, orphans, and widows, while giving them justice; and protecting subjects from every kind of attack and evil, establishing and preserving peace.[31] Luther then condemned three princely vices: doing nothing to promote God's word; not giving proper attention to their governing responsibilities and thus not providing justice and protection to the poor and needy; and practicing a sinful way of life. Such a way of life could be seen in their conducting their office in a selfish manner, as if God had given them their authority for their own use and honor, their own desires and arrogance, their own pride and splendor. This sinful way of governing could also exhibit itself in their acting as if they have no obligation to help or serve anyone.[32]

Four years later, in 1534, Luther again wrote a commentary on Psalm 101, and again fashioned it into a "mirror of the prince." In this work the reformer did not hesitate to criticize John Frederick's advisors and even the elector himself.[33] That criticism emerges gently but firmly in the commentary on the psalm.[34] Throughout the treatise secular princes among the readers are admonished to follow the pattern of life described

What follows is largely paraphrased in summary form from Robert Kolb, "Die Josef-Geschichten als Fürstenspiegel in der Wittenberger Auslegungstradition: 'Ein verständiger und weiser Mann' (Genesis 42,33)," in *Christlicher Glaube und weltliche Herrschaft. Zum Gedenken an Günther Wartenberg*, ed. Michael Beyer, Jonas Flöter, and Markus Hein (Leipzig: Evangelische Verlagsanstalt, 2008), 41–55.

30. Barbara Maigler-Loeser, *Historie und Exemplum im Fürstenspeigel: Zur didaktischen Instrumentalisierung der Historie in ausgewählten deutschen Fürstenspiegeln der Frühmoderne* (Neuried; ars et unitas, 2004), 11.

31. WA 31,1: 199, 4–5, 200, 5–6, 201, 26–27; cf. 205, 19–18.

32. WA 31,1: 214, 20—215, 12.

33. On the relationship between the electoral court and the team of reformers around Luther, see Günther Wartenberg, "Luthers Beziehungen zu den sächsischen Fürsten," in *Leben und Werk Martin Luthers von 1526 bis 1546*, ed. Helmar Junghans (Berlin Evangelische Verlagsanstalt, 1983), 554–561; Georg Mentz, *Johann Friedrich der Grossmächtige, 1503–1554* (Jena: Fischer, 1903–1908), 1:30–41. On the relationship of Elector Johann Friedrich and his court with the faculty at Wittenberg in introducing reforms, see Siegrid Westphal, "Die Ausgestaltung des Kirchenwesens unter Johann Friedrich—ein landesherrliches Kirchenregiment?" in *Johann Friedrich I.—der Lutherische Kurfürst*, ed. Völker Leppin et al., (Gütersloh: Gütersloher Verlagshaus 2006), 261–280.

34. WA 51: 200–264; on the implicit critique of the elector, see p. 198, in the introduction by F. Thiele und O. Brenner. Cf. Estes, *Peace, Order*, 193–205.

in the psalm; its descriptions of the ideal prince from David's pen serve as a textbook for ruling officials, according to Luther. King David is the true "model of the proper ruler."[35] In other works, Luther forthrightly discussed David's sins, including his sins in the conduct of his office of ruler of Israel, for example, in commenting on Psalm 51.[36] Here he ignored the king's flaws and vices: "dear David is so highly gifted and such a wonderful, special hero, that he is not only innocent of all the deception and murder that took place in his realm, but he opposed such liars and murderers and could not tolerate them. He turned on them so that they had to yield,"[37] an interpretation of the Israelite king's life that stands, at least in part, at odds with the biblical record and Luther's own judgment elsewhere.

Especially in commenting on Psalm 82, Luther emphasized that preachers of God's word are also obligated to call governing officials to repentance. "It would lead to much more rebellion if preachers would not condemn the vices of their rulers," he wrote. Failing to hold rulers accountable makes the mob angry and discontented, and it also strengthens the tyrants' wickedness. The preachers become accomplices of such evil and bring guilt upon themselves when they avoid such a preaching of repentance to government officials. They neither treat themselves nor let themselves be treated as mere servants of the prince, like hired men. They are the servants and representatives of God.[38] Luther's political theory in this treatise, as in all his comments on secular government, proceeded from his concept of the walks of life which constitute human existence and its social structures as well as the responsibilities God has built into each. God exercises his providence and his rule through his human creatures as they fulfill the callings that he has given them in life.

His admonitions to princes continued into his last years. In his *Admonition to Prayer against the Turk* (1541), largely a polemic against the papacy and against social ills in German-speaking lands, the reformer admonished secular rulers to ensure justice, curb usurers, and protect the people from the greed of nobles, merchants, and peasants. Governing officials should

35. WA 51: 227, 37–38. The phrase is from Heinrich Bornkamm, *Luther and the Old Testament*, trans. Eric W. and Ruth C. Gritsch (Philadelphia: Fortress, 1969), 9. Cf. Wolfgang Sommer, *Gottesfurcht und Fürstenherrschaft: Studien zum Obrigkeitsverständnis Johann Arndts und lutherischer Hofprediger zur Zeit der altprotestantischen Orthodoxie* (Göttingen: Vandenhoeck & Ruprecht, 1988), 23–73, and Robert Kolb, "David: King, Prophet, Repentant Sinner. Martin Luther's Image of the Son of Jesse," *Perichoresis* 8 (2010): 203–232.

36. See his draft of 1532, WA 31,1:539,5–540,2; the printed version of the 1532 lectures contains similar and more extensive comments, WA 10,2: 317,31–327,28; 330,22–350,28, 415,24–417,17.

37. WA 51: 234,12–16, 235,10–16.

38. WA 31,1: 196,19–198, 18, esp. 197,3–198, 2 and 198,12–13.

support, protect, and promote schools and churches and their pastors and teachers. They should nurture morality and honesty. Rulers should punish artisans, laborers, and servants for inappropriate actions. About the same time, in his Genesis lectures, he outlined how Joseph had modeled God-fearing, prudent, and just rule. Joseph's example provided Luther a framework for sharp criticism of princely tyranny and negligence in office.[39]

Quite important in his own life in Wittenberg was also the institution of the town council. He had witnessed positive benefits from good civic administration as well as its potential for corruption and injustice in Erfurt (and probably in Magdeburg). He seldom addressed the manner of governance in the towns in print apart from his concern that the town councils promote education. His *Open Letter to the Town Council Members of all Towns in the German Territory, That They Establish and Maintain Christian Schools* (1524) recognized that the power to implement his wishes for public education lay with the council members, so he turned to them.[40] In 1530 he published his *Sermon, That Children Should Be Kept in School* as an address to those with responsibilities as government officials of all ranks as well as parents, urging them to invest in education and keep its standards high, for the good of the society and the church.[41] We presume that as a prominent citizen of Wittenberg, Luther played certain roles as an informal advisor to the town council, applying the same standards there as he did in other places. Such interactions, however, have left few traces.

CALLED TOGETHER IN THE CHURCH

The institutional form and activity of the local congregation of Christ's people contrasts with twenty-first century congregations in North America in significant aspects of the life of Christians in social gathering and in serving others. At Luther's time, the local congregation in village, town, or neighborhood was integrated into the civic community in countless ways, so that the congregation as church shared responsibility for social welfare, education, care of the sick and dying, with the civil governing authorities. The pastor, as representative of the congregation, played a

39. See chapter 6, p. XX.

40. WA 15: 27–53, LW 45: 347–378; cf. Irene Dingel, "Luthers Schrift *An die Ratsherren aller Städte Lands* (1524)—Historische und theologische Aspekte," and Henning P. Jürgens, "Luthers Schrift *An die Ratsherren aller Städte deutsches Lands* (1524)—Entstehungskontext und Druckgeschichte," in Dingel and Jürgens, eds., *Meilensteine der Reformation, Schlüsseldokumente der frühen Wirksamkeit Martin Luthers* (Gütersloh: Gütersloher Verlagshaus, 2014), 180–190, 190–197.

41. WA 30,2: 517–588, LW 46: 213–258.

vital role in the civic community, and the lay people all functioned as members of the body politic, even though many had little ultimate say in determining village or municipal policy or piety.[42]

Luther understood the church not only as the gathering of the people of a specific place around preaching and the sacrament but also as the church of a region, for instance, the church of electoral Saxony. He worked with Melanchthon and other colleagues in organizing that territorial church and advised other towns and principalities on the reform of their churches, institutions that embraced the governance and coordination of the congregations within the jurisdiction of the prince or town council.[43] Beyond that, he recognized the entire people of God, those alive at his time and those who had died, as the holy Christian church, and he also felt a part of the contemporary church throughout the world, which encompassed believers in Christ in every corner of earth.

In his preaching and teaching Luther cultivated the awareness of his hearers and readers that they participated in this wider family of God that spread across the earth as well as in the congregation of their own locale. In his Small Catechism Luther taught children that the Holy Spirit does his sanctifying work not only "in me" as an individual but also in "the whole Christian church on earth and [the Holy Spirit] keeps it with Jesus Christ in the one common, true faith. Daily in this Christian church the Holy Spirit abundantly forgives all sins—mine and those of all believers."[44] The children were to recognize that they had a personal relationship not only with the Spirit who called, enlightened, and sanctified them, but also with the larger body of Christians throughout the world.

Luther clarified the terms used for the local congregation and that larger church in the Large Catechism.

> The word *ecclesia* properly means nothing but an assembly in German. We are accustomed to using the word *Kirche*, which the common people understand not as an assembled group of people, but as a consecrated house or building. But the house would not be called a church if it were not for the single reason that the group of people come together in it. . . . Thus, the word "church" really means nothing else than a common assembly and is not of German but of Greek origin, like the word *ecclesia*. In that language the word is *kyria*, and in Latin *curia*. Therefore, in our mother tongue and

42. On Luther's teaching on the church, cf. David P. Daniel, "Luther on the Church," in OHMLT, 333–352.
43. *Der "Unterricht der Visitatoren" und die Durchsetzung der Reformation in Kursachsen*, ed. Joachim Bauer and Stefan Michel (Leipzig: Evangelische Verlagsanstalt, 2017).
44. BSELK 872/873,19–24, BC 355–356.

> in good German it ought to be called "a Christian community or assembly," or best and most clearly of all, "a holy Christian people."[45]

He went on to define *communio* as "community," a fellowship that certainly embraced the local congregation but included believers all across the earth,

> a holy little flock and community of pure saints under one head, Christ. It is called together by the Holy Spirit in one faith, mind, and understanding. It possesses a variety of gifts, and yet is united in love without sect or schism. Of this community I also am a part and member, a participant and co-partner in all the blessings it possesses. I was brought into it by the Holy Spirit and incorporated into it through the fact that I have heard and still hear God's Word, which is the beginning point for entering it. Before we had come into this community, we were entirely of the devil, knowing nothing of God and of Christ. The Holy Spirit will remain with the holy community or Christian people until the Last Day. Through it he gathers us, using it to teach and preach the Word. By it he creates and increases holiness, causing it daily to grow and become strong in the faith and in its fruits which Spirit produces.[46]

The church exhibited Luther's conviction that reality rests on relationships. Not an abstract concept nor a distant institutional governance, his church in its several forms lived and breathed within the web of mutual support that constitutes the worshiping congregation and the larger community of believers at his time and throughout history.

As noted in chapter 4, Luther expected all Christians to give witness to their faith whenever they could, bringing the gospel to bear on the lives of others. He also expected them to be dwelling in God's word in their homes as parents instructed their children and servants in the Christian faith through the use of the catechism and the cultivation of daily meditation and prayer. He expressed his expectation that they regularly gather for worship in the church. In Wittenberg, services filled the week, and though attendance was sporadic at the week-day services, congregational worship framed the town's schedule and rhythm. He emphasized the need for frequent enjoyment of preaching, absolution, and the Lord's Supper. In 1523 he wrote, "a Christian congregation should never gather together without the preaching of God's Word and prayer . . . when God's Word is not preached, one had better neither sing nor read, or even come together."[47]

In a reformed order of worship written for the church in German in 1526, he declared his intention to purify but not abolish the traditional

45. BSELK 1062/1063,13–20, BC 437.
46. BSELK 1062/1063,27–1064/1065,11, BC 437–438.
47. WA 12: 35,19–21, LW 53: 11.

liturgy. He cleansed it from medieval accretions that fostered reliance on worshippers' dependance on their participation in the liturgy as a means of gaining God's favor or on the form of ritual performed by the pastor.[48] Liturgy should nourish the faith and give opportunity for praise of God. Therefore, the reformer expressed his wish that no one make a specific liturgical form "a rigid law to bind or entangle anyone's consciences but that all use it in Christian freedom as long as, when, where and how you find it to be practical and useful."[49] Luther envisioned a day when in addition to the worship of any from the local community who wished to participate in public worship, "those who want to be Christians in earnest and who profess the gospel with hand and mouth" should come together for praying, reading Scripture, enjoyment of the sacraments, and doing good works. They would also be ready to "reprove, correct, cast out or excommunicate" those who do not lead Christian lives.[50] He did not live to see a day when such a gathering within the village or town congregation was possible.

German princes and towns did not venture into the continents outside Europe and thus Luther's followers did not share the advantage of other European Christians, who could carry their faith to Asia, Africa, and the Americas supported by empire-building secular governments. However, Luther did recognize the need for constant outreach with God's word to those outside the faith by going beyond one's own geographical limits to other peoples. But he dedicated his own life to what was possible for him: restoring the proper understanding of the gospel and the proper practice of faith in Christ to the baptized who had lived in the darkness and deception within Christendom.[51]

Luther recognized that the church as an assembly was *simul justus et peccator*, both because it embraced more than just those who trusted in Christ and because even those who trusted Christ at times made ungodly decisions for the institutional life of the people of God and failed to reflect their faith properly in the activities of the congregation or larger form of

48. WA 12: 206,15–21, LW 53: 20.
49. WA 19: 72,3–20, LW 53: 61. Cf. Joseph Herl, *Worship Wars in Early Lutheranism: Choir, Congregation, and Three Centuries of Conflict* (Oxford: Oxford University Press, 2004) 3–22, Robin Leaver, *Luther's Liturgical Music: Principles and Implications* (Grand Rapids, MI: Eerdmans, 2007), Vilmos Vajta. *Luther on Worship* (Philadelphia: Muhlenberg, 1958).
50. WA 19: 73,32–75,30, LW 53: 62–64.
51. Gustav Warneck, *Abriß einer Geschichte der protestantischen Mission von der Reformation bis auf die Gegenwart* (Berlin: Warneck, 1910), 6–23 criticized Luther for not making efforts to carry the gospel beyond the German-speaking lands, an argument demonstrated to be false by Ingemar Öberg, *Luther and World Mission: A Historical and Systematic Study with Special Reference to Luther's Bible Exposition*, trans. Dean Apel (St. Louis: Concordia, 2007).

the church. Preaching on Matthew 22: 1–14 in 1533, Luther used the proverbial German in noting that one finds mouse excrement in the pepper:

> there are some evil people who bear the name of Christian because they have been baptized, receive the sacrament, hear the sermon but have nothing more from all that than the label. They do not regard it all as the truth. We must accustom ourselves to this. For our preaching will never produce a completely pious village, or household. . . . [into the church] come both the good and the bad. We have to suffer that and grant them that they can be called Christian. For even though they are not pious, they are invited guests. That will go on to the Last Day, and the judgment will turn out differently [than they expect].[52]

Furthermore, he recognized that even in the papacy the church had continued because the presence of God's word in preaching and baptism had continued to produce believers. For like individual believers, the church is the battleground in Satan's rebellion against God.

Christians proceed from their worship together into the world. Luther's understanding of God's callings to all people in their responsibilities within the situations of family, occupation, society, and church imposed a life of service to others, a life of self-sacrifice following Christ's example, upon his own chosen children. Luther strove to instruct his hearers and readers in how to carry out God's calling from the fountain of Scripture and from common sense formed by experience, one's own and that of one's society. For he believed that trusting God's sinner-embracing word of forgiveness and restoration of life leads to living out that life that Christ has won for sinners.

LUTHER'S USE OF GOD'S WORD IN BRINGING CHRIST'S LOVE TO OTHERS

Luther personally embodied faithfulness to his callings in his relationships with family and friends. He provided spiritual care for the suffering and grieving through letters[53] and in person in his circle of acquaintances

52. WA 52: 512,2–14.
53. Neil R. Leroux, *Martin Luther as Comforter: Writings on Death* (Leiden: Brill 2007); Ute Mennecke-Haustein, *Luthers Trostbriefe* (Gütersloh: Mohn, 1989); and Stephen Pietsch, *Of Good Comfort: Martin Luther's Letters to the Depressed and their Significance for Pastoral Care Today* (Adelaide: ATF, 2016). On Luther's use of letters for pastoral care in general, cf. Gerhard Ebeling, *Luthers Seelsorge. Theologie in der Vielfalt der Lebenssituationen* (Tübingen: Mohr/Siebeck, 1997).

and friends.[54] Melanchthon fell deathly ill in Weimar after consultations on the bigamy of Landgrave Philip of Hesse in 1540. At the request of Elector Johann Friedrich, Luther came to Weimar for consultation on other matters as Melanchthon lay unconscious in his sickbed there. Martin Brecht describes Luther's reaction in finding his colleague near death: "He turned at first to the window and stormed God in a manner that was unusual and outrageous, even for him."[55] He complained to God for imposing this suffering on him and "rubbed [God's] ears with all the promises that he would hear prayer, which I could recall from Holy Scripture, telling him that he had to listen to me if I were to trust his promise any other time." He took Melanchthon's hand and told him, "You will not die." Deathly sick though Melanchthon was, Luther instructed his colleague to not give an inch to the spirit of depression or he would be a murderer himself. As Melanchthon became conscious, he did not want to eat, and Luther told him that he had to take nourishment or "I will excommunicate you." Gentleness did not always mark his pastoral care. He wrote to his wife Katherina that Philip had really been dead and like Lazarus had risen from the death, for God had heard his prayer.[56]

Four years later their mutual friend Georg Spalatin, pastor in Altenburg, who had stood at Luther's side during the difficult years around 1520 when he served Elector Frederick the Wise as an advisor, was suffering from "a spirit of sadness," melancholy or depression. Luther had heard that he was even on the edge of death. "God does not want the sinner to die but to live and turn to him," he wrote his friend, whose conscience was being plagued by guilt over his approval of the marriage of a fellow pastor with the stepmother of his dead wife, contrary to canon law regulations that continued to determine public standards. Luther had the pastoral wisdom to take Spalatin's feelings of sin and guilt as seriously as Spalatin himself did. He assured Spalatin of forgiveness for his bad judgment, arguing that if he viewed himself as a real sinner, he should believe that Christ is a real savior. Spalatin was bombarded with comfort and counsel, not only from Luther but also from their mutual friends Nikolaus von Amsdorf and Melanchthon. They sent assurance that Elector Johann Friedrich also was

54. For example, Robert Kolb, "Seelsorge for the Cranachs," *Lutheran Forum* 42/1 (Spring 2009): 34–37.

55. Martin Brecht, *Martin Luther and the Preservation of the Church, 1532–1546*, trans. James L. Schaaf (Minneapolis: Fortress, 1993), 209–210.

56. Brecht, *Martin Luther and the Preservation*: 210, cf. Luther's report to his wife, WA Br 9: 168, 172, 22–24, WA 50:215.

graciously disposed toward the Altenburg pastor—who lived five more months after this bout with depression.[57]

Fourteen years earlier the student who was tutoring Luther's children, Hieronymus Weller, had been suffering the "spirit of sadness," and Luther encouraged him in a similar manner to do battle against Satan's afflicting attacks, just as the ancient Israelites had had to endure the attacks of the serpents in the wilderness. "God is not a God of sadness but of joy," he insisted.[58] Two subsequent letters continued with words of support and comfort, explaining that Satan's assaults were proof of Weller's faith that the devil wanted to destroy. Luther shared details of the aid from his Augustinian mentor Johannes von Staupitz which he had received when similar doubts and depression had had him in grip in the monastery.[59]

Weller must have found comfort in Luther's words, for he urged his mentor to write to his sister, Barbara Lißkirchen, who was married to a leading citizen of their native Freiberg, a mining center near Dresden. She was also suffering depression because she had become convinced that she was predestined to damnation. Luther did not mince words but with a firm tone counseled her to resist this despair.

> First of all, you must resolutely fix in your heart the point that thoughts like yours are certainly the whisperings and fiery darts [Eph 6:16] of the wicked devil. Scripture says in Proverbs 7 [25:27], "He who searches out the lofty things of majesty will be cast down." Now, such thoughts as yours are pointless, searching into the majesty of God and his high providence.[60]

His second argument began instructions on what to do concretely when such doubts struck Barbara.

> When such thoughts assault you, you should learn to question yourself like this: "Please, in which Commandment does it say that I should think about and deal with this?" When it is clear that there is no such commandment, learn to say: "Get away with you, tiresome devil! You are trying to make me worry about myself. But God says everywhere that I should let him care for me. He says, 'I am your God' [Exod 20:2]." That is, "I care for you; depend upon me, wait for me, and let me take care of you." This is what St Peter taught: "Cast all your worries upon him, for he cares for you" [1 Pet 5:7] And David taught, "Give your burden to the Lord, and he will sustain you" [Ps 55:23].

57. WA Br 10: 638–640, Nr. 4021, cf. Pietsch, *Of Good Comfort*, 27–100, 137–254.
58. WA Br 10: 373–375, Nr. 1593.
59. WA Br 10: 518–520, Nr. 1670, 10. 546–547, Nr. 1681.
60. WA Br 6: 86–88, Nr. 1811, cited in the translation of Pietsch, *Of Good Comfort*, 269–272.

Luther knew from his own experience that he dare not oversimplify the situation.

> Thirdly, if despite this, these thoughts continue (for the devil does not like giving up), you too must refuse to give up. You must always turn your heart away from them and say: "Don't you hear, devil? I will have nothing to do with such thoughts. In fact, God has forbidden me to. So stop it! I must now think of God's commandments, and in doing so, I will let him take care of me. If you are so smart, go up to heaven and dispute with God himself; he can answer you well enough." In this way you must always reject these thoughts and turn your heart to God's commandments.

Luther's comfort for Barbara Lißkirchen rested ultimately on the person and work of Christ.

> Fourthly, of all God's commands the highest is this, that we hold up before our eyes the image of his dear Son, our Lord Jesus Christ. Every day he will be our reliable mirror in which we can see how much God loves us and how well, in his endless goodness, he has cared for us by giving his dear Son for us. In this way, I say, one can learn the right art of dealing with predestination. This way, it will it be clear that you believe in Christ. And if you believe, then you are called. And if you are called, then you are most certainly predestined. Do not let this mirror and throne of grace be torn away from the eyes of your heart. If such thoughts still come and bite like fiery serpents, pay no attention to these "serpent-thoughts". Turn away from them and look at the bronze serpent, that is, Christ given for us. Then, God willing, you will feel better.

This wrestling with doubt and devil would go on, Luther was certain. He wrote further,

> But, as I have said, it is a struggle to get rid of such thoughts. If they enter your mind, throw them out again, just as you would immediately spit out some filth that fell into your mouth. God has helped me to do this in my own situation. It is his critical command that we keep before us the image of his Son, in whom he has revealed himself to be our God (as the first commandment teaches) who helps and cares for us. So, God will not allow us to help or take care of ourselves, which would be to deny him, and to deny the first commandment, and Christ as well. The wretched devil, who is the enemy of God and Christ, tries to use such thoughts . . . to tear us away from Christ and God and to make us think about ourselves and our own worries. If we do this, we take upon ourselves the role of God, which is to care for us and be our God. In paradise the devil wanted to make Adam equal with God so that he would be his own god and care for himself, robbing God of his divine work of caring for him. The result was Adam's terrible fall.

That was sufficient, he concluded, for the time.[61] In this way Luther used the medium of the letter to show his consideration and support for a woman he knew only from her relationship with his student Hieronymus and his brothers.

It is unclear what kind of satanic onslaught Else von Kanitz, a fellow nun who had escaped from Cloister Nimbschen with Katharina von Bora, was suffering, but Luther wrote her that the wearisome thoughts that the evil foe was imposing on her were evidence that she was only sharing the suffering of Christ and many other prophets and apostles, as the psalmists also demonstrated. In addition, he asked her to come to Wittenberg to teach in the girls' school there, perhaps sensing that she needed a change of scene and a more active life.[62] She decided not to come for reasons unknown, but Luther had tried to go beyond his words of comfort to provide support in concrete actions.

In his calling as professor, Luther not only consciously prepared his lectures and interacted with his colleagues, but also was in lively contact with students at various levels. Some lived with Luther's family in the Black Cloister; some of those recorded the evening conversations he conducted with them and others from the town who assembled there.[63] As professor, he had the sad task of informing parents when some students had died in Wittenberg.[64] Lewis W. Spitz Jr., noted that Luther always viewed human beings holistically: "His concern for students went well beyond the intellectual and theological to include their personal problems and social well-being." Spitz observes that his interest in his students extended long after they left Wittenberg, giving counsel and advice, celebrating family births and mourning deaths with them, intervening in their behalf when governmental authorities threatened them. He sought financial aid for them, accompanied their search for marriage partners, and fended off parental complaints that their sons had not returned to marry hometown girls but had found wives in Wittenberg.[65] His was a life lived for others.

61. WA Br 6: 86–88, Nr. 1811, cited in the translation of Pietsch, *Of Good Comfort*, 269–272.
62. WA Br 4: 236, Nr. 1133.
63. Ingo Klitzsch, *Redaktion und Memoria .Die Lutherbilder der "Tischreden"* (Tübingen: Mohr/ Siebeck, 2020) treats the memorialization of Luther and the monumentalization of his teaching by his students in great detail.
64. WA 6: 212–213, Nr. 1876; WA 6: 300–302, Nr. 1930; WA 8: 484–486, Nr. 3354; WA 10: 698–699, Nr. 4049.
65. Lewis W. Spitz, Jr., "Luther's Social Concern for Students," in *The Social History of the Reformation*, ed. Lawrence P. Buck and Jonathan W. Zophy (Columbus: Ohio State University Press, 1972), 249 (249–270).

BY FRIENDS BETRAYED

The same Luther who comforted even those whom he had never met personally could, however, display impatience and anger with friends, chiefly when they had betrayed the gospel and behaved in ways that threatened the reform efforts of the Wittenberg team. His impatience and anger with all whom he thought should know better than to deny important parts of the biblical message flamed up against those whom he had not met in person, to be sure, but his associates, when they taught falsely, aroused particular critique.[66] His fervor for the clear proclamation of the gospel of Christ ignited in him a fervor that impelled him to attack those who threatened that gospel and its spread. Mark U. Edwards has probed the elements of his anger, especially as he vented it with a ferocity arising from his sense of the life and death nature of the biblical message, often coupled with a sense of betrayal by figures from the pope to unfaithful colleagues.[67]

After initially trusting his friend to lead properly, for example, Luther finally realized the negative impact of Andreas Bodenstein von Karlstadt's rush to alter Wittenberg religious life. His concern for leading the innocent astray moved him in such an instance to bridle Karlstadt. Luther felt betrayed when his colleague and fellow comrade in arms called for fast-moving radical changes in the public life of the church while Luther was in the Wartburg. He perceived that the infant Wittenberg reform could be crushed by the reaction of civil authorities to the abolition of the mass, iconoclastic disturbances, and Karlstadt's open criticism of university learning. Karlstadt reverted to a medieval vision of reform that was moralistic and anti-sacramental. His rejection of the medieval priesthood led him to abandon vestments and other elements of medieval practice that he found superstitious. He claimed that "the gospel" demanded that of others as well. Worst of all, he turned away from dependence on the externally delivered word of God and interpreted the sacraments in symbolic fashion. Karlstadt abandoned his professorship and became pastor in the village of Orlamünde but continued to sow seeds of unrest.

The government of electoral Saxony banished Karlstadt as a dangerous agitator, and he left Saxony. When in the midst of the Peasants' Revolt authorities in Frankfurt am Main detained him, he appealed to Luther for

66. Mark U. Edwards, Jr., *Luther and the False Brethren* (Stanford: Stanford University Press, 1975).
67. Cf. Edwards, *Luther's Last Battles*, for an investigation and analysis of his reaction to the Roman Catholic party, the Jews, the sacraments, and political opponents. On the Jews, cf. the work of Stephen Burnett, "What Luther Could Have Known of Judaism," in *Juden, Christen und Muslime im Zeitalter der Reformation*, ed. Matthias Pohlig (Heidelberg: Verein für Reformationsgeschichte, 2020), 133–146, and other essays.

help in reconciling himself with the Saxon government. Luther asked for a rejection of his aberrant ideas; Karlstadt complied. Luther opened his home, first to Karlstadt's wife and then to his former colleague himself. Karlstadt came to Wittenberg under cover and stayed for eight weeks hidden away in the Black Cloister. However, Karlstadt returned to his contrary views, and the two could not reconcile their theological differences. In 1534 Karlstadt returned to the university world by accepting a professorship in Basel. Luther included Karlstadt among those whose sacramental views he critiqued and rejected in defending his own interpretation of the words of institution.[68]

In the late 1520s and again a decade later, Luther's and Melanchthon's former student and close friend Johann Agricola interpreted his mentors' theology in such a way that he eviscerated the distinction of law and gospel. This threatened the consolation that the gospel gives. Luther worked patiently with him to clarify his own key to pastoral care and the proper proclamation of the message of forgiveness, life, and salvation in Christ. Agricola expressed agreement with Luther but then returned to his own dismissal of the law's role in calling believers to daily repentance. He did this not just once but several times. Finally, Luther felt betrayed by a person whom he had repeatedly helped and in whom he had seen great promise as a theologian. By making the good news of Jesus Christ responsible for calling sinners to repentance and by labeling this call to repentance "gospel," Agricola turned the term "gospel" into an accusation and gave it crushing force alongside its being truly good news. He repeatedly demonstrated that he rejected the fundamental hermeneutical rule of his friends in Wittenberg. Luther became irreconcilable because of his deep pastoral concern and his disappointment at his friend's failure to understand what Luther thought should have always been clear to him.[69]

In the cases of Karlstadt and Agricola the feelings of betrayal illustrate the significance of the breakdown of trust and cooperation at the personal level of friendship in Luther's biography, especially when the reformer felt that these co-workers were betraying the gospel at the same time.

68. Amy Nelson Burnett, *Karlstadt and the Origins of the Eucharistic Controversy: A study in the Circulation of Ideas* (Oxford: Oxford University Press, 2011), 10–36; Scott H. Hendrix, *Martin Luther, Visionary Reformer* (New Haven: Yale University Press, 2015), 168; Edwards, *Luther and the False Brethren*, 34–59.

69. Hendrix, *Visionary Reformer*, 256–258; Edwards, *Luther and the False Brethren*, 156–179; Timothy J. Wengert, *Law and Gospel. Philip Melanchthon's Debate with John Agricola of Eisleben over Poenitentia* (Grand Rapids, MI: Baker, 1997).

Those who, in Luther's sight, should have known better than to oppose the faith included not only acquaintances but also those who opposed the gospel of Christ and the proper interpretation of Scripture as he understood them. As his conviction that Satan was endeavoring in more crafty ways to lure God's children away from the true faith in Christ, he attacked individuals and groups including those he labeled "Schwärmer," "papists," and "the Jews." His fierce critique of "the Jews" emerged only at the end of his life when rumors of Jewish conversions of Christians and other falsehoods regarding activities of Jews reached his ears from sources he trusted. After his more open approach to Jewish believers in 1523 in *That Jesus Christ Was Born a Jew*,[70] he showed little interest in the Jewish population of German-speaking lands during the later 1520s and 1530s. He did sharply critique individual Jewish interpretations of passages that he believed taught the doctrine of the Trinity or pointed to Jesus Christ. Increasingly hostile electoral Saxon policy and rumors of conversions and persecution of Christians impelled Luther into attitudes that betrayed his understanding of Christian love even for one's enemies.[71]

BY FRIENDS AND FAMILY SUSTAINED

Wittenberg Friends

The professor's relationships with several circles of those outside the Wittenberg theological collegium also enriched his life. The facets of his bonds to many of his printers exemplify a different sort of relationship than his ties to his theologian friends that extended to their families.[72] As noted above, his business relationships showed sensitivity and concern for his printers and with some of them he forged friendships. But with all his printers, he practiced symbiotic relationships that reflected a professional cooperation. This cooperation both enhanced the economic standing of individual printers and the entire town of Wittenberg and heightened Luther's ability to lead and direct reform in church and society immeasurably. Luther could be critical of his printers. For example, he openly displayed his discomfort with the type face of the first local printer with whom he worked, Johann Rhau-Grunenberg. He did not break their

70. WA 11: 314–336, LW 45; 199–229.
71. I am indebted to Professor Steven Burnett, University of Nebraska-Lincoln, for his sharing of his research for a soon forthcoming study of Luther's relationship with the Jews. Cf. Steven G. Burnett, "What Luther Could Have Known of Judaism," 133–146.
72. See chapter 6, p. 204.

relationship but let Rhau-Grunenberg know of his disgust for his sloppiness in producing his wares. Luther worked with several printers, with sensitivity for their economic plight, and with a willingness to hurry manuscript to them when they had begun to set a treatise in print while he was still writing the next few pages. He mobilized and transformed several medieval genres, the familiarity of which served as a bridge to the reading public, and he and his friend Lukas Cranach worked together to combine text with illustration.[73] His relationship with the Cranach family extended over two generations. The elder Lukas Cranach and Luther had formed a bond in the 1510s as the artist, a leading figure in the town council as well as at the electoral court, and the popular Augustinian preacher found common concerns. Luther brought comfort in his own unique way to Cranach and his wife when they received word of the death of their elder son, Johannes, on a journey to Italy.[74] The family friendship extended to Lukas the Younger, who after his brother's death, joined his father in the management of their studio.[75]

Similarly, Luther's barber Peter Beskendorf and he had formed a bond already by 1517. In 1535, Beskendorf told Luther of his plans to write a book on Satan's battle against believers, and Luther wrote for him a catechetical exploration of prayer.[76] Soon after this gift lay in Beskendorf's hand, the barber was celebrating with his family. Apparently, alcohol flowed. When Beskendorf's son-in-law, Dietrich Freyenhagen, a professional soldier, boasted of his body's magical powers to resist all weapons, the barber tested his claim, killing him with his sword. Luther and others intervened with the electoral court and attained a commutation of his sentence of death. Beskendorf lived out his last days in exile in nearby Dessau in destitution. Luther remained in contact with him, giving counsel and aid.[77]

Luther and his Family

Among the most telling of Luther's "face to face" relationships were those in his own family. His relationship with his parents is often defined based

73. Pettegree, *Brand Luther*, 39–46, 104–114, 143–163, 267–280.
74. Kolb, "Seelsorge for the Cranachs."
75. On the relationship between the Cranach family and Luther, see Steven E. Ozment, *The Serpent & the Lamb: Cranach, Luther, and the Making of the Reformation* (New Haven: Yale University Press, 2011).
76. WA 38: 358–375, LW 43: 193–211.
77. Martin Brecht, *Martin Luther and the Preservation*, 14–15.

on his complaints about their harsh treatment of little Martin, but such complaints can be found in the recollections of most people. His dedication of his treatise *On Monastic Vows* to his father, "my dearest parent," in November 1521 did not outright say, "you were right in opposing my entry into the monastery," but it amounted to that.[78] The cordial relationship between the two generations of Luthers, enhanced by the coming of the third generation with the birth of Hans and his siblings, suggests that the dynamic in the Luther family resembled the positive dynamic of many families as adult children and their children enjoy visits from grandparents.

As word reached Wittenberg that his father lay dying, Luther wrote that "from the bottom of my heart," he was praying to the heavenly Father, "who made you my father . . . and gave you to me that he strengthen you with his boundless goodness and his Spirit so that you recognize with joy and thanks giving the blessed message of his Son, our Lord Jesus Christ . . ."[79] News of his father's death reached him at the Coburg during the Diet of Augsburg. He wrote to Melanchthon,

> Even though it comforts me that my father, strong in faith in Christ, fell gently asleep, yet sadness of heart and the memory of the most loving dealings with him have shaken me in the innermost parts of my being, so that seldom if ever have I despised death as much as I do now . . . Since I am now too sad, I am writing no more, for its right and God-pleasing for me as a son to mourn such a father, from whom the Father of mercies brought me forth and through whose sweat [the Creator] has fed and raised me to whatever I am. I rejoice that he has lived until now so that he could see the light of truth.[80]

His companion at the Coburg, Veit Dietrich, a student and trusted editor of the reformer, reported Luther's mourning to Katharina: after two days he had recovered, although it was very hard. "While reading the letter [informing him of his father's death, from Hans Reinicke, his boyhood friend from Mansfeld], he said to me, 'So my father is also dead.' Then he promptly clutched his Psalter, went into his room, and wept so profusely that the next day his head hurt. Since then he has betrayed no further emotion."[81]

When his mother was suffering her final illness, Luther wrote to her, expressing his wish to be with her and reminding her that Christ had won the victory over death and all other enemies of the believer through his

78. WA 8: 573–576, preface omitted in LW 44.
79. WA Br 5: 239,22–26, Nr. 1529, WA 49: 269.
80. WA Br 5: 351, 20–36, Nr. 1584, LW 49: 318–319, translation from Hendrix, *Luther*, 216.
81. WA Br 5: 379, 16–19; Nr. 1595, translation from Hendrix, *Luther*, 216.

resurrection. In her baptism she had received God's seal and guarantee of her salvation, as it had been confirmed in her receiving the Lord's Supper and hearing the preaching of God's word. He ended by assuring her of the prayers of his wife and children: "Some are crying; others are eating and saying, 'Grandmother is very ill.'"[82]

The relationship of Luther and Katharina von Bora provided a model marriage for the students at the University of Wittenberg and many others. Luther's status as excommunicated outlaw made him seem less than a good match, especially in his own eyes. He was, in fact, a target for anyone who wanted to serve pope or emperor by delivering him to the authorities for burning or simply assassinating him wherever they might have the opportunity. The nun who had sought and found her freedom from the life of the cloister thought otherwise. Genuine love developed between the two, and they served one another with spiritual counsel as well as material assistance. In the latter category Katharina was quite superior to Martin, and she held her own in giving spiritual care and encouragement as well.[83] She managed a household with as many as forty residents and guests, including relatives, for a time with the assistance of her aunt Magdalena. She supervised hosting the residents and visitors in the Black Cloister. Her management of her own lands inherited from the von Bora family and her garden and brewery on the cloister grounds provided food for the residents. She cared for the sick, including plague victims. Among those who stayed for longer periods of time was Elisabeth of Denmark, electress of Brandenburg. She had fled the tyranny of her husband, Elector Joachim I, who despised her allegiance to the Wittenberg reform. Katharina nursed her through long periods of depression.[84] Though her assertiveness could raise hackles, she took part in the evening conversations her husband conducted[85] and had good relationships with Luther's circle of colleagues, especially Philip Melanchthon and Johannes Bugenhagen.[86]

82. WA Br 6: 103–106, Nr. 1820, LW 50: 18–21.
83. Sabine Kramer, *Katharina von Bora in den schriftlichen Zeugnissen ihrer Zeit* (Leipzig: Evangelische Verlagsanstalt, 2016) provides an excellent overview of the sixteenth-century sources extant on Katharina von Bora.
84. Hendrix, *Luther*, 201–202.
85. WA TR 2:303, Nr. 2047.
86. Kramer, *Katharina von Bora*, 73–74, 76–114. Contrary to what is frequently written, Katharina von Bora and Katharine Krapp, Melanchthon's wife, had a good relationship, see Stefan Rhein, "Katharina Melanchthon, geb. Krapp. Ein Wittenberger Frauenschicksal der Reformationszeit," in Stefan Oehmig, ed., *700 Jahre Wittenberg. Stadt, Universität, Reformation* (Weimar: Böhlau, 1995), 501–518.

Luther clearly enjoyed Katharina's company; as he prepared lectures or sermons, she sat near him at the spinning wheel, he mentioned.[87] She was often present and involved in the evening conversations that her husband conducted in the Black Cloister.[88] They corresponded on the finances of their household,[89] and he proudly described the produce of Katharina's agricultural enterprises, including her brewing (and selling) of beer.[90] When traveling, he kept his wife up to date on the state of his health,[91] and when she suffered serious illness, he shared his serious concerns with his evening conversation partners.[92]

Their correspondence reflected a lively, loving relationship. Luther designated his wife "my Doctor [of Theology], preacher in Wittenberg,"[93] "my lord,"[94] and an "empress."[95] He said of her, "I am an inferior lord, she is my superior; I am Aaron, she is my Moses."[96] He set her worth to him as greater than lordship over France and Venice would be,[97] and expressed his regard for the epistle to the Galatians by labeling it his "Katharina von Bora."[98] Family matters formed topics of conversation in their correspondence as well. During his longer stay at the Coburg castle in 1530, during the Diet of Augsburg, his devoted follower Argula von Grumbach visited him and gave advice on nursing the newborn Magdalena, which Luther passed on to Katharina.[99]

Luther entrusted Katharina with the handling of his scholarly work. From the Coburg in 1530 the reformer dispatched his manuscript of his commentary on Psalm 118 to Katharina for delivery to his printer Georg Rhau and entrusted her with the task of having Caspar Cruciger and

87. WA TR 3: 211, Nr. 3178, interpreted by one of those recording this conversation as a negative comment.
88. Kramer, *Katharina von Bora*, 173–175.
89. WA Br 9: 171–172, Nr. 3511.
90. WA TR 2: 290, Nr. 1995, WA TR 3: 300, Nr. 3390b, WA TR 2: 144–145, Nr. 1591.
91. WA Br 8: 51, Nr. 3140.
92. WA TR 4: 568, Nr. 4885, 4: 602, Nr. 4991.
93. WA Br 5: 154, Nr. 1476.
94. WA Br 5: 154, Nr. 1476, 5: 545, Nr 1683, 7:91, Nr. 2130.
95. WA TR 1:554, Nr. 1110.
96. John Witte Jr, "'The Mother of All Earthly Laws': The Lutheran Reformation," in *Encounters with Luther. New Directions for Critical Studies*, edited by Kirsi I. Stjerna and Brooks Schramm (Louisville: Westminster John Knox Press, 2016), 119. He cites this quote from Steven E. Ozment, *Ancestors: The Loving Family in Old Europe* (Cambridge, MA: Harvard University Press, 2000), 37.
97. WA TR 2: 281, Nr. 1965.
98. WATR1: 69, Nr. 146.
99. WA Br 11: 276, Nr. 4195.

Johannes Bugenhagen evaluate his manuscript *On the Keys*.[100] He sent her reports of political events.[101] He encouraged her study of Scripture[102] and praised her command of the psalms.[103] His reports on the theological negotiations conducted at Marburg in 1529,[104] at the imperial diet in Augsburg in 1530,[105] and at the imperial diet in Hagenau in 1540[106] demonstrate the depth of their partnership in thinking and planning the progress of reform.

Luther could be strict with his children, but the warmth of his relationship with them comes through in texts handed down to us. While he was at the Coburg during the Diet of Augsburg in 1530, Luther wrote a playful letter to his four-year old son, promising to bring him a *Jarmarkt* (a special gift from a trade fair), and enticing him to behave with a picture of a wonderful garden for children, where he could play and ride little ponies with golden reins and silver saddles. It was a garden "for children who like to pray, learn, and are good." Luther wrote that he had asked the keeper of the garden whether Hans might play there, too, and the man had said, "If he likes to pray, and learn and is good, he, too, will be welcome in this garden. And he should bring Lippus and Jost [Hans's playmates, Melanchthon's son Philip and Justus Jonas's son Justus, who were about Hans's age] with him, too," as well as his great aunt Lena. There they would play with pipes, drums, and crossbow.[107] Hans would later experience his father's strict discipline, but he also enjoyed this parent`s playful and loving interaction with his children.

The depth of Luther's emotions in his personal relationships is nowhere clearer than in his reaction to the death of his daughters, Elisabeth and Magdalena. After Elisabeth died at age eight months in 1528, he wrote, "My little daughter, Elisabeth, has died. I am amazed that my soul is so sick . . . I never imagined that parents could love their children so much."[108] Fourteen years later, as Elisabeth's sister lay dying, he asked his fourteen-year-old, "Sweet Magdalena, my little daughter, would you rather stay with me, your father, or go to your other father." Magdalena answered, "As God wills," and Luther said, "you dear sweet daughter." He added, "the

100. WA Br 5: 608, Nr. 1713.
101. WA Br 9: 172, Nr. 3511, Br 9:175, Nr. 3512.
102. WA TR 3: 648, Nr. 3835.
103. WA TR 4: 610, Nr. 5008.
104. WA Br 5: 154, Nr. 1476.
105. WA Br 5: 347–348, Nr. 1582, 5: 544–546, Nrs. 1682 and 1683, 5: 608–609, Nr. 1713.
106. WA Br 9: 205, Nr. 3519.
107. WA Br 5: 377–378, Nr. 1595, LW 49: 323–324.
108. WA Br 4: 511, Nr. 1303, LW 49: 203.

spirit is strong, but the flesh is weak. I love her so very much."[109] Especially touching are his thoughts when she died. In the words recorded by Luther the father at her death September 20, 1542: "I love her very much. But if it is your will, dear God, that you take her, I will gladly know that she is with you." He composed an epitaph for her, cast in words she was uttering:

I, Lena, Luther's dear, dear child,
Am sleeping now with all saints mild
And lie in my own peace and rest
For now I am our God's own guest.
A mortal child I was indeed
Was born of mother's mortal seed,
But now I live so rich in God
Because of Christ's dear death and blood.[110]

Luther's personal relationships reflected the heights and depths of his emotions and the nature of his understanding of being human. In these relationships he found a fullness of the gift of his humanity. These passionate expressions of emotion made him something less than an easy person to live with at times, but the devotion expressed by his students[111] reflects the embodiment of the gospel in those still engaged in the eschatological struggle against the devil, the world, and their own sinful desires. Not only his proclamation of Christ's saving work but also his practice of the faith and his sometimes-boisterous piety demonstrate what he believed God intended when he created human creatures: not to live alone but face to face with others, in God's callings, following his commands, because of their trust in Christ.

109. WA TR 5: 189–192, Nr. 5494.
110. WA, TR 5: 186,19–26, Nr.5490c,
111. Robert Kolb, *Martin Luther as Prophet, Teacher, and Hero: Images of the Reformer, 1520–1620* (Grand Rapids, MI: Baker Books, 1999), 17–134.

Conclusion: Martin Luther's Relational Ontology

This volume presents a portrait, not a photograph, of the Wittenberg reformer Martin Luther. Its impressionistic look aims to sketch a clear picture of the man and his thought within the framework of his perception of human existence and what is real—his view of the truth of God, his human creatures, and the rest of creation.

Martin Luther grew up with a conception of being Christian that prescribed a path to God's favor through his own performance of commands from God and from the church. These works, especially those of a religious or sacred nature, were to demonstrate to God that, unworthy though he might be, he was at least worthy of grace. This grace, he learned, would enable him to please God sufficiently to earn him a place on the path to heaven.

As a child and in adolescence, Luther's deeply emotional personality assimilated the depiction of God as angry judge and Jesus as the Lord with sword of judgment in his hands that altars portrayed, and sermons described. His own strong emotions encountered an emotional Creator—wrath produced fear. His parents' and priests' instruction found reinforcement in professors' lectures and in the counsel and rule of his Order and his Brothers in the cloister. However, his superior, Johannes von Staupitz, not only recognized Brother Martin's abilities and set him on the road to a professorship at the University of Wittenberg, but also assured him that based on God's predestination and Christ's sacrifice on the cross, his tortured fears of God's wrath could be set aside. Slowly during the 1510s, the oppressive weight of this wrath and the condemnation it imposed began to lift. In the context of his reading of the psalms and then the epistles to the Romans, Galatians, and Hebrews to prepare for his lectures, the latest in insights into the Hebrew and Greek texts from writings of biblical humanists, most prominently Johannes Reuchlin and Desiderius Erasmus, fermented in his mind. Out of the depths of his despair, he cried to God, in comment on Psalm 130 in 1525, "You forsake me. You despise my cry of desperation. You are the only one, however, who can help me." Luther found his place of refuge;[1] he found there a God who identified himself through steadfast mercy and loving kindness to his chosen people (Psalm 118.)[2]

Particularly his immersion in Hebrew texts, aided by Reuchlin's tools for grasping the language, led Luther out of a theological way of thinking bound by Aristotelian presuppositions and into a vision of reality in which all being came into existence through God's speaking. He recognized that God is always intensely personal throughout the Old Testament's unfolding of Israel's history, and in-the-fleshly personal when he came as the Word in human person as Jesus of Nazareth (John 1:18). This speaking Creator is, Luther discovered, a God of conversation and community. Human life, its design and its fulfillment, originated in conversation with God. He fashioned human creatures not to be alone but in community with himself and with other human creatures. God's plan, his regard or reckoning, and his confrontation with the mystery of the challenge of the realm of Satan through Christ's death and resurrection determined human life.

Luther had grown up with the habit of carefully calculating his own performance on the basis of laws and regulations set in place by Scripture and by ecclesiastical decree. He abandoned his own calculations to rest easy in God's calculation, his imputation, regard, or reckoning of a new-creature-nature for those to whom he has given the gift of a relationship of trust and love with himself.

Luther did not abandon the medieval sense of the goal of human life: obedience to God. But he recognized that the faithful—for example, Abraham or Paul—lived a life typified by love, joy, peace, forbearance, kindness, goodness, faithfulness, gentleness, and self-control based on their relationships with God that their Creator had established as pure, undeserved gifts. That life unfolded based on God's re-creative word: Luther was a listener. He hearkened to the word of the Lord before he spoke himself, in normal everyday earthly conversations and in his proclamation of the gospel of Jesus Christ, to which his order and his university had called him in 1512 with the bestowal of his doctorate in Bible. Trusting in God and what he said through the prophets and apostles became the

1. WA 18: 517–518, LW 14: 199–191.
2. A favorite of Luther's, cf. his 1530 commentary, WA 31: 68–182, LW 14: 47–106.

source of his identity as God's child. His trust in his Lord and Savior, his Creator and his Sanctifier, led him to respond to God's faithfulness to him with his own faithfulness to God. This faithfulness exhibited itself not only in praise and proclamation, but also in confrontation with God's foe, the liar and murderer, Satan. That confrontation took place in both his relationship with the Creator and his relationships with himself and all other creatures.

Luther recognized God's design for humanity and for his entire creation, interpreted in terms of Aristotle's substance and accidents when that seemed useful and reasonable, within the context of the word of the Creator that brought all things into existence. That creative word placed reality in every aspect of God's world in relationship with the Creator. His creatures also were designed to stand in relationships with each other that reflected the nature of reality reflecting God's own identity as the good God whose steadfast love endures forever, and who demonstrated that love above all by coming into human flesh as Jesus of Nazareth. In this reality Martin Luther lived as a trusting, faithful child of God.

Bibliography

PRIMARY SOURCES

Editions

The Annotated Luther, edited by Hans J. Hillerbrand, Kirsi I. Stjerna, and Timothy J. Wengert. Minneapolis: Fortress Press, 2015–2017.

Die Bekenntnisschriften der Evangelisch-Lutherischen Kirche, edited by Irene Dingel. Göttingen: Vandenhoeck & Ruprecht, 2014.

The Book of Concord, edited by Robert Kolb and Timothy J. Wengert. Minneapolis: Fortress Press, 2000.

The Complete Sermons of Martin Luther, edited by John Nicholas Lenker 1905–1909. Grand Rapids, MI: Baker, 2000.

D. Martin Luthers Werke. Weimar: Böhlau, 1883–1993.

Die evangelischen Kirchenordnungen des XVI. Jahrhunderts, edited by Emil Sehling et al. Leipzig/Tübingen: Reisland/Mohn-Siebeck, 1902–2016.

Luther's Works. St. Louis/Philadelphia: Concordia/Fortress Press, 1958–).

Melanchthons Werke in Auswahl [Studien-Ausgabe], edited by Robert Stupperich. Gütersloh: Bertelsmann, 1951–1975.

Printed Works Pre-1800

Altenstaig, Johannes. *Vocabularius Theologie . . .* Hagenau: Gran, 1517.

Amsdorf, Nikolaus von. "Vorrede," in *Der Erste Teil aller Bu[e]cher vnd Schrifften des thewren/ seligen Mans Doct: Mart: Lutheri/vom XVII. jar an/bis auff das XXII.* Jena: Christian Rödinger, 1555.

Mathesius, Johannes. *Historien/ Von des Ehrwirdigen in Gott Seligen thewren Manns Gottes, Doctoris Martini Luthers/anfang/lehr/leben vnd sterben* . . . Nuremberg: Johann vom Berg's heirs and Ulrich Neuber, 1566.

Reference Works

Grimm, Jakob and Wilhelm Grimm. *Deutsches Wörterbuch.* Leipzig, 1854–1961, consulted on October 11, 2021, at https://woerterbuchnetz.de/?sigle=DWB#1.

SECONDARY LITERATURE

Adams, Marilyn McCord. *Some Later Medieval Theories of the Eucharist: Thomas Aquinas, Gilles of Rome, Duns Scotus, and William Ockham.* Oxford: Oxford University Press, 2010.

——. *What Sort of Human Nature? Medieval Philosophy and the Systematics of Christology.* Milwaukee: Marquette University Press, 1999.

Alfsvåg, Knut. "Deification as Creatio ex nihilo. On Luther's Appreciation of Dionysian Spirituality," in *Hermeneutica Sacra. Studien zur Auslegung der Heiligen Schrift im 16.- und 17. Jahrhundert / Studies of the Interpretation of Holy Scripture in the Sixteenth and Seventeenth Centuries*, edited by Torbjörn Johansson et al., 59–84. Berlin: de Gruyter, 2010.

Antilla, Mikka E. *Luther's Theology of Music: Spiritual Beauty and Pleasure.* Berlin: de Gruyter, 2013.

Arand, Charles P. *That I May Be His Own: An Overview of Luther's Catechisms.* St. Louis: Concordia, 2000.

Aubel, Matthias. *Michel Stifel, ein Mathematiker im Zeitalter des Humanismus und der Reformation.* Augsburg: Rauner, 2008.

Aulén, Gustav. *Christus Victor: An Historical Study of the Three Main Types of the Idea of Atonement.* Translated by A. G. Hebart. New York: Macmillan, 1961.

Barth, Hans-Martin. *Der Teufel und Jesus Christus in der Theologie Martin Luthers.* Göttingen: Vandenhoeck & Ruprecht, 1967.

Batka, L'ubomír. "Luther's Teaching on Sin and Evil," in *The Oxford Handbook of Martin Luther's Theology*, edited by Robert Kolb, Irene Dingel and L'ubomír Batka, 233–253. Oxford: Oxford University Press, 2014.

Bauer, Joachim and Stefan Michel, ed. *Der "Unterricht der Visitatoren" und die Durchsetzung der Reformation in Kursachsen.* Leipzig: Evangelische Verlagsanstalt, 2017.

Bayer, Oswald. "God's Hiddenness," *Lutheran Quarterly* 28 (2014): 266–279.

——. "God's Omnipotence," *Lutheran Quarterly* 23 (2009): 85–102.

——. *Living by Faith: Justification and Sanctification*. Translated by Geoffrey Bromiley. Grand Rapids, MI: Eerdmans, 2003.

——. *Promissio: Geschichte der reformatorischen Wende in Luthers Theologie*. 2nd ed. Darmstadt: Wissenschaftliche Buchgesellschaft, 1989.

——. *Martin Luther's Theology. A Contemporary Interpretation*. Translated by Thomas H. Trapp. Grand Rapids, MI: Eerdmans, 2008.

——. "Toward a Theology of Lament," in *Caritas et Reformation. Essays on Church and Society in Honor of Carter Lindberg*, edited by David M. Whitford, 211–220. St. Louis: Concordia, 2002.

Bender, Martin. *Allein auf Gottes Wort, Johann Walter, Kantor der Reformation*. Berlin: Evangelische Verlagsanstalt, 1971.

Beutel, Albrecht. "Antwort und Wort," in *Luther und Ontologie*, edited by Anja Ghiselli, Kari Kopperi, and Rainer Vinke, 70–93. Helsinki: Luther-Agricola-Gesellschaft, and Erlangen: Martin-Luther-Verlag, 1993.

——. "'Gott fürchten und lieben.' Zur Enstehungsgeschichte der lutherischen Katechismusformel," in Albrecht Beutel, *Protestantische Konkretionen. Studien zur Kirchengeschichte*, 46–55 Tübingen: Mohr Siebeck, 1998.

Bienert, Wolfgang. "'Im Zweifel näher bei Augustin?' Zum patristischen Hintergrund der Theologie Luthers," in *Oecumenica et Patristica*, edited by Damaskinos Papendreou et al., 281–294. Stuttgart: Kohlhammer, 1989.

Blankenburg, *Johann Walter: Leben und Werk*. Tützing: Schneider, 1991.

Bluhm, Heinz. *Luther, Translator of Paul: Studies in Romans and Galatians*. New York: Peter Lang, 1984.

——. *Martin Luther, Creative Translator* (Saint Louis: Concordia, 1965).

Boettcher, Susan R. "Cyriakus Spangenberg als Geschichtsschreiber," in *Reformatoren im Mansfelder Land. Erasmus Sarcerius und Cyriakus Spangenberg*, edited by Stefan Rhein and Günther Wartenberg, 155–170. Leipzig: Evangelische Verlagsanstalt, 2006.

Bollbuck, Harald. *Wahrheitszeugnis, Gottes Auftrag und Zeitkritik: die Kirchengeschichte der Magdeburger Zenturien und ihre Arbeitstechniken*. Wiesbaden: Harrassowitz, 2014.

Bolliger, Daniel. *Infiniti contemplatio: Grundzüge der Scotus- und Scotismusrezeption im Werk Huldrych Zwinglis*. Leiden: Brill, 2003.

Bornkamm, Heinrich. *Luther and the Old Testament*. Translated by Eric W. and Ruth C. Gritsch. Philadelphia: Fortress, 1969.

Bräuer, Siegfried. "Cyriakus Spangenberg als mansfeldisch-sächsischer Reformationshistoriker," in *Reformatoren in Mansfelder Land. Erasmus Sarcerius und Cyriakus Spangenberg*, edited by Stefan Rhein and Günther Wartenberg, 171–189. Leipzig: Evangelische Verlagsanstalt, 2006.

Brecht, Martin. *Martin Luther: His Road to Reformation, 1483–1521*. Translated by James L. Schaaf. Minneapolis: Fortress Press, 1985.

———. *Martin Luther: Shaping and Defining the Reformation, 1521–1532*. Translated by James Schaaf. Philadelphia: Fortress Press, 1983.

———. *Martin Luther: The Preservation of the Church, 1532–1546*. Translated by James L. Schaaf. Minneapolis: Fortress, 1993.

Brosseder, Claudia. *Im Bann der Sterne: Caspar Peucer, Philipp Melanchthon, and andere Wittenberger Astrologen*. Berlin: Akademie-Verlag, 2004.

Brown, Christopher B. "*Deus Ludens*: God at Play in Luther's Theology," *Concordia Theological Quarterly* 81 (2017): 153–170.

Bultmann, Christoph. "Paul Ebers Gelehrsamkeit," in *Paul Eber (1511–1569): Humanist und Theologe der zweiten Generation der Wittenberger Reformation*, edited by Daniel Gehrt and Volker Leppin, 258–287. Leipzig: Evangelische Verlagsanstalt, 2014.

Burnett, Amy Nelson. *Debating the Sacraments: Print and Authority in the Early Reformation*. Oxford: Oxford University Press, 2019.

———. *Karlstadt and the Origins of the Eucharistic Controversy: A Study in the Circulation of Ideas*. New York: Oxford University Press, 2011.

———. "Luther and the *Schwärmer*," in *The Oxford Handbook of Martin Luther's Theology*, edited by Robert Kolb, Irene Dingel and L'ubomír Batka, 511–524. Oxford: Oxford University Press, 2014.

———. "Revisiting Humanism and the Urban Reformation," *Lutheran Quarterly* 35 (2021): 373–400.

Burnett, Stephen. "What Luther Could Have Known of Judaism," in *Juden, Christen und Muslime im Zeitalter der Reformation*, edited by Matthias Pohlig, 133–146. Heidelberg: Verein für Reformationsgeschichte, 2020.

Cargill Thompson, W. D. J. *The Political Thought of Martin Luther*, edited by Philip Broadhead. Sussex: Harvester, 1984.

Cary, Phillip. "Why Luther is Not Quite Protestant. The Logic of Faith in a Sacramental Promise," *Pro Ecclesia* 14 (2005): 447–486.

Cummings, Brian. *The Literary Culture of the Reformation. Grammar and Grace*. Oxford: Oxford University Press, 2002.

Daniel, David P. "Luther on the Church," in *The Oxford Handbook of Martin Luther's Theology*, edited by Robert Kolb, Irene Dingel and L'ubomír Batka, 333–352. Oxford: Oxford University Press, 2014.

Danielson, Dennis. *The First Copernican: Georg Joachim Rheticus and the Rise of the Copernican Revolution*. New York: Walker, 2006.

Dannenfeldt, Karl H. "Wittenberg Botanists during the Sixteenth Century," in *The Social History of the Reformation*, edited by Lawrence P. Buck and Jonathan W. Zophy, 223–248. Columbus: Ohio State University Press, 1972.

Dieter, Theodor. *Der junge Luther und Aristoteles. Historisch-systematische Untersuchungen zum Verhältnis von Theologie und Philosophie*. Berlin: de Gruyter, 2001.

———. "Luther as Late Medieval Theologian: His Positive and Negative Use of Nominalism and Realism," in *The Oxford Handbook of Martin Luther's Theology*, edited by Robert Kolb, Irene Dingel, and L'ubomír Batka, 31–48. Oxford: Oxford University Press, 2014.

Dingel, Irene. "Luthers Schrift *An die Ratsherren aller Städte Lands* (1524)—Historische und theologische Aspekte," in *Meilensteine der Reformation, Schlüsseldokumente der frühen Wirksamkeit Martin Luthers*, edited by Irene Dingel and Henning Jürgens, 180–190. Gütersloh: Gütersloher Verlagshaus, 2014.

———. "Philip Melanchthon and the Establishment of Confessional Norms," in, *Philip Melanchthon: Theologian in Classroom, Confession, and Controversy*, by Irene Dingel, Robert Kolb, Nicole Kuropka, and Timothy J. Wengert, 161–177. Göttingen: Vandenhoeck & Ruprecht, 2012.

———. "Pruning the Vines, Plowing Up the Vineyard: The Sixteenth-Century Culture of Controversy between Disputation and Polemic," in *The Reformation as Christianization. Essays on Scott Hendrix's Christianization Thesis*, edited by Anna Marie Johnson and John A. Maxfield, 397–408. Tübingen: Mohr/Siebeck, 2012.

———."Von der Disputation zum Gespräch," *Lutherjahrbuch* 85 (2018): 61–84.

Ebeling, Gerhard. *Luthers Seelsorge. Theologie in der Vielfalt der Lebenssituationen*. Tübingen: Mohr/Siebeck, 1997.

———. *Lutherstudien*, volume 2, *Disputatio de Homine*, issued in three separate parts. Tübingen: Mohr/Siebeck, 1977, 1982, 1989.

———, "Luthers Wirklichkeitsverständnis," *Zeitschrift für Theologie und Kirche* 90 (1993). 409–424; ET: *Lutheran Quarterly* 27 (2013): 56–75.

Edwards, Mark U., Jr. *Luther and the False Brethren.* Stanford: Stanford University Press, 1975.

———. *Luther's Last Battles. Politics and Polemics, 1531–46.* Ithaca, NY: Cornell University Press, 1983.

———. *Printing, Propaganda, and Martin Luther.* Berkeley: University of California Press, 1994.

Elert, Werner. *Morphologie des Lutherums. I. Theologie und Weltanschauung des Luthertums hauptsächlich im 16. und 17. Jahrhundert.* Munich: Beck, 1931.

Elliger, Georg. *Die neulateinische Lyrik Deutschlands in der ersten Hälfte des sechzehnten Jahrhunderts* (Berlin: de Gruyter, 1929).

Erickson, Erik. *Childhood and Society.* 2nd ed. New York: Norton, 1963.

———. *Identity, Youth, and Crisis.* New York: Norton, 1968.

Estes, James M. *Peace, Order and the Glory of God: Secular Authority and the Church in the Thought of Luther and Melanchthon, 1518–1559.* Leiden: Brill, 2005.

Evener, Vincent. "Wittenberg's Wandering Spirits: Discipline and the Dead in the Reformation," *Church History* 84 (2015): 531–555.

Ferel, Martin. *Gepredigte Taufe, eine homiletische Untersuchung zur Taufpredigt bei Luther.* Tübingen: Mohr Siebeck, 1969.

Fish, Stanley. *Is There a Test in this Class: The Authority of Interpretive Communities.* Cambridge, MA: Harvard University Press, 1980.

Flogaus, Reinhard, *Theosis bei Palamas und Luther.* Göttingen: Vandenhoeck & Ruprecht, 1997.

Forde, Gerhard O. *Justification by Faith: A Matter of Death and Life.* Mifflintown, PA: Sigler, 1991.

———. *On Being a Theologian of the Cross Reflections on Luther's Heidelberg Disputation, 1518.* Grand Rapids, MI: Eerdmans, 1997.

———. *Theology is for Proclamation.* Minneapolis: Fortress Press, 1990.

Fraenkel, Peter. "Revelation and Tradition, Notes on Some Aspects of Doctrinal Continuity in the Theology of Philip Melanchthon," *Studia theologica* 13 (1959): 97–133.

Garcia, Javier. "A Critique of Mannermaa on Luther and Galatians," *Lutheran Quarterly* 27 (2013): 33–55.

Gensichen, Hans-Werner. *We Condemn, How Luther and 16th Century Lutheranism Condemned False Doctrine.* Translated by Herbert J. A. Bouman. St. Louis: Concordia, 1967.

Gerrish, Brian. *Grace and Reason, a Study in the Theology of Luther.* Oxford: Clarendon, 1962.

Graham, William A. *Beyond the Written Word: Oral Aspects of Scripture in the History of Religion.* Cambridge, MA: Cambridge University Press, 1987.

Grislis, Egil. "Luther's Understanding of the Wrath of God," *The Journal of Religion* 41 (1961): 277–292.

Grönvik, Lorenz. *Die Taufe in der Theologie Martin Luthers.* Åbo: Åbo Akademi, 1968.

Gutiérrez, David. *Geschichte des Augustinerordens* 2. Rome: Historisches Institut des Augustinerordens, 1975.

Haar, Johannes. *Initium creaturae Dei. Untersuchung über Luthers Begriff der "neuen Creatur" im Zusammenhang mit seinem Verständnis von Jakobus I,18 und mit seinem "Zeit-Denken".* Gütersloh: Bertelsmann, 1939.

Hägglund, Bengt. *Theologie und Philosophie bei Luther und in der occamistischen Tradition. Luthers Stellung zur Theorie von der doppelten Wahrheit.* Lund: Gleerup, 1955.

Hamm, Bernd. *The Early Luther: Stages in a Reformation Reorientation.* Translated by Martin J. Lohrmann. Grand Rapids, MI: Eerdmans, 2020.

———. *Frömmigkeitstheologie am Anfang des 16. Jahrhunderts. Studien zu Johannes von Paltz und seinem Umkreis.* Tübingen:Mohr/Siebeck, 1982.

———. *Religiosität im späten Mittelalter. Spannungspole, Neuaufbrüche, Normierungen*, edited by Reinhold Friedrich and Wolfgang Simon. Tübingen: Mohr/Siebeck, 2011.

Hamm, Bernd and Volker Leppin, ed. *Gottes Nähe unmittelbar erfahren. Mystik im Mittelalter und bei Martin Luther.* Tübingen: Mohr/Siebeck, 2007.

Hartmann, Martina. *Humanismus und Kirchenkritik. Matthias Flacius Illyricus als Erforscher des Mittelalters.* Stuttgart: Thorbecke, 2001.

Hasse, Hans-Peter. "Paul Ebers Calendarium historicum (1550)," in *Paul Eber (1511–1569). Humanist und Theologe der zweiten Generation der Wittenberger Reformation*, edited by Daniel Gehrt and Volker Leppin, 288–319. Leipzig: Evangelische Verlagsanstalt, 2014.

Headley, John M. *Luther's View of Church History.* New Haven: Yale University Press, 1963.

Hendrix, Scott H. "Deparentifying the Fathers: the Reformers and Patristic Authority," in *Auctoritas Patrum. Zum Rezeption der Kirchenväter im 15. und 16. Jahrhundert,* edited by Leif Grane, Alfred Schindler, Markus Wriedt, 1: 55–68. Mainz: von Zabern, 1993.

———. *Luther and the Papacy, Stages in a Reformation Conflict.* Philadelphia, Fortress Press, 1981.

———. *Martin Luther, Visionary Reformer.* New Haven: Yale University Press, 2015.

Herl, Joseph. *Worship Wars in Early Lutheranism: Choir, Congregation, and Three Centuries of Conflict.* Oxford: Oxford University Press, 2004.

Herrmann, Erik. "Luther and the Importance of the Hebrew Heritage for His World of Thought," in *Simul: Inquiries into Luther's Expression of the Christian Life*, edited by Robert Kolb, Torbjörn Johansson and Daniel Johansson, 49–61. Göttingen: Vandenhoeck & Ruprecht, 2021.

———. "'Why then the Law?' Salvation History and the Law in Martin Luther's Interpretation of Galatians 1513–1522," Ph. D. Dissertation, Concordia Seminary, St. Louis, 2005.

Herms, Eilert. *Luthers Ontologie des Werdens. Verwirklichung des Eschatons durchs Schöpferwort im Schöpfergeist. Trinitarischer Panentheismus.* Tübingen: Mohr/Siebeck, 2023.

Hiebert, Paul. "The Flaw of the Excluded Middle," *Missiology* 10 (1982): 35–47.

———. *Transforming worldviews: An Anthropological Understanding of How People Change.* Grand Rapids, MI: Baker Academic, 2008.

Hoffmann, Gottfried. *Kirchenväterzitate in der Abendmahlskontroverse zwischen Oekolampad, Zwingli, Luther und Melanchthon.* Göttingen: Edition Ruprecht, 2011.

Irwin, Joyce. "Luther, Mattheson, and the Joy of Music," in *Lutheran Music Culture. Ideals and Practices*, edited by Mattias Lundberg, Maria Schildt, and Jonas Lundblad, 115–133. Berlin: de Gruyter, 2022.

Janz, Denis. *Martin Luther's* The Church Held Captive in Babylon: *Latin-English Edition with a New Translation and Introduction.* Oxford: Oxford University Press, 2019.

———. "What did Luther understand by 'Faith'," in *Reforming the Reformation. Essays in Honour of Principal Peter Matheson*, edited by Ian Breward, 69–80. Melbourne: Scholarly Publishing, 2004.

Jensen, Gordon A. *Experiencing Gospel: Martin Luther's 1534 Bible Project.* Minneapolis: Fortress Press, 2023.

———. *The Wittenberg Concord: Creating Space for Dialogue.* Minneapolis: Fortress Press, 2018.

Joest, Wilfried. *Ontologie der Person bei Luther.* Göttingen: Vandenhoeck & Ruprecht, 1967.

Johnson, Anna Marie. *Beyond Indulgences: Luther's Reform of Late Medieval Piety, 1518–1520.* Kirksville, MO: Trueman State University Press, 2017.

Juntunen, Sammeli. "Luther and Metaphysics. What is the Structure of Being according to Luther," in *Union with Christ: The New Finnish Interpretation of Luther*, edited by Carl E. Braaten and Robert W. Jenson, 129–160. Grand Rapids: Eerdmans, 1998.

Jürgens, Henning P. "Luthers Schrift *An die Ratsherren aller Städte deutsches Lands* (1524)—Entstehungskontext und Druckgeschichte," in *Meilensteine der Reformation, Schlüsseldokumente der frühen Wirksamkeit Martin Luthers*, edited by Irene Dingel and Henning Jürgens, 190–197. Gütersloh: Gütersloher Verlagshaus, 2014.

Kam, Vincent. "Luther on God's Play with His Saints," *Lutheran Quarterly* 34 (2020): 138–151.

Karimies, Ilmari. *Martin Luther's Understanding of Faith and Reality (1513–1521): The Influence of Augustinian Platonism and Illumination in Luther's Thought.* Tübingen: Mohr/Siebeck, 2022.

Kaufman, Peter Iver. "Luther's 'Scholastic Phase' Revisited: Grace, Works, and Merit in the Earliest Extant Sermons," *Church History* 51 (1982): 280–289.

Kegan, Robert. *In Over Our Heads: The Mental Demands of Modern Life.* Cambridge, MA: Harvard University Press, 1994.

Kim, Min Hwan. "Luther's View of Purgatory," Ph.D. dissertation, the Toronto School of Theology, University of Toronto, 2022.

Klitzsch, Ingo. *Redaktion und Memoria. Die Lutherbilder der „Tischreden".* Tübingen: Mohr/Siebeck, 2020.

Köhler, Walter. *Zwingli und Luther.* 2 vols. Leipzig: Heinsius, 1924, Gütersloh: Bertelsmann, 1953.

Kolb, Robert, ed. *The Alien and the Proper: Luther's Twofold Righteousness in Controversy, Ministry, and Citizenship.* Irvine, CA: 1517 Legacy, 2022.

Kolb, Robert. "'The Armor of God and the Might of His Strength.' Luther's Sermon on Ephesians 6 (1531/1533)," *Concordia Journal* 43 (2017): 59–73.

———. *Bound Choice, Election, and Wittenberg Theological Method: From Martin Luther to the Formula of Concord.* Grand Rapids, MI: Eerdmans, 2005.

———. "David: King, Prophet, Repentant Sinner. Martin Luther's Image of the Son of Jesse," *Perichoresis* 8 (2010): 203–232.

———. "God Kills to Make Alive: Romans 6 and Luther's Understanding of Justification (1535)," *Lutheran Quarterly* 12 (1998): 33–56.

———. "God's Gift of Martyrdom: The Early Reformation Understanding of Dying for the Faith," *Church History* 64 (1995): 399–411.

———. "Die Josef-Geschichten als Fürstenspiegel in der Wittenberger Auslegungstradition. 'Ein verständiger und weiser Mann' (Genesis 42,33)," in *Christlicher Glaube und weltliche Herrschaft. Zum Gedenken an Günther Wartenberg*, edited by Michael Beyer, Jonas Flöter, and Markus Hein, 41–55. Leipzig: Evangelische Verlagsanstalt, 2008.

———. "'Ein kindt des todts' und 'Gottes Gast.' Das Sterben in Luthers Predigten," *Lutherische Theologie und Kirche* 31 (2007): 3–22.

———. "Das Kreuz—die wirkliche Befreiungstheologie," *CA Confessio Augustana* 2016, 4: 43–54.

———. "'Life is King and Lord over Death,' Martin Luther's View of Death and Dying," in *Tod und Jenseits in der Schriftkultur der Frühen Neuzeit*, edited by Marion Kobelt Groch and Cornelia Niekus-Moore, 23–45. Wiesbaden: Harrassowitz, 2008.

———. *Luther and the Stories of God, Biblical Narratives as a Foundation for Christian Living.* Grand Rapids, MI: Baker, 2012.

———. "Luther on Peasants and Princes," *Lutheran Quarterly* 23 (2009): 125–146.

———. "Luther's Hermeneutics of Distinctions: Law and Gospel, Two Kinds of Righteousness, Two Realms, Freedom and Bondage," in *The Oxford Handbook of Martin Luther's Theology*, edited by Robert Kolb, Irene Dingel, and L'ubomír Batka, 23–45. Oxford: Oxford University Press, 2014.

———. "Luther's Providential God," in *The Interface of Science, Theology, and Religion: Essays in Honor of Alister E. McGrath*, edited by Dennis Ngien, 48–65. Eugene, OR: Pickwick, 2019.

———. "Luther's Recollections of Erfurt: The Use of Anecdotes for the Edification of His Hearers," *Luther-Bulletin, Tijdschrift voor interconfessioneel Lutheronderzoek* 10 (2010): 6–16.

———. "Luther's Theology of the Cross Fifteen Years after Heidelberg: Luther's Lectures on the Psalms of Ascent," *Journal of Ecclesiastical History* 61 (2010): 69–85.

———. "Luther's Transformation of Scholastic Terms," in *Handing over the Goods: Determined to Proclaim Nothing but Christ Jesus and Him Crucified, Essays in Honor of James Arne Nestingen*, edited by Steven

Paulson and Scott L. Keith, 21–38. Irvine, CA: 1517 Publishing, 2018.

———. *Luther's Treatise* On Christian Freedom *and Its Legacy.* Lanham, MD: Fortress Academic/Lexington, 2019.

———. *Martin Luther and the Enduring Word of God: The Wittenberg School and its Scripture-Centered Proclamation.* Grand Rapids, MI: Baker Academic, 2016.

———. *Martin Luther as Prophet, Teacher, and Hero: Images of the Reformer, 1520–1620.* Grand Rapids, MI: Baker Books, 1999.

———. *Martin Luther, Confessor of the Faith.* Christian Theology in Context. Oxford: Oxford University Press, 2009.

———. "Niebuhr's 'Christ and Culture in Paradox' Revisited," *Lutheran Quarterly* 10 (1996): 259–279.

———. "'The Noblest Skill in the Christian Church': Luther's Sermons on the Proper Distinction of Law and Gospel," *Concordia Theological Quarterly* 71 (2007): 301–318.

———. "Old Adam, New Martin: The Fatal and Resurrecting Consequences of Baptism in Luther's Use of Romans 7," in *Simul: Inquiries into Luther's Expression of the Christian Life*, edited by Robert Kolb, Torbjörn Johansson, and Daniel Johansson, 63–78. Göttingen: Vandenhoeck & Ruprecht, 2021.

———. "The Person of Christ in Sixteenth-Century Lutheran Theology," in *Common Places in Christian Theology. A Curated Collection of Essays from* Lutheran Quarterly, edited by Mark C. Mattes, 159–192. Irvine, CA: 1517 Publishing, 2023.

———. "Seelsorge for the Cranachs," *Lutheran Forum* 42/1 (Spring 2009): 34–37.

———. "'This is My Customary Procedure,' Says God: Martin Luther's Use of Dialogue and Monologue in his Lectures and Sermons," in *Teach These Things. Essays in Honor of Wallace Schulz*, edited by Erik Rottmann, 25–40. Versailles, MO: Wild Boar Books, 2008.

———. "'What Benefit Does the Soul Receive from a Handful of Water?' Luther's Preaching on Baptism, 1528–1539," *Concordia Journal* 25 (1999); 346–363.

———. "The Wittenberg Impact on University Education and the Christian Liberal Arts," in *My Savior's Guest. A Festschrift in Honor of Erling Teigen*, edited by Thomas Rank, 91–108. New York: Lulu Press, 2021.

———. "Wittenberg Uses of Law and Gospel," *Lutheran Quarterly* 37 (2023): 249–267.

Korsch, Dietrich. "The Word of God and Music in Luther: Re-Reading Luther's 1538 Rhau Preface," in *Lutheran Music Culture. Ideals and Practices*, edited by Mattias Lundberg, Maria Schildt, and Jonas Lundblad, 21–33. Berlin: de Gruyter, 2022.

Kramer, Sabine. *Katharina von Bora in den schriftlichen Zeugnissen ihrer Zeit.* Leipzig: Evangelische Verlagsanstalt, 2016.

Kunzelmann, Adalbero. *Geschichte der Deutschen Augustiner-Eremiten 5, Die sächsisch-thüringische Provinz und die sächsische Reformkongretation bis zum Untergang der beiden* 5. Würzburg: Augustinus, 1974.

Laato, Timo. "Justification: The Stumbling Block of the Finnish Luther School," *Concordia Theological Quarterly* 72 (2008): 323–346.

Lane, Anthony N. S. *Regensburg Article 5 on Justification: Inconsistent Patchwork or Substance of True Doctrine.* Oxford: Oxford University Press, 2020.

Leaver, Robin. *Luther's Liturgical Music: Principles and Implications*. Grand Rapids, MI: Eerdmans, 2007.

LeBon, Gustave. *The Crowd, a Study of the Popular Mind*. French original, 1895. New York: Greenpoint, 2022.

Lehmann, Roland M. *Reformation auf der Kanzel. Luther als Reiseprediger.* Tübingen: Mohr Siebeck, 2021.

Leoni, Stefano. "Der Augustinkomplex. Luthers zwei reformatorische Bekehrungen," in *Reformatorische Theologie und Autoritäten. Studien zur Genese des Schriftprinzips beim jungen Luther*, edited by Volker Leppin, 185–294, Tübingen: Mohr/Siebeck, 2015.

Leppin, Volker. *Geglaubte Wahrheit. Das Theologieverständnis Wilhelms von Ockham.* Göttingen: Vandenhoeck & Ruprecht, 1995.

———. "Luther on the Devil," in *Encounters with Luther: New Directions for Critical Studies*, edited by Kirsi I. Stjerna and Brooks Schramm, 30–41. Louisville: Westminster John Knox, 2016.

———. "Luther's Roots in Monastic-Mystical Piety," in *The Oxford Handbook of Martin Luther's Theology*, edited by Robert Kolb, Irene Dingel, and L'ubomír Batka, 49–61. Oxford: Oxford University Press, 2014.

———. *Repräsentation und Reenactment: Spätermittelalterliche Frömmigkeit verstehen.* Tübingen: Mohr Siebeck, 2021.

———. *Wilhelm von Ockham: Gelehrter, Streiter, Bettelmönch.* Darmstadt: Wissenschaftliche Buchgesellschaft, 2003.

Leroux, Neil R. *Martin Luther as Comforter: Writings on Death.* Leiden: Brill, 2007.

Lienhard, Marc. *Luther: Witness to Jesus Christ, Stages and Themes of the Reformer's Christology*. Translated by E. Robertson. Minneapolis: Augsburg, 1982.

Linebaugh, Jonathan A. "'The Speech of the Death'. Identifying No Longer and Now Christ Living 'I' of Galatians 2:20," *New Testament Studies* 66 (2020): 87–105.

Lindberg, Carter. "Luther and Feuerbach," *The Sixteenth Century Journal* 1 (1970): 105–125.

Lotito, Mark A. *Reformation of Historical Thought*. Leiden: Brill, 2019.

Maigler-Loeser, Barbara. *Historie und Exemplum im Fürstenspeigel: Zur didaktischen Instrumentalisierung der Historie in ausgewählten deutschen Fürstenspiegeln der Frühmoderne*. Neuried; ars et unitas, 2004.

Malter, Rudolf. "Luther und die Geschichte der Metaphysik," in *Thesaurus Lutheri. Auf der Suche nach neuen Paradigmen der Luther-Forschung*, edited by Tuomo Mannermaa, Anja Ghiselli, and Simo Peura, 37–62. Helsinki: Luther-Agricola Gesellschaft, 1987.

Mannermaa, Tuomo. *Der im Glauben Gegenwärtige Christus: Rechtfertigung und Vergottung. Zum ökumenischen Dialog*. Hannover: Lutherisches Verlagshaus, 1989; ET: *Christ Present in Faith. Luther's View of Justification*. Translated by Kirsi Stjerna. Minneapolis, Fortress Press, 2005.

———. "Hat Luther eine trinitarische Ontologie?" in *Luther und Ontologie*, edited by Anja Ghiselli, Kari Kopperi, and Rainer Vinke, 9–27. Helsinki: Luther-Agricola-Gesellschaft, and Erlangen: Martin-Luther-Verlag, 1993.

Marius, Richard. *Martin Luther: The Christian between God and Death*. Cambridge: Harvard University Press, 1999.

Mattes, Mark. "The History, Shape, and Significance of Justification for Preaching," in *Justification is for Preaching*, edited by Vergil Thompson. Eugene: Pickwick, 2012.

———. *Martin Luther's Theology of Beauty, a Reappraisal*. Grand Rapids, MI: Baker Academic, 2017.

———. "Luther's Use of Philosophy," *Lutherjahrbuch* 80 (2013): 115–123.

Mennicke-Haustein, Ute. *Luthers Trostbriefe*. Gütersloh, Gütersloher Verlagshaus, 1989.

Mentz, Georg. *Johann Friedrich der Grossmächtige, 1503–1554*. Jena: Fischer, 1903–1908.

Mentzel-Reuters, Arno, and Martina Hartmann, eds. *Catalogus und Centurien. Interdisziplinäre Studien zu Matthias Flacius und den Magdeburger Centurien*. Tübingen: Mohr/Siebeck, 2008.

Meuser, Fred. *Luther the Preacher.* Minneapolis: Augsburg, 1983.

Michael, Angela. "'Quod Christus sit mea forma'. Zur Bedeutung des Wortfeldes *forma / formari* in der Rechtfertigungslehre Martin Luthers," *Lutherjahrbuch* 89 (2022): 14–47.

Midgley, Mary. *The Essential Mary Midgley.* London: Routledge, 2005.

Muhlhan, Brett. *Being Shaped by Freedom: An Examination of Luther's Development of Christian Liberty, 1520–1525.* Eugene, OR: Pickwick, 2012.

Nembach, Ulrich. *Predigt des Evangeliums: Luther als Prediger, Pädagoge und Rhetor.* Neukirchen: Neukirchener Verlag, 1972.

Nestingen, James A. *The Faith We Hold, The Living Witness of Luther and the Augsburg Confession.* Minneapolis: Augsburg, 1983.

Ngien, Dennis. *Fruit for the Soul: Luther on the Lament Psalms.* Minneapolis: Fortress, 2016.

Niebuhr, H. Richard. *Christ and Culture.* New York: Harper, 1951.

Öberg, Ingemar. *Luther and World Mission: A Historical and Systematic Study with Special Reference to Luther's Bible Exposition.* Translated by Dean Apel. St. Louis: Concordia, 2007.

Oberman, Heiko Augustinus. *The Harvest of Medieval Theology.* Cambridge, MA: Harvard University Press, 1963.

———. *Luther: Man Between God and the Devil.* Translated by Eileen Walliser-Schwarzbart. New Haven: Yale University Press, 1989.

Ocker, Christopher. *Biblical Poetics before Humanism and Reformation.* Cambridge: Cambridge University Press, 2002.

Oepke, Albrecht. Art. "ἔν" in *Theological Dictionary of the New Testament,* edited by Gerhard Kittel. Translated by Geoffrey W. Bromiley, 541–543. Grand Rapids, MI: Eerdmans, 1964.

Østrem, Eyold, "'Musicam semper amavi': What is Remarkable about Luther's Views on Music?" in *Lutheran Music Culture. Ideals and Practices,* edited by Mattias Lundberg, Maria Schildt, and Jonas Lundblad, 35–46. Berlin: de Gruyter, 2022.

Otto, Rudolf. *Das Heilige. Über das Irrationale in der Idee des Göttlichen und sein Verhältnis zum Rationalen.* Breslau: Trewendt & Granier, 1917. ET: *The Idea of the Holy: An Inquiry into the Non-rational Factor in the Idea of the Divine and its Relation to the Rational.* Translated by John W. Harvey. Oxford: Oxford University Press, (1923) 1950.

Oyer, John S. *Lutheran Reformers against Anabaptists: Luther, Melanchthon and Menius and the Anabaptists of Central Germany.* The Hague: Nijhoff, 1964.

Ozment, Steven E. *Ancestors: The Loving Family in Old Europe.* Cambridge, MA: Harvard University Press, 2000.

———. *The Serpent and the Lamb: Cranach, Luther, and the Making of the Reformation.* New Haven: Yale University Press, 2011.

Paulson, Steven. "Graspable God," *Word & World* 32 (2012): 51–62.

———. "Luther's Antidote to Apophatic Theology," *Lutheran Quarterly* 35 (2021): 249–272.

———. *Luther's Outlaw God: Volume 1, Hiddenness, Evil, and Predestination.* Minneapolis: Fortress, 2018.

———. *Luther's Outlaw God: Volume 2, Hidden in the Cross.* Minneapolis: Fortress, 2019.

———. *Luther's Outlaw God: Volume 3, Sacraments and God's Attack on the Promise.* Minneapolis: Fortress, 2021.

Pesch, Otto Hermann. "Existential and Sapiential Theology—the Theological Confrontation between Luther and Thomas Aquinas," in *Catholic Scholars Dialogue with Luther*, 61–81, 182–193. Chicago: Loyola University Press, 1970.

Pettegree, Andrew. *Brand Luther: 1517, Printing, and the Making of the Reformation.* New York: Penguin, 2015.

Pietsch, Stephen. *Of Good Comfort: Martin Luther's Letters to the Depressed and their Significance for Pastoral Care Today.* Adelaide: ATF, 2016.

Poulsen, Hanne Kolind. "Between Convention, Likeness and Iconicity: Cranach's Portraits and Luther's Thoughts on Images," in *Lucas Cranach 1553/2003: Wittenberger Tagungsbeiträge anlässlich des 450, Todesjahres Lucas Cranachs des Älteren*, edited by Andreas Tacke, 205–216. Leipzig: Evangelische Verlagsanstalt, 2007.

Reinert, Jonathan. "Das menschliche Herz und Luthers Theologie. Ein weiterer Blick auf den Denkweg des werdenden Reformators," *Lutherjahrbuch* 88 (2021): 44–68.

———. *Passionspredigt im 16. Jahrhundert: Das Leiden und Sterben Jesu Christi in den Postillen Martin Luthers, der Wittenberger Tradition und altgläubiger Prediger.* Tübingen: Mohr/Siebeck, 2022.

Rhein, Stefan. "Katharina Melanchthon, geb. Krapp. Ein Wittenberger Frauenschicksal der Reformationszeit," in *600 Jahre Wittenberg. Stadt. Universität. Reformation*, edited by Stefan Oehmig, 501–518. Weimar: Böhlau, 1995.

Rieske-Braun, Uwe. *Duellum mirabile: Studien zum Kampfmotiv in Martin Luthers Theologie.* Göttingen: Vandenhoeck & Ruprecht, 1999.

Rieth, Ricardo. *„Habsucht" bei Martin Luther: Ökonomisches und theologisches Denken, Tradition und soziale Wirklichkeit im Zeitalter der Reformation.* Weimar: Böhlau, 1996.

———. "Luther's Treatment of Economic Life," in *The Oxford Handbook of Martin Luther's Theology*, edited by Robert Kolb, Irene Dingel and L'ubomír Batka, 383–396. Oxford: Oxford University Press, 2014.

Rittgers, Ronald K. *The Reformation of Suffering: Pastoral Theology and Lay Piety in Late Medieval and Early Modern Germany.* Oxford: Oxford University Press, 2012.

———. *The Reformation of the Keys.* Cambridge MA: Harvard University Press, 2004.

Robinson, Paul W. "Lord, Teach Us to Pray. Preaching the Pater Noster in Germany and Austria, 1100–1500," Ph.D. dissertation, University of Chicago, 2001.

Rorem, Paul. *Pseudo-Dionysius: A Commentary on the Texts and an Introduction to Their Influence.* New York: Oxford University Press, 1993.

Rosin, Robert L. "Humanism, Luther, and the Wittenberg Reformation," in *The Oxford Handbook of Martin Luther's Theology*, edited by Robert Kolb, Irene Dingel, and L'ubomír Batka, 91–104. Oxford: Oxford University Press, 2014.

———. *Reformers, the Preacher and Scepticism: Luther, Brenz, Melanchthon and Ecclesiastes.* Mainz: von Zabern, 1997.

Saak, Eric L. *Highway to Heaven. The Augustinian Platform between Reform and Reformation.* Leiden: Brill, 2002.

Saarinen, Risto. *Gottes Wirken auf uns: die Transzendentale Deutung des Gegenwart-Christi-Motivs in der Lutherforschung.* Stuttgart: Steiner, 1989.

———. "Martin Luther and Relational Thinking," in *Oxford Research Encyclopedia of Religion*, https://doi.org/10.1093/acrefore/9780199340378.013.344.

Saleska, Tim. "The Clarity of Paradox. A Meditation on Exodus 34:6–7," in *Simul: Inquiries into Luther's Expression of the Christian Life*, edited by Robert Kolb, Torbjörn Johansson, and Daniel Johansson, 195–211. Göttingen: Vandenhoeck & Ruprecht, 2021.

Sasse, Hermann. *This is My Body.* Minneapolis, Augsburg, 1959.

Scheible, Heinz. *Melanchthon, Vermittler der Reformation: Eine Biographie.* Munich: Beck, 2016.

Schumacher, William W. *Who Do I Say That You Are?: Anthropology and the Theology of the Theosis in the Finnish School of Tuoma Mannermaa.* Eugene, OR: Wipf & Stock, 2010.

Schürmann, Reiner. *Broken Hegemonies.* Translated by Reginald Lilly. Bloomington: Indiana University Press, 2003.

Schwarz, Reinhard. *Martin Luther, Lehrer der christlichen Religion.* 2nd ed. Tübingen: Mohr Siebeck, 2016.

Schwarzwäller, Klaus. *Cross and Resurrection: God's Wonder and Mystery.* Translated by Ken Sundet Jones and Mark Mattes. Minneapolis: Fortress Press, 2012.

———. "Verantwortung des Glaubens. Freiheit und Liebe nach der Dekalogauslegung Martin Luthers," in *Freiheit als Liebe bei/Freedom as Love in Martin Luther,* edited by Dennis Bielfeldt and Klaus Schwarzwäller, 133–158. Frankfurt: Lang, 1995.

Siggins, Ian. *Martin Luther's Doctrine of Christ.* New Haven: Yale University Press, 1970.

Simon, Wolfgang. *Die Messopfertheologie Martin Luther: Voraussetzungen, Genese, Gestalt und Rezeption.* Tübingen: Mohr/Siebeck, 2003.

Söderlund, Rune. *Ex praevisa Fide: Zum Verständnis der Prädestinationslehre in der lutherischen Orthodoxie.* Hannover: Lutherisches Verlagshaus, 1983.

Sommer, Wolfgang. *Gottesfurcht und Fürstenherrschaft: Studien zum Obrigkeitsverständnis Johann Arndts und lutherischer Hofprediger zur Zeit der altprotestantischen Orthodoxie.* Göttingen: Vandenhoeck & Ruprecht, 1988.

Spitz, Lewis W., Jr. "Luther's Social Concern for Students," in *The Social History of the Reformation,* edited by Lawrence P. Buck and Jonathan W. Zophy, 294–270. Columbus: Ohio State University Press, 1972.

Springer, Carl P. E. *Cicero in Heaven: The Roman Rhetor and Luther's Reformation* Leiden: Brill, 2018.

Steiner, George. *Real Presences.* Chicago: University of Chicago Press, 1989.

Steinmetz. David C. *Luther and Staupitz: An Essay in the Intellectual Origins of the Protestant Reformation.* Durham, NC: Duke University Press, 1980.

Stolt, Birgit. *Martin Luthers Rhetorik des Herzens.* Tübingen: Mohr/Siebeck, 2000.

———. *Wortkampf. Frühneuhochdeutsche Beispiele zur rhetorischen Praxis.* Frankfurt: Athenäum, 1974.

Tentler, Thomas N. *Sin and Confession on the Eve of the Reformation.* Princeton: Princeton University Press, 1977.

Thomas, Keith. *Religion and the Decline of Magic.* New York: Scribner's, 1971.

Thompson, Mark. "Luther on God and History," in *The Oxford Handbook of Martin Luther's Theology*, edited by Robert Kolb, Irene Dingel, and L'ubomír Batka, 127–142. Oxford: Oxford University Press, 2014.

Trigg, Jonathan D. *Baptism in the Theology of Martin Luther.* Leiden: Brill, 2001.

Vajta, Vilmos. *Luther on Worship.* Philadelphia: Muhlenberg, 1958.

Walsham, Alexandra. "The Reformation and 'the Disenchantment of the World' Reassessed," *The Historical Journal* 51 (2008): 497–528.

Wannenwitsch, Bernd. "The Simultaneity of Two Citizenships: A Theological Reappraisal of Luther's Account of the 'Two Regiments' for our Times," in *Simul: Inquiries into Luther's Expression of the Christian Life*, edited by Robert Kolb, Torbjörn Johansson, and Daniel Johansson, 177–191. Göttingen: Vandenhoeck & Ruprecht, 2021.

Wartenberg, Günther. "Luthers Beziehungen zu den sächsischen Fürsten," in *Leben und Werk Martin Luthers von 1526 bis 1546*, edited by Helmar Junghans, 554–561. Berlin Evangelische Verlagsanstalt, 1983.

Warneck, Gustav. *Abriß einer Geschichte der protestantischen Mission von der Reformation bis auf die Gegenwart.* Berlin Warneck, 1910.

Watson, Philip S. *Let God be God: An Interpretation of the Theology of Martin Luther* Philadelphia: Fortress Press, 1966.

Weaver, William P. "Melanchthon's Rhetorics and the Order of Learning: A Case Study in Library Database Research," *Reformation* 22 (2017): 120–146.

———. "Triplex est Copia: Philip Melanchthon's Invention of the Rhetorical Figures," *Journal of the History of Rhetoric* 29 (2011), 367–402. https://doi.org/10.1525/rh.2011.29.4.367.

Weaver, William P., Stefan Strohm and Volkhard Weis, "Volume Introduction," in *Philipp Melanchthon: Schriften zur Dialektik und Rhetorik/Principal Writings on Dialectic and Rhetoric. Principal Writings on Rhetoric, Philipp Melanchthon. Opera Omnia. Opera Philosophica 2/2.* XXXIII–LIV Berlin: de Gruyter, 2017.

Wengert, Timothy J. *Law and Gospel: Philip Melanchthon's Debate with John Agricola of Eisleben over Poenitentia.* Grand Rapids, MI: Baker, 1997.

———. "'Per mutuum colloquium et consolationem fratrum': Monastische Züge in Luthers ökumenische Theologie," in *Luther und das*

Monastische Erbe, edited by Christoph Bultmann, Volker Leppin, and Andreas Lindner, 243–268. Tübingen: Mohr/Siebeck, 2007.

Westphal, Siegrid. "Die Ausgestaltung des Kirchenwesens unter Johann Friedrich—ein landesherrliches Kirchenregiment?" in *Johann Friedrich I.—der Lutherische Kurfürst*, edited by Völker Leppin et al., 261–280. Gütersloh: Gütersloher Verlagshaus 2006.

Westman, Robert S. *The Copernican Question: Prognostication, Skepticism, and Celestial Order.* Los Angeles: University of California Press, 2011.

White, Graham. *Luther as Nominalist: A Study of the Logical Methods Used in Martin Luther's Disputations in the light of Their Medieval Background.* Helsinki: Luther-Agricola Society, 1994.

Wisløff, Carl F. *The Gift of Communion: Luther's Controversy with Rome on Eucharistic Sacrifice.* Translated by Joseph M. Shaw. Minneapolis: Augsburg, 1964.

Witte, John, Jr. "'The Mother of All Earthly Laws': The Lutheran Reformation," in *Encounters with Luther: New Directions for Critical Studies*, edited by Kirsi I. Stjerna and Brooks Schramm, 111–125. Louisville: Westminster John Knox Press, 2016.

Wolgast, Eike. "Luther's Treatment of Political and Societal Life," in *The Oxford Handbook of Martin Luther's Theology*, edited by Robert Kolb, Irene Dingel, and L'ubomír Batka, 398–420. Oxford: Oxford University Press, 2014.

Scripture Index

Index of Names

Subject Index

Lutheran Quarterly Books

Living by Faith: Justification and Sanctification, by Oswald Bayer (2003).

Harvesting Martin Luther's Reflections on Theology, Ethics and the Church, essays from *Lutheran Quarterly*, edited by Timothy J. Wengert, with foreword by David C. Steinmetz (2004).

A More Radical Gospel: Essays on Eschatology, Authority, Atonement, and Ecumenism, by Gerhard O. Forde, edited by Mark Mattes and Steven Paulson (2004).

The Role of Justification in Contemporary Theology, by Mark C. Mattes (2004).

The Captivation of the Will: Luther vs. Erasmus on Freedom and Bondage, by Gerhard O. Forde (2005).

Bound Choice, Election, and Wittenberg Theological Method: From Martin Luther to the Formula of Concord, by Roberg Kolb (2005).

A Formula for Parish Practice: Using the Formula of Concord in Congregations, by Timothy J. Wengert (2006).

Luther's Theological Music: Principles and Implications, by Robin A Leaver (2006).

The Preached God: Proclamation in Word and Sacrament, by Gerhard O. Forde, edited by Mark C. Mattes and Steven D. Paulson (2007).

Theology the Lutheran Way, by Oswald Bayer (2007).

A Time for Confessing, by Robert W. Bertram (2008).

The Pastoral Luther: Essays on Martin Luther's Pastoral Theology, edited by Timothy J. Wengert (2009).

Preaching from Home: The Stories of Seven Lutheran Women Hymn Writers, by Gracia Grindal (2011).

The Early Luther: Stages in a Reformation Reorientation, by Berndt Hamm (2013).

The Life, Works, and Witness of Tsehay Tolessa and Gudina Tumsa, the Ethiopian Bonhoeffer, edited by Samuel Yonas Deressa and Sarah Hinlicky (2017).

The Wittenberg Concord: Creating Space for Dialogue, by Gordon A. Jensen (2018).

Lutheran Quarterly Books

Luther's Outlaw God: Volume 1: Hiddenness, Evil, and Predestination, by Steven D. Paulson (2018).

The Essential Forde: Distinguishing Law and Gospel, by Gerhard O. Forde, edited by Nickolas Hopman, Mark C. Mattes, and Steven D. Paulson (2019).

Luther's Outlaw God: Volume 2: Hidden in the Cross, by Steven D. Paulson (2019).

Minister's Prayer Book: An Order of Prayers and Readings, Revised Edition, edited by Timothy J. Wengert, Mary Jane Haemig, Chris Halverson, and Robert Harrell (2020)

The Augsburg Confession: Renewing Lutheran Faith and Practice, by Timothy J. Wengert (2020).

Luther's Outlaw God: Volume 3: Sacraments and God's Attack on the Promise, by Steven D. Paulson (2020).

Stories from Global Lutheranism: A Historical Timeline, by Martin J. Lohrmann (2021).

Teaching Reformation: Essays in Honor of Timothy J. Wengert, edited by Luka Ilić and Martin J. Lohrmann (2021).

Experiencing Gospel: The History and Creativity of Martin Luther's 1534 Bible Project, by Gordon A. Jensen (2023).

Face to Face: Martin Luther's View of Reality, by Robert Kolb (2024).

A New Song We Now Begin: Celebrating the Half Millennium of Lutheran Hymnals 1524–2024, edited by Robin A. Leaver (2024).

Sola: Christ, Grace, Faith, and Scripture Alone in Martin Luther's Theology, by Volker Leppin (2024).